Jefferson Davis

Jefferson Davis (Southern Historical Collection, University of North Carolina Library, Chapel Hill)

Jefferson Davis

Clement Eaton

THE FREE PRESS
A Division of Macmillan Publishing Co., Inc.
NEW YORK

Collier Macmillan Publishers
LONDON

The Free Press
A Division of Macmillan Publishing Co., Inc.
866 Third Avenue, New York, N.Y. 10022

Collier Macmillan Canada, Ltd.

Library of Congress Catalog Card Number: 77-2512

Printed in the United States of America

printing number
1 2 3 4 5 6 7 8 9 10

Library of Congress Cataloging in Publication Data

Eaton, Clement
   Jefferson Davis

Includes bibliographical references and index.
1. Davis, Jefferson, 1808-1889. 2. Confederate
States of America--Presidents--Biography. 3. United
States--History--Civil War, 1861-1865. 4. Confederate
States of America--History. I. Title.
E467.1.D26E24   973.7'13   77-2512
ISBN 0-02-908700-7

To
Professor Frederick Merk of Harvard University,
whose unselfish devotion as a teacher and critical
ability I deeply appreciate.

Contents

Preface

—◆◆◆—

The goal of a biographer of Jefferson Davis should be to find out the truth about his subject and tell it as it is. It is not easy to do this—because of three pitfalls. The first pitfall is in the mind of the biographer: Does he ask the right questions? (I am sure that revisionists will ask different questions than those I have asked, since a biographer usually asks only those questions in which his own age has a lively interest.) I am interested in the rise of women in my own generation, and accordingly I have asked some questions about Davis's relations with women, and the handicaps of antebellum women. In addition, one chapter is a discussion of slavery on the Davis plantations, which may throw some light on the complex and controversial subject of Negro slavery in the Southern states. I recognize that the anti-Vietnam feeling remains strong, especially among young Americans, but I do not think that this modern feeling should operate to distort any account of Davis's part in the Civil War. I happen to be a Southerner, born in North Carolina and educated at both the University of North Carolina and Harvard University. I realize, therefore, that I must guard against the danger of my Southern background affecting too strongly the writing of this biography. On the other hand, a scholar reared in a large urban community in the North would have perhaps a harder time than I in coping with writing about a Southern leader of the antebellum and Civil War periods and with the realities of Southern rural life.

The second pitfall in the writing of a Davis biography is the absence of adequate materials about him, particularly of his early life. A large part of Davis's papers were destroyed or lost when federal troops overran his plantation, Brierfield, in 1862. Moreover, Davis was careless about keeping his papers and important letters. The largest manuscript collection of his papers that remains is the Jefferson Hayes–Davis Papers given by Davis's grandson to Transylvania University in Lexington, Kentucky. I have been fortunate in living in Lexington, where I could use these papers at my leisure. They contain, however, only a few letters relating to his early life, and very few manuscripts of the Civil War period. As is the case of most collections of papers, they consist mainly of letters written to him. As I researched the Davis materials, I found that I gained a greater sense of reality, both as to the nature of the man and as to his times, from the manuscripts than from the formal documents, laws, and official reports. In addition, the manuscripts have added human interest and color to my account of Davis's life. Since 1946, when I received a Guggenheim Research Fellowship, I have traveled all over the South investigating the resources in Southern libraries on the antebellum and Civil War periods of Southern history. In this work on Davis and the Confederacy I have used over forty collections, some of them large and others small. They are listed under the headings for the different libraries in the Bibliographical Note.

The third pitfall of a Davis biographer is to comprehend Davis himself. He was a self-contained, reserved man who did not freely reveal his thoughts and feelings. Therefore I have entitled the last chapter seeking to evaluate him "The Sphinx of the Confederacy," a title suggested by his close associate and supporter during the Civil War period, Clement C. Clay, Jr., of Alabama, who found his personality a riddle.

Davis's career up to the Civil War was admirable, although it was vitiated by his ardent defense of slavery. Even this mistaken course is understandable, for he sincerely believed paternal slavery to be the best condition for the Negro at that time, and he and his brother Joseph were paternal masters. Unfortunately, he was not one of those few Southerners of his generation who could rise above sectional influences, though in this respect he was not unlike most Northerners. If he had done so, he could not have remained in politics. He was a highly honorable man, extremely devoted to his family, and his patriotism was genuine and high-minded. He loved the Union as it was in the days of Washington, Jefferson, and Madison, but he believed that it had been perverted by a selfish Northern majority. He was not, as misrepresented by hostile critics, in favor of secession, except as a last resort to preserve Southern rights. Perhaps the most able of the "Southern Triumvirate" in the Senate (Robert M. T. Hunter of Virginia, Robert Toombs of Georgia, and Davis of Mississippi), he was a splendid public speaker, though hardly an orator in the Southern sense; courageous, both physically and morally; above petty politics; and capable of supreme devotion to a cause. I feel sure that if I had been a member of the Montgomery convention in 1861, I would have voted for him for Confederate president.

But then came the stresses and strains of the Civil War, which brought out certain weaknesses that had been only hinted at in Davis's pre-Civil War career. It is fascinating to see these develop. Beneath the stoic façade was an extremely sensitive man: one possessed of unconquerable pride. Then, during the war, he showed the effects of being a Southerner. The weight of historical opinion is at present against him. One prominent scholar, David Potter, has gone so far as to claim that Davis was mainly responsible for the defeat of the Confederacy in the Civil War. But the tides of historical opinion change. Practically all the adverse opinions on Davis represent hindsight. The severely critical scholars do not adequately take into consideration the tremendous difficulties that faced him, which were far greater than the problems with which President Lincoln had to deal. Today we lack the historical imagination and the knowledge of the emotional atmosphere of the times, of the crosscurrents of public opinion that harassed his administration, of the powerful inertia of Southern traditions that held him back, and finally of the miserable health that handicapped him.

There has long been a need for a modern, scholarly study of Jefferson Davis: no such biography has been published since Professor William E. Dodd's in 1907—and that one was not deeply researched. There have been, however, a number of superficial and partisan biographies, beginning with the pro-Davis volume of Frank Alfriend and the anti-Davis work of Edward Pollard, and continuing with books by Elizabeth Cutting, Allen Tate, Robert Winston, and the better studies by Hamilton J. Eckenrode, Burton J. Hendrick, and Robert McElroy (although the lattermost is remarkably superficial for an attempt by a Princeton professor of history). The most valuable fairly recent works are the excellent scholarly consideration of Jefferson Davis and his cabinet by Rembert Patrick, and a three-volume work by Hudson Strode. Strode, a University of Alabama professor of English, has written an admiring, pleasing book, which (despite the fact that it had been composed in a political vacuum) I have found very useful. Bell Wiley's comments on Davis in *The Road to Appomattox,* as well as his introduction to his edition of Jefferson Davis's *The Rise and Fall of the Confederate Government,* also deserve the thoughtful consideration of modern historians, amateurs and professionals alike.

I wish to express my appreciation to Professor William Scarborough of Southern Methodist University, Professor Charles P. Roland and Professor Steven Channing of the University of Kentucky, Professor Stanley L. Engerman of Rochester University, my Harvard roommate Professor Ernst Helmreich of Bowdoin College, Miss Roemol Henry, librarian of Transylvania University (for her helpfulness in aiding me to use the Jefferson Hayes–Davis

Papers), Miss Mattie Russell, curator of the Duke University Manuscripts, Mr. Kenneth Elliott of the University of Kentucky Press, and Mrs. Carolyn Wallace, director of the Southern Collection of manuscripts at the University of North Carolina at Chapel Hill. To Natalie Schick, the incomparable secretary of the History Department of the University of Kentucky, I owe an especially large debt of gratitude for typing from the difficult handwritten version of the manuscript, and for her intelligent corrections and suggestions. I also wish to express my appreciation to Charles E. Smith, Editor-in-Chief of The Free Press, for his valuable suggestions and his encouragement for me to persevere, and to Dr. Barbara Chernow for her careful and intelligent editing of the manuscript.

Jefferson Davis

The Imprint of Kentucky and Mississippi

 He was admired, hated, and after the Civil War reverenced as the martyr and symbol of "the lost cause." Jefferson Davis of Mississippi, cotton planter, leading senator of the South after John C. Calhoun, and harassed president of the Confederate States of America, was probably a decisive figure in the unhappy history of the South. Too dignified and reserved to be loved by the people whom he served, he could never establish a rapport with them, so badly needed in the fight for Southern independence, as did Lincoln with the Northern people, using his keen sense of the ridiculous, his political art, and his common touch. A type of the self-made aristocrat produced by the plantation society of the Old South, of which there was a considerable number, he is a fascinating study of the influence of regional character and mores upon personality. The cast of mind of that society was deeply conservative, but it had great virtues, the most outstanding of which was a high sense of honor. Davis was an epitome of the strength of the society that went down to defeat at Appomattox.

This biographer does not have the advantage of the young Harvard professor, Doris Kearns, author of *Lyndon Johnson and the American Dream,* who interviewed her subject in depth. Johnson revealed to her the influence of his mother and father on him, and his feeling of deprivation at not attending Harvard University—facts that had a prominent bearing on his political life. No comparable evidence exists for Davis. Psychologists might infer from the few known facts of his childhood that being the youngest of ten children, and much adored, he tended to resent opposition and criticism and took for granted that his associates approved of his opinions.

It would be fascinating to trace the influence of his highly successful brother Joseph, twenty-three years older than he, who was like a father to him, but relatively few facts remain to enlighten us. There was a Jonathan-David friendship between the two that lasted until the older brother died in 1870. Jefferson wrote to Joseph from Congress on September 22, 1855, that "whosoever is your enemy must needs be mine," and that he trusted him entirely as his agent in selling the cotton of his plantation. In this same letter he expressed concern for the welfare of his slaves: "Please look after Bob (a very old slave) and the old people."[1]

Even the effect upon young Davis of the environment, which we can pretty accurately describe, is difficult to assess, for different individuals are affected differently by approximately the same environment. It is reasonable, however, to assume that Kentucky and Mississippi—the one, the state of his birth and college education, and the other, the state of his youth and young manhood—left an indelible imprint on Jefferson Davis's mind and personality. But, as much as the environment and society in which he matured conditioned him, the influence of his family was much stronger. Although his family did not belong to the aristocracy of either state, he, like Andrew Jackson, became a one-generation aristocrat. Davis's father was a yeoman, a member of the South's rural middle class, though he was a superior member of that class by force of mind and personality. His father, Samuel Emory Davis, was descended from a Welsh ancestor who emigrated to Philadelphia in the eighteenth century.[2] The Welsh have contributed some notable leaders of the South, including Thomas Jefferson, whose father was born in the shadow of Mount Snowdon in Wales, Chief Justice John Marshall, George H. Thomas of the Union Army, "called the Rock of Chickamauga," and William L. Yancey, "the Orator of Secession."[3] Jefferson Davis's grandfather left Philadelphia to settle in Georgia, where his father was born. Jefferson was proud of the fact that his father fought for four years in the Revolution, supporting the Patriot cause.

While Samuel Davis was soldiering in South Carolina he met and fell in love with Jane Cook, a girl of Scotch-Irish stock, and after the war he married her. Jefferson described his mother as a woman noted for her beauty, much of which she retained to extreme old age, and as having a graceful, poetic mind.[4] Varina Howell, Jefferson's second wife, in her memoir of her husband, tells of their visit to his mother immediately after their marriage, when Jane Davis was eighty-five years old. She was, Varina wrote, still fair to look upon: "Her eyes were bright, her hair was a soft brown and her complexion clear and white as a child's."[5]

Jefferson Davis's father was given a tract of land by the state of Georgia for his service during the Revolution, and he settled on a farm near Augusta. He had enough education to be chosen county clerk. But he did not stay long in one place; he appears to have been of a restless disposition and capable of impetuous action. In 1793 he moved his wife and five children to Kentucky—first to Mercer County in the Bluegrass region, and then to a farm in the western part of the state (Christian County), not far from the Tennessee boundary. Here he built a double log cabin of four rooms with a "dog run," or breezeway, between the two halves, equipped with glass windows, which was unusual among the log cabins of the neighborhood. In this rude cabin Jefferson Davis was born on June 3, 1808. The house in which he was born was a cut above the log cabin in which Abraham Lincoln was born a year later, less than a hundred miles away. His mother was forty-five years old when he arrived and could expect the birth of no other children, so that his father, in naming him Jefferson after Thomas Jefferson, whimsically added the middle name of Finis, but Davis, understandably, dropped the latter name after he graduated from the United States Military Academy.

Jefferson Davis had a great admiration and affection for his father, who influenced him both by example and by precept. In his autobiography he described his father as unusually handsome and as an accomplished horseman. He was, he wrote, "a man of wonderful physical activity."[6] He remembered the last time that he saw him before his tragic death. At that time Samuel Davis was sixty-four years old, but he was still so strong and agile that when he was annoyed in trying to mount a fractious horse, instead of seeking assistance, he suddenly vaulted from the ground into the saddle. Jefferson's father was a taciturn man of "a grave and stoical character," but he was so much respected by his children that his word was law to them. Despite his firmness, he pursued an intelligent and mild course of discipline in rearing his children. In an age in which most fathers were authoritarian, he adopted a more permissive attitude, recommended by modern psychologists as the best way to develop creativity in young children. Davis observed in his autobiography that his father's admonitions to his children were "suggestive rather than dictatorial."[7] In addition, the future Southern leader had the advantage of being surrounded by affection in his childhood. He wrote at the end of his life that he had never ceased to cherish "the loving care of that mother in whom there was so much for me to admire and nothing to remember save good."

When Jefferson was two years old his father took the family to Bayou Teche in Louisiana. Because of a plague of mosquitoes that made the place unhealthy, they moved to a farm in southwestern Mississippi near the village of Woodville. Davis described the region in which his father located permanently as "sparsely settled," situated between the rich land of the Mississippi River delta and the poorer soils of the pinelands. Whereas in Kentucky his father had raised tobacco and horses, in Mississippi he cultivated mainly cotton, working in the fields with his few slaves. With their aid and that of the local carpenters, he built a fine house with a large verandah, and Jane gave it the romantic name of Rosemont.

The large families of the time in the South often necessitated that the older brothers and sisters serve to some degree as surrogate parents. As stated, Jefferson was the youngest of ten children, and there was a difference in age of twenty-three years between him and Joseph Emory, the oldest child. Joseph had an almost paternal affection for his youngest brother, and it continued until Joseph's death after the Civil War. Sisters Anna and Lucinda also gave special attention to the youngest child. These strong, loyal family relations lasted throughout Jefferson's life. Even before he became a mature man, Jefferson had a deep feeling of responsibility for his sisters, and they in turn wrote him warm and affectionate letters. He showed his devotion to his widowed mother by sending from his pay as a cadet at West Point monthly contributions for her support. Indeed, all his life he remained a good example of the strength of family ties in the Old South.

When Jefferson Davis was eight years old his father decided to send him to a Catholic school, the College of St. Thomas Aquinas, in south central Kentucky near the villages of Springfield and Bardstown, the headquarters of Catholicism in Kentucky. He made this decision despite the fact that he was a Baptist, and the Baptists of that period felt a strong prejudice against Catholics. Jefferson's affectionate mother strongly opposed sending her son away from home at such an early age, but in the Old South the husband was a dictator. An opportunity arose for the boy to travel to Kentucky with the family of a friend of his brother Joseph, Major Thomas Hinds of Natchez; Joseph was practicing law in Natchez. Major Hinds was planning a trip to the North, and he invited young Jefferson to accompany his family. They journeyed along the famed Natchez trace through a wilderness inhabited by the Choctaw Indians. The trip was a great adventure for the young boy, especially enjoyable when the party stopped for a long visit at the Hermitage, the home of Andrew Jackson at Nashville. Jackson and his wife Rachel received them cordially, and as a result Davis formed a lasting admiration for "Old Hickory," who, though stern and formidable in battle, was courteous, kindly, and hospitable in his home.

At St. Thomas, Davis was the youngest and smallest boy, and soon he became the only Protestant in the school. The natural desire to be like the other students led him to seek to be taken into the Catholic Church. But the Fathers, with great kindness, persuaded him not to make this hasty decision. The memory of the pleasant years spent at this Catholic institution in his boyhood may have had an influence on his opposing the anti-Catholic nativist movement in the 1840s and 1850s. After two years of schooling, he returned to his home alone on one of the earliest steamboats plying the Mississippi River. As he approached the homestead he tried to play a practical joke on his mother by pretending that he was a stranger. When he arrived his father was working in the fields with his slaves, but as soon as he saw his son advancing toward him, his austere, undemonstrative nature succumbed and he surprised the ten-year-old boy by kissing him repeatedly.

After his return Davis attended Jefferson College near Natchez for a brief period and then entered the log-cabin county academy near his home, which charged fees (as was the usual practice). In his autobiography he remembered the log-cabin schools of Mississippi as teaching by primitive methods, such as the use of copybooks and emphasis on memory, as well as the frequent flogging of delinquent or indolent pupils. He counted himself unusually fortunate in having as head of his academy a well-educated Boston Yankee, greatly superior to the run of backwoods teachers, from whom the bright boy learned much.

An episode that Davis tells in his skimpy autobiography about his school days is indicative of the spirit of the youth—his resistance to what he regarded as tyranny and invasion of his rights as a person. His schoolteacher assigned him a piece to memorize that he regarded as excessive. He protested but the teacher refused to lessen the task and, the next day when Davis had failed to memorize the piece, threatened to whip him. Jefferson defied the teacher by taking his books and departing for home. His father quietly told him that he had a choice of going to school or working in the cotton fields, for he could not tolerate idleness. After two days of picking cotton with the slaves in the hot sun, Davis decided to go back to school. But he had demonstrated his independent spirit and his quick resentment toward what he regarded as injustice —qualities that characterized his later career.

An important turning point in his development occurred when in the spring of 1823 he entered Transylvania University. Founded in 1789, it was the oldest and most prestigious institution of higher learning west of the Appalachian Mountains.[8] Davis was then not yet sixteen years old. The university at that time had a most stimulating atmosphere. It had an enrollment of 418 students, larger than the enrollment of Harvard College. Its medical school, containing a distinguished faculty and 282 students, was famed throughout the South and the West. Its law school, headed by Professor Jesse Bledsoe, whom Davis characterized as "a real genius,"[9] was also famous. While Davis was a student there another professor was the eccentric botanist, Constantine Rafinesque, a pioneer in the history of American botany, who spent so much time away from the university collecting new species that young Davis does not mention him.

Thomas Jefferson thought so highly of Transylvania that, discouraged over the trouble of founding the University of Virginia, he wrote to a friend: "We must send our children for education to Kentucky [Transylvania] or

Cambridge [Harvard]. The latter will return them to us fanatics and tories, and the former will keep them to add to their population. If, however, we are to go begging anywhere for education, I would rather it should be to Kentucky than any other state, because she has more flavor of the old cask than any other."[10]

The president of the university was Horace Holley, a Boston Unitarian minister. Holley was notably liberal in his ideas, both on religion and social affairs—in fact, too liberal for the religious folk of Kentucky.[11] Not only did he preach a religion of love and tolerance, but he practiced a genial style of living that included card playing and dancing, and his home was ornamented with nude classic statues that caused fundamentalists to shudder at such depravity in the head of a university. Especially shocked were strict Presbyterians, and in 1828 after Davis had left Transylvania, they drove him from the university.[12] Young Davis did not share this bigotry, and even as a teenager he displayed a critical attitude toward revealed religion. In his autobiography he described one of his professors as having the faith of a child, not doubting or questioning, and believing in the Bible literally as it was written.[13]

There were no dormitories in the university when Davis was a student. He roomed at the home of the postmaster, a short distance from the university. The testimony of some college mates, given after his death and quoted by Varina Davis in her memoir, tended to idealize his conduct. Ex-Senator George W. Jones of Iowa, a close friend, wrote that Davis was a top student of his class, but the testimony of another classmate, Judge Peter of Mount Sterling, Kentucky, described him as only a good student, respectful of the faculty, not choosing to participate in athletics, and taciturn in disposition.[14]

The opportunities for entertainment in the university were various, but we do not know which ones Davis enjoyed since he kept no diary. A young law student, William Little Brown, who preceded Davis at the university by twelve years, did keep a diary in which he recorded most of the amusements of the students.[15] They included playing checkers, dancing, attending the theater, watching militia musters, listening to political orators, going to the races, "shooting for a beef" (marksmanship contests), taking walks in the woods, and playing practical jokes, such as Davis's one of placing an ad in the local papers, signed by "Many Voters," calling upon a certain pompous and conceited young man to run for the office of sheriff. Davis also participated in the activities of one of the rival debating societies, which were the centers of the extracurricular lives of the students and gave valuable training in public speaking. At commencement on June 4, 1824, he gave an address on "Friendship" that the local newspapers praised, reporting that Davis's "On Friendship" made friends of the hearers.[16]

Although there is no documentary proof, it is a reasonable supposition that the students with whom he associated had a strong influence on his developing aristocratic manners and a peculiarly Southern sense of values.[17] The student body generally came from aristocratic and wealthy families from all over the

South. Some of them, such as William Little Brown, brought along a slave valet. Davis paid tribute to the high caliber of the students, relating that when he first took his seat in the United States Senate, six of the senators were graduates of Transylvania University.[18] The graduate of Transylvania whom he most admired was General Albert Sidney Johnston, who was five years older and had preceded him as a student at the university, but whom he knew at West Point.[19]

While Jefferson was at Transylvania he received a sad letter from his father, dated June 24, 1823. Samuel Davis had made a journey to Philadelphia to try to collect an inheritance from his long-deceased grandfather. He sorrowfully reported his failure to his son, writing that if he had prosecuted his claim thirty years before he might have become immensely rich, but now he feared that his inheritance was lost through the lapse of time. He wished to tell his son that if he should die and never see him again, he had left at Harford, Maryland, his horses and the Negro boy, Jim Pemberton, who had accompanied him on his journey and whom he had given to Jefferson. His final words were the admonition: "Use every possible means to acquire useful knowledge as knowledge is power, the want of which has brought mischief and misery on your father in his old age—That you may be happy and shine in society when your father is beyond the reach of harm is the most ardent wish of his heart."[20]

The broken parent returned to his farm near Woodville and on July 4, 1824, he died under tragic circumstances. At sixty-eight years of age financial ruin came upon him as a result of his endorsing a note of a son-in-law, and he was forced to sell his plantation and dispose of his six slaves. His wealthy son at Natchez, Joseph, fortunately, bought them and saved Rosemont for his mother. The elder Davis had a violent quarrel with one of his sons, who was helping him farm the land at Rosemont, and impetuously left the plantation, although his cotton crop remained unharvested. He left in an open boat for the plantation of his oldest son Joseph—Hurricane—and was exposed to the broiling sun and to malarial mosquitoes.[21] After he landed he became ill with malaria and died. He was buried at Hurricane. At Lexington, Jefferson received notice of the death of his father in a letter from Susannah, his sister-in-law, residing at Joseph's plantation. In a rather formal letter, Davis wrote of his shock at hearing the news, and of his love for his father, "rendered more so (if possible) by the disasters that attended his declining years."[22]

Three days after the death of his father, Davis sent to Secretary of War John C. Calhoun an acceptance of an appointment as a cadet at the United States Military Academy.[23] Unknown to him, his father and Joseph had secured his appointment through their influence with a Mississippi congressman. The young student at Transylvania was opposed to leaving the university before he had graduated, and he still had a year to go. Furthermore, he had no desire for a military life, but wished to enter the law school of the recently opened University of Virginia and become a lawyer like Joseph. Joseph finally persuaded him to accept the appointment with the promise that after a year at the Military Academy, if he should still be dissatisfied, he could withdraw and enroll in the University of Virginia. He remained at Transylvania until he was formally admitted to the academy on September 30, 1824. Strangely, he did not go to Rosemont to see his mother and brothers and sisters, to whom he was devoted, before he proceeded to West Point.

One chapter of his life had ended, and in surveying it, the historian should note the influence upon him both of the semifrontier society of Mississippi and of the more cultured, refined society of Kentucky. In his youth Mississippi was a very young state, being admitted to the Union in 1818. Wilkinson County, in which the Davis family lived, was on the edge of the delta or river section, settled largely by immigrants from the upper South such as the Davis family, while the eastern part of the state was settled principally by yeoman farmers from South Carolina and Georgia, who brought with them certain characteristics that they had acquired in the older states. They were exceedingly proud of their native states, especially those from Virginia, and in making laws for the new state they sought to copy the institutions and legal systems to which they had been accustomed.[24] There was a significant mixture of aristocratic and democratic elements in this society in which Davis matured. Some of the immigrants into Mississippi were aristocratic planters, such as Colonel Thomas Dabney of Burleigh, who brought with them the culture, the sense of dignity, and the gentlemanly manners of the eastern Tidewater, an area of large plantations and slaveholdings.[25] Although the Davis family could boast of no aristocratic ancestors, coats of arms, or heirloom silver, Jefferson and his brother Joseph acquired aristocratic manners, tastes, and values.

The Mississippi of Davis's youth was a violent land. Some of its most prominent leaders were men like George Poindexter, an impecunious lawyer, who left his native state of Virginia to improve his economic position. Poindexter fought duels and in one encounter killed his opponent. In another confrontation he threw brickbats at a Mississippi editor seeking to demolish him. Yet the Mississippians elected such a violent character as their governor and United States senator from 1830 to 1835.[26] They admired virile men who defended their "honor" against detractors. One of the most extreme of these was Colonel James K. McClung, a tall, handsome, romantic man who fought many duels to preserve his honor. He was also the *beau ideal* of chivalry, so much so that he conceived a violent hatred of another prominent Mississippi politician, James L. Alcorn, because the latter was quicker than he in protecting a young lady at a ball from an annoyer.[27] So much violence prevailed in antebellum Mississippi, not only over points of honor leading to fatal duels, but in mobbing antislavery men, in fisticuffs, and in cutting affrays, in which editors especially were involved, that cartoonists portrayed editors with quills in one hand and dueling pistols in the other. In such an environment the young Davis developed a touchy sense of honor, but, surprisingly, no record has survived to indicate that he or his brother Joseph ever fought a duel or acted as a second. Yet Jefferson issued several challenges, and in the Senate he defended the code duello.[28] Also, he engaged in a discreditable brawl in a boardinghouse in Washington with the obnoxious senior senator of Mississippi, Henry S. Foote, though it was hushed up.[29]

One unattractive aspect of the rapidly developing exploitation of the rich Mississippi delta and black belt lands, that does not seem seriously to have affected either Jefferson or his brother Joseph in their conduct, was the rise of nouveau riche cotton planters with the repulsive characteristics of that class. D. R. Hundley, a pioneer Southern sociologist, scathingly described this class of people, whom he called "swell heads."[30] But a more earthy description of this class was given to the Northern traveler, Frederick Law Olmsted, in a conversation with a Mississippi overseer in 1854. The overseer described the hauteur of the "big bugs," as he called them, who since they must have ice for their wine did not live on their plantations, but in Natchez or New Orleans, and in summer went north to Saratoga and Newport. The young "swell heads" were especially obnoxious, for they swaggered, gambled, and drank their lives away. You could tell the new aristocracy, the overseer said, by their walk: "They sort o' throw out their legs as if they hadn't got strength to lift 'em and put them down in any particular place. They do want so bad to look as if they weren't made of the same clay as the rest of God's creation."[31] As a rising politician, Davis had to deal with these people, but he does not appear to have been as deeply interested in the common people as was Lincoln, whose parents moved to the North while Davis's chose to remain in the slave region of the lower South.

Davis was also influenced by his exposure to Kentucky society. In addition to the influence of the students and the university, the city of Lexington and the surrounding Bluegrass country had a cultivating effect upon him. Lexington in this early period was called "the Athens of the West." Aristocratic Tidewater Virginia had contributed to the town and to the hemp plantations around it some of its leading citizens and planters as well as a style of life. Travelers described the unique charm and grace of the privileged class of this oasis of culture in the crude West. When Samuel Allen of the *American Agriculturist* visited Lexington in 1843, he noted that the citizens thought that their town and the surrounding Bluegrass "approaches Eden."[32] The town had a diversified industry, but the processing of hemp in its factories and ropewalks dominated its industry.[33] Around the city were farms and plantations devoted to raising fine cattle, mules, and horses, and the people were obsessed with horse racing. Davis was undoubtedly influenced in his taste for fine horses and racing by his Kentucky background. Doubtless, also, the youthful student patronized the confectionery establishment kept by a Frenchman, Monsieur Giron, which was a gathering place for the students and townspeople. Outside of Lexington was Ashland, the imposing home and plantation of Henry Clay, and young Davis almost certainly visited it, for he was a friend of Clay's eldest son, Henry.[34] At the time that Davis was a student at Lexington, Kentucky's most famous painter, Matthew J. Jouett (d. 1827), was doing portraits of notable citizens, particularly those of Horace Holley and Henry Clay. Kentucky silversmiths in this early period of cultural florescence were making beautiful julep cups, candlesticks, and pitchers, some of them from coin silver. But the supremacy of Lexington declined after the steamboats began appearing on the Ohio and Mississippi rivers, and Louisville began to eclipse it.[35]

Whether Davis was affected by some of the cruder aspects of Kentucky life one can only guess; profanity, gambling, and heavy drinking were rife in Kentucky. William Reynolds, a Northern merchant selling Negro cloth, visited Louisville in 1839 and commented in his manuscript journal: "I have never seen any Town or City that appears more loose in morals than this one. Courtezans allmost flock the Streets and the most profane language may at all times be heard, indeed the Language of some here would make the Devil stand aghast and wonder at their profanity. Great quantities of Liquor is drank, which of course is well calculated to set every other Evil affloat."[36] Davis was profane at one period of his life, but he could easily have picked up profanity in the army as well as in Kentucky. The Northern merchant was impressed also with the passion of Kentuckians for horse racing, their furious betting, and the phrase "I'll Bet You," which was constantly heard. The Northern cloth merchant thought that the Kentuckians had a more fiery, ambitious spirit than the people living on the other side of the Ohio River, which he attributed to their sense of superiority induced by the institution of slavery that caused the richer class of slaveholders to think that "God has made him a little better than those who have the misfortune to be poor."

On the other hand, young James H. Atherton, son of a New Hampshire antislavery congressman, wrote letters to his father from Lexington in 1832 that gave a more favorable view of Kentuckians. Atherton described Kentucky as the most beautiful spot in America. The ladies, he observed, although they dressed extravagantly, bet on the horse races, and were passionately fond of dancing and music, were well educated. The Kentuckians, he wrote, were high-minded, generous, honorable, and extravagant, the warmest of friends and the bitterest of enemies.[37]

Whether a person is deeply influenced by his environment depends to a considerable degree upon his sensitivity. Davis was a highly sensitive person— thin-skinned as to criticism, quick to respond to insults, sympathetic to the well-being of his slaves, and later to the clerks under him in the War Department, and, above all, attuned to the needs of his wife and family. It is reasonable, therefore, to conclude that he was deeply affected, perhaps to a large extent unconsciously, by the environment of the two states in which he grew up. From his family, moreover, he had derived ideas of dignity of character and bearing and of gentlemanly conduct that were reinforced by contact with aristocratic planters, and with their sons at Transylvania University. His visit as a young boy to the Hermitage gave him an enduring impression of one of the great democratic leaders of his age, whose party he joined when he became a man. In these early years he acquired a strong interest in books that he was to continue and to expand in his mature years. Nevertheless, in his youth and young manhood Jefferson gave little promise of his later political distinction. As Bruce Catton has observed, he was a "late bloomer."[38] Altogether, he was an attractive, ambitious young man, anxious to elevate himself and his family in the esteem of the world.

2

A West Point Cadet and Frontier Soldier

*I*n addition to the influence of his native state of Kentucky and of his adopted state of Mississippi, one of the strongest agents molding the young Jefferson Davis was the tradition of patriotism and of military service in his family. In political campaigns and in the Senate he spoke often of this family tradition, especially in affirming his love for the Union and in denying that he was a disunionist. His father, he observed, had served in the revolutionary army for four years, three of his brothers had borne arms in the War of 1812, and the fourth was prevented from serving as a soldier because the enthusiasm for volunteering in his county was so great that the county court feared that the county would not be properly protected in the presence of a large slave population; therefore, it drafted men to remain at home, and this brother was among the drafted.[1] The military tradition among Southerners was so strong that a much larger proportion of Southern men entered the army as a profession than did Northerners; moreover, military schools flourished in the South and the militia, with its high-sounding titles and musters, was a prominent feature of Southern life.[2] An important reason for this militarism, greater in the South than in the North, was the existence of slavery, involving latent fear of slave insurrection,[3] easily aroused by rumors of plots.

Davis was admitted to the United States Military Academy at West Point on September 30, 1824, at the age of seventeen years and four months. He was given an oral examination for admission, and although he was deficient in mathematics, he managed to appear more knowledgeable in that science than was actually the case. He also passed his French examination by diverting the attention of the examiner from that language to the Greek language, in which he was more proficient. As a possible result of this haphazard entrance examination, Davis in his autobiography commented that he had little confidence in examinations as a means of determining the qualifications of a person.[4]

At West Point, Davis soon made congenial friends. Many of these cadets were destined to meet again in battle, first during the Mexican War and later during the Civil War. Among Davis's fellow students were the future Confederate generals, Albert Sidney Johnston of Maysville, Kentucky, who had been a student at Transylvania University, and Leonidas Polk of Tennessee, both of whom were older than he and were prominent among the cadets.[5] Both Johnston and Polk served together at the Battle of Shiloh, where Johnston was fatally wounded; Polk died at Pine Mountain during the Atlanta Campaign. Another cadet, Thomas F. Drayton of South Carolina remained a loyal friend of Davis, and became a brigadier general in the Confederate army in 1861. He commanded the military district around Port Royal when his brother led the attacking Union ship. After the war, Drayton returned to farming. Contrasting with these exemplary students were other Southern cadets in Davis's "set" who had a bad influence on him and caused him to get into trouble. The "green" Mississippi youth apparently had some expensive tastes, for as early as January 12, 1825, he wrote to Joseph requesting that he send some cash, although the regulations of the academy strictly forbade a cadet from receiving extra money from a parent or any other person. He apologized for this request by explaining that in the future he hoped his monthly pay would meet all of his expenses, but that this expectation would depend on the company he kept. He wrote contemptuously of the cadets from the Northern states: "The Yankee part of the corps find their pay entirely sufficient [,] some even more, but these are [not] such as I formed an acquaintance with on my arrival it having originated in the introductory letters I brought on with me. Nor, are they such associates as I would [illegible] at present select ... you cannot know how pitiful they generally are."[6] He had been a cadet a year when two Virginians of aristocratic families entered the academy; during the Civil War, as Confederate president, he was to command them—Robert E. Lee and Joseph E. Johnston. Although both were a year older than Davis, they were in a lower class, and both ranked much higher in scholarship than did their future commander-in-chief. Lee was second top cadet in scholarship in his class and had no demerits during his four years at West Point.[7]

After Joseph E. Johnston resigned his post of Brigadier General and Quartermaster of the United States Army, he ranked behind only Cooper, A. S. Johnston, and Lee in the Confederate Army. He feuded with Davis for many years and surrendered to Sherman contrary to Davis's orders. Ironically, he died at the age of 84 of pneumonia contracted by standing hatless in the rain at Sherman's funeral.

Nor was Davis as exemplary in conduct as they were. The young Mississippian, indeed, was arrested during his first year at the academy for violating regulations in patronizing, with some friends, Benny Haven's tavern, which sold spiritous liquors. Captain Ethan A. Hitchcock, who discovered the erring cadets, testified at a court-martial that Cadet Davis on perceiving him exhibited "extreme embarrassment bordering on weakness," which he attributed to the consumption of alcoholic liquors.[8] Major William J. Worth, later a senior officer in the Mexican War, was a witness for the defense, testifying that Cadet Davis's "deportment as a Gentleman has been unexceptionable." The young cadet defended himself in a specious argument, contending that he was accused of an *ex post facto* offense, the regulation on visiting the tavern not having been published, and that excessive rain had driven him from his tent to the shelter of the tavern.[9]

The court-martial, however, convicted him and sentenced him to dismissal from the academy, recommending at the same time that the sentence be remitted in consideration of his previous good conduct. Despite this close call, he was again arrested for attending, in violation of regulations, a Christmas eggnog party on the night of December 24, 1826, given by some Southern students. Following the party, seventy cadets were involved in a riot against the officers, and nineteen were tried by court-martial and expelled. Davis was put under arrest and confined to quarters from December 26, 1826, to February 8, 1827, for participating in the drinking party. Fortunately, he did not take part in the riot because he had been ordered to his room—and he fell asleep while the riot was occurring.[10]

The youthful cadet does not appear to have been very religious while he was at "the Point." He was given demerits for being absent from chapel on numerous occasions. He appreciated the grand oratory of Chaplain Charles McIlvaine, but unlike his friend Leonidas Polk, the future Episcopal bishop and Confederate general, he was not converted.[11] In fact, he did not join a church until the stress and anguish of the Civil War led him to do so, and it is significant that, instead of joining the Baptist Church, the religion of his family, he joined the Episcopal Church, favored by the Southern aristocracy.

His numerous demerits indicate that he was a rather worldly young man with careless habits. The Military Academy under the famous superintendent, Sylvanus Thayer, had very puritanical rules. Davis, for example, was given demerits for visiting during study hours, having long hair at inspection, failing to keep his room in order, spitting on the floor, absence from reveille, absence from class, making unnecessary noise during study hours, firing his musket from the window of his room, not marching from the mess hall, disobeying orders, using spiritous liquors, inattention on drill, cooking in his quarters after eight P.M., absence from evening parade, candlestick out of place, and "foul clothes not in clothes bag."[12] He does not appear in the record as being guilty of other punishable offenses such as irreverence at church, ungentlemanly conduct, "profanity and other immoralities," and odor of tobacco in room.[13] In his studies he does not seem to have aspired to excellence, for when he graduated on June 30, 1828, his rank was twenty-third out of a class of thirty-two, a mediocre record indeed.

He was commissioned brevet second lieutenant in the infantry in January, 1829, and ordered to report to Jefferson Barracks, St. Louis, for further training. According to custom, he was granted a furlough, but did not go immediately to his home in Mississippi. On August 26, two days before his furlough expired, he applied from Lexington for an extension until December 31, on the grounds that he had been unavoidably detained in the North until the season for malaria and yellow fever had commenced, which rendered it imprudent for him to visit Mississippi.[14] He stated that he had been absent from home and relatives for nearly six years. The extension of furlough was granted and signed by Samuel Cooper, the Northerner, who during the Civil War joined the Confederate army and was appointed by Davis adjutant general and inspector general.

On May 31, 1829, Davis was ordered to report to Fort Winnebago, in Michigan Territory, a frontier fort that had been established the year before at the portage of the Fox and Wisconsin rivers because of the threat of an Indian war. On June 3, 1829, while stationed here, he wrote a letter to his favorite sister, Lucinda Stamps, who was living with his mother at the family home near Woodville, Mississippi, in which he contemplated his future plans (the letter was discovered in 1972 in Paris, Kentucky). He admitted that he really did not like the army, but that it seemed best suited to him. Ironically he rejected the choice of politics, his future profession, as a career that usually ended in maledictions and disgrace—a premonition of the end of his career as Confederate president. West Point, he observed, rendered him unfit for civilian life, for it made him "a different creature from that which nature had designed me to be." The army, unfortunately, did not encourage the desire among officers to improve themselves, and at his post the officers were generally "men of light habits both of thinking and acting," yet their manners were genteel and they observed the rules of morality, dissipation being less common among them than in Mississippi, for drunkards were dismissed from the service. As for himself, he intended to pursue a course of study, especially of lawbooks, since if he should leave the service, he preferred the practice of law to any other profession. He also mentioned in his letter that the diamond breast pin which Lucinda had given him had been admired by the Missouri girls (at St. Louis) and drew attention in the ballrooms, thus supporting Hudson Strode's picture of him as a gay blade in his young manhood.[15]

In his first post in the army his pay was fixed at $62.50 a month, including an allowance for one servant. For most of this period his servant was the faithful slave, Jim Pemberton, who after Davis left the army acted as his overseer at Brierfield. One of Davis's earliest duties was to search for deserters in the Chicago region, and he also acted as recruiting officer. He was recorded as acting assistant quartermaster during his stay at Fort Winnebago. As such, in May, 1830, he bought 148 pounds of candles for the post and supervised the hauling of stone and lime for constructing new barracks. Later he also served as assistant commissary of subsistence, in which position he bought beef, beans, and whiskey for the troops. One of his most arduous duties was to build a sawmill on the Yellow River and cut lumber to be rafted down to erect buildings at Fort Winnebago. He accomplished this difficult task in the face of hostile Indians, but the severe winter further ruined his health. He contracted pneumonia and became terribly emaciated. Only the faithful service of Jim Pemberton saved his life, and this solicitous care for him by the black man caused Davis, according to his wife Varina's memoir, to love him almost as if he were his brother.[16]

The young lieutenant was quite spirited whenever he thought that he had been ignored or treated disrespectfully. An example of his spirit occurred when his request for stationery was ignored by the assistant quartermaster at St. Louis, who wrote him a businesslike letter stating that he would not pay future drafts by him unless they were properly authenticated. Davis promptly returned his letter with the haughty comment: "I shall avoid making any call on you, which it may be optionary for you to grant or refuse."[17] The officer was so indignant that he wrote to General Thomas S. Jesup, quartermaster general of the U. S. Army, describing Davis's letter as insubordinate and disrespectful. Jesup wrote to the commanding general of the army, Alexander McComb, recommending that the impudent young officer be reprimanded for conduct repugnant to every sound principle of the service.[18]

In the summer of 1831 Davis was transferred to Fort Crawford at Prairie du Chien in the Michigan Territory, a place known for its Indian trade, and there he remained for two years. While he was stationed in this remote post he was ordered to go to the region of Dubuques Mines (near present-day Galena, Illinois) to protect recent settlers and lead miners from hostile Indians. Although he remained there from the fall of 1831 to the following spring and made frequent reconnaissances, he never saw an Indian. He was also charged with the formidable task of preventing further intrusions upon Indian lands by lawless settlers and miners in the Galena lead mining district.

In assigning him this task his commanding officer, Colonel Willoughby Morgan, wrote that Lieutenant Davis was "a Young Officer in whom I have much confidence."[19] His orders were to remove, by force if necessary, those who had illegally settled upon Indian lands. These squatters were rough, even dangerous men. Davis found them armed to the teeth and in a truculent mood.

Nevertheless, he was able by diplomacy to persuade them to remove peacefully, meanwhile registering their claims and promising them that, as soon as the treaty in process of being negotiated should be concluded, they could return. On March 26, 1832, he left the Galena lead district, having obtained a furlough of two months.

He went to Natchez and Woodville, where he seems to have been on July 9 when his brother Joseph addressed a letter to him at that place. Jefferson had asked his advice about applying for a position as engineer of a Mississippi railroad company. Joseph advised against it. While Jefferson was on furlough, which at his request was extended, the second Black Hawk War was being waged. Whether he gave up his furlough and returned to participate in the last skirmish, the Battle of Bad Axe (August 21, 1832), is a moot question, although it is doubtful that he did.[20] There is no question, however, that he commanded a body of troops guarding Black Hawk and about a hundred of his warriors when in September they were taken as prisoners from Fort Crawford to Rock Island and then to Jefferson Barracks at St. Louis. In his autobiography Black Hawk praised Lieutenant Davis for his kindness and consideration when he was transported down the river to St. Louis. He especially appreciated the lieutenant's efforts to protect him, when the steamboat touched shore at Galena, from attempts of a "a gaping crowd" to invade his privacy.[21]

Shortly after the conclusion of the Black Hawk War, in the fall of 1832, South Carolina precipitated a confrontation with the federal government by nullifying the tariff acts of 1828 and 1832. On March 1, 1833, Congress passed the "Force Bill," giving President Jackson the authority to employ the armed forces of the United States to collect the customs in South Carolina and uphold the authority of the federal government. Thus the possibility arose that, as an officer of the army, Davis might be required to participate in a military action against the state of South Carolina. In Varina Davis's memoir of her husband, she quotes his reaction to such an eventuality: "By education, by association and by preference I was a soldier, then regarding that profession as my vocation for life. Yet, looking the issue squarely in the face, I chose the alternative of abandoning my profession rather than be employed in the subjugation or coercion of a State of the Union, and had fully determined and was prepared to resign my commission immediately on the occurrence of such a contingency."[22] Fortunately, South Carolina accepted the Compromise Tariff Act of 1833 presented by Henry Clay, and repealed her Nullification Act.

On March 3, 1833, Davis was appointed second lieutenant of dragoons. Although he accepted the new commission, he protested against being a subordinate to two officers in the regiment "who were formerly much my juniors."[23] In the summer he was sent to Lexington on recruiting service at a time when a severe epidemic of cholera was afflicting the town. This epidemic spread terror among the inhabitants of the lower Mississippi Valley. The doctors did not know how to treat the disease and citizens and planters tried various pragmatic methods to combat it, such as the prescription of Jefferson's brother Joseph, who advised his brother-in-law to pull up every melon vine and cut down the fruit trees on his plantation.[24] Despite the danger, Jefferson remained at his recruiting post in Lexington, where 502 persons died from the dread disease.[25]

When he returned in August, 1833, to the headquarters of his regiment, now stationed at Jefferson Barracks, he was appointed adjutant of the regiment. At the end of the year the regiment was sent to Fort Gibson and to Fort Jackson in the wilderness of the Arkansas Territory. Here the men suffered severe hardships throughout the winter. Moreover, there was friction between the commanding colonel, Henry Dodge, and his officers. Dodge wrote, on April 18, 1834:

> I find more treachery and deception practised in the army than I ever expected to find with a Body of Men who call themselves Gentlemen. My situation is unpleasant, Davis who I appointed my adjt. was among the first to take a Stand against me. Major Mason and Davis are now two of My Most inveterate enemies the desire of these Gentlemen is to Harrass [me] in small matters[;] they dont want to fight [a duel].[26]

Davis's life in the remote frontier posts of the Middle West was lonely and primitive, but it was not without compensations and amusements. Among these amusements were attending horse races and wolf fights, hunting deer and pheasants, chasing buffalo, and observing Indian customs when they came to the forts to trade.[27] Davis formed a high opinion of the rough but sterling qualities of the frontiersmen whom he encountered, but a low opinion of the Indians. While a senator, in supporting a bill on February 10, 1858, to increase the army, he spoke in opposition to Senator Sam Houston, who praised the character of the Indians, by forthrightly declaring: "Take them as a mass, they are as deceptive, as bloodthirsty, as treacherous, as cowardly a race of men as are to be found on the globe."[28] The loneliness of his life was greatly alleviated when in April, 1832, Colonel Zachary Taylor took command of Fort Crawford, to which he had been assigned, for he fell in love with his daughter Sarah, and despite the opposition of Taylor to the courtship they met secretly at the house of a friend.

On May 10, 1834, Davis was commissioned first lieutenant in the regiment of the dragoons. He had served less than a year in his new commission when his commanding officer, Major R. B. Mason, brought charges against him, and he was tried by a court-martial beginning February 12, 1835. Mason charged Davis with conduct subversive of military discipline. The charge arose from the fact that on a rainy day he did not answer reveille roll call. On that occasion the major spoke sharply to the young lieutenant. According to Mason, Davis responded in an insubordinate manner, abruptly turning away and saying "Hum!"[29] When he was called back and ordered to his quarters under arrest, Davis stared at his commanding officer, did not obey the order until Major Mason had repeated it a third time, and then asked in a contemptuous manner, "Now are you done with me?"

Ordered to appear before a court-martial, the young lieutenant conducted his defense in a spirited and skillful manner. He observed that he had been severely ill with pneumonia in the winter of 1833–34 while on duty in the Northwest, and that he had previously expressed a desire to leave Fort Gibson for fear of the effect of the severe winter upon his weakened constitution. He was especially resentful that Major Mason had spoken to him harshly in the hearing of the company that he commanded. In his defense, by questions and cross-examination, Davis brought out from witnesses that he had been correctly military in conduct and had been faithful in performance of his duties. The trial lasted six days, and on the last day he asked the proud question, "Can it be required of a Gentleman, is it part of the character of a soldier, to humble him self beneath the haughty tone, or quail before the angry eye of any man?"[30]

In this episode Davis displayed an extreme sense of pride, derived partly from his background of being reared among dueling Southerners. It was later to prove a dangerous characteristic during his administration as Confederate president when he had to deal with equally proud and sensitive officers, such as Joseph E. Johnston and Pierre G. T. Beauregard. Unlike Lincoln, who could ignore insults for the good of his country, Davis would bridle at any criticism that he thought impugned his honor or dignity. At his trial, he stated the credo of a high-mettled Southern gentleman. "When I learn," he said at the court-martial, "that the caprice of a commander can increase or decrease the obligations of my commission, can magnify or diminish the quantum of military offence contained in military acts, I shall cease to consider myself a freeman and no longer feel proud of my sword."[31]

He was pronounced not guilty of the charge against him by the court-martial. The same court tried Lieutenant Lucius Northrop for disobedience of orders and breach of arrest. Davis testified in behalf of the accused, whom during the Civil War he was to appoint commissary general of the Confederate army, although he had to remove him after the Confederate house had passed a bill demanding this step. On March 1, 1835, while the trial was in progress, Davis applied for a leave of absence, and upon its expiration he resigned from the U. S. Army, to take effect June 30, 1835. The reason for this resignation was his intention to marry Sarah Knox Taylor. Taylor's opposition to his daughter marrying a military officer presented a formidable obstacle to the marriage, for in the antebellum period a suitor was supposed to get the assent of the father of his betrothed. But Sarah was strong-willed and met her lover at the house of a married friend.

Although Davis's military life ended when he was twenty-six years old, his days as a West Point cadet and as a frontier soldier continuously influenced his career. The erect military carriage acquired as a soldier he retained to his old age, and the splendid horsemanship developed during service in the dragoons was a valuable consequence of his military training. Originally he had not wished to pursue a military career, and he was not an outstanding student at West Point. Nevertheless, in contrast to so many West Point graduates, who, after they had gotten their education at government expense and served a minimum time in the army, resigned to pursue more lucrative careers, he had decided to make a career in the army his profession. He was propelled toward this choice of a military career partly, as observed, by the military tradition of his family, as well as by the prestige that Southerners gave to military service.

In the army Davis had learned to manage men and exercise authority, particularly in removing hostile lead miners from Indian lands at Galena. At military posts he mainly conducted reconnaissances, rather than fighting Indians. He also learned the perfunctory duties of a peacetime army, serving in the varied positions of assistant quartermaster, assistant adjutant, assistant commissary, and company commander. During his years as a frontier soldier he had tested his courage, displaying extraordinary qualities of resourcefulness, poise, and self-reliance, and a stoical character. Among deficits that accompanied his early military life was the impairment of his health, so that he was never as robust after his severe bout with pneumonia in Wisconsin as before, and his eyes, Varina Davis wrote, were permanently injured by overexposure to the blinding snows of the Northwest. More important, however, were the intangible effects of military discipline on his personality, increasing his reserve and formality of manner and strengthening an overweening sense of pride (though not of conceit), and they were to prove definite weaknesses in his personality while he was the president of the Confederate States of America.

West Point and his life as a soldier on the frontier, strengthened by the military tradition of his family, inculcated patriotism and loyalty to the national government. But it was a conditional loyalty, dependent on the national government observing the compact of the Constitution strictly and honorably. When that government threatened to trample on the rights of a sovereign state by coercing South Carolina in the Nullification crisis Jefferson Davis opposed it.

3

The Women in Davis's Life

Davis's decision to abandon the army as a career, in 1835, was a turning point in his life. He became a planter and a politician destined to play a great role on the political stage of the nation. At this time he appears to have been quite different in personality from the dignified, inflexible, and stern Confederate president. In his young manhood he presented a handsome cavalier appearance—a tall, slender young man just under six feet in height, with strongly marked features, deep-set blue-gray eyes, blond hair, and a notably erect carriage.[1] Although he retained a certain aristocratic reserve throughout life, beneath the reserve there was an affectionate, affable personality that was most attractively displayed in his two great love affairs.

While he was stationed at Fort Crawford at Prairie du Chien in 1832, as noted in the previous chapter, he met Sarah Knox Taylor, daughter of the commander, Colonel Zachary Taylor, and fell in love with her. She was eighteen years old then and had just moved from her home in Louisville, Kentucky, to this rough frontier post. A portrait painted when she was sixteen years of age shows a very feminine Southern girl, with long blonde hair parted in the middle and falling in ringlets to her shoulders, an extremely thin waist, and a sweet, unsophisticated expression—a typical Southern girl of the gentry.

There are no letters extant from Sarah to Davis and only one during this period from him, dated December 16, 1834. It was written from Fort Gibson in Arkansas Territory and expressed the longing of a young man for his betrothed. It is permeated by the romantic ideal of the Southern woman popular at that time. He wrote that before he had received her letter he had dreams of losing her, but her letter had driven away the nightmares. Romantically he exclaimed, "Often I long to lay my head upon that breast which beats in unison with my own, to turn from the sickening sights of worldly duplicity and look in those eyes, so eloquent of purity and love."[2] He recalled her gift before parting of a flower of hearts ease, which had remained as bright as ever. He confessed that he had kissed her letter often and that she was the first woman he had ever wished to marry, and that he hoped soon to see her, never to part. He told her that he lamented the breach between her and her family caused by his courtship. He ended his letter with a French phrase, *"Adieu ma chère, très chère amie."*

After nearly two years of engagement Sarah Knox Taylor and Jefferson Davis were married on June 17, 1835, at the home of her aunt, a sister of Zachary Taylor, three miles from Louisville. In his autobiography he explicitly denied that the marriage took place "after a romantic elopement, as so often has been stated."[3] Neither the members of the Davis family nor Zachary Taylor and his wife were present. Knox, as Sarah called herself, wrote an affectionate letter to her mother on her wedding day in a plea for "affection for a child who has been so unfortunate as to form a connection without the sanction of her parents."[4] Nevertheless, Zachary Taylor sent her a liberal supply of money and may have finally given a grudging assent to the marriage.

After the wedding the bride and groom took passage on a steamboat for Hurricane, his brother's plantation, where Joseph and his wife Eliza welcomed them. From there Sarah wrote an affectionate letter to her mother in which she recalled her mother's homely activities: skimming the milk and feeding the chickens, and being annoyed by unwelcome visitors. Sarah was enthusiastic about a beautiful colt that Joseph had given her to ride. She ended her letter with "Mr. Davis [her husband] sends best respects to you."[5]

In the late summer Jefferson and his bride visited his sister Anna, who was married to a wealthy physician-planter in West Feliciana Parish, Louisiana. It seems strange that Davis should take his delicate bride into the lower South at this time, when earlier he had asked for an extension of a furlough so that he could visit his relatives in Mississippi after the dangerous malaria season was over. At the home of his sister both he and his bride had a severe attack of malaria. They were nursed in separate rooms, but Davis heard his wife in delirium singing a favorite song of hers, entitled "Fairy Bells." Realizing her desperate condition, he arose from his sickbed and struggled to her room just before she died on September 15, 1835.[6] She was buried in his sister's family graveyard in Louisiana on the banks of the Mississippi River.

Jefferson was in serious danger for a month. When he was well enough to travel, he went to his brother Joseph's plantation to recuperate. For a number of years afterward he continued to have recurring attacks of malaria. In order to recover his health, in the winter of 1835–36 he made a trip to Havana, Cuba. He was lonely and bored and his chief recreation was sketching, but this activity aroused the suspicions of the Cuban authorities since he was known to have been an officer of the United States Army, and they feared he was sketching military fortifications.[7] He returned to the United States on a ship sailing to New York. From there he went to Washington, where he enjoyed observing the debates of Congress and meeting various prominent politicians to whom he was introduced by his friend George W. Jones, then delegate to Congress from the Michigan Territory. In 1837–38 he returned to Washington for another visit to Jones, during which President Van Buren invited him to breakfast at the White House.

He did not remarry for ten years, but lived in seclusion on a plantation that his brother Joseph gave him. Jefferson called it Brierfield because of the abundance of briars on the uncleared land. With the help of a few slaves, he cleared the land, built a cottage, and cultivated cotton. During the Christmas holidays of 1843 he met his future second wife, Varina Howell of Natchez, Mississippi. Joseph Davis had invited Miss Howell, seventeen years old, the daughter of a friend, to visit his plantation, Hurricane. He had three young daughters and no sons, and a melancholy second wife who was often sick. By the invitation, perhaps, Joseph wished to provide agreeable company for the female members of his family, as well as for his young brother on an adjoining plantation.

Varina was a tall brunette with a very striking personality. She was well-educated for a Southern girl of the period, for she had attended a finishing school in Philadelphia, and in addition had been tutored for twelve years in the Greek and Latin classics by Judge George Winchester, a native of Salem, Massachusetts, who had settled in Natchez. Although her family had little wealth, she lived in an attractive house, The Briars, and had acquired aristocratic manners and notions from Natchez society and from the consciousness that her grandfather had been a governor of New Jersey.[8] Her family and her tutor were strongly partisan Whigs, the party favored by the aristocratic planters and lawyers of the region.

Jefferson's first meeting with Varina occurred after she had come up the river in a steamboat, chaperoned by Judge George Winchester, and landed at Diamond Place, the plantation of Joseph's married daughter, Florida McCaleb. Jefferson, on his way to a political meeting at Vicksburg, rode by Diamond Place to deliver a message from Joseph to the young miss, inviting her to come as soon as possible to Hurricane and sending a saddle horse to ride. Varina's first impressions of her future husband were conveyed to her mother in a very perceptive letter. "He impresses me," she wrote, "as a remarkable kind of man; but of uncertain temper, and has a way of taking for granted that everybody agrees with him when he expresses an opinion, which offends me." Thus, at their first meeting she detected a trait, being opinionated, that was to prove a serious weakness during his administration as Confederate president. "Yet," she continued, "he is most agreeable, and has a peculiarly sweet voice and a winning manner of asserting himself. The fact is, he is the kind of person I should expect to rescue one from a mad dog at any risk, but to insist upon a stoical indifference to the fright afterwards. I do not think I shall ever like him as I do his brother. Would you believe it, he is refined and cultivated and yet he is a Democrat."[9]

Varina paid a long visit to the hospitable family at Hurricane, as was customary in the Old South among plantation families. In January, 1844, she was engaged to Jefferson. Yet, strangely, when she returned to her family at The Briars in Natchez, she forbade her lover to come to see her for a period. As late as March 8 he complained about this interdiction, observing that it seemed proper to him in order "to justify my writing to you that I should announce to your parents my wish to marry you."[10] But the opposition of Mrs. Howell had to be overcome: she had reservations about the marriage of her youthful daughter to a widower who was eighteen years older than she. Davis had an advocate in the much-respected Judge Winchester, and a week later he received a letter saying that the mother had ceased opposing the marriage.[11]

Six of Davis's letters to Varina while he was courting her have been preserved. Written in the rather stilted language of love letters of the period, they are quite romantic and decorated with French phrases. For example, he wrote, "Pray dont read at night, or punish your angel eyes by keeping a light in your chamber at night."[12] The letters show that he was extremely busy, riding around the country making political speeches for the Democratic party in the presidential campaign of 1844. They indicate, too, that he was much concerned over Varina's frequent illnesses, apparently brought on by nervous excitement. In the letters he mentioned that she had given him a lock of her hair and some heartsease flowers, popular mementos of a romantic age. Though he was deeply in love with her, he may have detected in her a temperamental weakness that displeased him. He warned her against "such love of admiration, or excess of politeness as might induce one to fear that ridicule or even detractive remarks were secretly made." (In one love letter he referred to what would today be termed the Freudian slip of calling him by her father's name.) Referring to it, Davis asked, "Have you, my dear child, been sick again?" In another letter he forewarned his prospective bride to be prepared to yield to the necessities our fortune imposes, to be "prepared for the worst within the range of possibilities, as blessed are they who expect nothing, for surely they shall not be disappointed"—rather grim advice to a vibrant young fiancée.[13]

After a postponement of the wedding on account of Varina's illness, they were married at the bride's home in Natchez on February 26, 1845, in an Episcopal ceremony. None of Jefferson's family attended the wedding, although Varina had invited Joseph and his wife. Jefferson wrote to Varina that brother Joe thought it probable that he would attend the wedding but that he had not previously thought of it.[14] Indeed, Joseph seems to have had reservations about his brother marrying into a large family whose father had been unsuccessful in business, which presented the probability of being a financial burden on his brother. This foreboding proved to be justified.

Immediately after the wedding Davis and his bride took a steamboat to Bayou Sara in Louisiana, then rode to Locust Grove, the plantation of his sister Anna, where his first bride had died. Here he visited the grave of his first love, a perfectly natural act, but one wonders what Varina must have thought of such a pilgrimage on her honeymoon. From Locust Grove they went to Woodville to visit his mother, and then they took passage on a steamboat for New Orleans where they stayed for six weeks at the fashionable St. Charles Hotel. After their honeymoon they proceeded to the cottage at Brierfield that Davis and his slaves had built.

Varina, in her memoir of her husband, remembered this house affectionately, with its doors six feet wide to admit the circulation of air, its deep fireplaces, and around it a magnificent grove of oaks and fig trees and abundant game—wild geese and ducks and blue cranes standing on one leg among the lily pads, with their lemon-colored flowers. Here they lived for five years until they built a more pretentious house, enjoying the appeal of unspoiled nature, visiting, reading, writing, gardening, riding horseback, and attending to the slaves.

The city-bred girl seems to have adjusted well to the lonely life at Brierfield where the mail was delivered only twice a week by steamboat. She busied herself with a flower garden and a vegetable garden, for both she and Jefferson loved roses and ornamental shrubs and vines. Daily, she and her husband would go for a horseback ride, she on a woman's sidesaddle, for it was regarded as unfeminine at that time for a woman to ride astride a horse. Often, on level ground, they would race each other. One of the things that Varina admired about Jefferson was his superb horsemanship.

Although Varina had frequent spells of sickness, Davis wrote to her mother two months after their marriage that "she grows calmer, discreeter, happier and lovelier with each passing day."[15] When her mother, who had eleven pregnancies, wrote to her six months after her marriage asking if she did not need "a comfortable dress" (a maternity dress), she replied that she did not need one and probably never would require one. Her husband, she wrote, had "a horror of loose gowns," and since he did not wish her to wear one, she never did, and furthermore she had given up wearing nightcaps.

While her husband was away during the Mexican War, Varina began supervising the building of a larger and more elaborate house at Brierfield. She used the labor of their slaves in making brick for the walls of the house; the slaves also did much of the carpentry work under the supervision of local white carpenters. The house was not a grand mansion such as the rich planters who lived in Natchez built. It was a low, one-story house with a verandah extending across the front, and with French windows. During the construction she quarreled with Joseph because he wished two kitchens built in order to accommodate his and Jefferson's widowed sister, Amanda, with her large brood of children, who were expected to occupy half of the house, but Varina firmly rejected this idea.

Indeed, Varina developed a strong dislike for Jefferson's brother Joseph. While they were in Washington, she wrote to her mother on April 29, 1854, "Jeff is wretchedly thin, and at times very weak, but then he recovers, and is gay for a week or ten days. I think his Brother Joe's alienation preys upon his mind but he never speaks of it."[16] Varina was jealous of the deep affection of Jefferson for his brother. She bitterly resented also that Joseph had not given them a deed for Brierfield although it was clearly understood that he had given the land to Jefferson. Earlier, also, Mrs. Howell had written from Natchez to her daughter some "revelations" accussing Joseph of retaining some of the money from the sale of Brierfield cotton, but Varina had burnt the letter.[17]

Varina was a Victorian woman who condemned any display of sex. Although she loved parties and dress, she had a puritanical side that led her to judge harshly those who violated the decorum of society. In a letter to her mother she expressed outrage at the conduct of the wealthy Mrs. Gwin, the wife of a future senator, at a ball given in honor of John C. Calhoun at Vicksburg in 1845. She severely criticized this lady for wearing a black velvet dress cut so low that it exposesd her luscious person, causing Varina to blush and feel ashamed. While waltzing with a son of Calhoun, Mrs. Gwin apparently looked at the young man so licentiously in addition to exposing the upper part of her breasts that Varina wrote, "It made my blood run cold and I felt like kicking both of them out of the room for daring to conduct themselves in such a manner before innocent young girls."[18]

A letter that Jefferson wrote to his wife from the mouth of the Rio Grande River on August 16, 1846, throws some light on Varina's character, and at the same time reveals that he occasionally used profanity. She had asked him to refrain from being profane. He replied that he had remembered her request on the subject of profanity, but asked, "Have you remembered mine on the subject of prayer, and a steady reliance on the justice of one who sees through the veil of conduct to the motives of the heart. Be pious, be calm, be useful, and charitable and temperate in all things."[19]

Varina was a successful hostess, both as a congressman's wife at Washington and later as the president's wife in Richmond. A brilliant conversationalist, she enjoyed talking with prominent political leaders, who paid great deference to her. Within a few months after arriving in Washington she had gained poise and confidence in herself, writing to her mother that her manners were much improved. "Without the desire for any admiration but Jeffy's," she wrote, "I have lost a great deal of that embarrassed, angry looking manner which made me show to so much disadvantage."[20] In her first year as a young congressman's wife, she entertained by giving a "little hop" to which she invited some "sweet looking girls" and intelligent young men, and she herself participated in the dancing. Young girls with their beaus would call informally at the Davis home, and the hostess played cotillions on the piano until she was exhausted. On one occasion "Jeff" flirted with the girls in an elegant manner and with a smiling face.

She was fond of clothes, which she made herself, and often described minutely in her letters to her mother such dresses, for example, as a black watered silk and white polka dot creation made of bobbinet and trimmed with her wedding lace, with which she wore a white japonica in her dark hair. But this feminine side of her nature was balanced by a serious interest in politics and intellectual subjects. She frequently went to the House of Representatives to hear the speeches, but on one occasion in 1846 she reported that she heard nothing but empty vaporing about our abilities, or power to whip England.

Along with her ability to be very charming when she pleased, Varina could be critical of people and forthright in expressing her opinions.[21] She herself recognized her sharpness of speech with people who annoyed her as a fault to be controlled. What made her cutting remarks all the more painful was that she was often witty at the same time. Mary Boykin Chesnut of South Carolina, who belonged to her small coterie of friends in Richmond during the Civil War, commented in her famous diary that "she is as witty as he [Davis] is wise." This aristocratic Southern lady, the wife of a wealthy plantation owner and former senator, gave a very favorable description of Varina's personality: "clever, brilliant, warm-hearted, and considerate."[22]

After remaining childless for seven years, Varina gave birth to her first child in 1852 in Washington, named after Davis's father. It relieved her from the reproach of other Southern married women against a barren wife. Mrs. Chesnut, who was sad over not having a child, commented in her diary that Southern women looked down on a childless married woman. In the Old South women felt obligated to have a child within a year of marriage. After Varina had been married only six months she wrote to her mother, "We both regret to be condemned to live in single blessedness."[23] Varina had a hard time with the birth of her six children and dramatized her pregnancies. When her first child Samuel died, she said that her husband was so anguished that he walked the floor half of the night and worked fiercely all day to forget the tragedy. But tragedy was to strike the Davises again and again in the early deaths of their children (one little boy fell off the high porch of the White House at Richmond) until at last only two of their children outlived the parents.

When her fourth child was born in May, 1859, Varina wished to name him in honor of her father, but Davis insisted that he be named after his beloved brother Joseph. She wrote to her mother that she cried herself sick over the thought and had to take quinine, but male supremacy in the Old South dictated that the husband had the right to name the child, and Varina yielded. But it was repugnant to name her baby after "a man whose very name was only suggestive to me of injustice and unkindness from my youth up to middle age." Unfortunately for her, too, the baby boy looked like his uncle Joe: "small build, grey eyes, large nose, and black hair."[24] She prayed that he would grow out of the resemblance.

While she and her husband were in Washington they were in high favor with the various presidents, particularly Franklin Pierce, and consequently were much entertained. Varina was amused by the foibles and funny things she saw in Washington society. At an elaborate costume ball given by the wealthy Senator and Mrs. Gwin of California, Varina attracted much favorable attention by dressing as Madame de Staël. On December 16, 1857, she wrote to her mother that a new dance called "the lancers" was all the rage, and that the dancers looked so solemn as they did the complicated steps— "all the old married women danced but me [she was only thirty]," she reported.[25] Most of the Davises's friends were Southerners. Varina enjoyed talking with prominent political leaders, such as President John Tyler, with whom she drank warm milk at an agricultural fair in Washington.

Varina was in many respects different from the female members of Jefferson's family. They illustrated the position of upper-class rural women in the Old South. In the letters of Davis's sisters and nieces to him there is a sense of feminine inferiority, though theoretically women were placed on a pedestal. Davis's sisters were strong individuals like he was, yet they felt inferior to males. Varina, who had met them as a bride, described them as "spirited, intelligent women, with strong convictions of duty and a wonderful inborn dignity that is not to be acquired by education."[26]

There was a note of self-effacement, nevertheless, in the sisters' letters to their brilliant young brother, the hope of the family. His beloved older sister Lucinda wrote: "I know that you will not think of the bad writing and still worse composition (that is if you can read it) of a sister that time or circumstance can never change." And even more so, the letters of Eliza, Joseph's wife, who was only three years older than Jefferson, are tinged with the feeling of inferiority caused by living in a society dominated by males. She admitted that she was indolent, for she was the wife of a wealthy planter who had plenty of servants. Yet life was not satisfying, and she confessed, "I sometimes feel as if I had no motive to exertion—that this life is but a dream that will soon pass away."[27] In this letter to her brother-in-law, she expressed great affection for him and a desire to hear from him, at the same time disclosing a feeling of inferiority, condemning her "poor brain deficient" and her "miserable scrawl," but adding that she was not "the same foolish creature as heretofore."[28] Some of this melancholy was doubtless owing to the fact that she was childless.

And Florida McCaleb, the oldest daughter of Joseph, also deprecated her worth in a letter to Jefferson. "I am too dull and commonplace, too unweary in my perseverance, to be highly appreciated, and you have grown weary of receiving the stupid letters of a very stupid friend," she wrote, and further on in her letter, "But I, who am the very type of all obscurity whose life has been a tissue of misfortune from my very birth." From a fifteen-year-old girl, married to a planter, such a letter must have been an expression of romantic pathos in an age when Byron was the rage. But her advice to her twenty-five-year-old uncle was realistic and typical of the Southern devotion to honor: "Cherish Ambition, cherish pride and al[ways] run from excitement to excitement, it will prevent that ever preying *viper* melancholy, it will blunt your sensibilities and cause you to be unmoved among afflictions." Florida, like Eliza, remained childless.

With few exceptions, such as the famous female abolitionists, the Grimké sisters of South Carolina, women of the period did not protest, at least publicly, against the status of their sex. Varina, although at times she argued vehemently against her husband's decisions, accepted unquestioningly male dominance. Mrs. Chesnut, in *A Diary from Dixie,* protested against the immorality of the planters with their slave women and during the Civil War wrote that men got all the glory; nevertheless, she was far from being a feminist, as were some of the Northern women. The reasons for women's acceptance of their assigned role in society were that their religion consigned them to a subordinate role, as did the romantic ideal of the period and their economic dependence.[29] How many women would run counter to the mores of their society and subject themselves to the ridicule of liberated Northern women was expressed by one of the most prominent and liberal of Southerners, John Hartwell Cocke of Bremo, Virginia. To his friend, the famous Professor William Holmes McGuffey of the University of Virginia, author of the *McGuffey Readers,* he wrote after attending a World Temperance Convention in New York in September, 1853:

> You have doubtless seen in the newspapers the struggle we had with the strong-minded women as they call themselves in the World Temperance Convention. If you have seen the true account of the matter, you will see that we gained a perfect triumph, and I believe have given a rebuke to this most impudent clique of unsexed females and rampant abolitionists which must put down the petty-coats—at least as far as their claim to take the platforms of public debate and enter into all the rough and tumble of the war of words.

The professor of moral philosophy replied: "I most heartily rejoice with you in the defeat of those shameless Amazons who gave so much trouble at the World Convention—I trust and believe that it will be *final.*"[30]

The attitude of most Southern women of the period toward males was probably like that of the Davis women, but this did not mean that when emergencies arose, such as during the Civil War, they could not throw off the role assigned to them by their society as helpless, fragile creatures. Rather, many of them capably filled the vacancies left by the soldiers at the front; they managed farms, plantations, and businesses, worked in factories and government offices, taught school, and performed work that before the war would have been unthinkable for women. Nevertheless, even before the Civil War there were a number of independent Southern women, who defied the feminine stereotype, such as the remarkable Rachel O'Connor, who successfully managed a large slave plantation in Louisiana, although during crises even she depended upon her half brother for advice and for strength.[31]

Another striking characteristic of the society in which Varina lived, which contrasted with the more democratic society of the North, was the attitude of women of the upper class, and often of the middle class, toward doing domestic work. It was for Negro slaves. Although cultivating flowers in the garden (usually with the assistance of a Negro slave) was looked upon favorably, to wash clothes, wash dishes, and sweep floors was frowned upon as unbecoming to a white woman of quality. When at the close of the Civil War, Thomas Dabney of Burleigh had not a dollar, not even money to buy a postage stamp, one of his daughters wrote, "His chivalrous nature had always revolted from the sight of a woman doing hard work. He determined to spare his daughters all such labor as he could perform." When it was reported that General Sherman had said that he would like to bring every Southern woman to the wash-tub, the master of Burleigh, seventy years old, declared, "He shall never bring my daughters to the wash-tub. I will do the washing myself."[32] And for two years he did it. This episode makes one wonder at the artificial conditioning of upper-class women by Southern mores of the antebellum period that would permit his daughters to let their gray-headed father to do the work that the majority of Northern women did as a matter of course.

Varina, although accustomed to servants, was not as helpless as the ladies of Burleigh. Despite frequent illness she was more vigorous than her husband, and unusually assertive; yet her husband handled her with quiet authority, maintaining unquestioned male dominance. He expressed his idea of the proper role of a woman in a speech at the Augusta, Maine, fair in 1858: namely, that she should have the "gentle charms which graced a Penelope," but also engage in more active pursuits than being merely domestic, such as the ability to ride a horse and the development of "that mental and physical training which makes a woman more than the mere ornament of the drawing room."[33] In their early married life he indicated, somewhat didactically, one of the outlets for Varina's energy: "to one of exacting and devoted temper (such as Varina) the cultivation of shrubs furnishes an appropriate and inexhaustible field of employment."[34] Although Varina, until she became the Confederate president's wife, refrained from interfering in political appointments and affairs, she undoubtedly expressed forceful opinions, but Davis was too strong-willed and opinionated to be swayed by petticoat influence.[35]

After Varina became the wife of the Confederate president, she displayed new sides of her personality. At times she was accused of acting in a regal way with a court retinue. She put considerable weight on her tall, large frame, while her husband became thinner and more emaciated. Gossipers said that the president was informed that Mrs. Abraham C. Myers, wife of the quartermaster general, had remarked that Varina, because of her dark complexion, looked like an Indian squaw, and shortly thereafter, in mid summer 1863, Davis removed Myers from the position and in his place appointed his old classmate, General Alexander R. Lawton, later president of the American Bar Association.[36] Mrs. Davis was exceedingly sensitive to any criticism of her husband, and showed it. Secretary of the Navy Stephen R. Mallory observes in his diary on June 23, 1861, that "Mrs. Davis lacks refinement and judgment—has a riotous sense of humors-mimics," and, on July 10, that Mrs. Davis is "ill-bred."[37]

On the other hand, the sophisticated correspondent of the *London Times,* William H. Russell, who attended a reception of hers in Montgomery, was favorably impressed with her, describing her as "a comely, sprightly woman, verging on matronhood, of good figure and manners, well-dressed, lady-like and clever."[38] Perhaps the fairest and most discerning estimate of Varina was made by General Josiah Gorgas, chief of ordnance of the Confederate army, by birth and rearing a Northern man, who wrote in his diary on October 17, 1862: "She is a lady of great good sense and of much more than ordinary cultivation."[39] In the face of adversity, she displayed great fortitude, managed her household well despite inflation and scarcity, protected her husband from inquisitive and boring callers, took warm meals to his office to lure him to eat, tried to guard his frail health, and made an excellent wife.

The contrast between the personalities of Davis and his wife was striking. Yet they were happy in their married life, for conflict was dissipated by Jefferson's agreeable personality with his family, and by the fact of his male authority. Varina wrote to her mother a year after their marriage. "Jeff is such a dear good fellow. I might quarrel with him a month and he would not get mad."[40] Moreover, he gave her expensive presents—for example, a cameo engraved with his portrait, a gold pencil, and a gold pen—presents that indicated his prosperity as a cotton grower and slave master, for his salary as a congressman was low. Mrs. Giraud Wright, the daughter of the fire-eater Senator Louis Wigfall of Texas, relates how her father once visited Davis in his home and found him lying flat on his back playing with his young children.[41]

An attractive, appealing side of Davis's personality was his kindness and consideration for his family and relatives. When he married Varina he embraced her large, impecunious family. He supported and educated several of her brothers and sisters. Moreover, Varina was continuously sending hams, eggs, butter, and other farm produce to her mother in Natchez, as well as making clothes for her brothers and sisters. After they had been married less than two years Jefferson gave his wife $450 to buy a piano, but she unselfishly sent the money to her mother for the education of one of her brothers.

One characteristic of Davis's personality that appealed especially to women was his fastidiousness in personal habits; as Mrs. Davis expressed it, he was always delicately *soigné* in his own person. When Jefferson visited Van Buren in the White House, the president admired his fine shoes that he had custom made in New Orleans. Mrs. Davis told of a poor man asking her husband for

money, with Jefferson so impressed by the neatness and cleanliness of the sup-
pliant that he gave generously. On another occasion he was so disgusted by
the dirty fingernails of a congressman that he satirically remarked that he
wished the congressman would play in the sand instead of in dirt.

This pleasant picture of Davis as a devoted and agreeable family man
presents a stark contrast to the image he projected in public life. Mrs. Clement
C. Clay, wife of an Alabama senator, commented on this paradox when she
observed that Davis had the reputation of being cold and haughty, but in
private he was informal and frank.[42] Mrs. Chesnut thought that Davis as
president of the Confederate States of America was overly serious, although
she recognized his cordiality and kindness to her. When she talked with him
in Montgomery at the beginning of the Civil War she noted a sad refrain
running through his conversation, as he predicted a long and bitter war. She
wrote that she was too afraid to say much in his presence, and that he was "an
austere man, quiet, grave, devoted to his work, without a vice in the world."[43]

This was the man, as women saw him, who was to stand forth in the
Senate as the ardent champion of Southern rights and to lead his people in a
tragic struggle for independence.

Slavery on the Davis Plantations

Jefferson Davis has been studied in historical works as a politician and president of the Confederate States of America, almost exclusively, but he was also a successful planter. His activities as a planter are significant, for they add some evidence to the current debate on whether slave labor was profitable in the Old South, and they also present an important aspect of Southern slavery that is often neglected or minimized—namely, the paternal relation between many masters and their slaves.

Jefferson's plantation of Brierfield, containing 800 acres, was part of a 3,000-acre tract of land that Joseph had bought from the federal government and from small pioneer farmers.[1] This purchase of the land of pioneer farmers, who partly cleared the land and sold it to planters before emigrating westward, and then the consolidation of these small farms, was the typical way in which the plantation system developed in the Southwest.[2] The soil was rich, but the great drawbacks to owning a Mississippi River delta plantation were the problem of keeping up the levees that protected the land from being inundated and the danger from malaria-bearing mosquitoes.

In addition to giving his brother the land, Joseph lent him the money to buy ten slaves so that he could begin operations as a planter. Jefferson worked furiously to clear the land, plant a crop, and build a cottage. He was aided by his invaluable and faithful slave Jim Pemberton, who, as we have seen, had acted as his body servant while he was in the army.[3] His friend, Lewis Sanders, Jr., kidded Davis about his absorption in this work in a letter of November 30, 1839, remarking, "Your close application to business in the pursuit of planting is rather anomalous considering your late connection with the army; as military gentlemen are not much given to employment out of Service."[4]

The young planter was still working hard on his plantation ten years after he had established it, and Varina helped him. A few months after her marriage, this city girl wrote to her mother that she kept the books recording the daily amounts of cotton the slaves picked, and that the Negroes required constant attention. Some years later, after her husband had been defeated in his campaign for election to the governorship and had temporarily retired from public office, she wrote to her mother that Jefferson was so busy in his fields "that I scarcely ever see him except when he is too tired to talk."[5] Not only did he supervise his plantation, but he often gave Varina a hand in cultivating her rosebushes and flower garden.

He was fortunate that his brother Joseph lived on a nearby plantation, for Joseph took an active interest in attending to the affairs of the plantation when Jefferson was away. On January 19, 1838, Joseph wrote to inform him that he would send his cotton to market, but that since the commission house they both used had failed he would dispose of their crops through the bank (at Jackson), and that he would prepare his papers on the cotton transaction so that Jefferson would understand them. On August 27 Joseph wrote to his brother from the steamboat *Pavillon,* while on his way to St. Louis, that he had purchased a supply of linsey cloth sufficient for the slaves at Brierfield as well as at his own plantation. He planned to buy provisions at St. Louis, he wrote, stating that he had already shipped bagging and bale ropes for the cotton bales.[6]

On learning that Jefferson planned to stay on his plantation during the sickly season of the summer and early fall, when malaria and yellow fever threatened, he expressed anxiety for his health. As was the custom of many rich delta planters, Joseph, with his family, escaped from this danger by traveling to the White Sulphur Springs in the cooler climate of western Virginia, or to Hot Springs in Arkansas, or to resorts in the North. His brother, on the other hand, continued to expose himself to malaria-bearing mosquitoes. Varina noted on October 29, 1854, that "he had escaped his usual attacks of fever this fall for the first time since he has been in public life."[7]

Joseph was one of the largest planters in the South; he had acquired his wealth by his own efforts. In 1838 he reported that his cotton crop would be about 800 bales. His plantation consisted of over 3,000 acres of fertile land, located twenty-five miles below Vicksburg, and it fitted the romantic stereotype of the Southern plantation. The brick mansion, standing in a grove of oak trees, was three stories tall and nearly surrounded by wide verandahs with white columns; the rooms were extraordinarily spacious, and there was the rare luxury of bathrooms with running water fed from a tank in the attic which slaves pumped full of water.[8] When Varina visited Hurricane as a seventeen-year-old girl she was intrigued by a storeroom containing candy, slave shoes, field implements, calico dresses, new saddles and bridles, guns and ammunition for hunting, pocket knives, and a variety of plantation supplies. Joseph kept the key to this treasure chest.

In her description of Hurricane, Varina noted the office where the accounts of the plantation were kept and where the brothers talked politics and crops. She was also impressed by the huge stable that contained thirty stalls for horses, and by the variety of other buildings, such as one for a cotton gin, a blacksmith shop, and a slave hospital, as well as rows of whitewashed slave cabins.[9] Especially impressive were the immense garden of rare roses and shrubs, the orchard of eight acres, and a separate library built in the shape of a Greek Doric temple, from whose shelves Jefferson often took books on government and history to read to his older brother in the evening. During the middle of the Civil War when the mansion was burned, the library alone was saved.

The Davis brothers were avid horsemen. Joseph owned some famous racehorses, such as Highland Harry, Black Oliver, and Medley, of which Varina wrote with admiration. When Joseph made a trip to Kentucky in the summer of 1838 he visited some of the racehorse farms to observe famous imported stallions, and he engaged to buy a colt of fine lineage. Eliza wrote to her brother-in-law Jefferson while he was in the army, "Your horses are beautiful. I wish you had them to train."[10] On March 11, 1843, Jefferson attended the organizational meeting of the Vicksburg jockey club, which promoted and supervised horse races. In the Mexican War he rode a beautiful, spirited black horse of Arabian breed named Tartar.

From 1835 to 1843, when he began his political career, he seldom left the plantation. The two persons with whom he broke his solitude in conversation were his brother Joseph and his Negro overseer, Jim Pemberton. During this period of isolation on his plantation, he spent many hours in cultivating his mind by reading, as a result of which he was later recognized to be one of the best educated men in Congress. He used his brother's fine library extensively, reading such books as Adam Smith's *The Wealth of Nations, The Federalist,* and Elliot's *Debates on the Federal Constitution*. Still, we know very little of the books that he read and admired, except through an occasional reference in his speeches—for example, to Oliver Goldsmith's *The Vicar of Wakefield*. A letter to his wife in 1869, shortly after his release from prison, while he was visiting Scotland, indicated that he was an admirer of Sir Walter Scott's novels and poems, especially "The Lady of the Lake," which he called a great poem. Mrs. Davis says in her memoir that her husband's love for poetry was continuous throughout his life, and that he memorized passages from Moore's *Lalla Rookh* and Byron's *Childe Harold* and *Don Juan,* as well as

Robert Burns's poetry. Varina wrote of his literary culture: "He was also a very good Spanish scholar and was fond of reading Spanish literature in his younger days. He was also a fair classical scholar, and never forgot his Greek and Latin. Although he had a good command of the French language, he had learned the language simply to read military books and he pronounced it as though it were English."[11]

His absorbing intellectual interest was in the serious subject of American politics. He and his brother had many conversations on political subjects. They regularly read the debates in Congress reported in the *Congressional Globe*. Although both men were strong individualists, they seemed to have been in agreement on most political subjects. They were ardent believers in the compact theory of the Constitution, and strongly opposed to the centralization of the federal government. They agreed also in their violent condemnation of the Northern abolitionists. Both brothers were conservatives, and assumed that the person with whom they were talking recognized the soundness of their political judgment. The older brother was a shrewd observer of politics, but aside from participating in the first constitutional convention of Mississippi, he never became an active candidate for office, concentrating his energies on his law practice and running his plantation.

Jefferson Davis's career as a planter illustrated the salient characteristics of the superior planter class of the lower South. Like virtually all cotton planters, he was concerned with the fluctuation of the prices on the cotton market. These prices were determined by the Liverpool market; planters were helpless to control the price they got for their cotton. In 1839–40, when such a bumper crop was raised that it depressed the market, Jefferson satirically proposed that "our Yankee friends should get up a scheme to pay bounties to cotton planters, to balance the bounties given to the manufacturers."[12] During the 1840s cotton generally brought a very low price, reaching a nadir of 4½¢ a pound in 1845, but in the 1850s the prosperity of the cotton kingdom rebounded, with the fleecy fiber selling for from 10¢ to 12¢ a pound.[13] Accordingly, in 1860 the planters were optimistic about the future of their staple crop so long as the political threat to the existence of slavery could be repelled.

Jefferson suffered from all the drawbacks of being an absentee planter in the 1850s. His white overseers, whom he employed after the death of Jim Pemberton, had trouble controlling the slaves, as indicated in a letter from his brother Joseph in which he reported that the slaves at Brierfield, as well as his own slaves, had engaged in a contraband trade with a merchant in whiskey and corn. Joseph observed that Jefferson's overseer had apparently not exercised sufficient energy and vigilance.[14] In 1857, Jefferson wrote to Varina concerning the discharge of an overseer named Johnson because of incompetence, and also because his ignorant wife had administered large doses of calomel and quinine to a sick slave child, causing its death.[15]

When the Davis family returned to Brierfield in 1857 after a long absence while Davis was secretary of war, they found the house practically dismantled—even the locks to the doors were gone. Varina cried over the appalling desolation of their home: no knives and forks, sheets cut up for napkins, no towels or regular napkins, nothing to cook in, and the family forced to sleep without mosquito netting.[16] Later she wrote that, while the master was absent, there was a decrease every year in their income from the plantation.[17]

One of the great problems concerning Southern slavery which modern historians have investigated exhaustively has been whether the institution was profitable to the majority of planters. The experience of the Davis brothers serves to confirm the latest finding on the question by the cliometricians, Robert W. Fogel and Stanley L. Engerman, who conclude that Southern slavery on the eve of the Civil War had great vitality and was, in fact, highly profitable. Also, contrary to the stereotype of inefficient Southern plantation agriculture, they have found that it was considerably more productive than Northern agriculture, because of the common use of women and children in the labor force, because of the widespread use of incentives and rewards, and, more important, because of the organization of mass labor.[18] Eugene Genovese maintains, perhaps with some truth, that the slaves *forced* the planters to adopt a system of rewards and incentives.[19]

The soil of the Brierfield plantation was so fertile, Varina wrote, that the wild goldenrods grew large enough for walking canes to be made from them. In the old plantation area of the Atlantic seaboard, the average yield of cotton per acre was less than a bale; but on the delta lands and Black Belt of the Southwest, planters frequently made one-and-a-half to two bales per acre. Despite reverses that came from floods, tornadoes, sickness of the slaves, low prices of cotton, and such episodes as alligators eating some of his calves, Jefferson made a considerable fortune from his planting operation. By 1840 he had expanded the number of his slaves from 10 to 40, of whom 29 were reported as engaged in agriculture.[20] In September, 1846, while he was with his regiment in Mexico, Joseph wrote to him that the black overseer estimated that the cotton crops at Brierfield would be about 300 bales, which would indicate that it was a profitable enterprise, even to an absentee landlord. In 1845 the tax rolls of Warren County listed Jefferson as owning 22 cattle, 61 slaves between five and sixty years of age and 13 under five years of age, and he paid a tax of $56.82 on personal property; at the same time Joseph owned nearly 200 slaves and paid a tax of $140.25. In 1856 Jefferson's tax bill had nearly tripled, and by 1860 Brierfield and its slaves were assessed for a value of $225,000, a sum that indicated he had profited greatly from slavery.[21]

The best indication of Jefferson's expanding wealth from planting is furnished by the manuscript records of the censuses of 1850 and 1860.[22] They indicate that in 1850 he had 450 improved acres and 350 unimproved acres, while Joseph had 1,600 improved acres and 1,200 unimproved. The cash value of Jefferson's plantation was then $25,000 and Joseph's, $100,000. But in 1860 the cash value of Jefferson's plantation had risen dramatically to $75,000 for his 800 improved and 1,000 unimproved acres, while the cash value of Joseph's remained the same. This great improvement in value of Jefferson's landholdings may have reflected to some extent the inflation of the decade of the 1850s and the rise in cotton prices. The census returns also indicate a dramatic decline in the value of Jefferson's farm implements and machinery from $3,000 in 1850 to $400 in 1860, a decrease which the available records do not explain.[23] The census records indicate, too, that during the decade Jefferson had shifted the emphasis of his working animals from horses and oxen to mules, employing in 1860 30 mules and 18 oxen, retaining only 7 horses. The cash value of his livestock had increased during the decade from $1,500 to $5,000, which included an increase of milk cows from 5 to 25. In 1850 he had raised 5,000 bushels of Indian corn, in 1860 only 1,000 bushels, a decline which may indicate that in the latter year he bought corn to feed his slaves. Although his brother had 275 sheep in 1860, he had only 5. In 1850 he and his brother each raised 100 swine, but the census record of 1860 omits the number held in that year. The same sheet of the manuscript census record of 1860 lists the holdings of fourteen other plantations in Warren County, which show that only three surpassed Jefferson's plantation in value, and that all except one were large plantations.

Like other planters, Jefferson Davis sought to increase his land and labor force. But in 1859 Varina lamented that they could not do this on account of the heavy destruction wrought by the great flood of that year, which had utterly destroyed their garden and orchard. As a consequence of the severe losses from the flood, she wrote, she had "never known Jeff so distressed and broken down."[24] Many planters in their greed to acquire more land and more slaves went into debt and were therefore in vassalage to their factors, as the commission agents in the seaport were called. But as far as can be determined from the records, Davis escaped this species of economic slavery, for he was financially conservative.

He belonged to that rather large group of planters known as "improving planters," who sought scientific ways to increase the production of their crops, especially by experimenting to find the most productive strains of cotton. He talked and corresponded with the noted scientific planter, Dr. Martin W. Phillips of Log Hall in Mississippi. Dr. Phillips, who made fun of "parlor planters," sent him records of the yields from different seeds of cotton, such as the varieties of "Banana," "Jethro," "Silk," and "Sugar Loaf" cotton.[25]

The life of the Southern planters, such as the Davis brothers, was far from the tranquil and leisured existence depicted in the romantic legend of the Old South. Actually the great majority of the planters were working farmers who supervised their slaves themselves with the aid of a Negro driver or overseer. Only 30 percent of the very large plantations employed white overseers, while a much smaller percentage of those planters owning less than a hundred slaves employed overseers.[26] But the figure of 30 percent seems too large. Absentee planters did usually employ white overseers, but they represented only a small proportion of the planters, except in the Mississippi delta region.[27]

Fogel and Engerman concluded that a large proportion of the planters used black overseers or themselves supervised their plantations, as did Jefferson Davis until after 1850, when he was absent serving in Congress or as secretary of war. Yet their startling contention has been very recently disputed, and they seem to have exaggerated the extent of slave overseership.[28] The use of black overseers declined between 1850 and 1860, which Professor Engerman attributes to political rather than economic factors.[29] The rising prosperity of the planters in that decade, and the good prices they received for their cotton, seems to have been a more important cause for the phenomenon, for the planters could better afford white overseers to relieve them from the hard work of supervising their slaves with only Negro assistants. Davis, as well as the majority of planters, employed his own slaves as carpenters and brickmasons, but he also hired a Northern white man to repair his cotton gin and domestic spinning jennies.

Davis was at different times both an absentee planter and a working planter. When he was absent from his plantation in Washington he constantly worried about its management. In the spring of 1859 he had to rush from Washington to his plantation to direct the efforts of his slaves in bolstering the levee to prevent a crevasse that would have flooded the plantation. He was not successful, for the high floods rendered his pastures unavailable and he had to board his cattle on the Gulf Coast. All of this occurred while Varina remained in Washington, expecting hourly the arrival of another baby. On November 24, 1859, Davis wrote his father-in-law from Brierfield, "My days here have been days of constant toil," and, on account of the needs of the plantation, he was reluctant to leave for the opening of the session of Congress.[30] Although he was desirous of preserving his plantation and the profits from his cotton fields, he was also deeply concerned with the welfare of the human beings on it.

Indeed, Jefferson and Joseph Davis illustrated the virtues of the better planters and slavemasters in their relations with their slaves, and therefore are not to be taken as typical of the slavery regime as a whole. Joseph established slave juries to try offenses of slaves on his plantation. The older and more responsible slaves held trials of accused slaves and sentenced them. Frequently Joseph reduced the sentences of the slave jury or pardoned the convicted culprit. Also, Joseph permitted one of his most intelligent slaves, Ben Montgomery, to keep a variety store on the plantation in which he sold goods to the slaves and the white family, and on occasions Ben purchased the entire peach crop at Hurricane and sold it at a middleman's profit. Ben was a remarkable slave who had learned to read and write, and his sons, Isaiah and Thornton, also learned at an early age to read, write, and do arithmetic. They copied letters for their master and filed papers and letters in the plantation office. Isaiah told an interviewer for the Boston *Transcript:* "We just barely had an idea of what slave life was."[31] The Montgomerys were so capable that in 1867 Joseph sold his own plantation and Brierfield to them for $300,000, although they had little cash and eventually had to surrender the plantations.

The Davis plantations were perhaps exceptional in respect to having literate slaves. Jefferson Davis undoubtedly overstated the amount of literacy among Southern slaves in his debate with senators Collamer of Vermont and Wilson of Massachusetts on April 12, 1860, when he asserted that the laws against teaching slaves to read and write in the South had not been enforced: "but I tell the Senator what, perhaps he does not know, that he will scarcely find a plantation on which he will not find many negroes who can read and who can write a little too."[32] A large proportion of the free Negroes in the South could read and write; the census of 1850 recorded 43 percent of the adult free Negroes in North Carolina as being able to read, and these literate Negroes, as well as some indulgent masters and their children, must have taught a number of slaves to read.[33] Carter Woodson, the eminent black historian, estimated that by 1860, 10 percent of the adult slaves could read.[34]

Jefferson followed the example of his brother in introducing slave juries at Brierfield. Whenever a slave was accused, the master would say, "I will ask him to give me his account of it."[35] He was such a mild master that the neighboring planters said that his slaves were spoiled. Varina, who played an important role in the management of the slaves, was much more strict. When she thought that a slave was malingering on the plea of being sick, she would go into his or her cabin with a bottle of castor oil and another of quinine, and as a result a slave who was pretending to be sick would return to work in the fields. With her own hands she made clothes for the slaves. During her first year as mistress of Brierfield, she wrote to her mother, she had cut out cloth for twenty-five pairs of pantaloons for the slaves and helped Jefferson distribute the clothing supplies to them.

Contrary to the usual practice of planters, Davis did not keep a lock on the corn crib, but allowed the slaves to help themselves to as much corn as they wished to feed themselves and the chickens that they were allowed to raise to supplement their regular food allowance or to sell to the white family. The slaves ground their corn meal from the unrestricted supply of corn in the crib on Saturday afternoons. The paternalism of the master was also shown in providing feasts at wakes (upon the death of a slave), at weddings, at Christmas, and on other occasions. A letter from his overseer to him while he was in Washington, dated January 31, 1859, mentions that the master had written in the "Book of Instructions" that it was the overseer's duty to provide the slaves with coffee, sugar, molasses, and flour.[36]

Davis solicitously cared for the old, the sick, and the handicapped slaves on his plantation. He employed a dentist to come from Vicksburg to care for their teeth, which was a rare thing for a planter to do. He sent a sick fieldhand, whom he described as "a good girl in every sense of the word," to the celebrated Dr. Cartwright in New Orleans to be cured.[37] In order to take proper care of his slaves in sickness he studied medicine. Both he and his brother had slave hospitals. When Davis was secretary of war he got into a discussion with James Campbell, postmaster general in Pierce's cabinet, over some aspect of medicine, and he showed such a knowledge of it that Campbell expressed astonishment. Davis replied, "Judge, you forget that I have had to learn something of medicine so as to take care of the Negroes on my plantation."[38]

Jefferson established such kindly relations with his slaves that, according to Varina, when he went to their quarters, the slaves, even the children, would greet him enthusiastically, and the master was in the habit of shaking hands with them. In her memoir she wrote affectionately of "Old Bob," who was well taken care of by the Davises. After the Civil War, Davis heard of the old Negro's losing his cabin and wrote to Varina from Fort Monroe: "What a beast he must have been who turned Uncle Bob out of his house, to find where he could a shelter for the infirmities of more than a hundred winters."[39] According to the manuscript census of 1860, however, there were surprisingly few old slaves on the plantation. Companionably, Jefferson and his brother hunted deer and bear with their slaves. Varina observed that Joseph had ten or twelve guns in his house which he gave to the slaves when master and slaves were hunting and the master was proud of their marksmanship. There was not the slightest hint of a fear of insurrection in the Davis households. It was against the law for slaves to possess firearms but the Davis brothers, like many of the planters, had a cavalier attitude toward the slave laws and violated them when it suited their interests to do so.[40]

The apparent contentment of "the people," as the slaves were euphemistically called, was owing not only to their paternal treatment, but to the wisdom and character of the black overseer, Jim Pemberton. Varina wrote of Jim's relations with his master: "They were devoted friends, and always observed the utmost courtesy and politeness in their intercourse, and at parting a cigar was always presented by Mr. Davis to him. James never sat down without being asked, although his master always invited him to be seated. James was a dignified, quiet man, of fine manly appearance, very silent, but what he said was always to the point."[41] When Jefferson was preparing to leave for the Mexican War, he gave this devoted slave the choice of going with him or remaining to manage the plantation. Jim decided to remain on the plantation, where he thought he could be of most service. When Davis was in Washington as a member of Congress, Jim Pemberton managed the slaves as overseer. His death from pneumonia in 1850 was such a great loss that he could never be satisfactorily replaced. The white overseers that Davis hired were not as good or as reliable as the black Jim Pemberton.

From the available records there is no indication that Davis ever sold a slave, but he bought slaves for plantation and domestic use. His factors in New Orleans wrote to him on August 9, 1852, informing him that they were sending molasses and a Negro cook about twenty-five years of age, who was also a fine washer and ironer.[42] Her previous master had sold her to a slave trader for no fault of her own, but because her husband was a rascal who stole things from him. The price was $850. Although most planters of the Old South had no scruples about buying slaves, they were reluctant to sell slaves, except for drunkards and incorrigibles. Humanitarian planters, such as the Charles Colcock Jones family of Georgia, were reluctant to sell to slave traders for fear that the slaves would fall into the hands of purchasers who would mistreat them.[43]

Such paternalism was not exceptional, but a fairly normal practice of many Southern slave owners.[44] Kenneth Stampp, representing a neoabolitionist point of view, maintains that the policy of the planters in regard to their slaves was "to Make Them Stand in Fear."[45] There were some exceptional planters who undoubtedly followed this harsh regime, but the usual practice was to treat the slaves humanely, and to recognize their customary rights. Keeping the slaves healthy was obviously the best economic policy.[46] John A. Quitman, later to become governor of Mississippi wrote that he had enormous debts but would rather be reduced to abject penury than to sell one of his 160 slaves, to whom he was deeply attached, for they were faithful, obedient, and affectionate. To his brother Albert, a Louisiana sugar planter, he suggested the rationale for a kind treatment of the slaves such as he and the Davis brothers practiced:

> Clothe them well, make them be clean and neat in their persons and dwellings, encourage them to have gardens and fruit-trees and vines, regulate their little domestic dissensions, and grant them every indulgence consistent with discipline. Harshness makes the negro stubborn; praise, even flattery, and, more than all, kindness makes them pliable and obedient. Keep them cheerful. I love to hear a gang of negroes singing at their work, whistling on their way home, and fiddling and dancing at night. . . . Pray attend to the sick and let them have every possible comfort.[47]

When he was absent in Washington, Davis gave orders to his overseer not to flog his slaves. Many planters followed his example, but the majority of planters probably did flog their slaves on occasions, because they regarded the use of the lash as necessary to maintain firm discipline.[48] Frederick Law Olmsted, one of the most realistic of Northern travelers in the South, rejected the myth, perpetrated in the North by abolitionists and by some neoabolitionist writers of our time, that the Southern slaves were savagely treated. Rather, he found in his three journeys into the South in the 1850s that the slaves of the South were better fed and housed than any proletarian class in the world. Although on large plantations in the Southwest he saw Negro drivers cracking whips over the heads of negligent and lazy workers, he noted that they seldom whipped them. In all of his travels in the South he saw only one case of a severe flogging of a slave by an overseer.[49] Masters tended to rebuke or dismiss overseers for brutality and to limit the number of lashes applied to offenders. William K. Scarborough, in his study, observes that "the majority of southern overseers treated the Negroes in their charge fairly well.[50] And only a minority of slaves in the South were under the charge of overseers, who in general were harsher than the master in treatment of slaves.

A balanced and realistic picture of slavery in the South, nevertheless, must include those planters who, unlike the Davis brothers, pursued a harsh and, in some cases, a cruel regime. In marked contrast with the Davis brothers, for example, was Dr. Richard Eppes, owner in 1860 of three plantations and 127 slaves in Virginia, a planter who personally whipped his slaves for offenses against "the laws of the plantation." A graduate of the University of Virginia and a devout Episcopalian, Eppes was a Virginia aristocrat. His manuscript diary (in the Alderman Library at the University of Virginia) details some of the whippings. On April 2, 1852, he whipped William for leaving the plantation without a pass; on Sunday, April 13, he recorded that he planned to whip one of his slaves for negligence, but after attending church decided to let him off, and commented that he was becoming more lenient than formerly. "Why?" he asked himself, and he philosophized that "the spirit of God is at work in my bosom." But the spirit of God seems to have left him on subsequent occasions: on April 16 he whipped George "for not bringing over milk for my coffee, being compelled to take it without"; on Sunday, July 21, 1852, he flogged Dick for stealing sugar and telling a lie, and he corrected Tom for galloping one of his carriage horses; on August 18, 1859, he ordered a whipping for Giles for letting the cows get into a cornfield; and on September 2 he personally administered to Henry, who had violated the plantation laws, a whipping of fifteen lashes.[51]

These frequent floggings should be viewed in the context of the normal practice during that age of parents and schoolmasters of flogging children for offenses. Catherine C. Hopley, an English woman, tutor to the children of Governor John Milton on his plantation near Tallahassee, Florida, observed that the slaves were seldom whipped, but that the children of the master were frequently flogged.[52] Somewhat in extenuation, also, of Eppes's apparently cruel behavior was the fact that he often rewarded his servants for good work with money payments.

In contrast with the paternalism of the Davis brothers, also, was the record of frequent whippings of the slaves that the diary of Bennett Barrow, a Louisiana cotton planter, reveals. Barrow personally flogged slaves for picking trashy cotton, for laziness, for keeping themselves or their cabins filthy, and for running away. His diary shows that he engaged in whippings two or three times a week. Indeed, the muscles of his right arm must have been strengthened by this frequent exercise. But at times, in lieu of whipping, he substituted other punishments, such as imprisonment in the plantation jail on weekends and holidays, or humiliating male offenders by making them don a red flannel cap while confined to the stocks, wear dresses, wash clothes, and so on. On the other hand, Barrow seems to have been generous to slaves in granting holidays, providing feasts, and encouraging work by various incentives such as money, gifts, and clothes.[53]

Curiously, Varina, in her account of paternalism on the Davis plantations, does not mention this common practice of offering incentives to get more work out of slaves. Nor is there mention of slave religion on the plantation, or of miscegenation. Apparently Jefferson (who was not a member of a church) and his wife did not promote religion among their slaves, as many planters did, notably Charles Colcock Jones of Georgia, who published a book on the religious instruction of slaves.

As for miscegenation, the immorality of planters with their slave women was vastly exaggerated by the abolitionists. Most of the planters were Victorians like Davis, puritanical in their attitude toward sex, and further restrained from sex relations with slave women by the need of keeping discipline on the plantation, as well as by fear of public opinion, racist aversion, and the precepts of Christianity. After the long contact of planters with slaves for well over two hundred years, the census of 1850 reported that only 7.7 percent of the slaves were mulattoes (that is, having as much as one eighth white blood). Moreover, the huge collection of narratives of ex-slaves made by the Works Progress Administration, 1936–39, revealed that only 4.5 percent of the slaves interviewed said that one of their parents was white.[54]

Nevertheless, recent studies of sexuality should make one skeptical of these figures, particularly since the census takers of 1850 and 1860 cannot be trusted as accurate reporters. Rachel O'Connor, a remarkable woman cotton planter of Louisiana, for example, found that one of her greatest problems was to keep her overseers from "sneaking after those negro girls," and in disgust she made two of her slaves overseers; she said they were more satisfactory than any of the white overseers.[55]

The manuscript slave schedules of 1860 of the Davis plantations, at first glance, might be regarded as disturbing to the thesis of this book as to the Davis's paternalism. But since the statistics on slavery in this census appear to be much less reliable than those of the 1850 census, which was directed by J. D. B. DeBow, they raise serious questions as to the reliability of quantitative studies of slavery resting on these statistics. In 1860 the Jefferson Davis plantation was reported to have 113 slaves. The 1850 manuscript census reported that, in addition to his plantation slaves, Davis had in Washington one black slave, twenty-five years old, and two female black slaves, twenty years old.[56] In 1860, presumably, he had brought slaves to Washington as servants, for a Southern lady had to have slaves to do the domestic work. Of his plantation slaves, there were 67 females and 56 males; only 6 were sixty years of age or older. These Negroes dwelt in 28 cabins, a number which would seem to indicate overcrowding, but probably the great majority of poor whites and humbler yeomen of the period fared no better. The surprising statistics—as reported by the assistant marshal—were that the plantation had 31 mulattoes and 29 fugitives out of the state.[57] At the same time Joseph's slaves, who numbered 355, were listed as having 104 mulattoes and 86 fugitives out of state. If these statistics are correct, it would mean that nearly one third of the slaves of the Davis brothers were both mulattoes and fugitives, raising the question of how then could Jefferson and Joseph be regarded as paternal masters.

These figures seemed so incredible to the author that he sent the photostats to William K. Scarborough of Southern Mississippi University, an able and objective scholar, knowledgeable both as to Southern slavery and the use of census statistics of this period. As for miscegenation, he replied that Warren County, where the Davis plantations were located (the county seat was Vicksburg), had a very high percentage of mulattoes as compared with the other counties of Mississippi, which ran about one mulatto in 10 slaves. In regard to the astonishing number of fugitives recorded in 1860 on the Davis plantations, he observed that the census cannot be trusted at all in this figure.[58] The fact that the number of fugitives and mulattoes is approximately the same, as given by the manuscript census of 1860, is puzzling, and would seem to cast further doubt on the credibility of the census figures. To make the imbroglio more incomprehensible, Stanley Engerman has written to the author that, according to the *Preliminary Report of the Eighth Census* (p. 137), there were only 68 fugitives in the entire state of Mississippi, while the *Population* volume for 1860 (p. xiii) has recorded only 8.39 percent of the state's slave population as mulatto.[59]

In common with the great majority of their generation in the South, Jefferson, Joseph, and Varina seemed to have had no qualms of conscience about holding slaves. There were a few Southerners who, after the relatively liberal period of apology for the institution had passed, made some efforts to abolish slavery, but their fate as extremists discouraged others from following their example.[60]

Following the war Jefferson Davis, in prison at Fort Monroe, expressed a very liberal opinion that he had held before the war when he wrote to Varina: "There is, I observe, a controversy which I regret, as to allowing negroes to testify in court. From brother Joe many years ago, I derived the opinion that they should then be made competent witnesses, the jury judging of their credibility."[61] Then why did not he and Joseph, men of influence in Mississippi, try changing the law that left Negroes defenseless against harsh, sadistic masters such as Lilburne Lewis, nephew of Thomas Jefferson, who hacked one of his slaves to death in 1811 before his assembled slaves but because, according to law, they were incompetent witnesses, the murderer went scot free?[62]

In addition to the need to change the slave code in regard to slave testimony, three other reforms were urgently needed to humanize the code: namely, acts to forbid the selling of children from their parents, to allow slaves to be taught to read and write, and to forbid the selling of slaves from their spouses. I have seen no evidence that Jefferson Davis favored these changes of the law. Although Southerners of that generation realized that the whole civilized world outside of the South condemned the institution of slavery, they made no concerted effort to reform the laws or abolish the slave system in a gradual way—and this is the tragedy of the South.

Did the absolute power of the master over his slaves tend to corrupt? The perceptive Mrs. Chesnut seemed to think that it had this effect on South Carolina planters. The vivid pen picture that she draws of her father-in-law portrays both the evil and the benign effects of slavery on those planters who had long been exposed to its subtle influences. She wrote in her diary: "My husband's father is kind, and amiable when not crossed, given to hospitality on the grand scale, jovial, genial, friendly, courtly in his politeness. But he is as absolute a tyrant as the Czar of Russia, the Khan of Tartary, or the Sultan of Turkey." Of his love for his fine estates with their slave property, she commented: "These are his Gods; he worships his own property."[63] But the Davis brothers, like many Mississippi planters, were recently arrived planters, and had not been exposed to the long-time effects of slavery. As far as one can judge, they were not corrupted by the institution, except perhaps in being somewhat arrogant on rare occasions, and intolerant of contradiction. Rather, they exhibited the better side of the consciousness of responsibility toward their slaves.[64]

The experience of Jefferson Davis with slavery and with the successful operation of a large cotton plantation made a distinct contribution to his development as a Southern politician. From experience he could sincerely present the most favorable side of slavery in defending the institution in Congress. Unfortunately, his experience with slavery tended also to make him somewhat autocratic and impatient with opposition. Success in politics is frequently based on the art of compromise. In rejecting the means of parliamentary adjustment and conciliation, Davis proved to be adamant when it came to upholding Southern rights and protecting Southern slavery, as subsequent chapters will show.

The Young Politician

$\mathcal{I}$n the antebellum South a gentleman was expected to participate in politics as a social duty. When men got together politics ranked with crops, the weather, and slaves as the staples of conversation. Unlike the situation of the "solid South" after the Civil War, there were two vigorous competing parties in the Old South which tended to increase political interest. Moreover, Southerners felt the danger of their minority status in the Union, so that they recognized the need of able politicians to defend their sectional interests. Although many of the wealthy, aristocratic planters of Mississippi were Whigs, Jefferson and Joseph Davis were Democrats, partly because their father was an admirer of Thomas Jefferson, regarded as the founder of the Democratic party, and partly because they were admirers of Andrew Jackson.[1] Accordingly, the first political notice of Jefferson Davis that appears in the records is his attendance at the State Democratic Convention in Jackson on February 22–24, 1842, as a delegate from Warren County, where his plantation was located.[2] During the next year he was thrust into a position of active campaigning by being unanimously nominated by the Warren County Democratic Convention to be its candidate to represent the county in the lower house of the legislature. Since the Whigs had a decided majority of voters in the county, Davis's candidacy represented a forlorn cause.

The absorbing issue of the campaign was whether the state should repudiate its bonds, issued during a period of speculation in 1837, to support the Union and the Planters banks. The Whigs generally opposed repudiation while a majority of the Democrats favored it. Davis took a moderate position, advocating the state paying the bonds of the Planters Bank but leaving the question of payment of the Union Bank bonds to the courts rather than to a vote of the legislature, which eventually repudiated the bonds.[3] The Whigs of Vicksburg called on the noted orator and politician, Sergeant S. Prentiss of Natchez to come to Vicksburg to engage in a public debate in the courthouse with the youthful Democratic candidate.[4] The Democratic newspaper of Vicksburg reported the debate between the seasoned orator and the green young candidate as a struggle between David and Goliath, as an honorable, gentlemanly, and fair discussion of the constitutionality of the Union Bank bonds, in which Davis came out triumphant and unscathed.[5] Nevertheless, the debate had a damaging aftermath for him. Robert J. Walker, born in Pennsylvania, though a former Mississippi senator acting as an agent of the federal government in England during the Civil War, falsely accused the Confederate president-to-be of being a repudiator.[6] In this, his first campaign for office, Davis was defeated, and never did he hold a state office except as colonel of militia; his whole political career prior to 1861 was spent in Washington.

Although in his initial try at politics Davis was defeated, he had gained credit with his party as a future standard-bearer. In late 1843 (December 20) he was chosen a delegate from his county to the State Democratic Convention held in Jackson on January 3, 1844. Here he made an impressive speech in which he stated that, although he had been instructed to vote for Martin Van Buren as the presidential candidate of the Democratic party, he personally favored the nomination of John C. Calhoun. He desired the selection of a Southern presidential candidate. He advocated the adoption of a platform favoring the annexation of Texas, free trade, and giving the South a fair share of federal appropriations for defense by establishing navy yards at Pensacola and Dry Tortugas. He urged the federal government to encourage the development of "the nautical feeling" of the Southern youth. Thus early in his political career he displayed a sectional spirit, especially in complaining of the disproportionate federal expenditure in the Northern states. He indulged in some sophomoric, purple patches of oratory that delighted the taste of Southern audiences of the time, such as his reference to the benefits of free trade from which "the nation may expect the extension of amicable relations with foreign nations until our canvas-winged doves shall bear us across every sea, olive branches from every land."[7]

His speech was so impressive that the convention chose him by acclamation as a presidential elector for the state at large. Davis anticipated that Van Buren would be the standard-bearer of his party, and in order to prepare himself for campaigning for the Democratic candidate he wrote on the same day,

March 25, 1844, a letter to ex-President Van Buren and one to Senator William Allen of Ohio, whose friendship he had made during a visit to Washington in 1838, requesting information useful in campaigning. He asked Van Buren to state his position on the annexation of Texas, on the constitutional power of Congress over slavery in the District of Columbia, and on whether his vote on the tariff of 1828 was owing to instructions that he received.[8] On all these points the New York politician was vulnerable in the South. The letter to Allen asked for facts that he might use to refute Whig charges of defalcations and extravagance during Van Buren's presidency, as well as evidence of Van Buren's attitude toward the United States Bank and the tariff.[9] Even before he wrote these letters he had joined with Henry A. Foote and John A. Quitman in addressing, on January 9, 1844, a public meeting in Jackson, the capital of the state, demanding the annexation of Texas. This proved to be the overriding issue of the campaign, and because of it the Democratic convention at Baltimore rejected Van Buren and nominated the "dark horse" candidate James Knox Polk of Tennessee.[10]

Davis made a number of speeches on behalf of the election of Polk in various towns and villages throughout the state. He traveled at his own expense by buggy and on horseback, staying at night in the homes of friends and Democratic partisans. At times he traveled with another canvasser, Henry S. Foote, a small, voluble, and coarse man, formidable in debate, who later became governor and senator from Mississippi and an enemy of Davis. He spoke at courthouses, at open-air barbecues, and in pastoral scenes where some of the audience sat on fence rails or leaned against trees. Free barbecues and public speaking were like a magnet in attracting large crowds, including Negroes, who feasted at the dinner stands, "groaning under the weight of Pigs, lambs, beef, well barbecued and seasoned with loaves of bread of all sizes and descriptions." At the time he had become engaged to Varina, he warned her not to be upset by Whig reports, and said that he was new at public speaking. Indeed, Whig papers depreciated Davis, declaring that his speech at Port Gibson was a schoolboy declamation, deficient in argument, and that his colleague, Henry S. Foote, made gestures like "a galvanized frog."[11] The Whig paper of Vicksburg criticized Davis for applying a vulgar simile in a speech comparing the Whigs to "tumblebugs rolling balls of dung"—this in the presence of ladies in the audience.[12] Foote, as was his custom, attacked the opposition candidate personally, but Davis confined himself to issues.

Varina in her memoir described the strenuous campaigning for Polk of her fiancé of a few months: "Riding in the sun and late in the dew in midsummer always gave him [a recurrence of] malaria fever. So the journeys were generally succeeded by long attacks of illness, and the fever affected his eyes; finally, they brought on an attack of amaurosis and impaired the sight of one."[13]

From newspaper accounts we gain a view, although partisan, of Davis as a public speaker.[14] They described his voice as musical and his demeanor as calm and dignified. Some Democratic papers, while praising him, expressed the wish that he would show more passion and more animation in his speeches.[15] He impressed people with his utter sincerity and his confidence in his opinions as the only right ones, which Varina admitted caused his opponents to accuse him of being domineering.[16] Reuben Davis (no relative) thought that, from the time he first heard him speak in 1844 at a barbecue at Holly Springs in northern Mississippi, Jefferson was a superb speaker. Reuben praised his beautiful voice, his lucid argument, his poetic fancy, and his use of ridicule and denunciation of the Whigs before an excited crowd.[17]

On the question of the annexation of Texas, Jefferson struck a responsive chord in his audience. A letter published in the Democratic newspaper of Aberdeen described the effect of Davis's speech on behalf of the annexation of Texas as *electrical,* causing the audience to cheer throughout his discourse.[18] In his various speeches during the campaign, besides advocating the annexation of Texas, Davis used as his main argument the unconstitutionality of such Whig measures as establishing a national bank, their distribution proposal, and passing a protective tariff. The argument of unconstitutionality dominated his thinking and speeches throughout his political career. He also attacked the infant Native American party, whose program was repugnant to his feelings of democracy and of true Americanism.

While Davis was campaigning for the election of Polk, he made a speech in Vicksburg at the organization of the Mississippi Anti-Dueling Society on May 27, 1844, that placed him in the conservative camp of opinion on that question. The background of the meeting was a strong public reaction against the killing of three editors of Vicksburg newspapers in duels and the stabbing and shooting of other citizens that had occurred in 1843–44. The meeting resolved that it would sustain any person who refused a challenge, asserting that to give or accept a challenge was not a proof of courage; condemned the carrying of concealed weapons; and recommended the appointment of a court of honor when a duel was threatened. The minority members of the meeting declared that the day had not arrived to do away with the code duello, which protected gentlemen from gross abuse. As a substitute for the majority resolutions, Davis offered resolutions that condemned street brawls and encounters as well as the habit of carrying concealed weapons. One of his resolutions read: "Resolved, That dueling, however irrational and immoral, can only be suppressed by the progress of intelligence, morality and good breeding; Therefore as the nearest approximation to the end we all desire, that the effort be made to prevent, *unnecessarily,* a resort to deadly weapons, and to regulate such a resort when it cannot be prevented by principles of fairness and as far as may be equality between the combatants."[19]

After Davis had come out of his seclusion as a planter he began to move up rapidly in the political world. His strenuous campaigning for the election of Polk had introduced him to the people of Mississippi and revealed his power as a speaker and political thinker. Accordingly, in the summer of 1845 he was nominated by the Warren County Democratic Convention as its candidate for representative in Congress, and a few days later the citizens of Vicksburg invited him to deliver a eulogy upon the recent death of Andrew Jackson. His speech was a conventional eulogy in which his praise of the departed Democratic chieftain had no critical remark.[20]

After his nomination he made a statewide canvass, for at that time the state had not been divided into congressional districts. In his speeches he advocated the popular side of the annexation of Texas, the occupation of the whole of Oregon, opposition to reestablishing a national bank, free trade, the establishment of navy yards on the Gulf Coast and at Memphis, the founding of military academies. During the campaign the politically dangerous issue of repudiation came up. In order to state his position, he stayed up all night to prepare a public letter for the printer. His position, as noted previously, was a compromise one: payment of the Planters Bank bonds and fair adjustment of the Union Bank bonds. He declared that he was in favor of a hard money currency, and that he was against any measure for the benefit of speculators. He then made a forthright statement: "I have never owned a share of bank stock, nor borrowed a dollar from a bank." At the very close of his letter to the public, he struck a popular note in discussing the relevance of the common law of England to the bank controversy: "My thoughts, my feelings are American; to England, the robber nation of the earth, whose history is a long succession of wrongs and oppressions, whose tracks are marked by the crushed rights of individuals—to England, I cannot go for lessons of morality and justice."[21]

Davis was one of four congressmen elected on November 3–4, 1845, obtaining the second highest popular vote.[22] Varina wrote regretfully of his entrance into politics: "Then I began to know the bitterness of being a politician's wife, and that it meant long absences, pecuniary depletion from ruinous absenteeism, illness from exposure, misconceptions, defamation of character; everything which darkens the sunlight and contracts the happy sphere of home."[23] If this was so, why did Davis and his wife sacrifice so much to hold political office? Certainly it was not for money, for congressmen were paid very low salaries. Davis never revealed his motivation, but it seems probable that he entered political life primarily for the honor and prestige of being a member of Congress. There must have been a higher motive also: to serve his state and region, which he loved and believed was threatened by "the fanatical spirit" of the North. In pursuit of his position as congressman, he once said that he did not spend as much as five dollars in campaigning, a far cry from the situation of today.

Before he left for Washington with Varina to take his seat in Congress, Senator John C. Calhoun, perhaps cherishing the ambition to attain his long-wished-for goal of becoming president, came to Vicksburg by river boat on his way to the Memphis Commercial Convention. In his speech there, un-anticipated by the young congressman, Calhoun was to depart from the strict construction view of the Constitution that he had so earnestly championed, by advocating that the federal government appropriate money for internal improvements of the large interior rivers on the grounds that they were virtually "inland seas."[24] Although Davis was an ardent follower of Calhoun, he could not accept this reversal of strict construction of the Constitution. He gave the speech of welcome, which he carefully wrote out and Varina copied. It was ornamented with metaphors, tropes, poetry, and florid rhetoric, and young Varina greatly admired it. He had asked his wife not to look at him during the speech, and he seemed nervous when he began to deliver it. At first he spoke haltingly, as though he was groping to remember the written words, but he soon abandoned the written text and gave an eloquent extempore address, praising Calhoun, but mentioning neither nullification nor the dramatic change of ideas on internal improvements. He tried to bring Calhoun out on certain subjects, but the experienced old politician evaded committing himself.

Varina was deeply impressed by Calhoun's forceful personality, his "eagle eyes" that looked straight ahead, his great mane of white hair pushed back from his forehead, his strong emaciated countenance, his tall slender figure, and his kindly manner in speaking to her. Nevertheless, she noted that his voice was not pleasant and that he spoke rapidly and in the manner of a professor of mathematics, with no attempts at rhetoric or ornament or appeal to the emotions, and with few gestures. She did not perceive him as dominated by personal ambition, only by his theories and sense of duty, and in her memoir of her husband she wrote, "He always appeared to me rather as a moral and mental abstraction than a politician."[25] Calhoun paid special attention to the young bride, the wife of a promising young politician.

As an orator, Davis had the advantages of a sweet musical voice with great carrying power and an imposing, dignified presence. After his speech welcoming Calhoun, which he had so carefully prepared, he never again, according to Varina, wrote out a speech before he delivered it, but always spoke extemporaneously from notes on two or three inches of paper.[26] He spoke rapidly and adapted the discourse to his audience, for he had a remarkable ability to sense the mood of a popular or senatorial audience. In his early political career his speeches were ornate, with frequent references to poetry and fiction for illustration, but later he changed to a plain, largely unornamented style. Mrs. Davis wrote that he was a parenthetical speaker, a fact that made his reported speeches (and they were indifferently reported in the newspapers) appear less effective than they actually were. Southern orators in this period took as their model the style of Demosthenes. Although Davis praised this style in the speech of a friend, he thought that it was not suited to discussing finances or questions of expediency in Congress. At the same time he criticized Calhoun's speech on the Independent Treasury as being "too sententious."[27]

The day following the Calhoun speech the young congressman-elect, his nineteen-year-old bride, and his niece Malie, twenty years old, departed by the northern route for Washington. It was late November and their steamboat became stuck in the Ohio River by floating ice; they had to transfer with their trunks to a rough wood sleigh that slid alarmingly on the precipitous, icy road. Later in the journey they were thrown out of a stagecoach down a twenty-foot embankment; they were bruised and an elderly congressman from Mississippi, who was accompanying them, broke a rib. The trip from Mississippi to Washington, in a day when the state had only one short railroad, took three weeks. Davis had planned to be in Washington for the opening of Congress but arrived a week late. After arrival, they had to find a congenial boarding house and join a "congressional mess." Varina apparently enjoyed social life in Washington, but she was concerned about the health of her husband as well as about her own. She wrote to her mother on January 30, 1846, when her husband had been only five weeks in Congress, that he sat up writing letters until two or three o'clock at night, and that his eyes "look so red and painful."[28]

Davis made his maiden speech in Congress two weeks after he took his seat in the House of Representatives. It was an attack on the Native American party. He opposed, he said, any laws to limit the political rights of foreign-born citizens of the United States for the purpose of purifying the ballot box, and he warned against adopting the foolish policy of China and excluding foreigners, a policy which had kept that nation from progressing. He observed that foreign-born citizens had made a notable contribution to American liberty during the Revolution, citing the fact that eight of the signers of the Declaration of Independence were foreign-born and nine others were immediate decendants of foreign parents.[29]

Davis worked very hard as a new member of Congress. He presented petitions of his constituents, franked letters to them, introduced a resolution for converting a portion of United States forts into schools for military instruction, sought to secure new mail routes in Mississippi, fought for federal appropriations to remove the bar in the Gulf channel near Pass Christian and to build a levee on the Mississippi, wrote recommendations for appointments to office, spoke in favor of raising two regiments for service on the western frontier, in which foreigners as well as native Americans should be recruited, and followed the instructions of the Mississippi legislature in regard to advocating a graduation of the price of public lands. Moreover, he served on two special committees, one to establish the Smithsonian Institution and the other, a committee to investigate the charges of defalcation against Daniel Webster, the secretary of state.

Davis was handicapped by bad health. He had severe earaches and inflamed, red eyes. Varina wrote to her mother that her husband was not as happy as he used to be. In recalling this early period of their life in Washington, Varina wrote: "Now began Mr. Davis's earnest work. He visited very little, studied until two or three o'clock in the morning. . . . Between us we franked all the documents sent to his constituents and all the letters, and the calls upon him for service he scrupulously attended. He was a working member."[30]

His second important speech was in opposition to a rivers and harbors improvement bill. He opposed Calhoun's doctrine of the Mississippi and its tributary rivers being equivalent to an "inland sea," and thus a proper subject for congressional appropriations for their improvement. Rather, he argued for retaining the Democratic creed of opposition to internal improvements by the federal government, on the ground of a strict interpretation of the Constitution. He deplored the rage for internal improvements by the federal government spreading like an epidemic over the country, threatening to level the barriers of the Constitution to the ground. He pointed out the sectional character of the bill before the House: namely, that nearly one half of the money to be appropriated was for the Northern states while only a trifling amount was reserved for the southeastern coast. He condemned the practice of "log rolling," or combinations of special interests to secure appropriations, but he himself urged appropriations for internal improvements in his own section, especially building a naval yard at Ship Island near New Orleans.

Davis's most notable speech by far during his five months in Congress was delivered on the Oregon question on February 6, 1846. The Democratic platform had demanded that the United States should abrogate the treaties with Great Britain of 1818 and 1827, which provided for the joint occupation of Oregon, and should assert a claim to the whole of Oregon as far as the Russian boundary of 54 degrees, 40 minutes, north latitude. Shortly after Davis became a member of Congress, a spirited debate over Oregon took place in the winter and spring of 1846. Davis did not join the extreme expansionists who popularized the slogan "54°40' or Fight," which became popular during the 1846 debate in Congress rather than during the preceding presidential campaign of 1844.[31] This group of expansionists was very strong among the congressmen of the Middle West, led by Senator Edward A. Hannegan of Indiana, but it was also supported by a number of young congressmen from the South, among them Jacob Thompson of Mississippi, motivated by extreme sensitivity on preserving national honor and anti-British prejudice.[32]

Davis made his major speech in the House of Representatives on the Oregon question.[33] He spoke in favor of acquiring not only Oregon but also California, "that key to Asiatic commerce." Nevertheless, he maintained that the country should not risk the danger of war by insisting on occupying the whole of Oregon, but should compromise the issue by extending the 49th parallel to the Pacific. He referred to sectionalism in the debate, yet he himself boasted of the patriotism and martial exploits of the Mississippians. He spoke of honor as motivating himself and his region, maintaining, however, that the Oregon question did not involve national honor, but was purely a question of expediency. He praised the American people as having a record of being haughty toward the strong but generous toward the weak, as exemplified in our conduct toward Mexico, and claimed that American history was unstained by an act of injustice or perfidy—in other words, the country was as yet an innocent nation. Congress finally adopted President Polk's proposal to extend the line of 49 degrees, the northern boundary of the Louisiana Purchase, to Puget Sound. As a whole Davis's speech on Oregon was sober and sensible, revealing that he was well informed on the exploration and diplomacy of Oregon, but it did have passages of rhetoric, especially the peroration, which Varina admired. She wrote to her mother that the speech was well written, and that she thought it was great.[34]

Davis ardently supported the declaration of war against Mexico on May 13, 1846. He had no qualms of conscience such as troubled many antislavery Northerners and Whigs as to the justness of the war. He accepted as a simple fact Polk's statement in his war message to Congress that "American blood had been shed on American soil," although this claim was based on the flimsy pretext that General Taylor's army north of the Rio Grande border was defending itself and American territory. Ironically, in this war of aggression, Congress maintained that the United States was fighting a war of defense, and Davis, in accepting a commission, said that the American volunteers would fight to defend the interests and *honor* of their country.[35] Even the fact that his political hero, John C. Calhoun, opposed the war as unwise and the great Whig leader, Henry Clay, opposed it as unjust did not deter Davis from giving his wholehearted support to the war.

Shortly after news arrived of the clash between Taylor's troops and the small Mexican army above the Rio Grande, Davis took the occasion to deliver a eulogy of his former father-in-law. In the course of his speech, he made a thoughtless, unfortunate remark that aroused the anger of Andrew Johnson, representative from Tennessee. In defending West Point graduates in the army against the criticism of an Ohio congressman, he asked a rhetorical question as to whether a blacksmith or a tailor serving as a soldier could have fought against the Mexican army as well as the trained officers and soldiers of General Taylor's army.[36] He meant only to illustrate the value of a military education, but Johnson, who had been a tailor and was very sensitive to any criticism of plebeians, reacted bitterly.[37] The next day Johnson accused the Mississippi senator of making an invidious distinction against the mechanic class to which he belonged. He referred to "the illegitimate, swaggering, bastard, scrub aristocracy," to which he implied Davis belonged. Heatedly, he vindicated the respectability of the mechanic class, making the ludicrous observation that Adam was a tailor who sewed fig leaves together for clothes.[38] Davis replied that he was "incapable of wantonly wounding the feelings or of making invidious reflections upon the origin or occupation of any man." He wished only to illustrate the value of a military education and to point out that preparation for a civil pursuit did not qualify a man for the duties of a soldier. This clash between Davis and Johnson was insignificant in itself, but it initiated a lasting hostility toward Davis in the man who was to serve as president while the Confederate ex-president was a prisoner at Fort Monroe, seeking a pardon.

The freshman rule, by which a first-year congressman was expected to remain silent, was ignored by the bold, independent congressman from Mississippi. He spoke freely and ably, under the compulsion of upholding Southern interests. Varina reported that ex-president John Quincy Adams, then a member of the House of Representatives, listened attentively to one of Davis's early speeches and said to one of the members, "We shall hear more of that young man, I fancy."[39] In his first year in Congress Davis developed self-confidence and poise, and when he delivered a speech he demonstrated that he had prepared well and was master of his subject.

For Glory and for Country

$\mathcal{D}$avis's life as a planter with its out-of-doors activity, its hunting, horsemanship, and command over a slave force, tended to prepare him for the greatest adventure of his life: his participation in the Mexican War. Mexico was a difficult neighbor. The frequently changing government repeatedly refused to pay the claims of citizens of the United States. When the United States sent John Slidell as minister plenipotentiary to Mexico City in 1846, Mexican officials refused to receive him. Although Texas had maintained its independence for nine years, the Mexicans refused to recognize its status and, moreover, they denied, perhaps correctly, that the Rio Grande was the boundary of the province of Texas, as the Texans claimed.

On May 13, 1846, the United States, following a clash with Mexican troops north of the Rio Grande, declared war against Mexico. Davis had no qualms of conscience over his country fighting an offensive war against a weak nation for aggrandizement of its territory. Many of his contemporaries, however, including John C. Calhoun, Henry Clay, Abraham Lincoln, many Northern Whigs, and the abolitionists, opposed the war, doubting its expediency or believing it to be a war for the extension of slavery.[1] Liberal historians, as well as the author, condemn it as an unjust war of conquest, but

57

the ablest student of the war, Justin H. Smith, has exonerated the United States.

On the day of the declaration of war, Davis wrote to a friend in Mississippi that he expected a war also with England over Oregon, but that before this occurred the United States should quickly defeat Mexico, dictating a treaty of peace in Mexico City. Noting that his military education and service should make him valuable in the war just declared, he expressed a strong desire to command a regiment from Warren County; if elected, he would join the regiment as soon as possible.[2]

The enthusiasm of the young congressman for military service in the war reflected a remarkable movement for volunteering among the Mississippians. John A. Quitman of Natchez, also eager to obtain a commission, wrote to Davis on May 22: "Our people are in a state of the highest excitement. Old and young, rich and poor, democrats and whigs, are ready to volunteer. They fear, however, that Mississippi will not have a fair chance." He pointed out that Mississippi was foremost in advocating annexation and that her people regarded the war with Mexico as their war: "We want no aid from the abolitionists." The brave Mississippians in volunteering, Quitman observed, were motivated by a desire to confer honor on our much abused State and win laurels for their own fame by participating in the "glory and danger of the war."[3] He neglected to observe that, in addition to glory, many of them expected a good time, a relief from the monotony and isolation of the plantation.

So great was the enthusiasm for volunteering in Mississippi that the Pontotoc Dragoons, for example, were outraged that the president called for only one regiment from their state. They were indignant, they wrote in a letter to Representative Jacob Thompson on June 8, 1846, "at the low estimate which has been put upon the chivalry and patriotism of our citizens" by denying them the privilege of fighting for their country. They protested against calling for a larger proportion of volunteers from the "icy states," than from the South. The Northerners, they maintained, were not as well suited for combat in Mexico as were Southerners.[4] But their plea presented by the Mississippi delegation in Congress was rejected, as Polk called for only 50,000 volunteers, apportioned to the different states, and Mississippi was assigned one regiment.

Davis was elected colonel of the First Mississippi Rifles at Camp Independence, near Vicksburg, on June 18, 1846, but not without considerable opposition. On the first ballot of the assembled volunteers, Militia General Alexander Bradford received 350 votes, Davis, 300, and three other candidates, 263 votes. Davis was elected on the second ballot, and news of his election was sent to him by a special messenger. Davis gladly accepted the commission issued by Governor Albert Gallatin Brown, but he concealed this fact from his wife.

Varina had just passed her twentieth birthday when she discovered that her husband had committed himself to volunteer, despite his promise that he would not. After war had been declared, there was a bitter struggle between the strong-willed young wife and her husband over the question of his volunteering. She tried passionately to dissuade him from going to war, but he prevailed in his resolution. She wrote to her mother on June 6 that she had just found out accidentally that "Jeff" had committed himself about going, and had "cried until I am stupid" over the decision.[5]

Although Davis rejected his young wife's passionate plea that he not volunteer but stay with her, he was very solicitous about her welfare while he was away. In one of his most remarkable letters that has survived, he wrote to his beloved sister Lucinda: "To you and your family alone of all the world could I entrust her and rest assured that no waywardness would ever lessen kindness." He was distressed, he continued, that she could not get along with the sweet but boring wife of his brother Joseph, and feared that her living with his brother's family at Hurricane would only increase the incompatibility of the two women. However, his sister, he felt, would "love her too much to take heed of the weaknesses which spring from a sensitive and generous temper."[6]

Davis sent a letter to his constituents that was published in the Vicksburg *Sentinel* on July 21, 1846, explaining why he was leaving his job in Congress to volunteer. He felt, he wrote, that because of his military training it was his duty to volunteer, and he could not wait until the close of the congressional session. He and the country in general believed that the war would be short, indicated by the term of service for volunteers being for either three or six months. He gave an account of his short career in Congress, noting that it included the support of a new tariff law designed for revenue, not for protection, and of the graduation land bill, by which the price of public lands should be decreased according to the length of time they had been on the market and not sold; he also stressed his moderate course in regard to the Oregon question and his support of a declaration of war against Mexico.[7] Naturally he did not admit that in serving his country he wished also to serve himself by winning glory, but in a letter to Lucinda dated July 8, 1846, he wrote: "It was felt by me as a real compliment to be chosen [colonel of volunteers] over a field of competitors when absent, and if the occasion offers it may be that I will return with a reputation over which you will rejoice as my Mother would have done" [she had died two years before].[8]

Davis joined the Mississippi regiment at New Orleans on July 21, 1846. His contemporary, Reuben Davis, a Mississippi congressman, described the First Mississippi Rifles as composed of the best born, best educated, wealthiest young men of the state, "going out to find glory upon the battlefield, and to do honor to the State of Mississippi."[9] Among its officers were the famed duelist–romantic adventurer, Colonel Alexander K. McClung, and Major

Alexander Bradford, whom Jefferson Davis had defeated for election as colonel, and whom Reuben Davis described as heartbroken because during the war he failed to get a bullet wound, as did Jefferson Davis and McClung.

Many Mississippi volunteers took their slaves, and they had to provide their own horses. Having hunted frequently, they were superb marksmen. Their uniforms were ridiculous for warfare, consisting of red shirts, white duck pants, and black slouch hats, and each man carried a bowie knife. One of the privates was Jefferson's brother-in-law, Joseph Davis Howell, whose family worried that his height of six feet six inches would make him a vulnerable target. Jefferson took along a slave provided by his brother Joseph to serve as a valet, as well as a magnificent Arabian horse named Tartar. He insisted on equipping his men with the most modern rifles available, fired by percussion caps instead of the old flintlock muskets that most of the other troops carried. In this selection of weapons he resolutely held out against the advice of General Winfield Scott, the most experienced officer in the army, who maintained that they had not been sufficiently tested. President Polk, in urging him to delay his departure for his regiment in order to vote for a tariff bill before Congress, promised in return to provide one thousand of the new rifles.[10]

Jefferson was a strict disciplinarian. His brother Joseph wrote to him, after he had been with his regiment less than two months, that some complaints had been made against him by soldiers because of the severity of training.[11] In Mexico the young commander would not tolerate the plundering of civilians and held his soldiers to a stern code of honor. Varina, in her memoir of her husband, wrote that when his soldiers stole corn from the field of a Mexican farmer, he rebuked his regiment and paid for the stolen corn. She also recorded that, although his men could easily have taken the silver vessels of the churches and the jewels that adorned the dress of the statue of the Virgin of Guadeloupe as spoils of war, they returned without an article belonging to the church or to a Mexican private citizen.[12] In his autobiography, Davis recalled with pride that during the attack on Monterrey his men found some much prized Mexican blankets, but not one was taken.[13]

Despite his strictness, his men were devoted to him. His young brother-in-law wrote from camp near Monterrey on October 13, 1846, in hyperbolic strain, that Davis's gallant conduct in battle had raised him so high in the estimation of his regiment that if he wished them to continue in service after their period of enlistment expired, "not a man in his regiment . . . would not sacrifice his life to obey him." He described his brother-in-law as always in front of his regiment, ready to be the first to expose himself to the enemy's bullets, and as demonstrating great coolness under fire, courage, decisiveness, and discretion.[14]

Jefferson Davis was much more fortunate than Albert Sidney Johnston who led a Texan regiment which, when their three months of service was up, undeterred by considerations of patriotism or honor or the moving appeal of their commander, voted to leave. When a delegation notified General Zachary Taylor of their decision while he was shaving, he brusquely told them to go, since he did not wish anybody serving under him who did not want to stay. Though bereft of his command, Johnston remained, and so did Major Ben McCulloch with his spy company of Texas rangers.[15]

In Mexico, Davis won the glory he was seeking. His success was partly owing to the generalship of the commander, his former father-in-law, Zachary Taylor. Taylor was not a scientific general; he made some egregious errors both in strategy and tactics in the Mexican War that might have been fatal if he had not been fighting against a weak foe. He paid too little attention to logistics or sanitation, with the result that his army suffered severely from disease, especially from dysentery and diarrhea. But he had other compensating qualities. Unlike the other prominent general of the war, Winfield Scott, he cared little for form and ceremony. A rough-looking, homely individual, he was short and squat and swarthy, with pronounced facial lines and gray hair. He looked and dressed the part of a plain farmer, and was fond of talking about crops and his Mississippi cotton plantation tilled by many black slaves. An Illinois volunteer described him as wearing "an old oil cap, a dusty green coat, a frightful pair of trousers and on horseback looks like a toad."[16] In the midst of battle he sat calmly on his white horse, "Old Whitey," and directed his troops. His constant exposure to the enemy's bullets seems foolhardy today, but it had a beneficial, reassuring effect on his green troops, who admired his reckless courage and called him "Old Rough and Ready." Indeed, he possessed the supreme attributes of a general in inspiring his troops with confidence, exemplifying the trait that General Grant exhibited in the Civil War: being "a fighting man."

Before the declaration of war against Mexico, Taylor had been ordered to move his army from north of the Nueces River, the old boundary of Texas, to the Rio Grande—where he had a series of minor clashes with Mexican troops that were hailed as glorious victories in the United States. After the declaration of war he crossed the Rio Grande and began the invasion of Mexico. Establishing his base at Camargo, an unhealthy and uncomfortable town, where many of his men became sick, he advanced toward Monterrey, the capital of Nuevo León province. His army numbered 6,640 men, of whom well over half were relatively untrained volunteers. He had two divisions of regular army troops commanded by General William J. Worth and General David Twiggs. It is interesting to note that foreigners made up 47 percent of the regular troops—mainly Irish, 24 percent, and German, 10 percent.[17]

Monterrey, a town of 16,000 inhabitants, lying in a valley, and flanked by the high Sierra Madre Mountains, was stoutly defended. During the attack, Taylor divided his force, sending General Worth to the northwestern end of the town in order to cut the road with Saltillo, which was the principal road for supplies and reinforcements, while he created a strong diversion with his troops at the northeastern part of the town. Worth's men succeeded in capturing the high hill called Independencia, which gave the Americans control of the route to Saltillo. John A. Quitman's brigade, which included the Mississippi Rifles, was also successful in storming Fort Teneria on the northeastern edge of the town.[18] Davis's lieutenant colonel, Alexander K. McClung, was the first to climb its ramparts in a feat of derring-do. Reckless charges, rather than skillful tactics and planning, characterized the battle, in which at one time General Taylor fought on foot in the midst of his men. Davis, like Taylor, seems to have taken delight in exposing himself to danger as he led his men. After his troops had participated in the capture of Fort Diabolo (also called the "Black Fort"), he led them through lanes and gardens of the city crossing streets swept by artillery, until they reached the Great Plaza, where the Mexicans had concentrated their forces.[19]

Faced by defeat, the Mexicans proposed an armistice, which General Taylor accepted. Taylor appointed Colonel Davis, Governor J. Pinckney Henderson of Texas, and General Worth as representatives of the United States to meet with representatives of the Mexican army to draw up terms of truce. They agreed to an armistice of eight weeks, allowing the Mexican army to evacuate the town with most of their arms and equipment, and stipulating that the Mexican army was to retire beyond an agreed-upon line, while Taylor's army was not to advance beyond the line during this period. Taylor ratified the agreement because the Mexican general told him that the government of Mexico had changed and that negotiations for peace had started. Jefferson's brother Joseph, in a letter of September 17, 1846, sharply questioned the wisdom of allowing the enemy an armistice of eight weeks in which to recover, especially after the expenditure of so much blood, and when the American army had an opportunity to force an unconditional surrender.[20] Jefferson defended the action in a letter to the *Washington Union,* saying that the Mexican army could have withdrawn by three routes regardless of American action, and that the amount of time given the enemy was determined by the long delays needed to receive answers from the two governments.[21] This astonishing generosity toward the enemy caused much criticism in the United States, and the administration rightly rejected the terms of the armistice.

After the capture of Monterrey, Davis obtained a sixty-day furlough to return to his home. The reason that Varina gives for this absence from the army was that her health was so greatly impaired by anxiety and depression that she needed his presence.[22] When he arrived at Brierfield, bringing his charger Tartar with him, he found many things neglected, although his black overseer, Jim Pemberton, had done his best. During her husband's absence Varina had remained mostly with her mother in Natchez or alone on the plantation, and this fact indicates not only her self-reliance and courage, but that she and her husband considered her safe on a lonely plantation surrounded by slaves. After attending to his affairs, Davis made a will granting, if he died while he was away, freedom to Jim Pemberton, as well as a bequest of land or money at his choice.

When he returned to his regiment on January 4, 1847, Davis found General Taylor's army at Saltillo, a town sixty miles south of Monterrey, which it had taken without opposition. Taylor had begun gathering supplies and transportation for a further advance into Mexico when he learned that President Polk's administration had changed its plans and decided to make the main thrust of the armed forces toward the Mexican capital, appointing the vain but able Winfield Scott to command an expedition which was to land at Vera Cruz and to advance from that port toward Mexico City. On January 17, Scott ordered Taylor to turn over to him all of his experienced troops and general officers. Among the troops that Taylor retained were the Mississippi Rifles and the battery of Major Braxton Bragg. Although the new plan seems to have been the correct one from a military point of view, it evoked great resentment in Taylor and in the soldiers left behind. Taylor regarded it as a conspiracy against him by the president, Secretary of War William Marcy, and General Scott, because he was gaining too much popularity and was being talked of for election to the presidency.[23]

Santa Anna, the president of Mexico and its ablest general, learned of the stripping of Taylor's army and decided to attack.[24] He led forward 18,000 troops, though claiming 20,000, while Taylor's force, after General John E. Wool with his troops had joined him, numbered only 4,759 men, a large part of whom had never been under fire. Only 517 of these men were regulars.[25] Thus the Mexican superiority over the American army was more than four to one. But the Mexican army was poorly led by its officers, including Santa Anna, and it conducted war with a medieval pageantry. While the band played, the cavalry attacked with raised lances, decorated with tricolored streamers, and the blades gleaming in the sun. At the beginning of the battle, fought before the hacienda of Buena Vista on Washington's birthday, Santa Anna sent an arrogant message to Taylor saying that with his numerical superiority of 20,000 men, the American army would inevitably have to surrender. Taylor's defiant reply was "forcible"; according to the soldiers, he told the Mexican general "to go to hell."

As the Mexican army advanced, Taylor withdrew his troops to a strategic position before La Angostura pass in the mountains, "the very spot for a small army to fight a large one." The Mississippi regiment, now composed of only 358 men, played a crucial role in the defeat of the Mexican army. The Mexican troops in great force attacked the left flank of the American army, causing some Indiana volunteers to retreat in panic, gravely endangering the American rear. General John Wool galloped up to Taylor at this time and said, "General, we are whipped," but Taylor was unperturbed. In this crisis he ordered Davis's regiment to attack. As the Mississippi colonel advanced he pleaded with the demoralized Indiana troops to fall in behind him and return to the battle, but without effect. Ordering his soldiers to hold their fire until the charging enemy was within close range, he succeeded in stopping the enemy with the deadly marksmanship of his men. When a large force of

Mexican cavalry then bore down upon his regiment, he arranged his men, along with some Indiana troops, into a V formation with the open end facing the enemy cavalry. In beautiful, massed order the Mexican Lancers rode at a gallop toward the Americans until they were nearly inside Davis's formation and then, unaccountably, slowed down and halted instead of launching a charge that might have won them a victory. Davis's men, cool and staunch, directed a devastating fire at the Mexicans, who fled.[26] Davis's V formation later became a subject of controversy. The arrangement was contrary to the orthodox method of opposing cavalry, but it was partly dictated by the nature of the terrain as well as by brilliant tactics. Early in the battle he was shot in the right foot, the bullet carrying pieces of his brass spur into the wound, yet he remained on his horse until the battle was over. As a result of his wound he had to use crutches for two years, and the wound affected his nervous system.

Thus Davis became "the hero of Buena Vista." President Polk appointed him a brigadier general of volunteers but he refused the commission on the ground that the president had no authority to make such an appointment, since it was a prerogative of the state. When the regiment returned to New Orleans in the middle of June, 1847, the men were received with wild enthusiasm. As they marched through the streets, they were showered with garlands of flowers by beautiful Creole women. One of the greatest orators of the South, Sergeant S. Prentiss, made the welcoming address, and Davis replied in an appropriate speech. At Natchez the reception was especially joyful and romantic. The young girls of the Natchez Institute, a private school, presented each of the veterans with a bouquet of flowers. The leading citizen, Colonel Adam Bingamon, gave an oration, replete with references to classic history and medieval chivalry, to do honor to the returning soldiers. He called the battle of Buena Vista the "American Marathon," and declared: "Never, even in the palmiest days of chivalry did more stalwart and devoted knights enter the lists of the proudest tournament; never were the interests and honor of a country entrusted to more valiant and determined hands."[27]

Diminishing the joy over the victory at Buena Vista were the battle deaths of many brave soldiers and officers, including Lieutenant Colonel Henry Clay, the oldest son of the great statesman, who, according to Varina, was one of her husband's friends at West Point. When the Mississippi Rifles returned to the United States there were only 376 men left of the 926 men who so eagerly went to war. Mrs. Davis, in her memoir of her husband, attributed this great loss in strength to death in battle and disease, but almost certainly some of it was owing to desertions and to men who for various reasons left the regiment. In the supposedly bloody battle of Monterrey, Davis reported that during the three-day conflict he lost only 8 men killed and 54 wounded or missing, and at Buena Vista, the other battle in which his regiment fought, approximately 30 were killed and 40 wounded.[28]

After the war came letters of criticism and discussions of how the glory should be distributed. One officer claimed that at the storming of the forts at

Monterrey, not Davis's regiment, but his, deserved the honor of reaching the forts first, to which detraction Davis hotly replied and a duel was narrowly averted. In 1850 W. H. Bissell, a colonel of Indiana troops in the battle of Buena Vista, cast aspersions on the role of the Mississippi regiment that Davis commanded, and Davis, defending his own honor and that of the regiment, sent him a formal challenge to a duel. The duel was prevented only by the offending colonel acknowledging "their gallant and distinguished service in that battle."[29] As late as the fall of 1858, Davis was still replying to detractors of his glorious exploits and those of his troops in the Mexican War. In a speech before the Mississippi legislature, he repelled the accusation that the formation of the "V" line of battle was an accident, and paid glowing tribute to the valor of Mississippi troops.[30]

The Mexican War did not end until after the capture of Mexico City by General Scott's army and the signing of a peace treaty on February 2, 1848. It was signed with Santa Anna by Nicholas Trist, a diplomatic agent, who accompanied the army. Although he negotiated the treaty after being recalled, the president accepted it reluctantly. The treaty gave the United States a vast territory including California, New Mexico, and Utah, but not as much territory as Davis wished.

Before the debate on the Mexican treaty, Davis's strong expanionist feelings had been displayed in the campaign to annex Texas, and to a lesser degree in the debate over the Oregon boundary. In the debate over acceptance of the treaty, he was one of the most prominent Southern expansionists. After the easy victory over Mexico a strong movement arose to acquire all of Mexico, a movement that President Polk resisted. Davis took an intermediate position, opposing the All-Mexico movement, but urging that the United States take a slice of northern Mexico as far as the Sierra Madre Mountains. He was in the Senate when the treaty of *Guadalupe Hidalgo* was being debated in 1848 and introduced an amendment to that effect, maintaining that the additional territory was needed to give the United States control of the whole Rio Grande valley as well as of an easily defended mountain barrier as a boundary. He finally voted for the treaty as submitted by the president in order to end the war and head off the All-Mexico movement.[31]

The terms of the treaty left vague the southwest boundary line between Mexico and the United States. To rectify this condition and to acquire a desirable site for the terminus of a transcontinental railroad, Davis persuaded President Pierce in 1853 to send his friend James Gadsden of Charleston, South Carolina, a Yale graduate and president of a railroad, as minister to Mexico. Gadsden was successful in negotiating a treaty for the purchase of a slice of Mexican territory of approximately 45,000 square miles, below the Gila River in the present state of Arizona. The purchase price of $10 million was regarded as excessive by Northern antislavery men in comparison with the mere $20 million or so paid for the vast territory of California and New Mexico ($15 million plus the assumption of approximately $6 million in claims of U.S. citizens against Mexico), and they dubbed it "conscience money." The treaty for the acquisition of the Gadsden Purchase was narrowly passed in the Senate.[32] When later, in 1858, Senator James Wilson of Massachusetts attacked the purchase during a debate on a transcontinental railroad, Davis stoutly defended it, maintaining that the acquisition of a transcontinental railroad outlet was not the only advantage of the Purchase, but that it also gave the United States a rich silver-mining district which would be valuable in a trade with Asia. This mirage wavered before the eyes of America throughout the nineteenth century and beyond.[33]

The Mexican War enormously aggravated sectional tensions, for it reopened the debate between the North and South over the status of slavery in the lands recently acquired from Mexico. Furthermore, the Mexican War provided a training ground for many of the men who were to be commanders on both sides during the Civil War. Among the relatively junior officers who served were the Southerners Lee, Bragg, Stonewall Jackson, A. S. and J. E. Johnston, Beauregard, and Longstreet, and among the Northern officers were Grant, Sherman, McClellan, Thomas, and Meade, to name several.

Davis came out of the Mexican War a national hero, and this reputation probably affected his belief that he had extraordinary ability as a military leader, so that in 1861 he preferred to become a general of Confederate armies rather than the Confederate president. The war also strengthened his tendencies toward expansionism. His role in the victory of Buena Vista so advanced his popularity with Mississippians that upon the sudden death of Senator Jesse Spreight in August, 1847, Governor Albert Gallatin Brown appointed him to fill out the unexpired term, and in January, 1848, the Mississippi legislature unanimously elected him to a full term. Here he became the most notable and outspoken defender of Southern rights.

The Champion of Southern Rights

In December, 1847, Jefferson Davis entered the Senate chamber on crutches, but with the aura of a military hero. The Senate in the 1840s and 1850s had far more prestige than it has today. It was the era of the mighty orators—Clay, Webster, Calhoun, and Benton—and people crowded the Senate chamber to hear them. The senators dressed in formal, courtly style, and their sense of the dignity of the Senate and of themselves caused them to waste time in personal attacks and defenses. Furthermore, these orators, as well as the lesser ones, believed that their speeches had real power to change things. It was perhaps an illusion; for men are influenced primarily by economic interests and partisan and regional loyalties rather than by speeches. Although Senators were ordinarily "coldly punctilious" to new members, they received Davis cordially and unreservedly. Varina did not like to go to the Senate chamber, because she dreaded the critical remarks that might be made of her husband by thoughtless, vulgar people sitting near her. On occasions when she did attend the speech of a notable man, she would send a servant to reserve a seat for her.[1]

The Davises rented a house near the United States Hotel, which they shared with the Armisted Burts and the McWillies, congressmen and their wives from South Carolina and Mississippi, taking their meals in the hotel where they enjoyed the company of the Toombses of Georgia. Varina and her husband occasionally attended fashionable dinners and balls; at the president's dinner she wore a sky-blue silk dress, "ruffled up to the waist, and made with train, with scarlet rosettes in my hair, and short sleeves." On one of those social occasions, she wrote with a keen sense of the ridiculous:

> I laughed until I almost died at the Mexican Minister. He left his cards for us, and we returned the visit New Year's day (1850), and when we went in I took him for a mulatto. First is "pass this way," second is a cup of eggnog, the third, his bow to me. He could not say one word but "pass this way," and every time he said "pass this way," I thought he felt as triumphant as Mouse Hedrigg did when she had "luppen a ditch."[2]

In her memoir she drew wonderfully perceptive portraits of the great men of the Senate whom she met, particularly of Calhoun, Benton, Clay, Webster, and Sam Houston. One of the prominent foreigners who visited their home was the filibusterer Narciso Lopez, who offered Davis $200,000 to lead an expedition to liberate Cuba from Spanish rule, but Davis turned down the tempting offer. His prestige in the Senate was indicated by his selection to be a member of "the escort of honor" to accompany the body of Calhoun, who had died on April 5, 1850, to Charleston. Also he was chosen chairman of the Senate Military Affairs Committee.

The great question that concerned the Senate during 1846–50 was the political organization of the western lands obtained from Mexico and by the Oregon treaty. The Wilmot Proviso, providing that any territory to be acquired from Mexico should be free of slavery, had been introduced in Congress by David Wilmot, a Pennsylvania Democrat, in the summer of 1846 after Davis had left Congress and was in Mexico. To Southerners, to use an appropriate cliché, it was like waving a red flag before a bull. It renewed sectional bitterness and a serious threat of Southern secession. In a letter of September 19, 1847, shortly before beginning his service in the Senate, Davis proposed that Southerners should demand of their political brethren in the North "a disavowal of the principles of the Wilmot Proviso, an admission of an equal right of the South with the North to the territory held as the common property of the United States, and a declaration in favor of extending the Missouri compromise [line] to all States hereafter to be admitted into our confederacy."[3] He followed these political principles throughout his senatorial career.

He delivered his first important speech in the Senate on July 12, 1848, on a bill to establish a territorial government for Oregon. On June 23 he had introduced an amendment to the Oregon bill declaring that "nothing contained in this act shall be so construed as to authorize the prohibition of domestic slavery in said territory while it remains in the condition of a territory of the United States."[4] In this speech he elaborated his views on the institution of Southern slavery. Davis did not believe, as did Calhoun, that slavery was to be the permanent condition of the Negro in the United States, but he thought that it would require several generations before it would be practicable to emancipate the Southern slaves. "The slave," he said, "must be made fit for his freedom by education and discipline and thus made unfit for slavery. And as soon as he becomes unfit for slavery, the master will no longer desire to hold him as a slave."

Yet he warned that "slavery could not be abolished without a long series of preliminary preparations; and during these preparations great dangers would menace the peace of the South."[5] Although Southerners apparently had little fear of their slaves when under control of the master, supported by patrols sent out every two weeks to search for arms in the cabins and to arrest Negroes out on the roads at night without passes, they envisaged great disorder if these controls should be relaxed. But Jefferson's position of gradually preparing the slaves for freedom was an enlightened one for his time and section; he practiced it on his plantation, and so did his brother Joseph. As a consequence some individuals, such as his black overseer, Jim Pemberton, and the Montgomerys on Joseph's plantations, were ready for freedom. Unfortunately, Southern masters as a whole, and the state legislatures, made no significant provision for the gradual elevation of the slaves.[6]

But Jefferson denied that slavery as it existed in the South was a sin or an evil; rather, he said that it was an "institution for the preparation of that race [the Negroes] for civil liberty and social enjoyment." He declared that slavery's origin was in the "divine decree—the curse upon the graceless son of Noah."[7] Furthermore, he pointed out that Northern ships had imported the African slaves into the South. In comparison with the wretched condition of the free blacks in the North, he observed, the Southern slaves were cared for in a paternal fashion, and an attachment generally existed between master and slave. His advice to the North was to "leave natural causes to their full effect, and when the time shall arrive at which emancipation is proper, those most interested will be most anxious to effect it."[8] But when that time should come (he suggested it might come as a result of the pressure of cheaper labor), it would be necessary to separate the Negroes from the superior white race.

On virtually every occasion that Southern slavery was attacked by Northern senators or by resolutions of state legislatures, Davis vigorously defended Southern institutions. When a resolution was introduced to admit the famed Irish temperance reformer, Father Theobald, to a seat in the Senate chamber, he vehemently opposed it (December 20, 1849), because the priest had been critical of Southern slavery, but the other senator from Mississippi, Henry S. Foote, a violent enemy of Davis, took an opposite position.[9] He was indignant when the Vermont legislature sent some resolutions to Congress condemning Southern slavery. He replied in a speech of January 10, 1850, satirizing the "highly moral" people of New England—"such superior samples of humanity" —and suggesting that such antislavery resolutions and petitions were for electioneering purposes. The Southern states, standing strictly on the defensive and wishing to preserve the constitutional Union, he declared, would resist aggression and insults. "They will march up to this issue and meet it face to face."[10]

Nowhere in Davis's speeches or private letters does he seem to have been aware of the depth of Northern feeling against Southern slavery, constituting a moral imperative for their representatives in Congress to do away with it— it was a blind spot in his vision. He considered that Northern politicians in agitating against slavery were motivated solely by a struggle for sectional power. When Senator John P. Hale of New Hampshire attacked the institutions of the South in 1849, presenting offensive antislavery petitions, Davis replied with devastating irony. Even Varina was critical of the vehemence of his remarks, writing to him from Natchez on January 25, 1849, that she had read in the papers "your very forcible little speech in partial answer to Mr. Hale's vituperations. It was a little too violent, more so than I would have liked to hear you be, however well deserved the censure."[11]

The Mississippi senator was among the foremost in criticizing the self-righteousness of New England, for he did not believe, as some Southerners did, that the abolitionists represented only a minority in that region. He condemned those Northerners "whose piety is so great that they must always be appropriating to themselves other men's sins." He called the abolitionists "these latter day saints," who sought to instruct Southerners in their moral duties.[12] He emphasized on several occasions that it was the New Englanders who brought enslaved Africans to the South. But he did not use the most telling criticism of the North, namely, that in its factories capitalists cruelly exploited women and children. This charge became the most potent ammunition in the Southern arsenal to counter the abolitionists after 1854 when George Fitzhugh, a lawyer from Virginia, published his *Sociology for the South,* and after 1856 when William J. Grayson of South Carolina published his *The Hireling and the Slave.*

Jefferson Davis was a party man. He believed that the two-party system was necessary for the functioning of democracy. His devotion to party was illustrated by his action in the presidential campaign of 1848. His personal inclination was to vote for Zachary Taylor, with whom he had established cordial relations after the death of his first wife, the daughter of Taylor. Nevertheless he believed that it was his duty to support Lewis Cass of Michigan, the candidate of the Democratic party, whose principles and platform accorded more with his principles than did those of the Whig candidate. Davis maintained that it was in the interests of the South to support the Democratic party, since the South constituted the minority section of the country, and its security in the Union depended upon preserving "the constitutional curb with which we check the otherwise unbridled will of the majority." The Democratic party, he held, because it was the party of strict construction of the Constitution, of "checks and balances, and of constitutional constraints," offered the greatest safety for the South.[13]

His allegiance to the Democratic party, beginning with his vote for Andrew Jackson for president, illustrated an important fact about antebellum Southern politics. The large planters of the delta and Black Belt generally supported the Whig party, and Davis and his brother belonged to this economic class; but family tradition also played an important role in party allegiance, and Davis followed his father's affiliation with the Jeffersonian party, later represented by Andrew Jackson.[14] He was not, however, a blind adherent of all the party's legislative proposals, as illustrataed by his support in 1849 of the establishment of a Department of the Interior, which was opposed by Calhoun, James M. Mason, and other Southern senators, who feared that it would mean an extension of federal power. When Mason pointed out that it was favored by "the other side," namely, Northern senators, Davis declared that he was not influenced by partisan considerations.[15] In the 1850s he consistently advocated a transcontinental railroad, which was not popular in the South.

During Davis's first year in the Senate gold was discovered in California, and so many people rushed to the gold fields that a movement arose to organize a state, skipping the territorial stage. Early in 1850 California applied to Congress for admission into the Union as the thirty-first state with a constitution forbidding slavery. If California had been admitted into the Union as a free state, it would have had serious consequences for the South, because it would have upset the sectional equilibrium in the Senate, depriving the South of its veto over legislation hostile to slavery. So alarmed was Calhoun by the prospect that he sought to form a Southern bloc in Congress composed of both Democrats and Whigs. For this purpose he summoned a meeting of the Southern congressmen in Washington, but the Whigs opposed his plan, and his "Address of the Southern Delegates in Congress to Their Constituents," portraying the danger to the Southern states from the antislavery crusade, and urging the union of all Southerners into a single party, was opposed by the Whigs and finally adopted by only one vote.[16]

Davis supported Calhoun's movement to unite the South in resisting the attempt of the North "to monopolize" the federal territories by excluding slaveholders from settling there. He did not say it, but it was a fact that the effort of the North to keep out slavery from the federal territories was motivated in part by a desire to keep out Negroes. The Northern states were almost as racist in feeling as the Southern states.[17] Faced by the probability that California would be admitted into the Union as a free state, skipping the territorial stage, especially since President Taylor adamantly supported this solution, Davis and his constituents were aroused. Davis had two major objections to such a prospect: (1) it would destroy the equilibrium that had been maintained in the Senate, so essential to ward off hostile attempts against slavery; and (2) it would deny to the South equal treatment of its citizens in the settlement of the federal territories. Therefore, shortly before he left for Congress, he addressed a letter to the people of his state expressing his defiant opposition to the Northern majority's position on the California and territorial questions. He warned: "The generation which avoids its responsibility on this subject sows the wind and leaves the whirlwind as a harvest to its children; let us get together and build manufactories, enter upon industrial pursuits and prepare for our own self-sustenance."[18]

In that same month a bipartisan convention in Mississippi, deeply aroused, called a convention of the Southern states to be held in Nashville on the first Monday in June, 1850, to devise and adopt some mode of resistance against the impending measures in Congress. In case of the adoption of these measures denying the South equality of treatment in the federal territories the convention threatened secession, or, as Cleo Hearon in his able study of "Mississippi and the Compromise of 1850" observed, "made the first formal expression in Mississippi looking to secession as a final resort in the defense of slavery."[19] The Mississippi legislature ratified the action of the convention by appointing delegates to the Nashville convention, resolving at the same time that there should be no discrimination against slaveholders and their property in the settlement of the territories acquired "by the common blood and common treasure of the citizens of the several States." Calhoun was generally credited with instigating the Nashville convention, but in a Senate speech Davis ascribed it to the spontaneous feeling of the people of Mississippi assembled in two conventions.[20] He declared that its purpose was not disunion but an appeal to the North. To Franklin H. Elmore of Mississippi he wrote that the convention should not be postponed but should meet for preventive purposes: "to check aggression, to preserve the union, peaceably to secure our rights, requires prompt action."[21]

In the critical situation that threatened the Union in 1850, Henry Clay presented on January 29 his famous compromise. It provided for the admission of California as a free state; the organization of two huge territories, Utah and New Mexico, out of the remainder of the territory acquired from Mexico, with no mention of slavery, leaving the question of slavery to the territorial legislatures with an ultimate appeal to the courts; the abolition of the slave trade, but not slavery, in the District of Columbia, a resolution that Congress had no right to interfere with the interstate slave trade; the reimbursement of Texas for the loss of its territory added to New Mexico; and a new fugitive slave law. Clay's proposals had little originality for their provisions had been offered before.[22] A sinister aspect of the Compromise called for the payment of $10 million to Texas for the loss of half of its territory; sinister, because its inclusion in the final compromise settlement was to enable Texas to pay its bondholders, located mainly in the North, who formed a powerful lobby for the passage of the compromise measures.[23]

Clay, after an absence of four years, had returned to the Senate in 1849, much to the disappointment of Davis, who regarded him as an antislavery man at heart, dangerous to Southern interests. Though seventy-three years old, the Kentucky statesman had retained a peculiar charm, was irresistible to women, though he was not handsome, and used his charisma effectively on many men, but not on Davis when Southern interests were at stake. While the great debate on the Compromise was going on Clay happened to visit Hill's boardinghouse, where Calhoun was staying, and met Amelia Burt, the pretty, twenty-year-old niece of the Carolina statesman, in a darkened corridor where to her surprise he kissed her; whereupon she rushed to tell her uncle, "I have been kissed by the great Mr. Clay." Calhoun replied, "Amelia, don't you put your trust in that old man."[24] Clay, whose son, killed at Buena Vista, had been Davis's friend, tried also to exert his charm on Davis to support his compromise. Meeting him on the Capitol grounds on March 7, Clay urged him to join those in favor of the Compromise that he said would give peace to the country for thirty years. But Davis declared that he was unwilling "to transfer to posterity a trial which they would be relatively less able to meet than we were," and he passed on his way.[25]

On January 21, 1850, the Mississippi delegation in Congress, headed by Davis, sent a joint letter to Governor Albert Gallatin Brown stating their opinion that the admission of California would be equivalent to adopting the Wilmot Proviso "in another form." They requested the opinion of the governor, the legislature, and, if practicable, the people as to the proper course the delegation should take in this emergency.[26] Governor Brown was an ardent fire-eater, in favor of the strongest measures of resistance, but the legislature held back until March 6 before sending its instructions to the Mississippi delegation. Davis read them to the Senate, instructing the senators and representatives of the state to resist the admission of California into the Union by "all honorable and constitutional means."[27]

The introduction of Henry Clay's compromise measure on January 29 precipitated one of the great debates in American political history. It was essentially a debate between the sections. The South was represented by Calhoun and Davis, the border states by Clay, the West by Stephen A. Douglas, the Northern antislavery forces by William H. Seward of New York, and the moderates by Daniel Webster. Davis tried immediately to answer Clay's speech in support of his compromise proposals but he could not get the floor until February 13. His speech on that date and on the following day was one of his greatest efforts in behalf of Southern interests, but it contained little eloquence.[28] He began by saying in the chivalric terms often used then that he took up the gauntlet that Clay had thrown down. The Kentucky senator had made much of the fact that the Mexican law governing the territories ceded by Mexico prohibited slavery, but Davis contended that this law was superseded by the laws and Constitution of the United States. Clay, Webster, and Douglas maintained that the expansion of slavery into the semiarid country acquired by the treaty of Guadalupe Hidalgo was interdicted by the laws of nature, but Davis asserted that the institution of slavery was adaptable to this region, especially being capable of use in gold mining and in agriculture based on irrigation.

The Mississippi senator declared that the South needed room for the expansion of its population. Admitting that slavery was a wasteful system of labor (recently denied by *Time on the Cross*), he argued that the South's labor force required fresh territory in which to expand. He could deduce the need for expansion from actual observation of the relatively rapid exhaustion of rich cotton lands in his state of Mississippi and the consequent migration of planters and farmers to fertile lands farther west. Not only did the South need a further supply of fresh agricultural land, he maintained, but it required room for an expanding population of both whites and Negroes. Take out "the accession from foreign immigration" into the North, Davis said, and the rate of increase of population in the two sections was practically the same, and to coop up the slave population in the old states would be to invite disaster. William L. Barney, in his recent study, argues that this fear of containment of the slave population was one of the main causes of secession.[29]

Davis's defense of slavery in his speech in Congress in 1850 was no different from what ordinary people constantly do—rationalize the status quo. He saw the Negroes as children, needing the protection and guidance of their white masters. Unfortunately, they continued to remain children, with whites making halfhearted efforts to educate them and enable them to attain the status of adults. Davis was probably right in maintaining that the condition of slaves in the South was far better than the condition of the Negroes in the North—certainly physically—but the Northern Negroes had no fear of their children and wives being sold away from them or of whipping. Davis was one of the most influential of the proslavery propagandists and contributed to the legend of the romantic South, perpetuated after the Civil War by Thomas Nelson Page, Joel Chandler Harris, and other writers.[30]

Rather than appealing to the need for protecting human rights, Davis appealed to economic considerations and legal and constitutional rights. He observed that slaves were suited to working in the hot sun, and that their labor was necessary to produce cotton—for Northern factories. He maintained that slaves were property under the Constitution, and should therefore be protected as property in their transferral into the federal territories. But he did not treat his own slaves, as noted, solely as property, and Southern laws recognized slaves as persons as well as property.

His main argument was constitutional: namely, that Congress had no right to discriminate between different kinds of property in the territories, nor did a territory composed of "first-comers, a conglomerated mass of gold hunters, foreign and native" have a right to exclude slaveholders; that, he said, was worse than applying the Wilmot Proviso. He expatiated on the unfairness to Southern soldiers who had fought in the Mexican War that they should be excluded from settling with their slaves in territory acquired by common blood and common treasure. Although he argued for no restrictions against slavery in the territories, he was willing to extend the Missouri Compromise line to the Pacific. Vehemently, he denied that he was a disunionist, protesting his devotion to the flag of the Union.

Clay's Omnibus Bill, presenting his compromise in one package, was defeated on July 31 in Congress. It was finally divided into its components, and the different measures were passed separately. Davis voted against the passage of all of them except the Fugitive Slave bill, and he did not regard this provision as much of a concession to the South, for he predicted correctly that it could not be enforced in the North.

In addition to his main speech of February 13 and 14, he spoke tenaciously through the summer against the enactment of the various compromise bills. He maintained that California did not have the requisite population for the admission of a state into the Union, and that its constitution had been drawn up by gold hunters, sojourners, adventurers, and soldiers from a disbanded New York regiment sent there by President Taylor, men who were not valid citizens of the state. He argued that California should go through the normal process of obtaining statehood, completing the organization of a territorial government before being admitted. In regard to the Texas–New Mexico settlement, he held that it injured Southern interests because the subtraction of such a large area from the slave state of Texas and the addition of it to New Mexico reduced the opportunity of the South later to acquire additional slave states.[31]

Davis's speech on the Compromise of 1850 does not rank with those of Clay, Webster, and Calhoun, or even of Seward, who at this time propounded his doctrine, which so enraged the Southerners, that there was a higher law than the Constitution. Not Davis, but Calhoun, in his notable speech of March 4, stated the extreme demands of the South. The South Carolina statesman took an uncompromising position that the Southern states could not remain in the Union without constitutional guarantees of their equality of rights, and he appealed to the North to stop agitation on the divisive slave question. Sixty-eight years old, haggard, worn, wrapped in flannels, Calhoun was too weak to deliver his last great speech but turned it over to Senator James M. Mason of Virginia to read, while he sat in his seat glaring defiantly at those he regarded as the enemies of the South. Nevertheless, the next day he dragged his long, thin frame up to the Capitol to defend his speech from attacks by Senator Henry S. Foote of Mississippi, a turncoat who had at first violently opposed the Compromise, but now supported it.

When the Omnibus Bill was defeated Calhoun said that he gloried in its defeat, but this proslavery victory had little significance because all of its provisions were later passed as separate laws. In the final passage of the separate bills, Clay played only a small role. Rather, Stephen A. Douglas, who formed various combinations of interests and politicians, was the master architect of the passage of the Compromise, while its originator, Henry Clay, was vacationing in Newport, Rhode Island. The death of Taylor on July 9 and his replacement by a doughface (Northerner with Southern principles) vice president, Millard Fillmore, advanced the cause of the adoption of the Compromise. Its passage was completed on September 17. Davis voted against every provision except the Fugitive Slave Law. After this last desperate effort to uphold the rights of the South, Calhoun returned to his boardinghouse, soon to die.

The Fugitive Slave Law of the Compromise proved to be the Achilles heel of this great sectional truce, for the Northern states refused to enforce it. It is amazing today that fair-minded Southerners, such as Jefferson Davis, promoted the patently unjust act, which James Ford Rhodes describes as "one of the most assailable laws ever passed by the Congress of the United States."[32] Congressman Albert Gallatin Brown of Mississippi, an extreme state rights and proslavery man, wrote to Jefferson Davis on May 1, 1852, that a "finality" resolution in Congress stating the Compromise to be a final settlement of the controversies between the Northern and the Southern states was designed to commit the Northern Whigs to a support of the Fugitive Slave Law.[33] Despite Davis's overwhelming defeat on the compromise measures of 1850, he still commanded a position of leadership in the Democratic party and had a following outside of the South, as indicated by the fact that in the Democratic National Convention of 1852 Illinois voted for him for vice president.

In the fall of 1851 the Compromise of the preceding year was presented to the states in convention for their acceptance or rejection. Davis's strong proslavery stance was not enough to save him from a humiliating defeat on this issue. He had strong reason to believe that the people of Mississippi supported him enthusiastically in his advanced position on Southern rights, for in 1850 the legislature had elected him to a full six-year term in the Senate. Furthermore, in December of that year the Mississippi legislature had also passed resolutions praising Davis and the other members of the congressional delegation, except Senator Henry Foote, for opposing the Compromise of 1850, thereby upholding the rights and honor of the state. The resolutions publicly castigated the course of Foote in voting for the compromise measures, despite his instructions, as not representing the will and interests of Mississippi.[34] On this issue Foote had pursued a vacillating course, at first violently opposing the admission of California as a state, and then backing down. His failure to resign after he had disobeyed instructions was clearly a violation of the customary Southern practice of a senator resigning his seat when his conscience would not permit him to obey instructions.[35]

After the passage of the Compromise, Davis had an opportunity to state his position on secession publicly when a group of citizens of Woodville, on November 17, 1850, published a series of questions in the Woodville *Republican* to which they requested answers from him. He replied that he was in favor of calling a state convention to decide on proper measures to be adopted and to prepare for the armed defense of the state, if needed. He also favored calling a convention of the slaveholding states for the same purpose. This convention should demand from the nonslaveholding states guarantees to protect Southern rights and insure Southern equality in the Union. If these demands were refused, the South should apply the last remedy: peaceful separation. He declared that he would prefer to go out of the Union, with the Constitution, rather than to remain in the Union and abandon the Constitution. In other words, he was in favor of manly resistance, rather than slavish submission to a majority who sought to violate the Constitution and deprive the South of equality in the Union. He did not state specifically what were the guarantees that he demanded from the North. At the same time he vigorously denied that he was a disunionist who sought to establish a Southern Confederacy upon the ruins of the Union.[36]

The question of whether Mississippi should accept the compromise measures would be determined by a convention that was to meet in the fall of 1851. Davis made a speech at Aberdeen in northern Mississippi during the latter part of May, 1851, outlining the course that he thought Mississippi should take. Since the border states had refused to cooperate with the lower South in opposing the compromise measures and thus preventing the encirclement of the slave states with a cordon of free states, he favored excluding the slaves of the border states from entering the planting states. He argued that the poor people of his state would not support the submissionists to the compromise measures because they wished to uphold slavery, that made race, rather than property, the basis of distinction of the classes and thus insured equality of all white men. He recommended nonintercourse with the Northern states to every extent practicable: the South should build factories and Southern merchants should patronize Southern suppliers in Southern ports, educate Southern youths in Southern schools, and employ teachers devoted to Southern rights. He retreated somewhat from his previous extreme position because the sentiments of the people of his state had changed. He did not think South Carolina should secede because of the enactment of the compromise measures, although she had the right to do so, and if the federal government used force against her she should secede, and he was in favor of the state of Mississippi going to her assistance.[37] In expressing his defiance, an observer noted, his eyes expanded, brightened, and flashed forth a fire of patriotic fervor.

In May, 1851, a combination of Union Democrats and Whigs in Mississippi nominated Senator Henry S. Foote for governor. Thereupon, Foote resigned as senator and launched a vigorous campaign for election to the governor's office, stressing acceptance of the compromise measures by Mississippi. This demagogue played such an important role in Davis's political career that it is pertinent to portray the character of the man.[38] He was born in Virginia and graduated from Washington College (now Washington and Lee), studied law, and migrated to Alabama and Mississippi. He was a little man with a big voice and a combative nature. His eloquence thrilled the Mississippi rural audiences and he was a master of sarcasm and invective. But he was distrusted as being an ambitious opportunist.

Following the nomination of Foote, a Democratic State Convention meeting in Jackson in June nominated the Northern-born statesman John A. Quitman as its candidate for governor. Quitman had attained fame as a brigadier general of Mississippi volunteers in the Mexican War, and had acquired wealth as a lawyer that enabled him to live in princely style in Natchez. He had also won popularity as a supporter of filibuster expeditions against Cuba, and had recently been indicted by a federal court on this account. (Filibuster expeditions were military forces that violated U.S. neutrality; in the Southern states they tried to enlist Davis as the commander.) The federal court acquitted him, but he had resigned as governor of Mississippi while he was under the cloud of violating federal laws. He was a poor public speaker, dull and prosy, and during a joint canvass (speaking from the same platform) he was easily eclipsed by the fiery Foote. Because of his extreme views on secession, he was regarded as a liability by many in the Democratic party.

In the midst of the gubernatorial campaign, the legislature called a state convention scheduled to meet in November, 1851, to consider the state's course with regard to accepting the Compromise. The election for delegates took place in September and resulted in a resounding victory for the Union party, which polled 28,402 votes to 21,242 for their opponents. As a result Quitman resigned as the candidate of the Democratic State Rights party, considering his chances for election hopeless. It is significant that the State Rights candidates for the convention drew their main strength from the southern part of Mississippi, an area of pine lands and poor people who had few slaves and little to lose in a confrontation with the federal government.

When Quitman withdrew, the state Democratic committee on September 16 named Davis to take his place and lead a desperate cause. Davis accepted the call, and resigned his seat in the Senate on September 23 to engage in the campaign. It was a great personal sacrifice. He much preferred to remain in the Senate than to become governor. Moreover, he was sick, and he did not relish a speaking contest with the slashing, rough-and-tumble campaigner, Henry S. Foote. For three weeks after his acceptance Davis was ill, suffering from pneumonia and confined to his room. His eyes were so affected that he could not read print or write, and he wore goggles when he came out of the darkened room. Nevertheless, his exalted sense of honor compelled him to accept the disagreeable and forlorn task, although only a few weeks were left to campaign. In a weakened condition, he tried to rally the people of Mississippi to oppose acceptance of the Compromise. But the tide of sentiment in the state had already turned, and such shrewd politicians as Albert Gallatin Brown, a candidate for reelection to Congress who had been foremost in advocating resistance, now turned with the tide. But not Davis.

It was surprising that the sentiment in the state for Southern rights, which had been so strong in 1850 during the debates in Congress, should within a few months change so markedly. The reasons for this reversal seem to have been: (1) the prosperity of the country—the Compromise has been called the

"Businessman's Peace," and the wealthy planters supported it; (2) the "finality" aspect—it was hailed as the final settlement of the disturbing slave controversy; and (3) by the summer of 1851, Georgia and Alabama had accepted it. Georgia, however, had warned the North that she would secede if the Compromise was violated, and its convention drew up the "Georgia Platform" listing those encroachments upon Southern rights that would justify secession; they served notice that their acquiescence was based only on a strict compliance by the North with all of its provisions, especially in regard to the enforcement of the Fugitive Slave Law.[39] Accordingly, Davis and the State Rights party were placed in an extremely awkward position, for only South Carolina seemed to be willing to act, and if Mississippi followed her, the two states would have no contiguous boundary but would be separated by two large states.

In the gubernatorial election Foote defeated Davis, but only with the help of the Whigs, and Davis lost by less than a thousand votes. After the election he maintained that he had been defeated by a false issue: namely, he was accused of being a disunionist, or as he stated it, his opponent and supporters had kept the "alarm bell of Disunion ceaselessly ringing." On the one hand, Foote accused Davis of being a secessionist, while Davis attacked his opponent as a changeling and defamer. The state was ablaze with emotion over the election. One person who campaigned for Davis and the State Rights party was the brilliant Lucius Quintus Cincinnatus Lamar, twenty-six years old, a lawyer at Oxford, and professor at the University of Mississippi. He condemned Foote for not resigning when he violated the instructions of the legislature and castigated him for changing his principles and abandoning the interests of the South.[40]

Although at the time Davis apparently did not realize the change of sentiment in his state, Varina did. She wrote shrewdly to her parents, October 28, 1851, shortly before the election: "the Southern Rights cause is a losing one now." She conceded that defeat would be the best thing for the family, citing the immense cost of the governor's office, entailing expensive entertaining, servants, and household expenses, silver, cutglass, linens, carriages and horses, dinner parties, brandy and wine. Furthermore, she could gain solace in defeat by realizing that she would not be forced to bear with insolence or to conciliate fools and busybodies, which she doubted that she could stand.

The victorious Henry S. Foote had an unsuccessful administration as governor and was not renominated for a second term. He resigned in disgust five days before his term ended in January, 1854, and emigrated to California. Defeated in this state in his bid for election to the Senate, he returned to Mississippi and located at Vicksburg; later he moved to Tennessee, where he opposed seccession. Here he was elected to the Confederate Congress to become a constant trouble-maker and virulent critic of Davis until he was finally expelled from the Confederate Senate in 1865.

Defeat for Davis meant retirement to Brierfield for a period of over fifteen months. Sitting on his verandah in the cool of the evening, smoking his pipe that later gave him so much pleasure as a prisoner at Fort Monroe, with the fireflies lighting up the gloaming, and breezes blowing the scent of honeysuckle, roses, and jasmine, he must have meditated on the bitterness of defeat and sought its causes. Although he had not actually recommended the secession of his state—but, rather, a convention of the Southern states for resistance—he was regarded by the people as a potential disunionist, and it was difficult for them to recognize the distinction that he made. He wrote later that he was a victim of false propaganda, but that was not the whole story—the Southern people wished peace and accepted the Compromise as a "final" settlement of issues.

Davis might well have meditated also on how starting his career as a nationalist, as did Calhoun, he had come to be a sectionalist, though not a fire-eater, for he had no desire to found a Southern republic. The single most important event that started him on his career as a sectionalist was the North's attempt to apply the Wilmot Proviso to the federal territories. Furthermore, the ceaseless agitation over slavery in Congress—"the denunciation heaped upon us by the press of the North, and the attempts to degrade us in the eyes of Christendom—to arraign the character of our people and the character of our fathers from whom our institutions are derived"—did much to make this proud, high-spirited man a sectionalist, though he wished to live in a spirit of fraternity with the North.[41]

The Power behind the Throne

Although Jefferson Davis felt bitter about his narrow defeat as a candidate for governor in 1851, he did not show it publicly. He had trained himself to be stoical in the face of adversity. Nevertheless, his pride was so wounded by this defeat that in a letter to a close friend nearly two years later he revealed his resolve never to return to public life until called by the people of Mississippi.[1] After his resignation from the Senate on September 23, except for a brief period of campaigning, he and Varina lived in retirement at Brierfield. He enjoyed the life of a planter and his wife was an enthusiastic gardener. She wrote to her mother that she was not depressed over the defeat for her heart was never in politics or soldiering.[2] During the period that her husband was out of politics, she became pregnant for the first time, with a baby expected in July, 1852. In the summer and fall her husband made some speeches advocating the election of the Democratic candidate for president, Franklin Pierce of New Hampshire, a "doughface," who was very favorable to the South.

After his election Pierce wrote to Davis from Concord, New Hampshire, on December 7, 1852, urging him to come to Washington to confer with him about Southern affairs and the formation of his cabinet. He hinted that he would like Davis to join the cabinet. Davis at first refused, but his sympathy for the president-elect grew after he received a letter from Pierce telling of the tragedy of a railroad accident that took the life of his only child, a boy eleven years old, and again suggesting that if his health were restored he wished to consult him.³ When Pierce asked him to attend the inauguration Davis felt that he could not refuse, and on this occasion he accepted the position of secretary of war. The other members of the cabinet were William L. Marcy of New York, secretary of state; James Guthrie of Kentucky, secretary of the treasury; James C. Dobbin of North Carolina, secretary of the navy; Robert McClelland of Michigan, secretary of the interior; James Campbell of Pennsylvania, postmaster general; and Caleb Cushing of Massachusetts, attorney general. Of these men, Davis felt closest to Caleb Cushing, a graduate of Harvard, a scholar, a polished orator, and a person of great versatility, a doughface favorable to the South.

Shortly after Pierce was inaugurated he and his cabinet made a tour of the large Northern cities. During this trip Davis spoke in favor of government aid in building a transcontinental railroad. Despite his opposition to the general principle that it was unconstitutional for the federal government to engage in internal improvements within the states, he justified his proposal as a military necessity to protect the Pacific Coast. He had made the proposal while still a senator. He also used the occasion of the speaking tour to promulgate his views on a strict construction of the Constitution: the preservation of state rights and free trade with the world, which were standard Southern doctrines.

Although Pierce was not a strong president, he was a delightful man to work with: sincere, considerate, handsome. He was a graduate of Bowdoin College and a friend of Nathaniel Hawthorne, a college mate who published an admiring campaign biography of him.⁴ Pierce's harmonious relations with his cabinet were indicated by the fact that he was the only president who had no changes in its personnel. The salaries of the cabinet officers, Varina wrote, were utterly inadequate for living expenses in Washington, and as a consequence the Davises grew poorer every day from neglecting the plantation. The members of the family in Washington included, besides the baby, Samuel Emory, and Varina's younger brother and sister, whom Davis was supporting while paying for their education. They lived in a twenty-three-room mansion rented from Edward Everett, the Massachusetts orator and statesman. Davis worked very hard at his job, sometimes returning home as late as two o'clock in the morning, and often forgetting to eat.

Nevertheless, the Davises enjoyed a very pleasant social life, especially since talent rather than money determined aristocracy in the nation's capital—so wrote Varina's mother after a visit.⁵ They were on intimate terms with President Pierce and his desolate wife. Varina's letters to her mother in Natchez described in detail the social occasions in which she shone, the dresses the ladies wore, the new dances. She and her husband played backgammon on occasional evenings "late and sometimes too late." Davis enjoyed being a trustee of the Smithsonian Institution, where he talked with learned scientists. When the first American expedition to Japan returned it brought back some exquisite presents, but Davis refused to let his wife accept any of those that Pierce offered her. Their happiness was broken when their twenty-three-month-old son died, and so grieved was the father that Varina wrote for many months afterward that he walked the floor half the night and "worked fiercely all day."[6]

Davis was an extremely efficient secretary of war, who maintained such high standards of public conduct that he would not allow his wife to employ any of his personnel to do errands for her or even to use the department's stationery. He had seven clerks under him, and one of them, William B. Lee, recalled: "He was one of the best Secretaries of War that ever served. He was a kind, social man, very considerate, and pleasant to serve under. I never heard a complaint from one of his clerks. Socially, he was a most charming man, officially, very pleasant. He was a warm friend and a bitter enemy. . . . He was a regular bull-dog when he formed an opinion, for he would never let go."[7] In her memoir Varina tells how he dispensed charity to numerous poor, weak, and friendless people.

Davis left office with unstained hands, so honest and faithful to duty that he repelled special interests trying to influence his decisions. Mrs. Clement C. Clay, Jr., wife of an Alabama senator, wrote that his reputation for honesty and vigilance was such that it would be impossible to cheat the government out of the value of a brass button.[8] It has always been a temptation to politicians in office to appoint political adherents to jobs under them. The only time, Davis wrote, when he violated his rule of not allowing sectional or party interest to control his appointments in the army, or in the department, even of clerkships, occurred when four new regiments were formed. In the appointments he followed the advice of the adjutant general, Samuel Cooper, a Northern man, but when the list of appointments was submitted to the president, it was found that in a purely military selection there was a preponderance of Southern men, for Southerners went into the army in greater proportion to population than did Northern men. For political considerations, the president counseled that the list should be revised in terms of geographical considerations. But Davis resisted attempts to collect political assessments from the clerks in his department.

When he became secretary of war the army numbered 10,745, but by December 3, 1855, when he made his third report to the president, it had been raised to 15,752 men. The main duty of the army was to defend the frontier against hostile Indians. In his report of December 4, 1856, Davis estimated that there were 400,000 Indians in the United States, of whom 40,000 were hostile warriors.[9] The discovery of gold in California and the advance of settlement in that region imposed new duties on the army of protecting settlers as they traveled across the plains. Davis proposed a new military organization on the frontier: namely, to abandon a number of small forts and concentrate the army into fewer forts and stronger detachments, especially of cavalry. Accordingly, when the grass grew in the spring sufficiently to support the horses, the cavalry could pursue, punish, and overawe marauding Indians. He sought to adopt the practice of the French army in Algeria where arid plains necessitated a new type of warfare. To encourage the enlistment of a good type of soldier, he constantly urged Congress to increase the salary, provide an attractive system of promotions, and pay pensions to widows and children of veterans.

One of his most troublesome problems was to try to remove the remnant of Seminole Indians remaining in Florida to reservations. Because of the difficulty posed by their escape to the Everglades, the army had been unsuccessful, despite a long and costly war in the 1830s, in removing all of them. On April 14 and 15, 1856, he wrote to Governor James S. Broome of Florida outlining the War Department's policy of dealing with the Indians still remaining in the state. It included: (1) efforts by agents of emigration to persuade them to leave voluntarily, which so far had proved unsuccessful; (2) prohibiting all trade with the Indians; (3) building military roads into the Indian country and exploring the Everglades, even though exploring parties had been attacked; (4) increasing the troops in Florida to 780 enlisted men and officers, as well as recruiting five companies of volunteers into the United States service; (5) paying rewards for the capture of living Seminole Indians.[10] But Davis left office with the problem still unsolved.

He was an innovative secretary of war. In 1855 he sent a commission of officers, including a future general, George B. McClellan, then a lieutenant, to study military developments in the Crimean War. He also dispatched the future Confederate general, William J. Hardee, to France to study tactics, a mission which aided him in writing a standard textbook on infantry tactics. In his autobiography Davis mentioned some improvements he had introduced, such as improved rifle muskets and rifles, the use of Minié balls, that became famed in the Civil War, the substitution of iron for wood in gun carriages, an advanced system of infantry tactics, and the use of heavy guns and large grain powder in the coastal defenses. He promoted experiments in breech-loading rifles; nevertheless, in the Civil War they were not adopted by the Confederate army, and only to a very limited extent by the Union army near the end of the war. He strongly recommended the manufacturing of arms for the army by the government, instead of awarding private contracts, as well as the establishment of a national armory in the West.[11]

Especially innovative was his introduction of a camel service for the army on the western plains. In response to his request, Congress on March 3, 1855, appropriated $30,000 for initiating this novel experiment. During the next year the officer whom he had selected to go to the Levant and Egypt to purchase camels, Major Henry C. Wayne, purchased thirty-three camels, and in the following year thirty-two additional ones. These exotic animals were landed at Indianola, Texas, and taken inland to Camp Verde. Davis was so intensely interested in this experiment that Varina wrote, he stayed up at night to translate a French work on the military use of camels. The camels traveled twice as fast as horses, ate smaller amounts of food, could go three days without water, and carried heavier loads, as much as 1,200 pounds.[12] But after Davis left office they were little used by the army, and the building of railroads superseded them.

In addition to supervising the army, the secretary of war was given other functions. He was placed in charge of building assembly halls in the wings of the Capitol for the Senate and House of Representatives, and was also entrusted with the completion of the dome. He had the able assistance of the chief of army engineers, Montgomery Meigs, but the dome was not completed until after the inauguration of Lincoln. He also had charge of building a conduit nine feet in diameter from the Potomac Falls to bring fresh water to Washington. He had charge of improving coastal harbors and of building military roads. His political philosophy, mentioned earlier, was opposed to the principle of appropriating money for internal improvements at government expense, and in such projects as well as in the operation of his department he sought to observe the strictest economy.

In 1853 Congress appropriated $150,000 for a series of surveys of the most practical route for a transcontinental railroad. As secretary of war, commanding a corps of able engineers, Davis was given the responsibility of directing these surveys. He sent out four exploring parties and in his instructions of July 25, 1854, directed them to make maps and topographical studies, as well as to report on depths of snow, supply of water and timber, and character of the soil. He also requested them to study the language and habits of the Indians and to make observations on the fauna and flora.[13] In his report he recommended the southern route (approximately along the 32nd parallel of north latitude) because it would encounter less formidable obstacles and be free of deep snow, but undoubtedly he was also influenced by sectional prejudices, believing that a railroad along this route would not only benefit the South economically, but hopefully would contribute to a political alliance between the South and the West.[14] He realized the dearth of water on this route but sought to obviate it by experiments in boring artesian wells along the route, and hoped that the experiments would indicate that on the western plains grass, timber, and agricultural products might be produced by irrigation.

Since he was a West Point graduate and had been a chairman of the Military Affairs Committee in the Senate, Davis took a special interest in the Military Academy at West Point. He strongly advocated higher standards of admission and increasing the time that a cadet spent at the institution from four to five years. He also proposed to establish a new professorship of "Ethics and English Studies."[15] His concern over the proper instruction of the cadets was further shown in a letter to the incoming president, James Buchanan, criticizing the instruction in English and protesting against the use of Wayland's text in moral philosophy, which condemned slavery. "To train the men who are at the head of the armies," Davis wrote, "to maintain the honor of the flag and in all circumstances to uphold the Constitution requires a man above sectional prejudices and intellectually superior to fanaticism."[16] Robert E. Lee was commandant of the academy while Davis was secretary of war, but his tenure was very unhappy, for he was too kindhearted and hated to discipline the boys. When some Southerners tried to get Davis to support a movement for establishing a military academy in the South, he refused on the ground that it would increase sectional jealousy. The advantage of West Point, he said, was that it developed "a national point of view in the young men from different states that attended it."[17]

The most distressing event during his tenure of office as secretary of war was a bitter quarrel with the general-in-chief of the army, Winfield Scott. It began in 1855 when Davis opposed promoting Scott to the rank of lieutenant general, as well as his claim for brevet pay in this rank. The quarrel was mightily increased by a petty incident: Davis overruled Scott's order granting a four-month leave of absence to Brigadier General Hitchcock, a lengthy leave that was not strictly in accordance with army regulations. Scott reacted in what Davis termed an "exhibition of peevish temper," and thereupon the proud, sensitive secretary of war and the vain, egotistical, quarrelsome old general began a combat in letters of Homeric proportions. Scott was a huge man physically, fond of impressive uniforms and pomp and ceremony, who proved to be a formidable warrior on paper as well as with his sword. Davis accused him of taking for himself a large share of indemnity extracted from the Mexicans while commanding in Mexico City. Scott's haughty reply to the secretary of war, in which he accused the latter of obstinacy and captious criticism, was only the beginning of a disgraceful correspondence between the two men. Scott wrote that Davis had "capped the climax of usurpation and absurdity." Davis replied in controlled anger: "Your petulance, characteristic egotism, and recklessness of accusation have imposed on me the task of unveiling some of your deformities." Sarcastically, the embattled general replied that the secretary of war had in "twenty-seven compacted pages of foolscap" poured out the full measure of his spleen and vengeance, whose slowly concocted venom was designed to kill him at once. He taunted Davis with being "the favorite" of the president and accused him of thrusting daggers into him, and of chicanery, arrogance, and scurrility. Davis in turn accused Scott of "grasping avarice" and of being a liar.[18] It is amazing that such accusations did not lead to a duel, although Scott was nearly seventy years old and Davis was only forty-seven. The incident is unimportant in itself, but it revealed the quick reaction of Davis to criticism, his personal pride, and his firmness in upholding army regulations, foretelling some of the difficulties he would encounter as Confederate president in dealing with egotistical, vain generals.

He did not confine his activities to the War Department, but he had so much influence in federal appointments and in foreign as well as domestic affairs that a Mississippi newspaper called him "the de facto president" and "the great Mogul."[19] In respect to patronage, he used his influence with the administration to aid the cause of the Columbus (Miss.) *Southern Standard,* which had supported him in the gubernatorial campaign of 1851, and was applying for the patronage to print the federal laws.[20] His great influence over the president was shown when he persuaded him to support the highly controversial Kansas-Nebraska Bill, ardently desired by Southern congressmen. This bill started innocently enough late in 1853 with the introduction in the Senate of a bill to organize a huge territory of Nebraska with no reference to slavery. The motives of Stephen Douglas, chairman of the Senate Committee on Territories, according to his own account, were to carry out the wishes of the people of the territory and to organize the territory so that a transcontinental railroad could be built with federal grants of land.

But a complex series of maneuvers took place that resulted in the originally huge territory being divided into two territories, Kansas and Nebraska. Moreover, a Whig senator, Archibald Dixon, successor to the seat of Henry Clay, caused consternation among the senators by attaching an amendment that canceled the Missouri Compromise line of limitation on the advance of slavery, an amendment to which Douglas reluctantly consented. In supporting this amendment, Davis explained later that it did not repeal the long-established line of 36 degrees, 30 minutes in the territories, for that line had been virtually repealed by the Compromise of 1850; the Kansas-Nebraska Bill merely recognized an existing fact, he claimed, in declaring that the prohibition of slavery north of 36 degrees, 30 minutes by the Missouri Compromise Act was "inoperative and void."[21] Such a semantic distinction was not understood by the mass of the Northern people, for they recognized that the practical effect of the Kansas-Nebraska Bill would be to open up the remaining western territory to the advance of slavery.

In order to secure the bill's passage through Congress it was necessary to get the support of President Pierce. The bill was scheduled to come up for a vote on Monday, January 23, 1854, and there was imperative need for haste in securing the president's support. Douglas appealed to Davis to secure an interview with the president for him and several accompanying senators. It was Sunday, and Pierce's scruples militated against doing any political business on that holy day. Nevertheless, Davis agreed to the request and led them into the executive mansion. While he left them waiting in the reception room, he went into the private compartment of the president and almost certainly persuaded him to support the bill. Then he introduced the senators to Pierce, who listened to their arguments and gave his assent to supporting the bill.

The three main actors in this drama had no idea of the tragic consequence of their act and of the tremendous uproar of opposition that it would provoke. It led directly to the formation of the Republican party, the destruction of the

Whig party, the civil war in Kansas, the rise of the American party, and the recalling of Lincoln to political life. The able Northern historian, James Ford Rhodes, pronounced the Kansas-Nebraska Bill "the most momentous measure that passed Congress from the day that the senators and representatives first met to the outbreak of the civil war."[22] The Compromise of 1850 had been hailed as a *final* settlement of the slavery question, but the enactment of the Kansas-Nebraska Bill reopened it with violence, beginning a bitter conflict between the North and the South in which Davis was to play a leading part.

The Aristocratic Type of Southern Politician

*S*hortly before his term as secretary of war ended in 1857, Davis became an unannounced candidate for reelection to the Senate. Some friends in Mississippi warned him that he would be defeated unless he came to Jackson to electioneer when the legislature met. To his friend Stephen Cocke of Aberdeen, he wrote a letter that reveals the mind of an aristocratic type of politician in the Old South, who would be a unique species today. He wrote that he was aware that he had no capacity, even if he wished, to engage in political intrigue and electioneering. His personal pride forbade it, and leaving his duties in Washington to solicit for his personal advantage would be violating the trust of his constituents. "This I know," he wrote, "is sometimes called impracticable theory, and sometimes attributed to a vain assumption of superiority, but in my own case at least cannot be properly assigned to the latter cause."[1] Also, in a letter to Franklin Pierce on September 3, 1859, he stated this high-minded view of seeking public office that has disappeared, namely, that "the presidency is an office that can never be properly filled by one who has sought it in the mode and by the means known as electioneering."[2] It was an old-fashioned concept of politics that the Jacksonian revolution overturned, although the practice was well established in elections to the Virginia colonial legislature of treating the voters to rum punch and liquor or, as it was called, "swilling the planters with Bumbo." Even George Washington found it necessary to do so; his agents in 1758 supplied 160 gallons to 391 voters, or more than a quart and a half to a voter.[3]

There were two types of successful politicians in the South during the period of Davis's participation in politics: the aristocratic type such as Davis himself, and the folksy, demagogic type who gulled unsophisticated rural audiences by affecting the language and manners of the common man and by telling jokes. Franklin E. Plummer, a Yankee who had emigrated to Mississippi, set a pattern for this type of demagogic political campaigner in his 1829 bid for election to Congress. This clever Yankee won the favor of rural voters by playing practical jokes on opponents; he curried favor with voters in the piney woods by kissing babies, by searching for red bugs that infested their clothing and crushing them, and by holding a calf by the tail while a voter's wife milked the cow, as well as by his plausible speeches. On one occasion he defeated an aristocratic opponent for office, Honorable Powhatan Ellis, by publishing an advertisement which he attributed to Ellis who was reputedly seeking to recover a portmanteau lost in crossing a swollen stream. The unscrupulous demagogue listed the following articles: 6 lawn handkerchiefs; 4 prs. silk stockings; 6 cambric shirts; 2 night do.; 1 nightcap; 1 pr. stays; hair brush; flesh-brush; razors and dressing glass; nailbrush; clothes brush; pomatum; perfume, etc. etc.[4]

Even some aristocratic candidates, men of culture, descended to demagogic tricks in order to win election. Virginia Clay, wife of Clement C. Clay, Jr., tells of a trick she used while her husband was trying to unseat Congressman W. R. W. Cobb who represented the Huntsville district of Alabama. Cobb, a man of little education and unpolished manners, won the votes of the common people by appealing to their affinity for a "rough diamond." Virginia borrowed from her landlady a very "tacky" sunbonnet, "a pea-green cambric bonnet, lined with pink, and stiffened with pasteboard slats," which she wore at political meetings, thus identifying her with the common people, winning votes for her husband in the rural counties.[5] But Davis and his wife scorned resorting to such tactics.

Davis stands out in marked contrast to the average Mississippi politician as a man of culture, of refined manners, and of stoical self-restraint. A number of the other Mississippi politicians were violent, often crude men. The governor of the state in 1848–50 was Joseph W. Matthews, who had supported himself in early life by digging wells, hence his nicknames "Joe the Well-Digger" and "Old Copperas Breeches." Henry S. Foote, who defeated Davis for governor in 1851, was a bald-headed little man, like a tiny, pugnacious "fice" dog, always barking and snapping, but a consummate demagogue. He issued challenges to duels, and once had a fistfight with John A. Quitman. The governor at the time of secession, John J. Pettus, was described by a British war correspondent as "a grim, blunt man who had for years hunted and trapped in the forest. The sovereign citizens walked freely through his office, with mildewed walls and broken panes, and acted," the correspondent reported, "in every respect as if they were in a public house save in ordering drinks." While the British visitor was talking to this extremely provincial-minded governor, the latter dropped "a portentous plug of tobacco just outside of a spittoon with the air of a man who wished to show he could hit the centre if he liked."[6] He must have truly represented the people of his state, for when he ran for reelection in 1861, he received 90 percent of the vote.[7]

The Southern institution of the political barbecue gave the demagogue (as well as a dignified speaker such as Davis) an opportunity to have a field day in applying his arts. Countrymen from miles away rode in with their families, and even the slaves joined in the fun. Tables were loaded with roast lamb, beef, ham, fried chicken, corn bread, and turnip greens. The audience roared approval when a speaker gave his opponent "hell" in a tongue-lashing, and laughed uproariously at jokes satirizing individual politicians or the opposite political party. It was an important occasion for politicians, and they circulated among the crowd, shaking the toil-hardened hands of their constituents.

A successful politician had to pay close attention to local and state politics. It was the base of his power, indispensable to his reelection. Davis, even in retirement and during the first few months in the cabinet, was actively engaged in seeking to preserve the unity of the State Rights party in Mississippi, which he led and which was threatened by "fermenting factions."[8] The intrastate selectionalism between the northern part of the state, the stronghold of the yeoman, and the delta region and south Mississippi, dominated by the slave-holding aristocracy, was intense. Davis's archenemy, Foote, was very strong among the voters in the North and, though recently victorious as governor, desired to return to the United States Senate, which led him to internal politics, for not only Foote, but Albert Gallatin Brown, the spokesman of the common man, coveted the election to the Senate. Various local politicians, particularly James Phelan of Aberdeen in the North, wrote to Davis in the summer of 1853 to learn whether he preferred to remain in the cabinet or be reelected to the Senate. Davis replied that he would like to resume his old seat in the Senate, but that he would not electioneer for it.[9]

Rumors had circulated that he would not accept an election to this post, and R. S. Tarpley, a Jackson lawyer and close friend, was so alarmed that he urged him to deny such rumors. Tarpley hoped to persuade him to run for president in 1856, but he believed that to attain this object Davis should first be reelected senator. Davis was willing to resign his position in Pierce's cabinet to return to the Senate, stating his belief that he could probably be as useful to the president in the Senate as in the cabinet. He revealed his bitterness over being repudiated by the voters in 1851 in a contest with Foote for governor: "It is the mortification of being beaten by such a man as Foote and by such shallovꞏ artifices as were used which have made the result of 1851 galling;

anything which would remove the barb would answer all the end I ever sought."[10]

Politics in Mississippi at this time was ruled by ambitious and opportunistic men. By 1852 the two wings of the Democratic party that had split during the controversy over the Compromise of 1850, the Unionist and State Rights factions, had reunited, and the Whigs were no longer a threat. The Democratic papers of the state urged the legislature to elect Davis as senator. But John A. Quitman also aspired to the position, as well as ex-Govenor Albert Gallatin Brown, Henry S. Foote, and John J. McRae, a fire-eater who was elected governor of Mississippi in 1853. The Natchez *Courier* described the differences between the three leading contenders as follows: "Others (than Quitman) may be better party men. Davis is a greater Machiavellian and Brown a greater demagogue, but Quitman is their superior in manliness, honor and candor."[11] But Davis was too proud to come to Mississippi to canvass or solicit votes.

His opponents, however, had no such scruples and were busy forming combinations and trading support. The master intriguer and demagogue on this occasion proved to be Brown. Although he had cooperated with Davis in 1851 in the contest over the governor's office and in opposing the Compromise of 1850, he developed a jealousy of his superior rival, partly because of Davis's aristocratic aloofness and dignity. In contrast with Davis's upbringing, Brown had risen from a poor-white pineland district of southern Mississippi. Unlike Davis, too, he worked hard in 1853 to win the coveted seat in the Senate. He made 115 speeches, traveled 3,200 miles, and spent $1,200, while Davis scorned such tactics. Brown compared himself, the advocate of the poor man, with the aristocratic Davis "sitting on an easy chair at Washington getting his $8,000 a year, and drinking champagne," while he was exposed to malarial fever, and drinking rotgut liquor.[12] Davis had great pride, while Brown was shameless in plying the arts of the demagogue.

The political situation in Mississippi in 1853 was vividly described later by J. J. Pettus in a letter to Davis in June, 1857. He observed that after Davis was defeated in 1851 "many State Rights men believed that all was lost," and that the legislature would submit to the large majority of the Union vote and send Foote in triumph back to the Senate. Nevertheless, Pettus wrote, he had secured enough members of the legislature pledged to you to give you the nomination, but Brown and his friends electioneered in the streets of Jackson, promising their support for Davis in 1856, and after many caucuses the majority of the State Rights senators agreed to postpone the senatorial election for a year, with the result that Mississippi was represented by only one senator.[13] The next year Brown was elected. Davis had to wait until 1857 for reelection to the Senate.

While a civil war was raging in Kansas over the application of Douglas's popular sovereignty doctrine to the unhappy territory, Davis remained aloof from the controversy, attending to his duties as secretary of war. He was deeply concerned over making plans to be elected senator after the expiration of his term as secretary. Accordingly, he wrote to one of his strong supporters in Mississippi that he feared that a proposal to run him for vice president in 1856 was actually a movement to defeat him for election to the Senate. He outlined the position that he wished for his friends to take in presenting his candidacy, namely, that he desired his position in the crisis of 1850–51 to be reaffirmed and his position as "a Southern rights" man endorsed.[14]

His principal rival for election to the Senate in 1857 was Jacob Thompson of northern Mississippi, an aristocratic type of politician, a graduate of the University of North Carolina, who held nearly the same position on political issues as did Davis, but was regarded as less of an "ultra." Sentiment in the state appeared to be evenly divided between the two men. Nevertheless, Davis did not cultivate the voters by appearing among them frequently, shaking hands, making speeches, or attending barbecues. One newspaper, the Port Gibson *Herald,* had earlier criticized this cavalier attitude by observing that a speaker should not assume "that he is a *great Jupiter* and his audiences pigmies."[15] In an indirect way, nevertheless, the Davises courted the voters. Varina franked hundreds of letters as well as printed congressional speeches, and her husband sent garden seed to his constituents.

The senatorial election was decided not by the people but in the caucus of the Democratic party, which by this time was overwhelmingly dominant, for the legislature would ratify its decision. The first ballot resulted in a tie vote, which was then resolved by the presiding officer, Davis's political friend R. S. Tarpley, voting for him.[16] Accordingly, on the day following the end of his tenure as secretary of war, Davis took his seat in the United States Senate.

A profile of the Mississippi Senate in 1850 and 1860 that elected Davis would reveal that it was composed largely of middle-aged farmers, planters, and lawyers. The Senate was a small body of 20 members, who were democratically elected by the people and apportioned on the white bases. In 1850 it was composed of 10 farmers or planters, 6 lawyers, and several merchants and physicians; in 1860, of 12 farmers or planters, 3 lawyers, and a sprinkling of the professions.[17] As a whole the members were not rich men, but well-to-do. In 1860 only three had real property or personal property (slaves) worth $100,000 or more. Davis, as we have seen, belonged to the middle class of planters. Only once in his political life did he solicit the votes of the people, when he ran unsuccessfully for the legislature. Therefore, he did not have to appeal to the people for votes, or struggle upward through the political process, as did Lincoln, who was several times defeated in his bid for political office. Thus, Davis lacked the invaluable experience of exercising the art of compromise and of dealing with all kinds of politicians and voters.

Whether being well educated, as was Davis, was at this time an advantage or a disadvantage in politics in the lower South is difficult to determine. College education was so heavily weighted with learning Greek and Latin that it hardly fitted a political aspirant with the ability to communicate with the common people in their language. Thomas Hamilton, a supercilious British traveler, observed in *Men and Manners in America* (1833) that one heard more Latin quoted in Congress than in the British Parliament, but that it consisted of hackneyed phrases and revealed no deep acquaintance with classical literature.[18] On the other hand, universities and colleges, with their debating and literary societies, gave training to graduates in public speaking.

Rural audiences were often suspicious of educated men, regarding them as inclined to skepticism and as being impractical. Andrew Johnson, the authentic representative of the way common people in the South thought, opposed a bill in Congress in 1846 to use the Smithsonian bequest to educate teachers, for he said that young men educated in such an institution would be rendered unfit for being teachers by "the extravagance, folly, aristocracy, and corruption of Washington" and would abandon the teaching profession to hang about a lawyer's office and become "a pack of drones instead of schoolmasters."[19]

Sam Houston also expressed a distrust for highly educated men. This Texas hero would sit in his seat in the Senate, clad in a spectacular red vest, whittling sticks and carving little wooden hearts, one of which he presented to Varina. He declared that scientific scholars were interested only in catching a bug of rare quality to immortalize their names and in writing books. "Who can read these books?" he asked. "A man who is industrious, or intends to make an honest living," he said, "has no chance to do it. You are throwing impediments in the way of industry when you are creating these books. You create a morbid appetite in children for pretty pictures. They will not learn their alphabets." The British officer, Arthur Fremantle, saw Houston in Texas after he had been deposed as governor for being opposed to secession, and was disgusted with his coarse manners, particularly his chewing and profusely spitting tobacco juice and blowing his nose with his fingers.[20] His remarks, although they seem absurd, and his coarse manners reflected the anti-intellectual attitude of thousands of poor Southern farmers—people to whom Davis had to appeal for votes.

The upper South, to a greater degree than the lower South, chose aristocratic representatives in Congress. John C. Breckinridge and J. J. Crittenden in Kentucky, for example, represented the aristocratic tradition. Patricians, also, were the Virginia senators in 1860, the sleepy-eyed, somewhat corpulent R. M. T. Hunter, proud of the Pocahontas blood flowing through his veins, and James M. Mason, of whom Mrs. Chesnut gave a colorful description in her diary, quoted later. Representing North Carolina in the Senate was the moderate gentleman, Thomas Bragg, whom Davis appointed attorney general, and South Carolina after the death of Calhoun was represented by the aristocratic Robert W. Barnwell, a Harvard graduate, and James H. Hammond.

The combined effects of slavery on the whites, illiteracy, and the rural isolation of the plantation society contributed to personal leadership in politics. John William DeForest, a Freedman's Bureau agent in South Carolina, observed: "Every community [of the state] had its great man, or its little great men, around whom his fellow citizens gather when they want information, and to whose monologues they listen with a respect akin to humility."[21] Although party ties were emphasized, these "great men" such as Davis, with some plebeians among them, who gathered in Washington answered the roll calls on questions relating to slavery, as Thomas B. Alexander has shown in his quantitative analysis, as sectionalists rather than as party men.[22]

The touchstone test that the Southern politician, whether plebeian or aristocrat, had to pass to hold office was whether he was sound on slavery. The test was applied to the Mississippi senator in the summer of 1859 when the burning issue of the revival of the African slave trade came up in Mississippi. At the Southern Commercial Convention at Vicksburg in 1859 a resolution for the reopening of the African slave trade was adopted by a large majority, but a minority led by Henry S. Foote, Davis's enemy, opposed it.[23] Among the latter were the representatives of the upper South, which had surplus slaves to sell, as well as many of the large planters of the lower South, the value of whose slaveholdings would be reduced by the success of this proposal. Davis, although not a very large slaveholder, also took a stand against the movement, as did Mississippi's other senator, Albert Gallatin Brown.

This position may seem inconsistent with Davis's proslavery philosophy, but he had valid, pragmatic objections to reopening the African slave trade as far as his state was concerned. He thought that Mississippi had a sufficient slave supply for its present needs. In a speech before the Democratic State Convention at Jackson, on July 6, 1859, he proposed that laws regulating the African slave trade be left to the states. He also declared that the act of 1820 making the participation in the foreign slave trade piracy, carrying the death penalty, should be repealed as unconstitutional. Likewise, he proposed that the treaty with Great Britain providing that the United States should keep a naval squadron on the coast of Africa to suppress the trade, as well as the right of the British navy to search American ships suspected of carrying on the illegal traffic, should be abrogated. Nevertheless, he argued that even if the federal laws prohibiting the African slave trade should be repealed, Mississippi should not repeal its state laws against the trade, solely because of the economic consequences of throwing open the market for wild African slaves. He was not against it for humanitarian or moral reasons, for he thought that it transferred slaves from a savage to a Christian master. Nor did his objections apply to Texas and New Mexico, or to any future acquisitions of territory south of the Rio Grande.[24]

On this explosive issue Jefferson Davis proved himself a conservative in opposition to the fire-eaters. He realized, however, that as a Mississippi political leader he must tread warily in regard to his position on the revival of the African slave trade, for a supporter from Vicksburg wrote him on June 7, 1859, that "the democratic party would be destroyed by the agitation of the question at this time."[25] It is likely that he hoped he would be the Democratic candidate for president in 1860. His conciliatory speeches in New England may have been inspired by this hope. Also, though some historians have regarded Davis's advocacy of a transcontinental railroad as designed to form an alliance between the South and the West, a more probable interpretation is that he thought it would form a basis for his bid to become a national statesman and a candidate for the presidency.

The political careers of Davis as well as other Southern politicians of this period were necessarily based on the preservation of the slave system and of state rights. Although Davis advocated state rights as a constitutional principle in which he sincerely believed, actually the main motivation for its support in the South was as a mechanism for the protection of slavery. Davis ranked with Calhoun and Senator James H. Hammond of South Carolina as an outstanding political protagonist of the slave interests in Congress. Why did these political leaders spend so much of their energy before this body in an elaborate and emotional defense of Southern slavery as a humane and righteous institution? There have been various explanations for the rise of the Southern proslavery propaganda, which had begun before the challenge of the abolitionist movement in the North. One explanation, popular among liberals today, was that Southerners recognized slavery as a sin and an evil, and tried to salve their consciences by an argument in its defense. Another view is that the proslavery propaganda was directed at securing the allegiance of the nonslaveholders of whom, incidentally, a large proportion could not or did not read. Still another ingenious explanation was offered by David Donald in his presidential address before the Southern Historical Association in 1970: namely, that some of the most prominent Southern defenders of slavery were motivated by a desire to attain distinction in a cause that would bring them honor in their region to compensate for earlier insignificance and failure.[26] None of these explanations applies to Davis. His reaction to Northern attacks on Southern institutions was a perfectly human one: to resist denunciations of his section that he thought unfair and to repel regional insults, just as he would defend his own honor, if necessary, by a duel.

Nowhere in his available correspondence and public speeches did he admit that the overriding concern of the slaveholders and their propagandists was to preserve a property investment estimated at between $3 billion and $4 billion in 1860. But many other slaveholders openly admitted that this was their principal motive. John Berkeley Grimball, a wealthy rice planter of South Carolina, wrote in his diary after the election of Lincoln: "The prospect before us in regard to our Slave Property, if we continue to remain in the Union is nothing less than utter ruin."[27]

Davis and his wife, as noted, had no feelings of guilt over holding slaves. By the 1840s he and most of his fellow slaveholders did not have to struggle with their consciences over the sin of slavery, as had a previous generation, and as had even a few of his contemporaries, notably Reverend Charles Colcock Jones of Georgia. In his young manhood Davis had not been exposed to Northern antislavery men as had Jones, who for three years had studied theology at Cambridge and Princeton. In letters to his fiancée in 1828–30 the Georgian revealed his strong antislavery feelings and his criticism of the South, especially for suppressing free discussion.[28] But as the minister grew older and became the paternal master of three plantations, he succumbed to the great change of public opinion that Davis described in a speech on July 6, 1859, before the Democratic State Convention at Jackson. The Mississippi senator observed that as a result of recent discussions by the press and on the platform the illusions of a previous generation in regard to slavery had been dispelled. Now, he asserted, the legal and moral right of slavery was not doubted by intelligent citizens. Nevertheless, he felt the need of strengthening the doubters and faint-of-heart who may have been disturbed by the propaganda of the abolitionists and the apparent incongruity of slavery with the Declaration of Independence. He frankly admitted: "We need to be assured of the rightfulness of Slavery."[29]

In his votes in Congress, to protect Southern interests, he adhered to a pattern of doctrinaire state rights and the strictest construction of the Constitution. A notable example of his increasing sectionalism was his opposition in 1860 to a homestead bill. Earlier in his political career he had pursued a liberal policy in regard to the public lands. In 1846 he had presented memorials of his state to Congress, favoring the graduation of the price of public lands and advocating a generous policy toward preemption. But in 1860 he joined other Southern senators, who in general, with the notable exception of Andrew Johnson, opposed the enactment of the homestead bill, offering a free farm to homesteaders. The Southerners feared that, by encouraging immigration, it would increase the Northern preponderance of votes in Congress. Davis shared this fear and spoke against the enactment of the bill, especially opposing the provision that placed European immigrants on the same footing with native Americans in obtaining a free farm in the public domain. He applauded President Buchanan for vetoing it in 1860. It was a courageous act on the part of the beleaguered president, although unwise politically, for it probably contributed powerfully to the election of Lincoln.[30]

Another striking example of Davis's conservatism was his opposition to the Morrill Land Grant Act, first introduced in Congress in 1857, but on account of Southern opposition not passed until 1862. This bill would have made grants of public land to the states in proportion to their representation in Congress for the purpose of establishing agricultural colleges. Of all the sections of the country the South would have profited most from this liberal, farsighted bill. Yet, on February 1, and 7, 1859, Davis spoke against its enactment, and he was joined in his opposition, surprisingly, by Andrew Johnson of Tennessee, the outstanding advocate in the Senate of the common man's interests, although Foote, and senators John Bell of Tennessee and John J. Crittenden of Kentucky, also conservatives, supported it. Davis, always the man of Southern pride, argued that the agricultural interests needed no federal aid and, neglecting to take account of the far greater educational importance of the bill, he stated his main objection to be the unconstitutionality of the measure that would invade the state's prerogative.[31]

His extreme conservatism on constitutional and racial matters was illustrated in his opposition to two bills that came before Congress in the spring of 1860. One bill provided for the enlargement of the Louisville and Portland canal around the falls at Louisville, Kentucky. Davis opposed it on grounds of a strict construction of the Constitution, although he admitted the need of the enlargement for a free flow of interstate commerce.[32] The other bill was for the establishment of free schools for both white and Negro children in the District of Columbia. The Mississippi senator opposed it because it would put white children and Negro children on terms of equality, and he maintained that the inferiority of Negroes was fixed by nature and by the law of God. He opposed using the money of taxpayers for this purpose or for eleemosynary purposes.[33] Yet, as a young congressman in 1846, he had supported a bill to use the Smithsonian bequest to educate teachers in the District of Columbia for teaching white children.

Except for his consistent support of a transcontinental railroad and of establishing in 1846 the Smithsonian Institution in Washington, Davis's votes in Congress rarely departed from the conservative and economical policies of his Southern colleagues. In 1850 he opposed Congress appropriating money for the navy to engage in the search for the lost British explorer, Sir John Franklin, in the Arctic Ocean, as not warranted by the Constitution. Also he resisted the abolition of flogging in the navy.[34] He opposed efforts of Northern congressmen and of Henry Clay to secure an appropriation to purchase the manuscript of Washington's Farewell Address, observing that it would be a precedent for buying his walking sticks, medals, Mount Vernon, and the battlefields on which he had fought. Congress should not surrender to sentiment, he declared, in using the people's money.[35] In the interest of economy he advocated making the Post Office self-sustaining and abolishing the franking privilege of congressmen. He urged Congress, however, to appropriate money to increase the army, a proposal that provoked the strong opposition of another leading Southern senator, Robert Toombs of Georgia.

The pattern of conservatism set by Davis and Southern congressmen in the antebellum period was followed by the representatives of the Southern states in Washington for many years after the Civil War.[36] It was based primarily on race, and on protection of the interests of plantation agriculture, both of which, until the Franklin Roosevelt era, relied upon restricting the expanding power of the federal government through the doctrine of state rights. Davis's seemingly contradictory course—he was a strong conservative in domestic policy and a liberal in foreign policy—also prefigured the course of Southern senators during much of the twentieth century. But the politics of the Old South was not plagued by the rise of a crop of demagogues, as was the New South after the Civil War with the emergence of the Populist Movement.

The Southern Imperialist

*E*xpansion was the mood of Mississippi and, indeed, of the lower South during Jefferson Davis's career in politics. It had blossomed luxuriantly during the 1830s, "the flush times of Alabama and Mississippi," when new cotton lands were opened for settlement, causing the planters to feel expansive and to speculate recklessly.[1] The demand for ever more fertile lands to take the place of exhausted and eroded soils that resulted from wasteful and careless agriculture put pressure on the politicians to annex Texas, then seek parts of Mexico, and finally to add the island of Cuba to the United States.

Davis was one of the most forceful advocates of expansion in Congress. During his second and last term in the Senate this issue, particularly the acquisition of Cuba, the advocacy of a transcontinental railroad, and the expansion of slavery into the western territories, absorbed his energies and depleted his frail health. In his first term he had advocated the building of a transcontinental railroad as a great national project, for the reasons that it was vital for military protection of our western coast and that it would tend to unify the country (a clear indication that he was not a fire-eater, as William E. Dodd pointed out).[2] Like Thomas Jefferson, who had constitutional qualms over purchasing Louisiana, so did Davis in regard to the federal government undertaking the building of a transcontinental railroad. He admitted that such a railroad could not be built across states without their consent, but he proposed to construct the railroad before the territories became states. He held the common illusion of his time that the western plains constituted the Great American Desert, and that it would be necessary for the government to provide financial aid to induce private companies to construct a railroad across it.

When a bill was introduced in Congress late in 1858 to construct a transcontinental railroad, it caused a lively sectional and constitutional debate. Senator Henry Wilson of Massachusetts branded Davis's recommendation of a southern route as a disunion route, pointing out that if the South dissolved the Union, it would lie wholly within a Southern Confederacy.[3] Davis defended his recommendation of a southern route by citing elaborate reports from engineering officers on the different routes surveyed. Wilson maintained, however, that the officers of the surveying parties were incompetent, and that Davis's recommendation of the southern route was colored by his sectional prejudices. The Massachusetts senator boldly declared, "I know of no man in the Senate or the country . . . who is more biased by sectional feeling than the Senator from Mississippi."[4] Davis had added, he asserted, to the estimates submitted for the cost of the northern route and subtracted from estimates of the southern route for the purpose of winning the selection of the southern route.

An acute lawyer, Senator Judah P. Benjamin of Louisiana, also took issue with Davis on the constitutional authority for building a transcontinental railroad. Senator Andrew Johnson of Tennessee, criticizing the expense of the surveys and of printing the reports, which he said cost the government over a million dollars, declared that there was no necessity for a transcontinental road through a desert country. In dealing with Johnson and answering Wilson's attacks, Davis revealed a keen sense of cutting irony and a devastating power of sarcasm. An example was his contemptuous reference to the proposal that the plebeian senator from Tennessee had made for a change of the Constitution in regard to the election of the president. Davis observed that such a change would make the presidential election process "a pony race, with a number of pony candidates running."[5]

On January 12, 1859, he submitted his version of a bill to construct a transcontinental road. He held that it was futile to get Congress to agree on a proper route; therefore, his bill provided for a company of capitalists, with government aid, to select the route that they judged most profitable. The federal government would grant to the company alternate sections of land for the space of six miles on each side of the road, a right of way two hundred feet wide, and a loan of $10 million to be paid back within ten years, the time given to build the road. He was sharply opposed to corporations or individuals enriching themselves from the sale of public lands, and his elaborately detailed bill of fourteen sections provided strong safeguards to insure that the road would be built in a substantial and workmanlike manner, that the grants of public land would be made only as sections of twenty-five miles each were completed, and that the government would be charged at a fair price for the transportation of mail, army supplies, and troops.[6]

This bill was a good demonstration of his practical mind (also shown in his efficient administration of his plantation and of the War Department). His practicality was curiously balanced or offset by his obsession with abstractions, such as regional honor, and a strict construction of the Constitution, when such an interpretation favored Southern interests.

In his advocacy of a transcontinental railroad Davis stood virtually alone among Southern leaders. "Mr. President," he said, two weeks before he resigned from the Senate, "it is well known that, for many years past, I have departed from those with whom I was usually associated, in advocating some plan of coupling the Pacific coast with the valley of the Mississippi."[7] His vigorous and persistent advocacy of this great national project must be accounted one of the most progressive and forward-looking measures promoted by any statesman of his generation.

As secretary of war and leading counselor in Franklin Pierce's cabinet, he pressured the weak president into urging an expansionist policy that would benefit the South, especially to acquire Cuba. He persuaded Pierce to appoint Senator Pierre Soulé of Louisiana, an ardent expansionist and proslavery propagandist, as ambassador to Madrid, and also John Y. Mason, a fat-headed old Virginian of strong proslavery convictions, who thanked Davis for securing his appointment to the French mission. Soulé, particularly, was selected for his post in order to acquire Cuba. Soulé proved to be the worst ambassador that President Pierce could have appointed. He was a fiery, flamboyant individual, with no talent for diplomacy, and blatantly outspoken in his sympathy for the Cubans.[8]

By the acquisition of this island teeming with slaves, the Southern expansionists hoped to add two slave states to the United States, counterbalancing in the Senate the free states of the North. The expansionists, however, did not publicly emphasize this motive, but maintained that by such an acquisition the United States would free the oppressed people of the island from Spanish misrule, stop the African slave trade which centered in the island, make the Caribbean a mare clausum, and benefit Northern commercial interests by providing a market for their manufactured goods.

Soulé had a lucky opportunity, nevertheless, to bring pressure to bear on the Spanish government to relinquish the island by the *Black Warrior* affair. On February 28, 1854, Spanish authorities in Cuba seized the American ship *Black Warrior,* carrying cotton to Havana, for violating port regulations. Soulé issued an ultimatum, demanding the dismissal of all officers concerned in the seizure and an indemnity of $300,000. Spain refused, and Soulé was left up in the air, but eventually Spain compensated the owners, removing a threat of war.

In the same year, Soulé was instructed to meet with Mason and James Buchanan at Ostend in Belgium to recommend a policy in regard to Cuba.

The three ministers drew up the outrageous Ostend Manifesto in which they advised Secretary of State William L. Marcy that Spain should be offered $120 million for Cuba, and if the offer were refused the United States would be justified in seizing it.[9] Davis, in a speech in Mississippi, later said that if the *Black Warrior* affair had not been mismanaged the United States would have owned Cuba.

While Davis was still secretary of war the presidential election of 1856 took place, resulting in the narrow victory of James Buchanan, a Pennsylvania doughface, over John C. Frémont, "the Pathfinder," the first candidate of the Republican party. This party was dominated by antislavery men, whose platform promised to prohibit in the federal territories "those twin relics of barbarism, polygamy and slavery." Southerners threatened secession if the "Black Republican" candidate won.[10] Buchanan carried every slave state except Maryland, which voted for Millard Fillmore, the American party candidate, and by a slender margin carried the crucial state of Pennsylvania. Buchanan was elected by a minority popular vote, and the prospects looked bleak for Southerners in the next presidential election. Although Davis did not actively campaign for Buchanan, he was happy over his victory that warded off the threat of disunion posed by the near victory of the party that Southerners called the "Black Republicans."[11] Grateful for Southern support, Buchanan appointed a cabinet containing Jacob Thompson of Mississippi and Howell Cobb of Georgia, and pursued a proslavery policy in which he often consulted Jefferson Davis.

When Davis reentered the Senate in the fall of 1857 after an absence of over six years, the first grave issue that confronted him was whether he would support the notorious Lecompton Constitution of Kansas. This constitution was drawn up in 1857 by a proslavery convention at Lecompton, Kansas, that was boycotted by the free-state settlers, who had set up a separate territorial government at Topeka. It was unfairly presented to the people in a territorial election in which most of the free-state settlers refused to vote. Nevertheless, President Buchanan in a message to Congress on February 2, 1858, recommended that the Lecompton Constitution be accepted and that Kansas be admitted as a slave state. Davis was seriously ill in the winter of 1857–58; he appeared in the Senate only at infrequent intervals, emaciated, head bandaged, leaning on a cane. Accordingly, he did not participate in the Lecompton debate until after Buchanan had presented his message.

On February 8, Davis spoke in praise of Buchanan's message. He complained of the unfairness of the action of Northern antislavery settlers (sparked by Eli Thayer's New England Emigration Society in 1856) flocking to the territory of Kansas to make it a free state. Instead of letting natural forces determine the course of settlement, he said, they had introduced a political element. Had you made no political war on Southern people and their institutions, he declared, the Southern people would have attended to their daily affairs little concerned "whether this species of property [slaves] or any other was held in any other portion of the Union. You have made it a political war. We are on the defensive."[12] He expressed doubt that even if slavery were introduced into this debatable area it would permanently remain there. In 1860 the census recorded exactly six slaves resident in Kansas.

During his second term in the Senate, Davis was a harassed man; he appeared to take nearly everything seriously, especially the cause of the South. In the summer of 1858 his health became so bad that his doctor advised him to seek a cooler climate in the North where he would be free of political tension. He decided to take a sea voyage, sailing to Maine. In early July he left Baltimore with his family for Portland, Maine, where the Montgomery Blairs, intimate friends of the family, had a cottage. On board ship, he made a short July 4 speech in which he condemned the actions of English patrol ships exercising the right of search of American ships suspected of smuggling slaves. Although they were proceeding under a treaty with this country, he claimed that their actions insulted the United States and stopped a lucrative American trade in ivory and other tropical products. Arriving at Portland he was serenaded, and he replied with a speech emphasizing the common historic traditions of both sections. At the same time, he criticized the attempt of European nations to prohibit privateering by international law. He argued that in peacetime the United States should keep a small navy, in wartime depending on the merchant marine to protect the nation by privateering. He also advocated his favorite proposal of government aid in building a transcontinental railroad.[13] He was so popular among the Democrats in Maine that Bowdoin College awarded him an honorary degree, and when a movement later arose to revoke it the faculty stood firm in opposing it.[14]

At Faneuil Hall, Boston, on October 11, 1858, he made his most important political speech in the North before a large crowd at the Grand Ratification Meeting of the Democratic party, presided over by his friend Caleb Cushing. Here he referred to the patriotic memories of both sections, to the great men of the Revolution from both regions, and bestowed high praise on the eminent Northern Democrat, Franklin Pierce. He observed that Massachusetts had a history of standing for state rights, state sovereignty, and community independence. He proceeded to ask why the bitter sectional controversy had arisen over slavery. Referring to the wisdom of maintaining diversity in the United States, he declared that agriculture and manufacturing complemented each other in this country rather than being antagonistic. He made a plea to his audience to arrest the dangerous agitation over the expansion of slavery into the territories. Slave property, he claimed, had the same status as any other property, and Congress had no authority for determining kinds of property. He expressed friendliness toward the Northern people, noting the large number of Democrats among them, and in return he received a cordial welcome.[15]

In a speech in New York a week later, he asserted that the South was not the aggressor in the slavery controversy. It demanded only the status of equality, which would give its citizens the right to emigrate to the federal territories with their slave property. The territorial legislatures had no authority to determine the status of slavery—only when a territory became a state could such a decision be made. Again he analyzed the sectional controversy as a struggle for sectional aggrandizement—a power struggle. In addition to the contest over the territorial issue, he observed, there was a struggle to change the naturalization laws. In this state of many immigrants, he shrewdly pointed out that the Southern cause had a similar basis with those opposing nativism, namely, observing the Constitution. He lashed out against those who maintained that there was a higher law than the Constitution and the Bible, of whom Senator William H. Seward was the chief exponent. The higher law advocates, he declared, should be tarred, feathered, and whipped, and the lynch law should be applied to them just as it was used during the Revolution.[16]

While Davis was speaking in the North, some ultra-Southerners condemned him as placating the Yankees. He returned to Mississippi to answer the charges. He had a favorable opportunity to do so when he made a speech before the Mississippi legislature on November 16, 1858. In this speech he explained the motive of his trip to the North. It was not, as alleged, to win support for the Democratic nomination for president, as some of his critics had charged, but in obedience to the advice of his doctors to seek a cooler climate and freedom from political tension. He referred to his physical condition as wasted by "protracted, violent disease," his brow as being furrowed, and his hair as frosted by the passage of time.[17]

Among the criticisms of Southern newspapers, which had repeated the calumnies of Black Republican editors, was the depreciation of the conduct of his regiment and of himself at Buena Vista, which he defended vigorously. Some Southern newspapers had also misrepresented his position in 1851, calling him a secessionist. He had not advocated secession, except as a last resort. Instead, he said, he had advised summoning a convention of all the Southern states for counsel over the course that they should take as a result of the passage of the Compromise of 1850. On this occasion he had declared that if an abolitionist should be elected president in 1860, the Southern states would secede. Therefore, he now urged the state to prepare for contingencies by increasing its ability to defend itself, by building an armory for manufacturing arms, constructing railroads, and strengthening levees on the Mississippi River.[18] Finally, he declared that in the North he had staunchly advocated the equality of the South with the North in the federal territories.

With health greatly improved, Davis returned to his seat in the Senate to back the purchase of Cuba. The collapse of efforts in 1854–55 to acquire the rich island teeming with slaves had come partly as a result of the uproar of bitter sectionalism caused by the Kansas-Nebraska Bill, as well as because of the intransigent attitude of Spain. After this fiasco Davis did not give up his struggle to acquire Cuba, efforts which came to a head again in Buchanan's administration. On January 10, 1859, John Slidell introduced a bill in the Senate for the appropriation of $30 million for the purpose of negotiating with Spain to purchase Cuba, and two weeks later it was reported favorably by the Foreign Relations Committee. Buchanan supported it, as well as another favorite project of Davis, the building of a transcontinental railroad. The Republicans were unalterably opposed. Old Ben Wade of Ohio, referring to this bill and to the homestead bill, which a large majority of Southerners opposed, sneered: "The question will be shall we give niggers to the niggerless, or land to the landless?"[19]

Davis spoke in and out of Congress for the purchase of Cuba. In an address before the Democratic Convention at Jackson in the summer of 1859, he urged it to adopt a resolution in favor of the acquisition of Cuba, on the grounds of commercial and political necessity. Acquisition of this slave territory would be vital to the South in case of the formation of a Southern Confederacy. He frankly admitted that his desire to annex Cuba and thereby increase slaveholding constituencies was motivated in part by the minority status of the South. He believed that Cuba could be obtained by negotiation, but he opposed the use of force to attain that objective as staining the bright escutcheon of the United States, unless the island became dangerous to this country. Furthermore, he observed that the acquisition of Cuba would secure a great military advantage to the United States in guarding over trade between the Atlantic and Gulf states; also, he pointed out that the weakness of Spain exposed her to the pressure of British reformers to abolish slavery and thus make Cuba another Jamaica.[20] He argued that our possession of Cuba would be of advantage to the inhabitants who were oppressed by a despotic rule.

In addition to Davis and Slidell, one of the strongest proponents of the measure was Robert Toombs of Georgia, who argued that the Cuba bill would benefit the entire country, particularly the Northern states. It would provide, he pointed out, a splendid market for their manufactures, and they in return could import to our shores tropical fruits, sugar, and coffee. With the acquisition of the "Pearl of the Antilles," with its fine harbors, the United States would be able to make of the Caribbean Sea a mare clausum. In his flamboyant way, Toombs declared, "Probably younger men than you or I will live to see the day when no flag shall float there except by permission of the United States of America. That is my policy." It should be, he said, "American policy to unite as fast as it can be fairly and honestly done all the tropics under our flag."[21] But the opposition to Slidell's bill was strong and, fearing it could not pass, Slidell withdrew it.

Davis also championed the cause of the filibusterers who sought to invade and seize, not only Cuba, but Nicaragua, which controlled the most accessible route to California. He supported William Walker, called "the grey-eyed man of destiny," in his efforts to make himself dictator of that volatile country, introduce slavery there, and unite it with the United States. Davis believed strongly in the Manifest Destiny of the United States to expand across the continent. But he and the Southern congressmen were not alone in urging expansion, for they had the sympathy of prominent Northern Democrats, notably Stephen A. Douglas. Douglas supported Davis and other Southerners in trying to get Buchanan to condemn Commander Hiram Paulding of the U.S. Navy for arresting Walker in Central America, and with them he sought to secure Walker's release.[22]

In a speech at the state fair at Augusta, Maine, on September 23, 1858, Davis predicted that the whole of North America would come under the control of the United States as a protectorate, although he opposed incorporating in the United States countries populated by a different race from the Caucasian people of this country.[23] He observed that, though the breed of horses and cattle could be improved by crossing different stocks, the mingling of races was a different thing. The reason for the advanced state of civilization in this country, he asserted, was that its people had kept pure the Caucasian blood that flowed in their veins. In the movement of Davis and the Southerners to expand the territory of the country southward, the strongest motive seems to have been, not so much to widen the area of slavery, but to acquire strength politically in the Senate by adding slave states.

Recently, scholars have debated the question of whether manifest destiny really represented the mood of the country in the nineteenth century. The respected Harvard historian, Professor Frederick Merk, has challenged the older thesis advanced by Albert K. Weinberg that Americans in the nineteenth century held to this doctrine.[24] Actually public opinion in this period, in the absence of Gallup polls, is extremely difficult to analyze, because the newspapers were an unreliable index of public opinion, and also because of the conflicting interests and aspirations of different regions.

Davis seems to have been considerably in advance of dominant Southern opinion in urging expansion. Robert May, in his study, while showing the importance of the Southern expansion movement, admits, "At best, a majority of Southerners supported expansion."[25] The Southern anti-imperialists included such powerful political leaders as Calhoun, Clay, and many leading Whigs who took a decidedly conservative position in opposing expansion. The great Carolina statesman declared at the time of the Mexican War, "Mexico is forbidden fruit, to eat of which is to die." He was concerned that the expansion movement threatened to break down the color line in the South, by absorbing what he called a mongrel population.[26] Davis was aware of this danger, for in 1848 he had opposed the absorption of all of Mexico.

The sympathy of Southerners for the filibusterers and the debate in 1859 over the Cuba bill probably had a powerful delayed effect in determining President-elect Lincoln to stand firmly against the acceptance of the Crittenden Compromise. Although the National Democratic party platform of 1860 advocated the annexation of Cuba, Lincoln doubtless exaggerated the danger of adopting such a policy. His party opposed even an amendment offered by Congressman Emerson Etheridge of Tennessee that surely would have obviated the danger of acquiring additional slave territory, namely, that any future annexation of territory must receive a two-thirds vote of Congress.[27]

Davis's policy of annexing territory to the southward posed an obviously great peril to the United States. The necessity of ruling semitropical possessions, with their ignorant populations, could have contaminated the purity of American institutions and weakened democracy in the United States. Davis skirted this issue, and there is reason to believe that he held Manifest Destiny as only an idea rather than as a practical policy. It was a part of the insularity of a young people who had conquered a wilderness, and believed that American forms of government were the best in the world and should be extended over the continent. But there was also the question of national honor being involved in seizing a helpless country or putting pressure on a weak nation such as Spain to sell. Buchanan said that our national character would not permit this country to acquire foreign territory except by honorable means. Jefferson Davis, however, like many other politicians, including Thomas Jefferson, could rationalize his desires and policies so as to accord with his notion of honor.

The Momentous Split of
the Democrats

As the outstanding leader of the Southern conservatives and of the expansionists, Jefferson Davis had a powerful influence in shaping the pro-Southern policies of the Pierce and Buchanan administrations. To his brother Joe he wrote as early as September 22, 1855, while secretary of war in Pierce's cabinet, that he "felt my services here may be more beneficial to the *South* [italics by the author] than those that I could render elsewhere."[1] His influence over Buchanan was also considerable in directing policy in a pro-Southern direction. Not only did he encourage Buchanan's policy in the Caribbean, but he supported his Kansas policy against Senator Douglas, and backed the efforts of Buchanan's lieutenants to defeat Douglas as the nominee of the Democratic party in 1860. Davis did not attend the Democratic convention at Charleston, but more than any other man he contributed indirectly to the breakup of the party at that convention, and thus to the ending of the hegemony of the Southern states.

He did attend the Baltimore convention of that year along with Stephen A. Douglas and Murat Halstead, editor of the Cincinnati *Commercial,* who has left a perceptive description of the Southern leader's appearance at that time. Davis, he reported, was tall, very erect, with prematurely gray hair (he was only fifty-one years old), and haggard-looking. Halstead noticed his hands; they were thin, bloodless, bony, and nerveless. He observed that it was painfully evident that he was ill but, nevertheless, he gave "a closely reasoned speech." Davis's career in Congress and as president of the Confederate states, in fact, was almost constantly marred by ill health. Douglas, on the other hand, was short and stocky, with duck legs, and leonine head, with black hair worn long and thinning, and in vigorous middle age.[2]

Halstead gave a surprising thumbnail sketch of the great fire-eater, William Lowndes Yancey—not at all like our conception of the fiery "Orator of Secession." He did not rant or breathe fire against the Yankees; rather, he was a mild, unassuming gentleman. Davis really did not sympathize with his extreme proposals. In one of his speeches he said that Yancey's "League of United Southerners" had only a small membership, chiefly in Alabama.

Yet, as to Davis's role in the intersectional conflict, Halstead observed that the speeches of Davis and Judah P. Benjamin against Douglas and Pugh after the Charleston convention of April, 1860, "deepened and exasperated the controversy and made it more personal."[3] The importance of Davis in raising sectional consciousness can easily be exaggerated. He was the most powerful spokesman of Southern interests and resentments. Most of the lesser Southern politicians expressed similar objections to Douglas's popular sovereignty doctrine. A few, like Governor Henry A. Wise of Virginia, condemned Davis's stand in favor of the Lecompton Constitution, but agreed with him in opposing the popular sovereignty doctrine. Wise maintained that the effects of the popular sovereignty doctrine were similar to the doctrine of the Republicans in excluding slaveholders from settling in the federal territories.[4]

Holding the views that they did, Davis and Douglas were bound to clash, although there would have been a chance of compromise if Davis had not been so inflexible and adamant. Their controversy was not over the question of the rightfulness of slavery but, rather, over the question of territorial democracy, which Douglas called "popular sovereignty," and which Davis branded as "squatter sovereignty." It was a tragic quarrel, because it contributed greatly to the Southern rejection of Douglas, the only viable Democratic presidential candidate in 1860. As a result, it split the National Democratic party; the unity of this party offered the only hope of defeating the Republican candidate, Abraham Lincoln, and of preserving the Union.

In addition to a conflict over ideology between Davis and Douglas, the Mississippi senator entertained a barely concealed contempt for the powerful leader of the Northern democracy. Although both men came from the same social stratum of the middle class, Davis had made himself a Southern aristocrat, while Douglas, born in Vermont and brought up in New York, had moved to Ohio where he was deeply influenced by the spirit of the Middle West which emphasized democracy.[5] In a letter to Franklin Pierce, Davis expressed his scorn for Douglas as "a little electioneering grog drinking demagogue."[6] His perception of the man agreed almost precisely with Harriet Beecher Stowe's description of him as a demagogue of wonderful vitality and ability as a debater, who if he had been gifted with wit would have been "too irresistible a demagogue for the liberties of our laughter-loving people."[7] But Mrs. Stowe, as well as Jefferson Davis, failed to gauge the depth of Douglas's nature, he was much more than a demagogue, as Robert Johannsen has shown in his recent biography of Douglas.

In his debate with Lincoln at Freeport, Illinois, on August 27, 1858, Stephen Douglas had announced his famous Freeport Doctrine, by which the people of a territory, despite the Dred Scott decision of the previous year, could determine for themselves whether they would allow slavery or prohibit it, simply by enacting or refusing to enact police protection for the institution.[8] In contradiction, Davis held that only at the time that a territory became a state, could it make this decision by its constitutional convention. Over the Douglas doctrine, called "squatter" sovereignty by Southerners, a mighty debate developed, both inside and outside of Congress, in which Davis became the main protagonist of the Illinois senator.

The issue came to a head in the Senate during the debate over the admission of Kansas as a state with its fraudulent Lecompton Constitution. President Buchanan used all his power and prestige to push the bill of acceptance through Congress.[9] Finally a compromise was worked out called the English bill, which resubmitted the Lecompton Constitution to the people of Kansas, giving them an alternative of accepting it with an unusually large grant of federal land that they had asked for, or rejecting it, in which case the territory would have to wait until it had the necessary population, and then the state would receive only the normal amount of federal land. The Republicans unfairly propagandized the English bill as a bribe to accept slavery, but Davis defended it as fair and reasonable. Douglas had a dangerous decision to make: Should he be true to his popular sovereignty doctrine or remain loyal to Buchanan and the administration party? He wavered desperately, at one time deciding to accept the English bill, but then the pressure of Illinois leaders forced him to rescind his earlier decision.[10] He chose, therefore, to oppose the controversial bill, and thereby broke with the Democratic administration, while Davis supported the administration.

Because of this rebellion, the Democratic Senate caucus, on December 9, 1858, deprived Douglas of his powerful position as chairman of the Committee on Territories. To make the blow more humiliating, the decision was made in his absence, while he was vacationing with his beautiful bride in Cuba. Davis was the leader of this dismissal, ardently supported by the embittered President Buchanan, while Senator Robert Toombs of Georgia, the second most powerful senator from the South, opposed it as impolitic.[11] This flagrant insult was probably the last straw in determining Douglas to become a candidate for the Democratic nomination for president. Davis's role in this episode, as well as his support of the corrupt Lecompton Constitution, form perhaps the most disreputable acts of his career. They can be explained only by his intense Southern partisanship that warped his judgment.

Whether the opening of the western territories to slavery would have resulted in the introduction of any significant number of slaves is highly doubtful. Even Davis took an ambiguous position on this question, partly for political reasons, partly because there was not adequate information on the agricultural and mineral resources of the West. In the Compromise debates he had held that slaves could be used in the southwestern territories in mining and in irrigation (a long way in the future). In the debate over the admission of Kansas as a state, however, Davis asserted that only household and family slaves would be taken into the debatable region, and that their owners would soon find it to their advantage to free them. Undoubtedly, he looked forward to the time when new slave territory would become available by means of expansion of the United States to the southward. Accordingly, he demanded not only that there should be no legal restriction on the expansion of slavery into the common territories, in compliance with the Dred Scott decision, but also that the federal government should protect slaveholders in the security of their slave property there.

The desperate debate between Northern and Southern senators over the expansion of slavery into an unsuitable semiarid land seems to have been over an abstraction. Yet to Jefferson Davis it involved a vital "principle," and to the Northern people at the time it involved a great moral principle upon which there could be no compromise. Many Northerners viewed the western territories as the Promised Land, in which they hoped to settle with no slave or even free Negro competitors. Thus their motives in seeking to curb the expansion of slavery were a mixture of materialism and idealism. The Southerners also, though generally ignorant of conditions in the West, looked upon the territories acquired from Mexico as a legitimate area of settlement. On February 28, 1860, the *Charleston Mercury* expressed this feeling in dismissing the argument of "barren abstractions." On the contrary, it maintained that the area in dispute had valuable agricultural and mineral resources adapted to slave exploitation, and especially pointed out the availability of the Indian Territory, after the removal of the Indians, as well as the rich semitropical lands to the southward for the expansion of slavery.[12] But the New Orleans *Bee* demurred, raising the question of where the slaves for such expansion could be procured, since the South did not have enough slaves for its own needs, as indicated by the exorbitant prices of slaves in the lower South.[13] Would that the heated debaters and orators on both sides of the subject could have read the persuasive essay of Charles W. Ramsdell, "The Natural Limits of Slavery Expansion," published in 1959! In this essay he maintained that, on account of inadequate rainfall for plantation agriculture and the lack of a supply of fertile land accessible to market, slavery had reached its natural limit by 1850.[14]

Nevertheless, there was more to Davis's struggle for Southern rights than a concern that the South should not be shut out of the southwestern territories. He had a larger objective, namely, to establish for all time an interpretation of the Constitution as a compact creating a *federal* republic, with limited powers, which he believed to be vital to the safety of the South. His able mind was thus severely limited by a legal fixation. Although he knew a considerable amount of history and frequently cited it, he did not apply it to the realities of his day. He never treated the Constitution as a growing, changing, dynamic institution; but he was no different in this respect than Calhoun and other Southern statesmen of his period.

It is doubtful if the great majority of the people attributed as much importance to the fervid speeches in Congress over the expansion of slavery, that congressmen such as Jefferson Davis and Stephen Douglas thought they did. Alexander H. Stephens wrote on January 5, 1860, that he believed the people of Georgia didn't care a button what Congress did. "There is really not the least excitement in the public mind upon public affairs," he observed. "No man that I have seen for weeks or months seems to take any interest in what is going on in Washington."[15] His words strike a familiar note, for today most ordinary citizens are interested only in what directly affects them, and show a remarkable apathy toward and ignorance of public affairs and voting.

Jefferson Davis did not believe that his great fight on the Senate floor in 1858–60 with Douglas and the Republican leaders that preceded the disruption of the Democratic party was over an "abstraction." Varina Davis, in analyzing the character of her husband, wrote that he was so dominated by conceptions of principle that he underrated the value of social life as a means of political advancement or as an agency of influencing other politicians. She contrasted her husband with the powerful Republican political leader, William H. Seward of New York, who once, while visiting the Davises in Washington, confessed that he never spoke out of conviction alone, but for the purpose of influencing the voters. Davis replied that he never spoke from any other motive but principle.[16]

When he entered the Senate chamber in January, 1860, he girded himself for an even greater and more provocative struggle over the territorial issue than he had fought during the two previous years. The situation in Congress was tense and explosive. The House of Representatives had just ended a bitter struggle to select a speaker following forty-four ballots and wrangling for two months between the Republican and Democratic members. A solution was made possible only by the withdrawal from the contest of the Republican candidate, John Sherman of Ohio, brother of the famous Civil War general, who had aroused bitter antagonism in the South by endorsing Hinton Rowan Helper's antislavery book, *The Impending Crisis of the South: How to Meet It.* In the course of the debates over the election of the speaker one member of Congress accidentally dropped his gun on the floor, leading to a wild fracas among the members. Senator James H. Hammond wrote to Francis Lieber,

"I believe every man in both houses is armed with a revolver—some with two —and a bowie knife," and this dangerous state of feeling was corroborated by Senator James W. Grimes of Iowa.[17] It was a time, therefore, for a statesman to seek to moderate sectional passion.

Moreover, the nation had been suddenly disturbed on October 16, 1859, when the New England fanatic, John Brown, and a small group of followers seized the United States arsenal at Harpers Ferry and sought to stir up a general slave insurrection. Davis was placed on the Senate Committee to investigate whether the bold assault at Harpers Ferry was instigated by a conspiracy of Northern antislavery men. A recent biographer has called Davis "the chief inquisitor" of the committee headed by Senator James M. Mason of Virginia; its purpose was to pin the blame for Brown's irrational act on the Republican party.[18] Although the committee interviewed a number of leading Republicans, it absolved them from blame.[19] Nevertheless, public opinion in the South widely believed that Brown was supported by Northerners in general, and a hysterical fear of abolitionist emissaries seeking to stir up the slaves swept the South, a kind of mass paranoia.[20] Davis unfortunately did nothing to tranquilize public opinion. Instead, his speeches in the Senate increased sectional bitterness, although he frequently expressed the wish to preserve fraternity with the North if only the antislavery agitators would leave the South alone.

Indeed, he pursued an opposite course. On March 1, 1860, he reintroduced some earlier resolutions, seven in number, slightly modified, which he described as "Resolutions on the Relations of the States." His opponents, however, branded them as a demand for a federal slave code in the territories. He held that intermeddling with the domestic institutions of the states (by which he meant slavery) by other states was subversive of the Constitution, insulting to the states, and tending to destroy the Union. Negro slavery, he declared, was an important part of the institutions of fifteen slaveholding states, and no change of opinion or feeling on the part of the North in regard to it could justify the attacks of Northern men on it. The heart, or core, of his resolutions (the famous fifth resolution) was his contention that neither Congress nor a territorial legislature possessed the power by the Constitution to deprive a citizen from emigrating into federal territory with his slave property, and that should experience prove the judiciary or executive authority did not provide protection for this right it became the duty of Congress to pass appropriate legislation. Only at the time when a territory became a state, could a decision be made by the people constituting the new state on the question of whether slavery should be permitted or excluded. Finally, the resolutions declared that any laws of the states to defeat the enforcement of the Fugitive Slave Law of 1850 (by the Personal Liberty Acts) were subversive of the Constitution and revolutionary in effect.[21]

The resolutions were a flat denial of Douglas's popular sovereignty doctrine, as interpreted by his statement in the Freeport debate. They did not win unanimous approval even in Mississippi, where anti-Davis critics described them as academic, impractical, a mere "Will o' the Wisp."[22] Albert Gallatin Brown, Mississippi's junior senator, introduced an even more extreme amendment calling on Congress to pass a slave code protecting slave property in the territories, but it received little support, even from the senators of the lower South. During a protracted debate, the hostility of the Mississippi senators for each other came out in the open, and Davis referred with contempt and sarcasm to his plebeian colleague.

Since the Democratic presidential convention was to meet in Charleston on April 23, critics accused Davis of trying through his resolutions to dictate that party's program. One of the most influential of the critics was Senator Robert Toombs of Georgia, who on February 10, shortly after the preliminary resolutions had been presented, wrote to Alexander H. Stephens that the Davis resolutions on slavery in the territories were approved by the president and were in the main good, but he observed, "It is the very foolishness of folks to raise and make prominent such issues now" (before the assembly of the Democratic convention to nominate a presidential candidate). Toombs argued that the Dred Scott case had already decided that Congress could not prohibit slavery in the territories. By pressing the abstract issue now, he maintained the Northern voters in the Democratic party would be driven off; it was "naked folly to turn out a quarter of a million at least of such men on such pretenses."[23] He was undoubtedly right, and his remarks show that he was much more pragmatic than Davis. He felt the Mississippi senator had advanced such extreme statements because of his hostility toward Douglas—a maneuver to defeat his nomination at the Democratic convention in Charleston. The sober-minded Alexander H. Stephens, always suspicious of low motives in men, agreed. Even the fire-eater, Senator Louis T. Wigfall, who had emigrated from South Carolina to Texas after killing a man in a duel, condemned the policy of alienating the Northern Democrats with the unnecessary Davis resolutions in an election year.

In a Senate speech supporting his resolutions, on May 16 and 17, Davis denied that they had been concocted to affect the decisions of the Democratic presidential convention; rather, they were introduced to obtain an expression of the Senate on sound political principles. He believed that his resolutions would have a beneficial effect by showing the public "the error of supposing that there was a purpose on the part of the Democracy, or of the South, to enact what was called a slave code for the territories of the United States."[24] It was a fine distinction to make, for the public could see little practical difference between Davis's fifth resolution and the threat of a federal code protecting slave property in the territories. Surprisingly, his resolutions were adopted in the Democratic Senate caucus, on May 24, with every Democrat except the independent Senator Pugh of Ohio voting for them—Douglas being absent.[25]

Just as Davis fought courageously and skillfully on the battlefields of Mexico, he waged a battle in the Senate for the extreme claims of the South, but not as effectively. During much of the time that he was a senator, as we have seen, he was handicapped by illness. Furthermore, he was hampered by a blind spot in his vision of American society. Like other Southerners of his generation, he could not see that slavery was an evil institution, bound to pass. He was unable, therefore, to understand the Northern senators who opposed him. But they, too, had a blind spot: while inveighing against slavery, they failed to recognize the exploitation of the workingman in the Northern states, and the labor movement was far too weak to force their cause upon the attention of the politicians. It was true, as Southerners charged, that many Northerners who were so zealous in backing the cause of the slave were self-righteous and complacent about the evils existent in their own region.

The majority of Northerners, however, were not abolitionists and, outside of New England, probably not even against slavery, for racism was widespread above the Mason-Dixon line. It would have been sensible, it seems today, for Southern politicians to have cultivated this large body of public opinion represented by the Northern Democrats, whose leader was Stephen A. Douglas. The Illinois senator agreed with Davis and the other Southern senators on most questions, including the building of a transcontinental railroad and Southern imperialism. His Southern-born wife, and after her death his children, had inherited a large slave plantation in Mississippi, which he administered. Like the Southerners, he thought that Negroes were inferior to whites and that they were better off under a regime of paternal slavery than in a state of freedom. The confrontation between Davis and Douglas was over the role of democracy in the western territories, especially in connection with the timing of the decision to accept or reject slavery by the territory. In this conflict Douglas proved the greater statesman than Davis, for he represented a broader vision, a national point of view, in seeking to reconcile the extreme Southern and the extreme Northern positions.[26] The attacks of Davis on this unquestioned leader of the Northern Democrats were disastrous to the real cause of the South, constituting one of the most serious mistakes of his career. They contributed largely to the disruption of the Democratic party during the presidential nominating convention at Charleston, South Carolina, on April 23, 1860.

In looking forward to the Democratic convention, Davis insisted that he was much more interested in the type of man that the convention should select than in its platform. He was determined, however, that Stephen A. Douglas should not be that man. As early as September 3, 1859, he had written to his friend, Franklin Pierce, that he hoped Pierce would be chosen by the party rather than "certain ambitious demagogues," undoubtedly meaning Douglas. Before the meeting of the nominating convention, when it seemed likely that the national party would split, Davis in a letter of January 30, 1860, proposed that the convention should dispense with a platform, as the Whigs had done in 1840, and nominate a man who would be accepted by both sections of the nation.[27]

Although Davis was nominated as a presidential candidate by the Democratic party of Mississippi, he made no effort to obtain the coveted office and did not attend the Charleston convention. He was not the man for conventions, political deals and combinations, and handshakings. He recognized that his extreme position on slavery prevented him from being a viable candidate, for it would impair the ability of the Democratic party to win the national election; accordingly, he did not wish the nomination. Nevertheless, at the Democratic convention his Massachusetts friends, Caleb Cushing, Robert C. Winthrop, and Ben Butler voted for him to the last ballot. Butler declared, "I voted fifty-seven times for the nomination of Jefferson Davis.[28]

As the delegates assembled, the air was tense with excitement in Charleston, the worst place that could have been chosen for a convention, for the city was the very citadel of Southernism, hostile to moderate decisions. The convention nominated a friend of Davis, the intellectual Caleb Cushing of Massachusetts, as permanent chairman, but significantly rejected the proslavery faction of New York delegates led by Mayor Fernando Wood and seated instead the pro-Douglas faction led by Dean Richmond. The main issue at the convention was the territorial one, and behind it lay the bid of Stephen A. Douglas for nomination as the presidential candidate of the Democratic party.

At the beginning of the proceedings, the convention made a vital decision: to adopt the platform first and then select a presidential candidate. The platform committee, unable to reach an agreement, offered a majority report and a minority report. The majority report presented a platform that incorporated the fifth of the Davis resolutions, demanding congressional protection of slavery in the territories. The minority report declared support for the Cincinnati platform of the party in 1856, which was ambiguous on the question of popular sovereignty, but it was the plank of the Douglas supporters. Subsequently, a pledge was added to abide by the decision of the Supreme Court on constitutional questions in regard to slavery in the territories. When the minority report was adopted by the convention, the delegations of the lower South led by Leroy Pope Walker bolted, and the national Democratic party, one of the strongest bonds holding the Union together, was tragically split. The disruption was not desired by either side but, as the poet Robert Burns has written, "the best-laid plans o' mice and men gang oft agley," or in more modern terms, as Roy Nichols has observed, everybody's plans at the convention went awry.[29]

The Southern delegates were determined, whatever came, not to accept Douglas as the party nominee, or his platform on the territorial issue. As Toombs expressed it, "The minority platform did not offer us the Dred Scott opinion." He also observed, "The Supreme Court have decided this case in our favor; but Douglas will not stand to it."[30] Actually, however, a modification of the minority platform went far toward conceding the Southern position, with the provision to abide by the decisions of the Supreme Court upon questions of constitutional law in regard to slavery in the territories, but it did not offer the protection of a slave code.

Davis tried to prevent the withdrawal of the Mississippi delegation from the convention. His agent was a brilliant young law professor at the University of Mississippi, recently elected as congressman, Lucius Quintus Cincinnatus Lamar. Lamar attended the Charleston convention in obedience to the wishes of Davis. He wrote to William S. Barry, a delegate to the convention and later president of Mississippi's Secession Convention, that he represented Davis's views. Davis instructed Lamar to prevent the withdrawal of Mississippi from the convention because of the adoption of the Douglas platform, for he believed that "the Southern states could achieve a more solid and enduring triumph by remaining in the convention and defeating Douglas."[31] When his advice was ignored, Davis later signed an address with Lamar advising the return of the delegates to the adjourned Baltimore convention. Here the split of the Democratic party, instead of being healed, was intensified by the creation of three parties: the National Democratic party, which nominated Stephen A. Douglas; the State Rights Democratic party, which nominated John C. Breckinridge; and the Constitutional Union party, which nominated Senator John Bell of Tennessee.

After the final split of the Democratic party into three factions, Davis exerted himself to get all three candidates to resign and unite on a compromise candidate, such as the New York governor, Horatio Seymour, a doughface.[32] Breckinridge and Bell authorized Davis to confer with Douglas, agreeing to withdraw their candidacies if he would, but Douglas refused, observing that if he did withdraw his followers would vote for the Republican candidate, Abraham Lincoln. Instead, breaking precedent, Douglas made a heroic canvass in the Southern states, boldly attacking disunion, motivated by an urgent sense of responsibility for preserving the Union (by this time he had exhausted his wonderful vitality in drink and strenuous activity; he was to die the next year at the age of forty-eight). In this crisis of the Union Jefferson Davis proved that, far from being a fire-eater seeking to break up the unity of the country, he was really a compromiser.

Braking Secession's Momentum

The consequence that Southerners had dreaded occurred on Election Day, November 6, 1860. The disruption of the Democratic party was followed by the election of Abraham Lincoln, the Republican candidate, on a platform advocating the containment of slavery. He received a popular vote amounting to only 39.2 percent of the electorate, winning with a very slender plurality; it was the smallest proportion by which an American president has been elected. Could Lincoln have been defeated if Davis's efforts to concentrate the anti-Republican vote on one candidate had succeeded? A scholarly study has calculated that if such a fusion had occurred, Lincoln would still have been elected by a majority of 17½ votes in the Electoral College, since he won 18 of the free states as well as 3 of New Jersey's votes.[1]

Great numbers of the Southern people now looked to Davis for advice on what to do in this crisis created by the victory of the Republican party. The year before, on July 6, 1859, in a speech before the Democratic State Convention of Mississippi, he had declared that if a president should be elected in 1860 on the platform of Mr. Seward's "irrepressible conflict" speech at Rochester, he favored the dissolution of the Union.[2] But when Edmund Rhett, son of Robert Barnwell Rhett, and editor of the Charleston *Mercury,* wrote him on November 10, 1860, a few days after the presidential election asking his opinion on secession, he wrote a discouraging reply. He doubted that the governor of Mississippi would call a secession convention; anyway, if a convention of the Southern states should assemble, Mississippi would probably not support secession. If South Carolina seceded alone, he doubted that his state would follow her; the geographical separation of the two states would be a powerful obstacle to the formation of an alliance with South Carolina. He found it difficult to reply to Rhett's last question, he wrote, as to whether South Carolina should secede alone, but if she were attacked by the federal government or had her ports blockaded, it would be a folly that would enlist every true Southern man in her defense. Davis personally favored seeking the cooperation of the Southern states on the question of secession before asking for a popular decision in the states upon that question. The letter therefore offered virtually no encouragement to the fire-eating Rhetts. Davis admitted, however, that he was living in isolation on his plantation and could not properly evaluate the effect produced on the minds of the people of his state by the result of the recent election.[3] His judgment proved wrong, as subsequent events demonstrated.

The mood of the people is difficult to fathom on the basis of the fragmentary evidence that has survived. Before the election of Lincoln—at least in the spring of 1860—only a small minority appeared to advocate secession. According to a recent in-depth study of approximately 200 Southern newspapers, the majority opposed secession.[4] At that time, even after Lincoln's election, three of the most influential newspapers of New Orleans—the *Picayune,* the *Bee* (the principal Creole newspaper), and the *True Delta*—were for compromise, not secession. After Lincoln's election, however, the press of the cotton states changed its attitude.[5] The mood of the people of the lower South veered sharply as they became conscious of the intransigence of the Republican leaders, who wrongly believed that the Southern threat of seceding was a bluff. On December 14, 1860, thirty Southern congressmen in Washington sent a telegram that undoubtedly had an important influence in increasing the growing secession sentiment in the lower South. This document, prepared in the room of Reuben Davis, the secessionist congressman from Mississippi, declared that because the Republican leaders would make no concession to the South, the honor and safety of the Southern states required that they should secede and form a Southern Confederacy.[6] Davis was among the thirty signers of the telegram.

Nevertheless, he tried to put the brake on the momentum toward secession. Even when he was campaigning for the election of Breckinridge and Lane, according to Percy Rainwater, an able student of the secession movement in Mississippi, Davis, alone of the campaigners, was "deliberate and guarded in his utterances on the question of secession in the event of Lincoln's election."[7] After the results of the presidential election were known in Mississippi, Governor J. J. Pettus issued a proclamation calling on the legislature to meet at Jackson on November 26 to consider the course of the state in this emergency.

He also invited Mississippi's delegation in Congress to meet with him in Jackson on November 22 to advise in respect to his forthcoming message to the legislature. Reuben Davis recommended that the governor advise the legislature to call a convention to take Mississippi out of the Union. A vote was taken on the radical proposal, and the group was evenly divided, Jefferson Davis opposing it, but when Governor Pettus cast the deciding vote in favor of a secession convention, he then voted with the other congressman for a unanimous recommendation calling for a secession convention.[8] By a vote of 4 to 3, also, the group advised the governor as to an answer to a telegram that he had received from the governor of South Carolina asking whether the South Carolina convention, which was about to meet, should have its ordinance of secession go into effect immediately or wait until March 4. They advised that the ordinance should go into effect immediately.[9]

After the Civil War, in commenting upon this meeting of the governor and the congressional delegation, Jefferson Davis explained why he differed with them in his reluctance to have his state secede, although he believed as they did in the unquestionable right of a state to secede. He thought that the state would not be permitted by the federal government peaceably to secede. The knowledge that he had gained in the War Department, he said, revealed the South's total lack of preparation for war in comparison with the Northern states. The odds against the South, therefore, because of lack of military equipment, would be far more prohibitive than if based solely on the proportional inferiority of its population. Since he believed that secession would be the precursor of war, he wanted to hold back from impulsive action. "It was stated to me afterwards [of the governor's meeting with the congressional delegation]," he wrote, "that my associates considered me too slow and it was probably true that they were right in their belief that I was behind the opinion of the people of the State as to the propriety of a prompt secession."[10] Davis denied emphatically the conspiracy theory of secession and wrote that the Southern states were not led into secession by a few ambitious and discontented politicians, but "the truth is that the Southern people were in advance of their representatives throughout" the secession movement.[11]

While Davis was meeting with Governor Pettus and the congressional delegation, he received a telegram from one of Buchanan's cabinet asking him to come to Washington immediately. The conference group decided that Davis should comply with the request. Buchanan wished to consult him on a message to Congress that he was preparing, and the fact that he summoned Davis instead of Toombs or Hunter, who composesd the other members of the "Southern Triumvirate" in the Senate, is indicative of Davis's preeminence as a Southern leader in 1860. Davis did offer counsel, and at the time he thought that Buchanan had accepted his suggestions, but when the message was delivered on December 4 it had been so changed that Davis felt compelled to criticize it, especially because it denied the right of secession.[12]

On December 20, the very day that South Carolina seceded, Vice President

Breckinridge appointed a Senate Committee of Thirteen to devise a compromise and head off the secession of the other cotton states. The venerable senator from Kentucky, John J. Crittenden, seventy-three years of age, who occupied Henry Clay's seat, was made chairman. The committee represented fairly the different sections and spectrums of opinion of the country. Davis was appointed one of the members from the South but at first declined to serve, finally, however, agreeing "at the solicitation of friends."[13]

Crittenden had a much more difficult task to accomplish than Henry Clay had in 1850, because the sectionalism between the North and South had become much more bitter and widespread. On December 18 Crittenden presented to the Senate his proposals, which were to become the basis for discussions in the Senate Committee of Thirteen. Essentially, they proposed to restore the Missouri Compromise to the eastern border of California, and to assure the Southern states by irrepealable constitutional amendments that slavery in the states where it was established would be safe. At the beginning of the committee's sessions, Davis introduced an unwise resolution that no report should be adopted that did not have the support of a majority of the Republican members and a majority of the other members; the resolution was adopted.

The key man in any attempt to effect a compromise would be William H. Seward, the Republican leader. This powerful, but supple man was favorable to a compromise that included restoration of the Missouri Compromise line, until he heard from Lincoln through his close confederate, Thurlow Weed, that the Republican president-elect was unalterably opposed to the main feature of the Crittenden Compromise, the restoration of the Missouri Compromise line. Then Seward and the other Republican members voted against a report to the Senate favoring the acceptance of the Crittenden proposals. The members from the lower South did likewise because the Republican members rejected it, although they were willing to accept the Crittenden Compromise. On December 31, the committee announced to the Senate that they could not agree on a report, and thus efforts at compromise ended. At this point Crittenden made a dramatic proposal in the Senate, suggesting on January 3 that his compromise be submitted to the vote of the American people in a national plebiscite, but the Republican members defeated this hopeful measure.[14]

In January, 1861, the states of the lower South, in conventions, began rapidly to pass ordinances of secession. But Davis apparently still hoped to delay the actual carrying out of these ordinances until March 4, and so advised Governor Pettus of Mississippi with regard to the secession of his own state. Announcing this date as the time of implementation of the secession movement, Davis believed, would "present in a palpable form the fact of our resistance to Black republican domination." He believed, moreover, that if the Southern congressmen remained in their seats they could prevent the enactment of an appropriations bill, or one giving the incoming president new powers, so that he would be relatively helpless until the meeting of another Congress. Did he hope for a reconciliation in the meantime? His brother Joseph wrote to him on January 2 that he had read to a friend a letter from him suggesting "the possibility of reconstruction."[15] The fire-eaters, headed by Robert Barnwell Rhett, feared that Davis would succumb to "the dread spirit of reconstruction."[16] Nonetheless, Davis's last days in the Senate were devoted to acting as agent for Governor Pettus in securing modern arms for Mississippi from a Northern manufacturer and to speaking on behalf of building a transcontinental railroad.

While other senators from the South were resigning, Davis remained at his post until he received official notice that Mississippi had seceded (on January 9). This notice arrived on January 20, but Davis was sick and delayed his farewell speech to the Senate until January 21. Mrs. Davis has vividly described the event in her memoir. Her husband was so sick that he could hardly walk to the Senate chamber. Every available space in which to sit or stand had been taken and women in their crinoline skirts sat on the floor. Dressed in black broadcloth appropriate to the occasion, the ailing senator began his speech in low deliberate tones, but as he proceeded his voice gathered strength, becoming loud and clear, "like a silver trumpet."[17]

He sought to establish his theory of state sovereignty as making secession a legal right. He stated that he approved of Mississippi's action in exercising this right rather than staying in a Union in which Southerners believed that they would be deprived of "the rights which our fathers bequeathed to us." Not once did he mention the election of a Republican president as the cause for secession. He refuted the use made of the Declaration of Independence to attack Southern slavery, observing that at the time of adoption it applied only to the political community and not to slaves, the same interpretation that Chief Justice Roger B. Taney had given to that instrument in his Dred Scott opinion. Davis concluded by affirming his friendly feeling for his colleagues from the Northern states and his hope for peaceful relations between the seceding states and those that remained in the Union. In spite of his powerful delivery, it was far from being a great or inspiring speech.[18]

As one surveys the secession movement and ponders whether it could have been defused, several facts stand out as particularly significant. First, it was carried out with remarkable swiftness, not by a conspiracy, which Davis stoutly denied, but by an extremist minority acting on an inert majority (the way so many movements have been effected in history). Second, even the lower South moved reluctantly toward secession and the founding of a new nation. The late Professor David Potter, in his book *The Impending Crisis, 1848–1861,* analyzed the votes for delegates to the secession conventions in the lower South, showing that the "cooperationists," of which Davis was one, came "remarkably close" to defeating immediate secession, particularly in Georgia and Louisiana —states that were necessary for founding the Confederate States of America.[19] Furthermore, in this crucial election, it is astonishing that the vote for delegates to the convention was considerably less than the vote in the recent presidential election.[20]

It would be hard to prove until further studies are made, but it seems likely that the secession movement was carried forward by the young, the adventurous, the planters on the make, and even the poor whites, who hated and feared the Negro. Lawrence Keitt, a young congressman from South Carolina, might be taken as representative of the reckless young secessionists. He wrote to "Sue" from Montgomery, where he was a delegate, on February 19, 1861, that he had "a vision of a great nation coming into existence."[21] The city populations in general, on the other hand, had voted in the election of 1860 against Breckinridge, the candidate of the secessionists, although he himself was not one of them, while the rural people tended to vote for him.

In the conventions of the lower South, the secessionists ultimately gained victory by wide margins. They won perhaps because of the contagious example of others states, who acted through interstate commissioners, because of a feeling of hopelessness in opposing secession, and because of the fear of being called "submissionists," or traitors to the South. The basic causes of the shift of opinion toward secession were a belief that the election of Lincoln constituted a *future* danger to the continuance of slavery and, of much lesser importance, a false sense of the obligation to uphold regional honor.

The Southern people were rushed into secession by an emotional wave. They would not listen to the words of wisdom of Alexander H. Stephens and Jefferson Davis who urged delay. Certainly one of the most statesman-like letters that Davis ever wrote was dispatched from Washington to Governor Pettus on January 4, 1861, recommending that the senators and congressmen remain in their seats until March 4 and block legislation hostile to the South and that the secession ordinances should not go into effect until March 4.[22] If the conventions had provided for their ordinances to go into effect after March 4, as Davis and some other prominent Southern leaders proposed, the result might have been different, for this would have bought time for emotions to cool, leading to the possibility of reconsideration and compromise.

Elected President of
the Confederate States

*J*efferson Davis went sadly back to Mississippi, not wishing to be president of a Southern confederacy, but preferring to hold high military rank in the army during a war that he felt was sure to come. Before he left his seat in the Senate, his colleagues held a meeting in Albert Gallatin Brown's room (Davis being absent because of sickness) to decide whether to withdraw at once or to wait until March 4 in order not to leave the Republicans in control of Congress to pass legislation hostile to the South. Senator Robert Toombs observed that to leave the Republicans in control of Congress would be worth a hundred thousand men to the North. In his valuable journal Senator Thomas Bragg of North Carolina, who opposed immediate secession, recorded on January 12, 1861, that at the meeting they decided to ignore pragmatic considerations and withdraw from the Senate immediately, motivated primarily by a sense of honor.[1] Such an emotional decision reflected an important aspect of the Southern mind in 1861, a devotion to honor regardless of consequences, that distinguished Southerners of the period from the more practical-minded Northerners.[2] At this meeting, Bragg recorded, they talked also about the formation of a provisional government for the seceded states and agreed that Senator Robert Toombs would probably be elected president of the Confederacy and "Davis in the opinion of all" would be general-in-chief of the army.

The legislature of Alabama had invited the seceding states to meet at Montgomery on February 4 to draw up a provisional constitution and to elect a provisional president and vice president. Accordingly, the so-called Montgomery convention of the six states of South Carolina, Georgia, Florida, Mississippi, Alabama, and Louisiana (the Texas delegation arrived late) drafted a provisional constitution that retained the basic elements of the United States Constitution with certain changes dictated by the desire to protect slavery and state rights more firmly. There were a few innovations, the principal ones being the election of the president for a single term of six years, the right of the president to veto items of appropriation bills, the provision that cabinet members could be given seats in Congress (which was not implemented), the establishment of a budget system, and the adoption of amendments to the constitution by a two-thirds vote of the states instead of a three-fourths vote as required by the United States Constitution. The fifty-five members voted by states, and they represented almost exclusively the wealthy, propertied class and slaveholders of their individual states.[3] They constituted during the first years of the Confederacy's existence a unicameral legislature that made such important decisions as opening the Mississippi River to the Northern states bordering on it. The opening of the Mississippi River was vital to obtaining the good-will of the Northwest, for it was a very important outlet for the trade of that region, and at this early stage of secession, there was hope that the states of the Ohio Valley and Upper Mississippi might form an alliance with the Confederacy.

In drawing up a constitution and choosing a president, the Montgomery convention acted in haste just as the secession conventions had done. It adopted a provisional constitution on February 8, four days after it had met, and the next day unanimously elected a president and vice president. There was hardly any campaigning for these two offices. Merton Coulter, an able historian of the Confederacy, states: "In this excessive zeal for unanimity and harmony seems to lie the explanation of why Jefferson Davis instead of Robert Toombs was elected President."[4] But this is too simple an explanation. Personal rivalries, ambitions, and animosities operated among some of the contenders to cancel each other, while Davis seems to have been exempt from the turmoil. Moreover, it was believed that his selection would be viewed favorably by Virginia, which was undecided. Robert Toombs and Howell Cobb of Georgia (the latter was elected president of the convention) were formidable candidates, but they were from a state that was divided by a surplus of aspirants, including the ever ambitious Alexander H. Stephens. Therefore the delegation from Georgia could not use its considerable power in choosing a president. Robert Barnwell Rhett and William L. Yancey, the great precipitators of the secession movement, were too extreme in their views to be in the running. It seems ironical that the convention selected Davis as president and Alexander H. Stephens as vice president—conservatives who had tried to delay the secession movement, men of such frail health that they were seriously handicapped in carrying out their overwhelming responsibilities.

Duncan F. Kenner, a wealthy sugar planter from Louisiana, a delegate to the Montgomery convention who became a Confederate senator and was chosen by Davis for a secret mission to France to propose the emancipation of the slaves in return for France's recognition and help, succinctly stated the reasons for the choice of Davis as Confederate president: "We were seeking the best man to fill the position, and the conviction at the time, in the minds of a large majority of the delegates, that Mr. Davis was the best qualified, from both his civil and military knowledge and experience, induced many to look upon Mr. Davis as the best selection that could be made."[5] Kenner added that Davis's known conservative views were also a factor in his election. Moreover, he was the outstanding senator from the Southern states in asserting Southern rights and Southern honor.

The selection by the Montgomery convention of Alexander H. Stephens for vice president was clearly a mistake. From the very beginning he had been opposed to secession, having little confidence that the experiment of establishing a Southern nation would succeed. Yet he accepted the job, apparently because he was intensely ambitious and loved honor and public office. A poor boy who had risen into the aristocracy, he had absorbed their chivalric ideals, and fought duels to maintain his honor. Stephens was a staunch supporter of slavery; shortly after his inauguration on March 21, 1861, at Savannah he made a speech in which he said that the Confederacy's "foundations are laid, its corner-stone rests upon the great truth, that the negro is not equal to the white man; that slavery—subordination to the superior race—is a natural and normal condition."[6] This forthright defense of slavery seems ironical today in a man whose slave plantation near Crawfordville, Georgia, was named Liberty Hall, and whose defense of civil liberties in wartime and advocacy of "constitutional liberty" did much to weaken the Confederacy. With his shrill voice and emaciated form, Stephens seemed unsuited to oratory, yet he was one of the great political speakers of the Old South. Attorney General Thomas Bragg described him in his journal: "so feeble frame yet such spirit and intellect."[7] Sick much of the time and dreading exposure to cold weather, he stayed away often from his duties in Richmond. Davis made a mistake by seldom consulting him. Yet, despite his fanatical support of state rights and civil liberties, Stephens advocated some wise policies, such as rushing cotton to Europe before the blockade became effective to set up a credit for purchase of supplies, a realistic tax policy, and efforts to obtain peace. In Georgia he and his younger brother Linton, a Harvard graduate with a handsome face and splendid physique, a striking contrast to Alexander, were focal points of the opposition to Davis and his nationalizing measures to win the war.[8]

Jefferson Davis was in his rose garden with his wife when a messenger arrived bearing the news that he had been elected president of the Confederate States of America. Neither he nor Mrs. Davis was elated, but he accepted the office as a duty imposed on him. Varina, in her memoir of her husband, expressed the opinion: "I thought his genius was military, but that as a party manager, he would not succeed. He did not know the arts of the politician and would not practice them if understood, and he did know those of war."[9] How right she was! Davis, who had recently been appointed major general of militia by the Mississippi governor, also believed that he was better suited to command in the field than to serve as president. But he loved glory and at the moment the office to which he had been elected was more prestigious than being a general in the Confederate army.

Before he left Brierfield on February 11 he provided for the care of his slaves and went ahead of Varina on a roundabout route over the disjointed one-track railroads, reaching Montgomery six days later. The difficult and cumbersome journey, necessitated by the fact that there was no railroad between Jackson, Mississippi, and Montgomery, was a vivid illustration of the decentralized, backward economy of the South that forebode ill for the success of the Confederacy in fighting against the much more centralized, industrialized North. At Montgomery the president received an enthusiastic ovation. All the way to the Confederate capital, except in Tennessee (which was significant also, for a vital railway ran through eastern Tennessee from Richmond), he made twenty-five speeches along the route. In Montgomery he was welcomed by the famed orator William L. Yancey, who proclaimed, "The man and the hour have met."

On February 18 Jefferson Davis was inaugurated. As this tall, slender man with the beautiful, far-reaching voice and dignified bearing delivered his inaugural address from the portico of the state house of Alabama, the crowd was gay and enthusiastic, not realizing that a long, disastrous war lay ahead. The band played a relatively new and lively tune, "Dixie"—composed ironically by a Northern man, Dan Emmett, a blackface minstrel—that was to become the unofficial anthem of the new nation. The thoughtful members of the crowd must have tried to estimate the president, whether he would measure up to his great responsibilities. In some respects they had more evidence than we have today regarding his career and abilities, but the historian has a valuable perspective that they did not have. Undoubtedly this perspective, the judgment of Jefferson Davis today, will change as revisionists arise in the future.

His inaugural address was not a great speech—in fact, it was not even equal to the demands of the occasion. He had little time to prepare it, and probably had no help from others, for statesmen wrote their own speeches then. It had the virtue of being very short in a day of long-winded orations. He appealed to the Declaration of Independence, which affirmed the American idea that governments rest upon the consent of the governed, as well as the right of revolution, which justified the Confederate states in establishing a separate government. The Confederacy wished peace with the North, he said, but it must be prepared, if need be, to defend its independence with the sword. If the people are called upon to make sacrifices, he declared, these are "not to be weighed in the balance against honor and right and liberty and equality." In humble tones he invoked God to guide the young republic.[10]

Davis's most immediate task was to appoint a cabinet. In making his selections he felt constrained by the strong state rights sentiment prevailing in the Confederacy to recognize the claims of the most prominent states. To recognize the claims of Georgia he appointed Robert Toombs secretary of state, although the two men did not like each other. For the position of secretary of the treasury, he was persuaded to appoint Christopher G. Memminger of South Carolina, who was recommended by Robert W. Barnwell, to whom Davis had first offered the post of secretary of state (he had declined). To what proved to be the most important position in the cabinet, the secretaryship of war, he appointed Leroy P. Walker, who had led the Alabama delegation from the Democratic convention in 1860 when it adopted the Douglas platform. Davis did not personally know either Walker or Memminger. The president selected Judah P. Benjamin, Louisiana senator in 1861, as attorney general, and as postmaster general, John H. Reagan, an ex-Texas congressman.

The South was regarded as an aristocratic society in the North, but it is significant that in 1860 few of the leading Southern statesmen were of aristocratic lineage. Postmaster General Reagan's father was a tanner, and at one time he himself had been an overseer. Stephen Mallory, the secretary of the navy, was the son of a Connecticut Yankee, who had aided his widowed mother in running a boardinghouse for sailors in Key West. Christopher G. Memminger of South Carolina was a German immigrant who had spent his early youth in a Charleston orphanage. Judah P. Benjamin was the son of a small Jewish merchant. The ablest diplomat of the Confederacy, John Slidell, was born in New York City, the son of a tallow chandler, who as a young man had emigrated to Louisiana. Davis, as noted, was the son of a substantial yeoman farmer, and was born in a house not much more imposing than the log cabin in which Abraham Lincoln was born. The same story of lowly origins could be told of many of the Civil War governors, such as Joseph E. Brown of Georgia, Zebulon B. Vance of North Carolina, John J. Pettus of Mississippi, John Letcher and "Extra Billy" Smith of Virginia. On the other hand, Davis's changing cabinet contained some representatives of the aristocracy, notably Robert M. T. Hunter, Robert Toombs, Leroy P. Walker, George W. Randolph, James A. Seddon, and John C. Breckinridge.[11]

In contrast with Lincoln's abler cabinet, the Confederate cabinet was constantly changing. There were fourteen different appointees for the six positions during four years. The fact that Davis had six secretaries of war can be partly explained by his continual interference with that department, but he generally allowed the other secretaries to have their way, and resignations from these departments occurred for a variety of reasons.

The ebullient Robert Toombs, despite his unquestionable ability, was miscast for the State Department. His restless energies found little outlet in this department, and he declared that the Department of State was contained in his hat. He chafed at performing such routine duties as issuing letters of marque and reprisal for Confederate privateers and publishing the acts of Congress. He longed for the more active and glorious life in the Confederate army. Also he resented the fact that the cabinet did not accept some of his opinions.[12] Consequently he resigned after five months in office, and Senator R. M. T. Hunter of Virginia replaced him on July 24, 1861. Toombs asked Davis to appoint him as a brigadier general although he had no military training, and Davis with misgivings humored him because of his prestige as a politician. Toombs was a miserable failure as a general, and his superior officers refused to recommend him for promotion. Because the president declined to nominate him for promotion, Toombs turned bitterly against him, resigned from the army, and went back to Georgia, where he was a leader of the opposition to Davis. Before his resignation Mrs. James Chesnut Jr., the wife of the South Carolina senator, wrote in her diary: "Toombs is ready for a revolution. He curses freely everything Confederate from a president to a horse boy and thinks there is a conspiracy against him in the army."[13]

As a member of Davis's cabinet, Toombs wrote the instructions for the first Confederate commissioners to Europe, and for the commissioners to Washington. But his chief significance was, along with Secretary of War Walker, to advocate an aggressive military policy of invading the Northern states at the beginning of the war. The rebel war clerk at Richmond, J. B. Jones, in his gossipy diary, has described his advocacy of this policy while drawing a vivid portrait of Toombs:

> He is a portly gentleman, but with the pale face of the student and the marks of a deep thinker. To gaze at him in repose, the casual spectator would suppose, from his neglect of dress, that he was a planter in moderate circumstances, and of course not gifted with extraordinary powers of intellect; but let him open his mouth and the delusion vanishes. At the time alluded to he was surrounded by the rest of the cabinet, in our office, and the topic was the policy of the war. He was for taking the initiative, and carrying the war into the enemy's country. And as he warmed with the subject, the *man* seemed to vanish, and the *genius* alone was visible. He was most emphatic in the advocacy of his policy, and bold almost to rashness in his denunciations of the merely defensive idea. He was opposed to all delays, as fraught with danger; the enemy were in the field and their purposes pronounced. Why wait to see what they meant to do? . . . he was for making the war as terrible as possible from the beginning.[14]

Christopher Memminger entered the cabinet with the reputation of being an able banker, an advocate of sound money, and a champion of the public school system in South Carolina. But his unfortunate personality produced friction. Chief of Ordnance Josiah Gorgas described him as follows: "Mr. Memminger treats others with rudeness, and is, besides, dogmatical, narrow-minded and slow. He places every fresh paper at the bottom of his pile and makes it await its turn patiently without regard to its importance. . . . Whenever I leave Mr. M. after an interview, I feel somehow as tho' I had been trying to do something very much out of the way, so injured and *put on* does he represent himself. He always assumes a bristly offensive, and makes you appear to be on the aggressive toward him." There was great opposition to Memminger among Congressmen, with whom he especially disagreed in regard to taxation policy. Toward the end of the war Gorgas observed that "Mr. Memminger has ruined our finances (with the able assistance of a weak Congress), and yet the President refused to the last moment to acknowledge that Mr. M. was the wrong man."[15] Although his religious devoutness may have had little to do with his efficiency as secretary of the treasury, and although it may have supported his incorruptibility, his fanaticism caused some critics to make fun of him. J. B. Jones recorded on June 22, 1861, that Memminger proposed that the War Department cease work on Sunday, but the secretary rejected his proposal.[16] Senator Louis T. Wigfall of Texas ironically observed that Memminger had proposed to finance the Confederacy by leaving collection bags in the church.[17] But Memminger applied system to the department and his strict rules caused the assistant secretary of the treasury, Philip Clayton, to resign.[18]

A far different type of man was the Secretary of War, Leroy P. Walker. William H. Russell, *London Times* correspondent and trained observer, described him as "tall, lean, straight-haired, angular, with fiery impulsive eyes and manner—a ruminator of tobacco and a profuse spitter—a lawyer, I believe, certainly not a soldier; ardently devoted to the Cause, and confident to the last degree of its speedy success."[19] Indeed, Walker predicted that soon the Confederate flag would be waving over the Capitol in Washington, if not over Faneuil Hall in Boston. He was a courteous gentleman but according to Mrs. Chesnut a "slow coach," and he himself declared that the War Department was not suited to a gentleman. He had the same fault attributed to Davis by his critics, namely, trying to attend to too many details that should have been left to subordinates. In addition, he was harassed by ill health (he constantly chewed and spat tobacco) and was swamped by many applications for commissions in the army. Davis had no confidence in his ability to give military orders, and so the president made the military decisions and reduced his war secretary to the status of a clerk. Accordingly, on September 16, 1861, Walker resigned as a result of severe criticism and the breakdown of his health from overwork. The president accepted his resignation and honored his request to be appointed a brigadier general.[20]

The man who succeeded him as war secretary was the Attorney General Judah P. Benjamin. He was without military experience but was probably the most intelligent man in the cabinet, often called "the brains of the Confederacy" and "that ever smiling Jew."[21] (His subtle and complex personality will be described in the chapter on Confederate diplomacy.) Like Walker, he

was unsuited to direct the War Department, and became thoroughly disliked by some of the outstanding generals. Beauregard had a quarrel with him
and he so antagonized General Thomas J. "Stonewall" Jackson that the latter
offered his resignation, but the quarrel was smoothed over by Davis. Benjamin
believed in enforcing the law and army regulations, but the men over whom
he had authority were highly individualistic, "touchy" Southerners, notorious
for their cavalier disregard of the law. The disasters of the surrender of
Roanoke Island and of Fort Donelson occurred while Benjamin was secretary
of war, and he was especially blamed for the lack of preparation and reinforcement of the roops on Roanoke Island. Finally he was glad to leave the hornet's
nest of criticism when Davis on March 24, 1862, appointed him secretary of
state, a position he held until the collapse of the Confederacy.

After Benjamin left the War Department Davis appointed to the post an
aristocrat, George W. Randolph, a grandson of Thomas Jefferson, who soon
quarreled with the commander-in-chief and resigned. Then Davis appointed
to the vacancy his ablest secretary of war, James A. Seddon, another Virginia
aristocrat. Seddon was a quiet, unassuming gentleman whose plantation,
Sabot Hill, near Fredericksburg was a center of classic culture and good
society. He had been a successful lawyer, a member of Congress, and a
Calhoun leader. He was tall, slender, and emaciated, with a face that looked
somewhat like that of a Jewish rabbi, especially as he habitually wore a black
scullcap. But beneath his scholarly demeanor was a man of rare intelligence
and decision-making capacity. He had great influence on Davis, not only because of his intellect, but because of his tact and his deferential manner
toward the president. Only his frail health and lack of humor impeded his
effectiveness; nevertheless, he performed the duties of his office with industry
and vigor. He was the cabinet member who recognized the tremendous importance of the West in the military plans of the Confederacy.

John H. Reagan, the postmaster general, was one of the three original
cabinet officers whom Davis kept to the very end. Yet he was the member of
the cabinet who frequently opposed Davis's decisions, confuting the criticism
that Davis kept only "yes men" around him. Reagan was a man of common
sense—rugged, forthright, and efficient. The Confederate Constitution required that after a brief period the postal department should be self-supporting,
and Reagan accomplished this remarkable feat in an inflated economy, but he
was able to do this only because mail carriers were willing to accept very low
compensation, because they were exempt from the draft. When Reagan first
conferred with the president after his appointment he bluntly told him that
he would not have voted for him for president, because he thought he was
better suited to have a career in the Confederate army. Also, in one of the
earliest cabinet meetings, the secretary of war said that he could raise and
equip an army of 10,000 men, and asked how they should be distributed.
Reagan advocated sending 5,000 men to Louisville and 5,000 to Covington,
Kentucky, despite the fact that Kentucky had not given permission and such a

movement would violate state rights. But it probably would have been a wise decision, and might have led to the Confederacy holding the Ohio River as well as obtaining a large accession of soldiers and valuable supplies. He was the only member of the cabinet who opposed Lee's invasion of Pennsylvania in 1863, and he was an early but unpopular advocate of arming the slaves to fight for the Confederacy.[22]

One of Davis's best cabinet appointments was Stephen R. Mallory of Florida as secretary of the navy. Yet Mallory was opposed by the Florida delegation because he had been tardy in joining the secession movement, and the president had to pressure the Senate to approve the appointment. Mallory had been chairman of the U.S. Senate Committee on Naval Affairs and proved to be an innovative secretary, especially in building powerful iron-clad ships such as the *Virginia,* which fought the *Monitor* outside of Hampton Roads, Virginia, in March, 1862. Also he was very successful in acquiring and using a fleet of commerce raiders that destroyed much of the Northern commerce. Less publicized were his promotion of using torpedoes against war ships of the enemy and the construction of the submarine, *H. L. Hunley,* that destroyed a warship off the coast of Charleston. He had the misfortune of seeing most of his iron-clad ships burned by the Confederate army to prevent their capture by the enemy.

The leader of the executive team of the Confederacy, Jefferson Davis, provoked controversy while he was president, and in the end he was accused of being a despot. Yet at the beginning of his administration when Russell of the *London Times* interviewed him in Montgomery, before the capital was removed to Richmond, he seemed to be universally admired within the Confederacy. He did not impress the British observer as favorably as he had expected, but in contrast with the Northern president he had the appearance of a gentleman. Physically, Russell wrote, he had a

> slight, light figure, little exceeding middle height, and holds himself erect and straight. He was dressed in a rustic suit of slate-colored stuff, with a black silk handkerchief round his neck; his manner is plain, and rather reserved and drastic; his head is well formed, with a fine full forehead, square and high, covered with innumerable fine lines and wrinkles, features regular, though the cheek bones are too high, and the jaws too hollow to be handsome; the lips are thin, flexible, and curved, the chin square, well defined; the nose very regular with wide nostrils, and the eyes deep-set, large and full—one seems nearly blind and is partly covered with a film, owing to excruciating attacks of neuralgia and tic. Wonderful to relate, he does not chew, and is neat and clean-looking, with hair trimmed, and boots brushed. The expression of his face is anxious, he has a very haggard, care-worn, and pain-drawn look, though no trace of anything but the utmost confidence and the greatest decision could be detected in his conversation.[23]

He did not mention that Davis had a short, grayish beard under his chin and covering his throat (as shown in a picture of him in the uniform of a major general of Mississippi militia).

Certain questions arise concerning Davis's administration of the Confederate government, two of which are pertinent to this chapter. Did he consult his cabinet sufficiently, and was he a good administrator? When W. M. Brooks, president of the Alabama Secession Convention, wrote him on March 13, 1862, a severely critical letter, accusing him of not holding cabinet meetings, Davis replied that he was wrong, for cabinet meetings were held nearly every week.[24] Confuting the charge that the president seldom held cabinet meetings, the secretary of the navy wrote, in his diary, that Davis conferred individually with his cabinet officers daily and held cabinet meetings two or three times a week, but that these meetings were not fruitful, involving four or five hours of tedium that failed to determine anything. One reason for their futility, he observed, was Davis's "uncontrollable tendency to digression."[25] At another time, he complained that the president did not consult his cabinet on military appointments or as to his plans of campaign, which was obviously an unfair statement: consider his consultation of the cabinet, extending through two or three days, before Lee's invasion of Pennsylvania in the summer of 1863. But Attorney General Bragg, shortly before he left the cabinet in April, 1862, confided to his diary a regret that he had been so little consulted.[26] Nevertheless, the president usually accepted the consensus judgment of his cabinet. Only in the War Department did he seriously interfere with the decisions of his cabinet officers; the other secretaries usually had their way. Furthermore, he stoutly defended them from criticism and as a rule supported their recommendations and proposals, which he submitted to Congress.

As president, was Jefferson Davis a good administrator? The critics (and they were many) maintained that he was a failure. Robert Kean, chief of the Confederate Bureau of War, who had considerable opportunity to judge him first hand, commented in his diary, June 14, 1863, that even Davis's friends admitted that he was no administrator—"the worst judge of men in the world, apt to take up with a man of feeble intellect or character and when he has once done so holds on with unreasoning tenacity."[27] Again, Kean was caustic in writing on July 28, 1863, that the president preferred to have around him "accommodating civil-spoken persons." Both secretaries of war under whom Kean served, he reported, complained to their intimates of the "endless tediousness of consultations which yield no results." He quotes the intelligent, spirited secretary of war, James A. Seddon, as saying that the president was the most difficult man to get along with whom he had ever known. Neither Davis nor Robert E. Lee, "a man of few words," was in Kean's judgment a great leader in council.[28]

But this brilliant young Virginian was hostile to Davis because of the quarrel between the president and Kean's superior, Secretary of War George W. Randolph (to be discussed later), and he undoubtedly exaggerated Davis's deficiencies. But another capable witness, the chief of Confederate ordnance, General Josiah Gorgas, a warm friend of the president, was comparatively free from prejudice in judging his chief, yet wrote in his journal on August 6, 1863:

The President seems determined to respect the opinions of no one; and has, I fear, little appreciation of services rendered, unless the party enjoys his good opinion. He seems to be an indifferent judge of men, and is guided more by prejudice than by sound discriminating judgment. I have been surprised to hear his condemnation of men and measures—yet apparently without any idea that it was for him to correct them. He sneers continuously at Mr. Mallory and his navy and is at no pains to conceal his opinions before that secretary; yet he never controls him in any respect; nor will he yield to the opinion of the country which has long since pointed to a change in that branch of the service.[29]

Secretary Stephen Mallory's testimony on the president as director of the government and manager of the cabinet was conflicting. He blamed Davis for devoting too much time to petty details that should have been handled by subordinates, with the consequence that he was constantly overworked and ill. Mallory thought that the president was a good judge of men (contrary to the conclusions of other critics, and of the author), but that his main fault as an administrator was a lack of prompt business habits. This fault was all the more strange since Davis had the reputation, derived from his administration of the War Department during Pierce's presidency, of being "a ready man prompt in making decisions and acting upon them." Actually, Mallory wrote, he was "singularly cautious and dilatory," "not only because he habitually undertook more labor than he could accomplish, but that much of his time was given to unimportant details." This absorption in details that others also noticed, the secretary of the navy attributed to "his exalted sense of justice and the desire to be right.[30]

President Lincoln was also a loose administrator, but he was a master at handling men. Davis had had little experience as a political administrator. As was the case with Lincoln, he had never been the governor of a state, and as secretary of war he directed only seven clerks and supervised an army of between 10,000 and 15,000 men. As Confederate president, his task was much more complicated. He presided over 70,257 civilian employees, the largest number being in the War Department and the smallest number, twenty-nine, being in the State Department.[31] Even as the master of a slave plantation, he was, like the majority of planters, far from being a tight, careful administrator. The Confederacy has rightly been compared to an underdeveloped country fighting today against a well-organized and comparatively powerful modern nation. It had to organize everything quickly from "scratch," and neither Davis nor many other Southern politicians had the capacity or training to do so effectively.

The First Great Decisions

The explosive point, where war was likely to start, was the unfinished Fort Sumter in the harbor of Charleston, three miles from the city. On the night after Christmas, 1860, Major Robert Anderson, a Kentuckian who was in command of several federal forts around the harbor, moved his garrison from the exposed Fort Moultrie to Fort Sumter. President Buchanan was upset by this sudden violation of the status quo in this area, for he had not given a specific order for this transfer of troops, and Secretary of War John B. Floyd, a Virginian, wished the president to order the enterprising officer back to his original post. Senator Jefferson Davis and other Southern representatives in Washington were excited, for they believed that Anderson had violated a gentleman's agreement with the president to maintain the status quo, and they went to the president to demand the recall of the bold officer to his original station. Although Davis had influence with Buchanan, he was unable to get him to recall Anderson, for not only was the latter following discretionary instructions, but the president realized that Northern public opinion would be outraged by such a surrender to Southern demands. To add to the tension, an unarmed merchant ship, the *Star of the West,* with troops and supplies to reinforce Fort Sumter, was fired upon by the South Carolinians as it attempted to enter Charleston harbor, and forced to turn back.[1] Jefferson Davis again went to see Buchanan and said to him, referring to the status quo agreement between the president and the South Carolina members of the House of Representatives, "Now, Mr. President, you are surrounded with blood and dishonor on all sides."[2]

President Buchanan did not believe that the Southern states had a constitutional right to secede, but he also did not believe that he had the authority to coerce them back into the Union. Therefore, he adopted a holding pattern until the new president took office on March 4. To negotiate with the government in Washington, President Davis appointed as commissioners Martin J. Crawford, a Georgia congressman, who had voted for Breckinridge in 1860, and André B. Roman of Louisiana and John Forsyth, editor of the Mobile *Register,* both of whom had voted for Douglas. They were instructed to negotiate for the recognition of the Confederate government, for the surrender of all forts and public property within the limits of the Confederacy, and for a fair division of the public debt. The Confederate Congress had declared on February 25 that the Mississippi River was freely opened to the navigation of all states, so this was not an issue to be settled. But the advisability of surrendering the federal forts in Confederate territory (most of which had already been seized, with the notable exceptions of Fort Pickens at Pensacola and Fort Sumter) was a burning issue.

President Lincoln's inaugural address was awaited with considerable anxiety in the Southern states. It was surprisingly moderate in tone, seeking to quiet the fears of Southerners on many subjects, but on the all-important question of the status of the forts he warned ominously that the government would hold all public property in the Southern states. Lincoln's inaugural, which seems so inoffensive today, must be considered in the context of the profound suspicion that Southerners had of any statement made by a Northern Republican.[3]

On March 8 the Confederate commissioners requested an interview with Secretary of State William H. Seward, but he flatly refused to see them. He did communicate with them unofficially, however, through Associate Supreme Court Justice John A. Campbell of Alabama, and gave to the latter assurances that Fort Sumter would be evacuated. At one time, all of Lincoln's cabinet, with the exception of Postmaster General Montgomery Blair, favored the evacuation of Fort Sumter. But Lincoln wavered, influenced in part by a mistaken conception of the strength of Unionist sentiment in the South that he believed would prevail, and on the other hand, by a fear of the effects of surrendering the fort on Northern public opinion and in dividing the Republican party.[4] On April 8 he ordered a relief expedition prepared under the command of Gustavus Vasa Fox, who had visited Charleston and had predicted that such an expedition would be successful. Lincoln sent a clerk in the State Department to inform Governor Francis Pickens that he was sending the relief expedition carrying both troops and provisions, but that only supplies, and not troops, would be landed unless the relief expedition should be fired on.

The moment of decision had arrived for the Confederate cabinet. Both President Davis and President Lincoln were extremely anxious to avoid a war. Charles W. Ramsdell has argued persuasively that Lincoln, foreseeing that a war would have to be fought to preserve the Union, adopted a shrewd, calculated strategy of forcing the Confederacy to fire the first shot, thus placing on the South the onus of starting the war, but such a Machiavellian strategy seems unlikely.[5] As the relief expedition was approaching, Beauregard telegraphed Davis for instructions on whether to take Fort Sumter before it arrived. The president called a cabinet meeting, which debated earnestly what to do. From a dubious source—namely, Robert Toombs's early biographer, Pleasant A. Stovall—the Georgian statesman was reported to have advised against any move to fire on the fort, saying that by so doing the Confederacy would activate a hornet's nest and lose every friend in the North. But the credibility of this colorful story is suspect.[6] It was completely out of character for the pugnacious Georgian, and contradicts his later actions.

Davis sent a telegram to General Beauregard to reduce Fort Sumter unless Major Anderson agreed to surrender. Accordingly, Beauregard dispatched his aides to the fort to demand this surrender. Major Anderson refused, but observed that he would be forced to surrender on April 15 because of lack of provisions unless prior to that time he received "controlling instructions from my Government or additional supplies."[7] The aides were fire-eaters and considered Anderson's terms unsatisfactory; they announced that the bombardment of the fort would begin at four-thirty in the morning on April 12. After thirty-three hours of bombardment, the fort was surrendered. The treatment of Major Anderson and his troops at the surrender reflected the chivalrous ideals of the South, as well as perhaps the respect of a student for his teacher, for Beauregard had been Anderson's student at West Point.

This momentous event was followed by Lincoln's request for 75,000 militia from the states and his proclamation of a blockade, ultimately of the eight Southern ports. Such acts meant coercion of the seceded states, with the result that Virginia, North Carolina, Tennessee, and Arkansas joined the Southern Confederacy. Kentucky remained neutral for a while, and one of the great achievements of Lincoln was his patient, shrewd handling of his native state. In early September General Leonidas Polk, on his own initiative and against the wishes of Davis, moved his army to seize the strategic position of Columbus, Kentucky, at the junction of the Ohio and Mississippi rivers, violating the neutrality of the state. Thereupon, Kentucky abandoned its policy of neutrality, declaring itself on the side of the Union.

The second important decision that President Davis had to make came right after the astonishing Confederate victory of Manassas, or Bull Run, in northern Virginia on July 21. At that time the Confederacy faced its first military test, when Brigadier General Irvin McDowell led an army of approximately 35,000 men, mostly green volunteers, from Washington to capture the Confederate capital, which had late in the previous May been unwisely moved from Montgomery to Richmond. Opposing the Union army was General Pierre G. T. Beauregard with approximately 30,000 equally green troops, stationed behind Bull Run Creek and in front of the village of Manassas, thirty-five miles distant from Washington. It was a strategic location because it lay at the junction of two railroads, one leading to the Shenandoah Valley, sixty miles away, where General Joseph E. Johnston commanded a force of 8,000 men against the Union general, Robert Patterson, seventy years old. The fortunes of the battle at Manassas wavered back and forth in a contest that has been described as "a battle of blunders."[8] About half of the men on each side were not engaged in the fighting. Thomas Jonathan Jackson, who before the war was an eccentric professor of mathematics at the Virginia Military Institute at Lexington, distinguished himself by his bravery and staunchness, winning the sobriquet of "Stonewall." The tide of battle was turned when Brigadier General E. Kirby Smith arrived with the first detachment of Johnston's army from Winchester in the valley on the Manassas Gap Railroad, attacking McDowell's troops from the flank and rear, leading to a rout of the Union army and its disorderly flight to the safety of Washington.[9] The order for the junction of Johnston's army with Beauregard's was given by President Davis, although Beauregard claimed credit for the idea.[10]

While the fighting was in progress Davis was "itching" to go to the battlefield but restrained himself, remaining in Richmond and directing reinforcements to the embattled army until the hour of victory. On the night of the encounter, after eleven o'clock, he conferred with his generals and was surprised that a pursuit had not been ordered. He sat down and began writing such an order, but when he was told that the officer who had reported the rout was known in the old army by the nickname of "Crazy Hill," he decided not to give the order of pursuit.[11] Both Beauregard and Johnston concurred in the wisdom of this decision. The opportunity to pursue the routed army was lost on that night, for in the morning it rained so heavily that the roads became impassable bogs of mud.

After the battle there was a disgraceful quarrel over whether the Confederate army should have pursued the enemy to Washington and captured the nation's capital. Some of the Richmond newspapers criticized Davis for the army's failure to pursue, thereby losing the glorious fruits of victory. Beauregard blamed the president for his inability to pursue the enemy because of inadequate food and transportation.[12] Against this charge Commissary General Lucius B. Northrop defended his department by replying (some years after the war) that "there was plenty of provision for a march on Washington." General Johnston, on the other hand, defended the decision not to risk defeat by a pursuit on the ground that the Confederate army was more disorganized by victory than was the defeated army. Furthermore, Washington was defended by formidable fortifications. To Beauregard's excuses Davis replied in a letter of August 1: "I think you are unjust to yourself in putting your failure to pursue the enemy to Washington to the account of short supplies of subsistence and transportation."[13] Rather, Davis remarked, the true cause was their ignorance of the extent of the enemy's rout, and this was undoubtedly correct—although the disorganization of the Confederate army was another factor. Davis's letter to the glory-seeking General Beauregard had a noble quality when he observed, "Enough was done for glory," advising him to ignore the criticisms of the uninformed (advice that he himself seldom followed). On August 10 Beauregard replied that he did not mean to say that Washington could have been taken immediately after Manassas, but later.[14] At the same time he assured the president that he had no desire to become a candidate for president, which some of his admirers were advocating.

The Southern people were deeply disappointed that so little had come from great expectations. Mary B. Chesnut, in her diary for early August, expressed not only her own feelings but probably those of a large majority of the Southern people: "Time and tide wait for no man, and there was a tide in our affairs which might have led to Washington. We did not take it, and so lost our fortune."[15] She wrote that Commissary General Northrop was the most abused man in Richmond. Actually, however, it was probably an illusion that the Confederacy had lost a golden opportunity. The Union army was not as badly defeated as portrayed; three of its brigades were intact and the fortifications of the city were a deterrent. Probably Major General George B. McClellan, who was called from West Virginia to take command, exaggerated in reporting that when he arrived at the capital the city was defenseless, he had no army to command, and the dash of a regiment of cavalry could almost have taken the city, a remark that circulated in the Confederacy.[16]

On October 14 Beauregard published a long grandiloquent official report of the battle of Manassas, or Bull Run. He attributed to himself rather than to Davis the plan of ordering Johnston's army to join his. Davis first read it in synopsis form in a newspaper, which caused a sensation. He was angered by its tone of self-congratulation. He observed in a letter to Beauregard that the newspapers claimed he had overruled Beauregard in a plan to advance after Bull Run, and that the newspapers were sustained by the general's report. He informed the general that his report appeared to be "an attempt to exalt yourself at my expense."[17] Thus began a quarrel that ripened during the course of the war. Abraham Lincoln, with his noble quality of self-effacement, would almost certainly have avoided such a petty quarrel, which may have had a negative effect on the war.

At approximately the same time, Davis had a bitter controversy with Joseph E. Johnston over the latter's rank. Davis nominated to Congress the ranking of the Confederate generals as follows: (1) Samuel Cooper of New Jersey as adjutant general, the position that he had held in the United States Army; (2) Albert Sidney Johnston; (3) Robert E. Lee; and (4) Joseph E. Johnston. In the United States Army J. E. Johnston had held the higher rank of brigadier general of the Quartermaster Department, while Lee was only a lieutenant colonel. The Confederate Congress had provided by law that when U.S. officers joined the Confederate army rank in this army should correspond with the rank held in the U.S. Army. Johnston resented Davis's recommendation to the Congress of a rank for him lower than he believed that he deserved.

Brooding over what he regarded as an injustice, Johnston sent to the president on September 12 a captious letter complaining of his ranking. Always supersensitive to criticism, Davis was angered by its tone and two days afterward replied: "Sir I have just received and read your letter of the 12 inst. Its language as you say, is unusual, its arguments and statements utterly one-sided and its insinuations as unfortunate as unbecoming."[18] Just the day before receiving Johnston's letter, Davis had written a letter to the egotistical general settling the question of command, placing Johnston clearly in top command over Beauregard and signing the letter "Your friend." But after this quarrel, relations between the two men became distinctly cool and eventually bitter. Thereafter, Johnston was uncooperative and annoyed the president by failing to give him necessary military information and neglecting to file reports with the War Department. Moreover, Johnston was constantly asking for reinforcements and, when given these, failed to fight, constantly retreating before the enemy.

The president, it now seems, made a serious error in withholding from Johnston the rank that he thought rightly belonged to him. In his diary, Secretary of the Navy Stephen Mallory wrote that Judah P. Benjamin, who had quarreled with both Johnston and Beauregard while acting secretary of war, constantly influenced the president in his low opinion of both generals. Benjamin's favorite theme, Mallory wrote, was their want of ability. He maintained that Johnston wouldn't fight, and thus it would do no good to reinforce him.[19] There is a relatively untold story of the quarrels, divisions, jealousies, resignations because of lack of promotion, selfishness, failure of generals to cooperate with each other, and drunkenness among the Confederate officers—but it is only the old story of human nature in all ages.

A third extremely important decision that Davis was called upon to make was necessitated by the declining enthusiasm in volunteering for army service. Since the founding of the American republic the United States had a tradition against a standing army but had relied for defense on the state militia, to which all able-bodied white men, 18 to 45 years old, were required to belong. President Davis observed to William H. Russell that although travelers made fun of the profusion of military titles (especially in the South), "the fact is, we are a military nation . . . perhaps we are the only people in the world where gentlemen go to a military academy who do not intend to follow the profession of arms."[20] The South was particularly martial-minded, partly because of the need to prevent slave insurrection, but also because of the tradition of the gentleman, the cavalier on horseback. This thesis, ably argued by John Hope Franklin, has been rejected by the English scholar, Marcus Cunliffe, who maintains that the South was no more military than other sections of the country.[21] But when one considers the fact that the Confederacy in 1860 had a white population of only 5.5 million while the North had a population of 21.5 million whites, or odds of four to one, and that 313 of the 1,108 officers in the United States Army in 1861 resigned their commissions at the beginning of the war, the statistics tend to confirm the conclusion that the South was more inclined to the military life than the North. Furthermore, although the proportion of Southerners and Northerners enlisted in the armies during the Civil War is in dispute, because of incomplete records, it would seem that the proportion of those that fought for the Confederacy sharply outnumbered the proportion that fought for the Union.

Volunteering, however, was enthusiastic both in the Confederacy and in the North at the war's beginning. Confederate Secretary Leroy Walker reported that so many men volunteered that he had to refuse 200,000 would-be soldiers because he could not arm them. A somewhat similar situation existed in the North. Local leaders and politicians recruited soldiers very much as did the Alabama planter, Daniel Hundley, a graduate of the University of Virginia, who had written a pioneer sociological study entitled *Social Relations in Our Southern States*. In his diary he has vividly described his experience in recruiting a company of volunteers in northern Alabama. He rode horseback through the country, making stump speeches at barbecues and political gatherings. Believing that "God manifestly is on the side of the South. May we by our acts in the future keep Him with us," he could urge men to volunteer with fervor and sincere conviction. By July 18, 1861, he was able to recruit thirty-seven men and to organize a company that elected him captain. On July 28 he got his men to camp at Memphis, but he was quickly disillusioned by observing the demoralizing influence of camp life on his simple, unsophisticated country boys: wickedness flourished. He recorded on December 6, 1861: "After pay day—nothing but gambling, drinking, swearing, and quarreling."[22]

From the beginning of the Confederacy, Davis had discounted the illusion of the Southern people that a Southern soldier was much superior to the city-bred Northern soldier. He observed in a cabinet meeting that, although "men of the South were as a rule more ready to resent personal insult than those of the North," in organizing its military forces the Confederate government should recognize the equality of Northern and Southern soldiers.[23] When the provisional Congress was considering enlistments, Davis advocated enlistments for three years or the duration of the war. Congress, however, anticipating a short war, at first wished to permit enlistments of a Confederate army of 100,000 men for as little as sixty days. Finally it accepted a compromise of twelve months. But as early as November 30, 1860, at a dinner in the White House of the Confederacy attended by the attorney general, Thomas Bragg, the president spoke of the discontent and mismanagement of the twelve-month volunteers, and his fear that they would not reenlist despite the offer of a $50 bonus and a two-month furlough. Their enlistments would expire in the spring of 1862, just when Richmond was threatened by a formidable Union army under General George B. McClellan. Faced by this danger and urged by generals Robert E. Lee and Thomas J. Jackson, Davis on March 29, 1862, recommended the passage of the first conscription act in American history, and on April 16 Congress responded by passing such an act.

This measure conscripted able-bodied white males between the ages of 18 and 35 years, and required three years of military service of those already in the army. It was seriously marred by allowing substitutes and by permitting the drafted men to elect their own officers below the rank of colonel. Exempted were industrial workers, railroad men and telegraph operators, state office-holders, schoolteachers of twenty pupils, professors, mail carriers, one editor for each newspaper, Quakers, apothecaries, and so on. To this list was added shortly, an exemption that caused much grumbling and discontent among the nonslaveholders, namely, the exemption of overseers of twenty slaves. Although necessary, it gave the poor people a handle to maintain that it was "a rich man's war and a poor man's fight." Actually, the number of slaveowners and overseers exempted was small: according to a report of the Conscript Bureau, only 200 in Virginia, 120 in North Carolina, 301 in South Carolina, and 201 in Georgia. In December, 1863, Congress abolished the system of allowing substitutes and placed stringent regulations in regard to the exemption of overseers, excluding only those overseeing fifteen slaves that delivered to the government certain specified amounts of meat. As the war went on so great was the need for more men to counterbalance the rapid increase of the Northern armies, that Davis recommended drafting those between 35 and 45 years of age and 18-year-olds, and such a law was passed, on September 27, 1862. A third law in February, 1864, drafted men from 17 to 50, though the boys of 17 and the men between 45 and 50 were to be employed only as home guards or reserves.[24]

In the latter part of the war Georgia and South Carolina enacted laws drafting for the state militia those men between 50 and 60 and youths 16 years old, but they were not to be used outside of their states.[25] One man alarmed by South Carolina's new draft law was the poet and novelist, William Gilmore Simms, who had been foremost in urging secession. On January 9, 1865, the elderly romancer sent to Governor Andrew Magrath a plea for exemption from military service. He was fifty-nine years old at the time and wore "a long gray beard, like a Jewish father or Swedenborgian." He was living alone with his slaves, who cheered him by their devotion, for his wife and fifteen children were dead. He based his plea for military exemption on the ground that he could hardly walk any distance because of hemorrhoids, from which he had suffered for thirty years and because of an enlarged testicle.[26]

As waging the war resulted in ever increasing demands for more soldiers, Davis supported a policy of scraping the bottom of the barrel for additional manpower. Modern historians have criticized this policy of "overmobilization," as they call it, by which too large a proportion of the manpower was withdrawn from the production of food crops, especially meat, as well as from industry and transportation. General Josiah Gorgas also questioned its wisdom, writing in his diary on January 31, 1864: "It is simply absurd to call on all to fight."[27] Those most unsuitable should stay on the home front and devote themselves to agriculture, the arts, mining, and manufacturing. Gorgas criticized calling his workingmen in the munitions shops at every alarm to defend Richmond. Also, Lee would not release badly needed skilled mechanics from the army. Mallory complained that the president refused to permit a man to leave the army to work on gunboats for the navy.

An unpleasant problem that arose early in Davis's administration was what the Confederate response should be to Northern atrocities. When the captured crewmen of the privateer, *Savannah,* were threatened with execution as pirates, Davis wrote on July 6, 1861, to President Lincoln that if the threat was carried out he would order a like number of Northern prisoners executed.[28] On August 1, 1862, he called his cabinet into session to consider what he should do about the atrocities committed by several Northern generals against Southern prisoners and civilians. The cabinet unanimously replied that retaliation should be used only in extremities. But in a second meeting held the next day Secretary Mallory reversed his opinion, holding that "federal prisoners in Southern hands should be held to answer for the barbarities threatened upon Southern people." We should not treat the Northern enemy, he said, upon "the basis of civilized warfare when they are waging upon us a war of desolation and extermination."[29] But later Mallory changed his opinion again and agreed that the Confederacy should wage the war on the basis of honor and avoid retaliations. Davis, dominated by Southern ideals of chivalry to women, declared that in the case of Benjamin Butler, who had issued the famous proclamation of June, 1862, that the women of New Orleans caught insulting his troops were to be treated as prostitutes, he was to be regarded as an outlaw and executed at the moment of arrest. Both sides accused each other of atrocities—the North cited the Confederate burning of Chambersburg, Pennsylvania, the "massacree" of Negro soldiers at Fort Pillow, and prison conditions at Andersonville, Georgia.

The president and the Confederate Congress were especially aroused to resentment by the North's using Negro troops led by white officers, and by the preliminary Emancipation Proclamation of President Lincoln. On December 24, 1862, Davis practically threatened death to slave troops and their white officers who were captured by ordering them to be turned over to the states and dealt with as agents to instigate slave war. The Confederate Congress on April 30, 1863, voted that white officers leading Negro troops should be "deemed as inciting servile insurrection," and when captured should be put to death. After Lincoln issued his Emancipation Proclamation on January 1, freeing the slaves in the seceded states, Davis condemned it as encouraging slaves to assassinate their masters, announcing that commissioned officers carrying it out would be dealt with as engaged in inciting slaves to revolt, and that captured slaves enlisted as soldiers would be treated as unwilling instruments and discharged to their homes on parole.[30] Yet within fifteen months the Confederacy itself was enlisting Negro soldiers.

Despite his vindictive feelings toward the atrocities of the Northern army, Davis was essentially a compassionate, humane man, a fact that was revealed in his attitude toward pardoning Confederate deserters. According to John H. Reagan, he never approved a single death sentence for deserters who appealed to him. To enforce the military code, Reagan reported, "General Lee found it necessary to have some deserters shot before the record was sent to the President, as he feared without doing this his army would become too much depleted by desertion."[31] Also, Davis disapproved of enlisting youths in the army as a practice that would use up the seed corn of the future, but when Senator William A. Graham presented a petition from the president of the University of North Carolina, David Swain, to exempt college students from the draft, his response was not encouraging. He observed that "it was among the calamities of war that breaks up all our institutions and that General Lee needed men in the army, and they must be supplied from somewhere."[32]

Davis considered the feelings of his generals, especially those of whom he liked, as General Gorgas noted in his diary. To the latter the president confessed that he was about to do an injustice to General Pemberton, "in obedience to popular clamor," in removing him from command of the artillery defense of Richmond, that he wished therefore to give him as high and honorable a position as possible, and accordingly was appointing him as inspector of artillery and ordnance in the field.[33] Likewise, he kept the unpopular General Bragg in command of the army of Tennessee as long as possible and then promoted him to be his military adviser in Richmond; also, he protected the unpopular Commissary General Lucius B. Northrop as long as he could. One of Davis's many virtues was this staunch loyalty to his friends, but it was also a serious administrative weakness.

Davis set a high tone for himself and for the Confederate army in seeking to keep the war a gentleman's war. Maybe the Confederate army was hampered by this philosophy. Indeed, Confederate history contains numerous examples of Christian gentlemen engaged in the art of killing men in the tradition of chivalry. Bishop Leonidas Polk, a lieutenant general in the western army, General Louis Pendleton, Lee's chief of artillery, who alternated between shooting Yankees and preaching, and E. Kirby Smith, commander in charge of the Trans-Mississippi Department, a soldier who longed to be a preacher but did not feel that he was good enough for the profession of saving souls, belonged to this unique species of military man. Even the ruthless Stonewall Jackson did not war against helpless civilians, women, and children as did some of the Northern generals.

One point that Douglas Southall Freeman has made in his biography of Lee was that this chivalric idea of war held by the Southerners as a whole partially explains the tremendous mortality among the officers of the Confederate army. They felt that they must lead their troops, get out there in front, and set an example. On occasion even the top generals led charges. Albert Sidney Johnston did, and even Lee wanted to do so. The Northern generals were not quite so chivalric; they had more sense. As the war went on, there was an enormous attrition among Southern officers. The Southerners were more old-fashioned than the Northerners; they were prone to reckless charges, shoulder to shoulder, using their bayonets, and the generals would make heroic speeches to their soldiers before battle. All of this passed away in the modern age.

The North, too, had its exemplars of waging war on Christian principles and according to the rules of honor and chivalry, but they seemed to have been less common, certainly less influential, than in the Southern army. The outstanding example of chivalry among Union generals was Major General George B. McClellan. In a notable letter to Lincoln while his army was stationed at Harrison Landing on the James River of Virginia, July 7, 1862, he outlined his philosophy of humane war, namely, that the war against the Confederates "should be conducted upon the highest principles known to Christian civilization"—a war not "upon population, but against armed forces and political organizations," involving neither forcible emancipation of the slaves nor confiscation of private property.[34] These were the principles of Jefferson Davis, but not of the successful Northern generals, Grant, Sherman, and Sheridan, or of the unsuccessful generals Hunter, Kilpatrick, and Pope. Was the hard-nosed policy of total war essential to defeat the Confederates?

Early Disaster

Euphoria in the Confederacy followed the glorious victory of Bull Run. Lawrence M. Keitt, the handsome young fire-eater and Confederate congressman from South Carolina, wrote to "Susie" on July 26, 1862: "I think by January the war will be ended," and he informed her that among the spoils of Bull Run were "ten wagons of handcuffs." "Isn't it atrocious," he exclaimed; already the atrocity stories mill had begun to operate. But by the first of January discontent among the army and disappointed expectations among the people had eroded the exuberance. The army under General Joseph E. Johnston had retreated in northern Virginia to headquarters at Fairfax Court House, Harpers Ferry had been abandoned, and the men, having suffered the inactivity and hardship of the winter camp, wished for action. They found that the war was no longer romantic, as many of them had imagined it would be.

Under these circumstances Beauregard urged Joseph E. Johnston to launch an offensive, especially in order to hamper the large concentration of enemy forces in front of Washington. To decide this critical question, President Davis traveled by special train to Fairfax Station, and from there rode horseback the four miles to Johnston's headquarters. He sat erect on a white horse, serenaded by a band playing "Hail to the Chief" and "Dixie."[1] At the con-

Birthplace of Jefferson Davis in Christian County, Kentucky. *Kentucky Historical Society*

Davis as a young man of 32. *Southern Historical Collection, University of North Carolina Library, Chapel Hill*

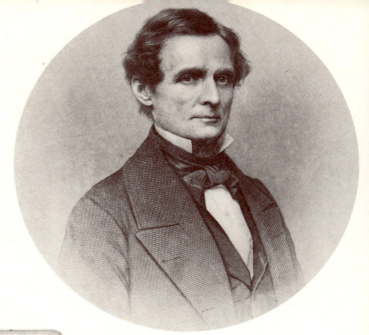

Mr. Davis as
Secty War,
with Peirce's
Cabinet —
Was handsome
as this when
I first knew
him
V. Clay-Clopton

Davis as Secretary of War, with a note in the handwriting of Virginia Clay-Clopton. *Duke University Library*

Varina Howell Davis, portrait attributed to Henry Byrd. *From the L. W. Ramsey Collection, courtesy of the Frick Art Reference Library*

GROUP OF PORTRAITS REPRESENTING THE CABINET OF PRESIDENT PIERCE.

Franklin Pierce's Cabinet, from upper left to upper right: William L. Marcy, James C. Dobbin, R. McClelland, James Campbell, Caleb Cushing, Jefferson Davis, and James Guthrie. *Library of Congress*

Opposite page, top: Davis as President of the Confederacy. *From the Anne Bachman Hyde Collection, Southern Historical Collection, University of North Carolina Library, Chapel Hill*

Opposite page, bottom: The White House of the Confederacy in Montgomery, Alabama. *Library of Congress*

Davis and his Cabinet with General Lee in the Council Chamber in Richmond. From left to right: Stephen R. Mallory, Judah P. Benjamin, Leroy P. Walker, Jefferson Davis, Robert E. Lee, John H. Reagan, Christopher Memminger, Alexander H. Stephens, and Robert Toombs. *Library of Congress*

Left: Judah P. Benjamin. *Library of Congress* Right: Albert Sidney Johnston. *Library of Congress*

Joseph E. Johnston. *Library of Congress*

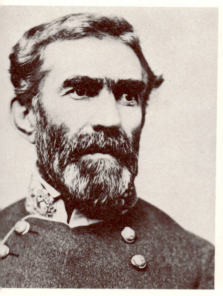

Left: Braxton Bragg. *Library of Congress* Right: Pierre G. T. Beauregard. *Library of Congress*

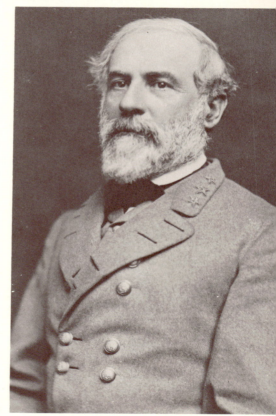

Robert E. Lee. *Library of Congress*

Jefferson and Varina Davis. *Duke University Library*

Davis (on left) and Clement C. Clay. *Duke University Library*

ference held on October 1, 1861, he considered the plan of Beauregard for an offensive through Maryland. When he learned that an army of 60,000 men—20,000 more than were then under the command of the generals—would be required, he vetoed the idea of the army going on the offensive, so ardently desired by the soldiers and the Southern people, on the grounds that he could not furnish that many troops and arm them.

In Kentucky there was bad news. On January 20, 1862, Confederate troops at Mill Springs, or Logan's Cross Roads, in the southeastern part of the state were defeated by General George H. Thomas. If there had not been bloodshed, the battle would have been a comedy. Major General George B. Crittenden, son of the famous Kentucky compromiser, who was in command, was accused of drunkenness and subsequently reduced to the rank of colonel. The second in command of the very, very green troops, Felix Zollicoffer, who had been a Tennessee newspaper editor, was nearsighted and with his white raincoat was a conspicuous target. In the confusion of battle he rode up to some enemy troops; he mistook them for Confederates and gave them some orders. Instead, they fired, killing him, and put his command to rout. Ridiculed by Stanley Horn, Zollicoffer was defended as "a capable strategist" by Thomas Connelly.[2]

Disaster followed disaster. General Henry A. Wise, ex-governor of Virginia, was sent with an inadequate force of 2,500 men to defend Roanoke Island on the coast of North Carolina. He was one of the worst of the political generals, brave but rash, noted for fiery oratory and tobacco chewing. Affairs at Roanoke Island were sadly mismanaged: Secretary of the Navy Mallory recorded in his diary that one half of the guns there were unmounted and only twenty rounds of ammunition were at the fort.[3] Wise lost his son in action and was forced to surrender on February 8, 1862, to a large army and fleet under the command of Ambrose Burnside. Several months earlier, the fine harbor of Port Royal, South Carolina, affording a superb base for the Union navy, had been captured by Admiral Samuel F. Dupont. Fort Pulaski at Savannah, Georgia, was also captured.

But the truly crushing disaster to Confederate army and morale came with the surrender on February 16, 1862, of 13,000 troops at Fort Donelson on the Tennessee River. Davis had sent the officer whom he regarded as the finest in the Confederate army, his classmate at West Point, General Albert Sidney Johnston, to defend the western frontier. Johnston established his headquarters in the center of a line of defense approximately 400 miles long, running from Cumberland Gap to Columbus, Kentucky, on the Mississippi River. He left the command of Fort Donelson to the incapable John Floyd, who had been secretary of war under President Buchanan. A much smaller fort, Fort Henry, on the Cumberland River twelve miles away, was commanded by the Kentuckian, Brigadier General Lloyd Tilghman. When the forts were threatened by General U. S. Grant with an army and a fleet containing some iron-clads advancing up the Tennessee River, Johnston assembled 15,000 troops to defend Fort Donelson. In the subsequent battle Floyd was swayed by conflicting counsels of his subordinate generals, Gideon J. Pillow and Simon Bolivar Buckner, deciding at last to surrender the fort and troops to the surrounding federal army. President Davis in his message to Congress on February 25, 1862, said that he was unable to believe that so large an army surrendered without a desperate effort to cut its way through the invading forces. The surrender of Fort Donelson was a failure, not only of generalship, but of character. Johnston had a trusting nature, and he left far too much discretion to incapable men; it seems that he himself should have gone directly to Fort Donelson to take command.[4]

The news of the disaster in Tennessee reached Richmond shortly before Davis delivered his inaugural address as the first and only president of the permanent government. He and Vice President Stephens, who had served provisionally since 1861, were elected, without opposition, by popular vote. Davis delivered his short inagural address in the rain before George Washington's statue at Richmond. The spirits of his audience were depressed not only by the inclement weather, but also because they had heard of the party of the North in disregarding the Constitution and threatening Southern disasters to the Confederate armies at Roanoke Island and at forts Henry and Donelson. In his address Davis referred to the despotism of a sectional rights. He compared the suppression of personal liberty in the Northern states by the Lincoln government (undoubtedly referring to the repression of Maryland during the secession movement) with the course of the Confederate government, stressing that no act on the part of the Confederate government had impaired personal liberty or freedom of speech, of thought, or of the press. He likened the struggle of the Southern people for self-government to the revolutionary generation fighting for independence from England. Although he admitted that the tide of battle had recently gone against the Confederate army, he said these reverses served only to stimulate the people to heroic resistance. Especially notable in the address was the expression of his reliance on the protection of the Providence of God, Who favors a cause that is just. Thus Davis expressed the deep religiousness of the Southern people at that time, so different from the rationalism of the leaders of the revolutionary generation, or even the secular spirit of today.[5]

After the surrender of Fort Donelson, Johnston withdrew General Leonidas Polk from Columbus, Kentucky, and he retreated from Bowling Green toward Nashville without attempting to defend it. Nashville, with its great depository of military supplies and railroads, occupied the importance in the West that Richmond did in the East, and its loss shocked the Southern people. Nashville should have had strong fortifications but these were not built, largely because the Confederates did not expect the North to begin its campaign until the spring. It was a case of being too late, as so often happened to the Confederates, who did not have the sense of time or the drive and organization of the Northerners. When the principal engineering officer, Jeremy Gilmer of

North Carolina, began desperately to try to make up for lost time in erecting fortifications before the advancing Union troops arrived, he was stymied. According to Attorney General Thomas Bragg, he could not get 500 hands for this purpose. Also, rather than transport Johnston's army in its flight southward, the railway men ran away, and the owner of a steamboat at Nashville refused to let Johnston have it to cross the Cumberland River, and before Johnston could commandeer it he removed vital machinery parts.[6]

The abandonment of Nashville to the enemy without a fight resulted in an enormous loss of military supplies that the Confederacy could ill afford. War is usually accompanied by great waste as well as corruption, but the South could not afford much waste, while the North, on the other hand, was comparatively rich. To the credit of Davis, it must be said that he strove hard to prevent military waste. He seemed, however, to have a double standard in this regard—one for his friends, and another for those generals he did not like. He condemned Joseph E. Johnston for not attempting to save military supplies, especially heavy artillery, when he abandoned Harpers Ferry, and a little later his position at Centreville, Virginia, close to the federal lines—and for his premature retreat before McClellan's army from the lower peninsula, exposing Norfolk to capture and resulting in the blowing up of the iron-clad *Virginia* in May, 1862, shortly after its dramatic battle with *Monitor*. But he withheld criticism when his friend and hero, Albert Sidney Johnston, showed a similar lack of concern in abandoning Nashville with its great store of supplies.

Indeed, the waste in the Confederate army, much of it avoidable, was never suppressed: huge supplies of food left at railroad depots, criminally allowed to rot, and equipment abandoned to deteriorate. When Colonel Arthur J. L. Fremantle of the English Goldstream Guards accompanied Lee's army in the invasion of Pennsylvania, he observed enormous piles of excellent captured rifles lying exposed to the weather, left to rust at Fairfax Court House. He also noted that after battles the Confederate soldiers recklessly threw away blankets, knapsacks, and other equipment.[7]

Following the debacle at Fort Donelson and the loss of Nashville, a great outcry arose in the Confederacy to remove Johnston from command. Johnston wrote a noble letter to the president admitting that the surrender of Fort Donelson was almost without remedy and offering to resign. For the good of the country, he wrote, he had not tried to defend himself from the uproar of criticism following the surrender of the fort and Nashville. As extenuation, however, he referred to the failure of the governors to send reinforcements desperately needed and his unwillingness to reveal to the enemy the weakness and vulnerability of the Confederate army in the West. Yet was it not as serious a mistake to fail to tell the people? But it was a Confederate policy not to do so, a policy that the newspapers, in exaggerating victories and minimizing defeats, also followed.

Davis refused to accept Johnston's offer of resignation and wrote him an affectionate letter expressing confidence in him. When a delegation came to Richmond demanding that the president remove Johnston from command, he replied, "If Sidney Johnston is not a general, the Confederacy has none to give you." And in a letter to the disconsolate general, he wrote, "My confidence in you has never wavered, and I hope that the public will soon give me credit for judgment rather than to continue to arraign me for obstinacy."[8] Nevertheless, in his message to Congress, February 25, 1863, he admitted that "the Government had attempted more than it had powers successfully to achieve," especially by attempting to protect "the whole of the territory of the Confederate States."[9] When he came to write *The Rise and Fall of the Confederate Government,* Davis called Sidney Johnston one of the noblest men and ablest soldiers whom he had ever known.[10] He defended him for remaining with his small force at Bowling Green and not taking command at Fort Donelson by observing that to have done so would have left no deterrent to General Don Carlos Buell's marching directly from Louisville into Nashville. The army at Fort Donelson, Davis explained, did not try to leave the fort after they had made one unsuccessful foray because the route to retreat found by the scouts would have involved wading through a branch of water three feet deep in a blizzard, and the army doctors said it would have meant death to one half of the men.[11]

Prominent among the critics of Davis's alleged mismanagement that led to the surrender of Fort Donelson was W. M. Brooks, president of the Alabama Secession Convention. In reply to his criticism, Davis on March 13, 1862, wrote a strong letter defending himself. He acknowledged the error in attempting to defend all the frontier of the Confederacy, both seaboard and inland. But, he observed, if the army had received the arms and munitions from the states that they had a right to expect, "the attempt would have been successful and the battlefield would have been on the enemy's soil." He stoutly denied that he had chosen a purely defensive military policy, claiming that it had resulted from necessity: the lack of military stores and the paucity of army reserves had necessitated a policy of defense. Furthermore, the country had supposed that the strength of the army was greater than it really was, he had borne criticism in silence, for "to reply would have exposed our weakness to the enemy." He felt, however, that it was necessary to defend himself from critics who had failed to get an office or who attacked him for other reasons in order to prevent a loss of confidence in him as president, thus injuring the cause.[12] This consideration remained constantly on his mind.

Johnston retrieved his reputation in the eyes of the Southern people when his army nearly defeated Grant in the battle of Shiloh, Tennessee, on April 6, 1862. After abandoning Nashville he had retreated to Corinth in northern Mississippi, an important railroad center. Here he joined his army with one commanded by Beauregard and prepared to advance against a federal army under Grant, who had established headquarters at Pittsburg Landing on the Tennessee River. Johnston's army was able to march the twenty miles from

Corinth to the enemy lines without detection, surprising both Grant and Sherman, the second in command. Johnston had let Beauregard organize the troops in faulty arrangement, so that in the confusion of battle, in rough terrain, the different units became mixed.[13] Nevertheless, on the first day of battle they were exultantly victorious, driving the Union army back several miles and occupying the camp of Sherman at Shiloh Church. But at the height of victory Johnston, who was unwisely leading his troops in the midst of the hottest fighting, in the so-called "Hornet's Nest," was struck at two-thirty in the afternoon by a Minié ball that cut an artery in his leg. Instead of having it attended to, he remained in the saddle, bleeding to death.[14]

Beauregard took over command just as some of Buell's troops arrived to reinforce Grant's army. Late in the afternoon Beauregard gave the controversial order to retreat, hoping to regroup his disorganized troops to fight the next day. In the night, however, Buell arrived in force, and the gunboats on the river poured shot and shell into the ranks of the gray-clad army. Beauregard retreated to his base at Corinth. For many years afterward critics argued that the order to discontinue the fighting when several hours of daylight remained had caused the Confederates to lose a great victory.

But General William J. Hardee, who commanded a corps in the battle, wrote to a lady friend what was probably a sounder analysis of the defeat, though, curiously, he did not mention the death of Johnston as a significant factor. The Confederates, he wrote, rushed into the battle with spirit, driving the enemy before them until the gunboats on the river "opened up a terrific fire, which tho' doing little injury, was perfectly appalling to our men." When the order came to fall back it was carried out in great confusion, and divisions and brigades became separated. The Confederates renewed the fight the next day; but the enemy had brought up fresh troops and Hardee's men did not fight with as much ardor as they had on the previous day.[15]

The Confederates believed, and Davis shared this belief, that Johnston was such an outstanding general that if he had lived the outcome of the Civil War might have been different, but most modern historians have their doubts. Not only did Albert Sidney Johnston fail to live up to his reputation in the defense of Fort Donelson, but he abdicated the proper role of a general at Shiloh in leading his troops from the front instead of remaining at a position to direct the entire army. The capable biographer of Albert Sidney Johnston, Charles Roland, however, defends Johnston's going to the front as necessary to inspire his green troops by giving them an example of courage.[16] Shiloh was a significant battle, for if Johnston could have smashed the army of Grant, who on this occasion was negligent, before Buell's army arrived in force, he might have changed the course of the war. Unlike Davis, Lincoln would hardly have chosen an unsuccessful general to be the commander of all the federal armies and to plan the campaigns that ended the war, although in the first half of the war he did choose a long line of incompetent commanding generals.

Fully as significant as the battle of Shiloh, if not more so in its long-term effects, was the capture on April 24, 1862, of New Orleans, the South's greatest port. For some unaccountable reason historians have neglected this event, certainly one of the most important of the Civil War. Davis left the responsibility for defending this vital port to his secretary of the navy. One of the president's serious limitations was his lack of appreciation of the importance of naval operations and amphibious warfare. It was the use of amphibious warfare, along with having superior generals in the West, that primarily explained the Union's successes in that theater of the war. There was only a small army of 3,000 men under the recently appointed, northern-born General Mansfield Lovell stationed at New Orleans to defend it from a land attack. Moreover, virtually no cooperation existed between the Confederate army and the naval forces in defense of the city. As so often happened with the Confederates, they were hampered by grave illusions and the lack of adequate intelligence. The Confederate naval and military officers were confident that New Orleans was safe from attack from the Gulf Coast, but believed that the principal danger would come from federal gunboats descending from above. After Admiral David G. Farragut's fleet crossed the bar at the main entrance to the Mississippi by lightening the weight of the heavy warships, the majority of Confederate naval and military officers believed that the fleet could not succeed in passing forts Jackson and St. Philip, located seventy-five miles below the city on opposite sides of the river.

When Farragut's fleet began the ascent of the river in April, 1862, the naval commander at New Orleans, W. C. Whittle, telegraphed the commander of the fleet of Confederate gunboats stationed at Fort Pillow on the Mississippi River above Memphis to hasten to attack the federal fleet before it reached New Orleans. The latter telegraphed Secretary Mallory for permission to join the New Orleans defense, but the secretary, despite the requests also of the secretary of war and General Mansfield Lovell, ordered him to remain at his post. Then a succession of mistakes and misfortunes befell the Confederate forces defending New Orleans. Before Farragut began the ascent of the river his own officers thought that the odds against their success favored the Confederates, their chief advantage being that the federal forces were unified while the Confederates were divided into three forces under separate commands. Actually, their chief asset was the bravery, skill, and resolution of their commander, Flag Officer Farragut, a Southerner who had elected to stay with the U.S. Navy, a man genial and kindly until the fighting began, proud of the physical agility that enabled him, after he was sixty years old, to turn a handspring on deck on his birthdays. As Robert Selph Henry expressed it, "Against them [the divided Confederate command] came a man singularly undivided."[17]

Undeterred by the difficulties and dangers, Farragut ordered his fleet to pass the dreaded forts on a dark night. He succeeded without any notable loss. Previously the commander of a fleet of mortars, David D. Porter, had bombarded the forts for five days, without any significant effect. President

Davis attributed the fall of New Orleans mainly to: (1) the failure to light up the channel between the forts by sending fire rafts adequate to light it, so that the gunners in the forts could see their targets; and (2) the failure to construct an effective line of rafts below the fort that would detain the enemy's ships under fire of the forts.[18] On the other hand, the brave and capable commander of the *Governor Moore,* one of the fleet of Confederate steamboats and tugboats, bows fitted with railroad iron to ram the enemy ships, boilers and engines protected by cotton bales, attributed the Confederate defeat to "the stupidity, tardiness, ignorance, and neglect of the authorities in Richmond."[19]

The fleet arriving at New Orleans met virtually no opposition. Brigadier General Lovell left the city with his small army in order not to endanger the women and children remaining there from being bombarded by the Union guns. The politician-general, Ben Butler, with an army of 18,000 men, took military command of the city, but before his troops were landed a howling mob raged, looting and setting fires. The Confederates surely had nothing to be proud of in their defense of the city, unless it was the bravery and steadfastness of the commander of the forts, Brigadier General K. Duncan, and several individual captains of small ships, notably of the ram *Manassas.* The commander of the naval forces at New Orleans and the officer in charge of the nearly completed iron-clad, *Louisiana,* was described by David D. Porter: "Fortunately for us, Commander (John K.) Mitchell was not equal to the occasion, and the *Louisiana* remained tied to the bank, where she could not obstruct the river or throw the Union fleet into confusion while passing the forts."[20] Both the *Louisiana* and the uncompleted *Mississippi,* which if completed would have been the most powerful iron-clad in the world, were destroyed by the Confederates to prevent their falling into the hands of the enemy.

A blue-ribbon congressional committee investigated the disaster at New Orleans in the middle of August, 1862. The principal object of inquiry was not the sad mismanagement of the defense but why the unfinished *Louisiana* and *Mississippi* had not been moved upstream to avoid their destruction, and whether Mallory had pushed their construction, and whether the Tift brothers, originally natives of Mystic, Connecticut, but long residents of the South, had acted energetically and patriotically in trying to finish the warships in time. The investigating committee, dominated by Davis supporters, and headed by his friend, Clement C. Clay, Jr., finally acquitted the navy and Secretary Mallory of all the charges brought by Senator Charles Conrad of Louisiana and Henry Stuart Foote, Davis's old Mississippi enemy, now congressman from Tennessee.[21]

Was Davis responsible for the loss of New Orleans? Yes, partly, but in his account of the tragedy he does not admit any personal blame. He had been given plenty of time to make adequate dispositions for the defense of the city. It was nearly a month from the date of Farragut's arrival at Ship Island, his base at the mouth of the Mississippi River, before he began the ascent of the river with his fleet and crossed the shallow bar. The president sent an officer to investigate; this man reassured him and Davis relied too much on his report and on Secretary Mallory. He was also assured early in January by General Mansfield Lovell that New Orleans could not be reached by land and was safe from the fleet at Ship Island.[22] The president's mind was doubtless occupied at the time with the safety of the Tennessee front. In fact, he admitted in *The Rise and Fall of the Confederate Government* that a large part of General Lovell's force in New Orleans, before the city was seriously threatened, was dispatched to the Tennessee front to help General Beauregard. Today it seems that Davis was remiss in not stationing a strong military force for the protection of New Orleans, placing it under the command of an abler general than Mansfield Lovell, and seeing to it that there was unity of command of the naval and land forces.

Secretary Mallory was distraught over the loss of New Orleans and was never able to replace the two fine iron-clads. To his Spanish Creole wife, to whom he was devoted, he wrote that the losses at New Orleans "almost killed me," and that night after night he lay awake thinking of them with tears in his eyes.[23] If Davis was as deeply affected he was too stoical to express it. Joseph Davis in Mississippi wrote to his brother that New Orleans was more capable of defense than any commercial city in the Confederacy and that it was shamefully abandoned by General Lovell, who had become "universally odious."[24] Mrs. James Chesnut, Jr., at Columbia, South Carolina, realized more fully than most of her compatriots the tragic significance of the loss of the city when she wrote in her diary on April 27, 1862: "New Orleans is gone, and with it the Confederacy! Are we not cut in two? The Mississippi [River] ruins us if it is lost. The Confederacy is done to death by the politicians."[25]

The Capital Saved and the Two-Pronged Offensive

At that time the capture of the capital was regarded as symbolizing the defeat of a country, and President Davis was so obsessed with the defense of Richmond that he neglected other parts of the Confederacy. It was a mistake from a military point of view to have moved the capital from Montgomery to Richmond, which was approximately a hundred miles from the frontier. Davis apparently did not see this, or at least I can find no record of his protesting against the change of site of the capital to an exposed position. Atlanta would have been much better and far safer. But there was a sound military reason for a staunch defense of Richmond, for the Tredegar Iron Works, by far the most valuable Confederate foundry for the manufacture of large guns and other munitions, was located there. It could, however, have been dismantled, with its machinery, and moved to a less exposesd position in the interior of the country.

In the early spring of 1862 Richmond was menaced by a formidable army, led by General George B. McClellan. President Lincoln and the Northern public were getting restless over the inactivity of the huge army at Washington that General McClellan had been training in the preceding fall and winter. McClellan was only thirty-six years old, but as a result of the adulation that he had received, he had developed a Napoleonic complex. Though well versed in military knowledge, he had two self-defeating qualities: he continually magnified the strength of the opposing army and he lacked the fighter instinct of a U. S. Grant.[1] Lincoln tried to prod him into action by issuing a foolish executive order: all armies must move forward on February 22, Washington's birthday. Nevertheless, McClellan took his time, and carefully trained the huge army of 120,000 men that he had assembled. He insisted, against President Lincoln's wishes, on carrying out his own plan for the invasion; instead of marching directly against Richmond, as McDowell had done, transporting his army to Fort Monroe and advancing against the rebel capital along the peninsula formed by the James and York rivers.

In order to safeguard Washington from attack while the army was away, the president ordered McDowell's corps of 30,000 men to remain behind—one of the causes, possibly, for failure of the campaign. Therefore, when McClellan landed at Fort Monroe he had only 90,000 men to oppose the Confederate army of less than half that number. The invading troops were different from the Confederate soldiers. William H. Russell saw a grand review of part of the troops of McClellan and McDowell in Washington and recorded in his diary that of the 55,000 soldiers in the parade that he saw, at least 20,000 were Germans and 12,000 were Irish, an estimate that over one half of McClellan's invading army were "foreigners," perhaps a large proportion of whom lived in the country before the Civil War started.[2]

In the face of the grave danger posed by the advance of McClellan's army, President Davis showed up at his best. As the clouds grew darker and criticisms of him wounded his vanity he rose to meet the emergency, writing his wife that he felt "the mustering clans" rise up in him in defiance.[3] He showed his constant concern for the defense of the capital when he visited Joseph E. Johnston's headquarters to consult the prickly general, riding through the rain to inspect the defensive works and obstructions of the James River at Drewry's Bluff against the advance of McClellan's gunboats. He displayed courage, recklessness, and disregard for personal safety when he visited the army guarding Richmond and took a real risk of being shot. His young aide, William Preston Johnston, wrote to "Rosa" on June 2, 1862, that when the president heard the sound of guns firing he and his staff rode toward them and the president tried to rally stragglers and retreating soldiers.[4] As the danger of capture of the city mounted, he sent Varina and the children to Raleigh, North Carolina, for safety. He wrote her that he would not allow the army to be penned up in the city. He would take lonely rides on horseback in the evening regardless of the possible dangers—which today would surprise the security-conscious world.

On April 14 he held a council of war with his generals to decide on whether to defend Richmond by holding up McClellan's army on the lower James, or as Joseph E. Johnston recommended, concentrating Confederate forces (including largely stripping the Atlantic seacoast of its defending troops) near Richmond. A heated debate took place between Johnston and Robert E. Lee, now Davis's military adviser, over this issue; Lee became very emotional and with tears in his eyes declared that Richmond must not be given up. Davis's decision was to fight on the lower James, which Douglas Southall Freeman, the great biographer of the general, declared was "undoubtedly a sound decision."[5] Johnston sulked and in the latter part of May twice refused a request from Lee and Davis to come to the capital for a conference. Lee, wonderfully tactful and self-effacing, acted as peacemaker between the president, dissatisfied with Johnston's behavior, and the general in command of the defense.

It is difficult to arrive at a balanced judgment of this high-ranking officer who had such notable virtues and at the same time such exasperating faults. Johnston was a proud, aristocratic Virginian, very intelligent, and skilled in military science. Of average height and impressive military bearing, he amused his Negro servant by keeping his hat on at the table, for he was partly bald. He was jealous of Lee, whom he felt always got the better deal in troops and assignments. He was secretive and hypersensitive, reluctant to communicate his plans to the Confederate commander-in-chief and the War Department—in other words, it was hard to secure his cooperation, as well as to get along with him. In Davis he was dealing with another man as jealous of his prerogatives, as proud, and as sensitive as he was.

Yet Johnston was well liked by his troops, for they felt that he would not expose them unnecessarily to the guns of the enemy. His supercautious military career was characterized by skillful retreats—certainly he was the best retreater in the Confederate army. Mrs. Chesnut in her diary tells a story that illustrates his caution and pride. When he came to South Carolina on a hunting expedition in his younger days he displayed a very human quality, exhibited in his later reluctance to engage his troops in aggressive combat. He had the reputation of being a very fine shot, but he brought back no birds. The situation was never just right for him to fire his gun—either the birds were flying too low or too high, the dogs were too far or too near, things never seemed to suit him, and he was afraid to risk his reputation for being a crack shot.[6] Such a mental attitude carried over into warfare; although a brave and accomplished general, he was also an egotist, afraid to launch what might be an unsuccessful adventure in battle. His biographers, Gilbert Govan and James Livingood, however, present a more favorable estimate of him.[7]

With his vastly inferior force, Johnston retreated skillfully up the peninsula, engaging the federal army briefly at Yorktown. He surprised Davis by his early withdrawal from the coastal region of Virginia. The president had ordered arrangements made to remove public property from the naval base at Norfolk, but Johnston's unexpectedly rapid withdrawal did not allow time for this. In a letter to the retreating general, Davis implied criticism for his not paying due regard to the saving of Confederate supplies at Norfolk for, he observed, the premature retreat "must involve enormous losses, including unfinished gunboats."[8] Perhaps the most tragic of these losses after the evacuation of Norfolk on May 9 was the destruction by the Confederates themselves of the famous iron-clad *Virginia,* which in the previous March had won renown by destroying some wooden Union warships in Hampton Roads and engaging the iron-clad *Monitor* in an indecisive battle.

By the end of May, McClellan had advanced to within five miles of Richmond, when Johnston turned upon his foe and severely checked the federal army in the battle of Seven Pines, or Fair Oaks. But in this battle he was seriously injured (he was prone to getting shot, being wounded ten times), and on June 1 Davis appointed Robert E. Lee commander of the Army of Northern Virginia. Strangely, during the first year of the war, Lee had been placed in the background, his talents largely wasted in a frustrating campaign in West Virginia and in supervising Atlantic Coast defenses. But on March 10 Davis had appointed him his military adviser in a maneuver, as Douglas Southall Freeman has observed, to preserve his presidential prerogative against the intention of Congress to name the Virginian commanding general of all Confederate armies. In the Seven Days battles around Richmond that followed Lee won the nickname of "King of Spades" because he insisted, despite the reluctance of Southern soldiers to work, that they should throw up fortifications with picks and shovels. At this early stage of the war they scorned such efforts as fit only for slaves.

While the Confederates were retreating before McClellan, General Thomas Jonathan Jackson was conducting his famous campaign in the Valley of the Shenandoah, May 4 to May 30, against several Union generals. Jackson was one of the great generals of the Civil War, but it may be surprising to learn that Davis, according to the diary of his Attorney General Thomas Bragg, said in a cabinet meeting that he was utterly incompetent.[9] Jackson was not of the aristocracy, but represented the energetic, respectable middle class of the South. Although he had many amazing eccentricities, he was a devout Presbyterian who would have fitted well into Cromwell's army.[10] He had such tremendous drive and led his men so furiously and so fast that they were called "foot cavalry." Within less than a month he had defeated four federal commands in the Valley—led, however, by distinctly inferior generals—and had threatened Washington.[11] He sent a dispatch to the adjutant general on May 26, 1862: "During the last three days God has blessed our arms with brilliant success." His army consisted of only 18,000 men, but by brilliant tactics he was able to bring to the battlefield at any one engagement a force superior to the enemy. Lee now called his army to Richmond to help defeat McClellan. But Jackson arrived late and displayed a strange lethargy during the Seven Days battles, which has been explained as due to lack of sleep.

By his generalship and the élan of his soldiers, Lee forced the Northern general to retreat down the peninsula to Harrison's Bar. Nearby, at Malvern Hill, the Confederates were unwisely thrown against the federal army in a furious battle that resulted in great and unnecessary loss of life. Although Richmond was saved at this time, splendid opportunities to destroy the enemy, never to recur, were lost. Davis explained this failure to crush the Union army as owing to lack of information, the incompetence of some subordinate generals and staff, and delays in carrying out Lee's orders. The federal army should have been destroyed, as Lee admitted, but it got away to the safety of its gunboats. In addition to the charitable reasons given by the president, it was also true that Lee was still an apprentice in commanding a large body of troops (he was only a lieutenant colonel when he resigned from the U.S. Army to join the Confederacy). He gave imprecise orders and left too much to subordinate generals. In these battles the Confederates suffered a tremendous loss of approximately 20,000 killed, wounded, or missing out of the 80,000 troops that defended Richmond.

Davis now had reason to breathe easier. He had found two generals who would fight and win—Robert E. Lee and "Stonewall" Jackson—soon to form a masterful team. Both of them were Napoleonic generals, determined to smash the enemy, not content merely to hold or gain territory. Davis left military decisions in Virginia largely to Lee. Lee was very polite and tactful and, above all, complaisant to his sensitive and proud commander-in-chief. He confined himself, however, almost wholly to the Virginia front.

For the first time now, the Confederacy had both the confidence and the men to engage in offensive warfare. President Davis does not seem, however, to have initiated the two-pronged offensive of invading Kentucky and Maryland simultaneously in the fall of 1862. Before this bold gamble, Lee, with the cooperation of Jackson, had defeated the boastful Union General John Pope in the smashing victory of Second Bull Run (August 23 to September 1, 1862), fought on the old battleground of First Manassas, but in the battle of Chantilly he had not succeeded in blocking the Union army's retreat to Washington.

Right after the Second Bull Run victory, Lee wrote to Davis that unless the president disapproved he would invade Maryland, and if victorious would enter Pennsylvania. There were several reasons for Lee going on the offensive; he proposed to threaten Washington and Baltimore and he thought that success on Northern soil would stimulate the peace movement in the North. Davis was fearful that by leaving Richmond uncovered the enemy might march into the city, but Lee reassured him that there was no danger. Finally Davis assented, for both he and Lee, as well as the Southern people, thought that Maryland was held in the Union by armed force and that when a Confederate army arrived, the Marylanders would gladly rise to welcome it and the army would receive a large accession of Maryland volunteers.

Lee was poorly prepared for the invasion. His army of 50,000 men needed shoes badly, but he hoped to get them in the North. Moreover, they wore tattered garments of all colors—butternut predominated over the traditional Confederate gray—and many of them wore homespun, which their mothers and sisters had weaved and dyed. Yet Lee had almost a mystic confidence in his ill-clad, ill-shod soldiers and they in turn thought that the team of Lee and Jackson was invincible. Unfortunately, for military rather than psychological reasons, Lee chose his area of entrance at Frederick in western Maryland. This was the part of the state inhabited to a considerable extent by German settlers and having few slaves; the people were strongly pro-Union, as contrasted with eastern Maryland, a land of plantations and slaves. Consequently, they were not aroused by the Confederate invaders singing the recently composed nostalgic refrain, "Maryland, My Maryland!" and they did not rise up to join the Confederate army. It was distinctly the wrong part of the state for that song. As Major Walter H. Taylor, one of Lee's aides, ruefully commented after the army returned, "Don't let any of your friends sing 'Maryland'— not my 'Western Maryland,' anyhow."[12]

Nor did Lee's proclamation to the Marylanders, made at the suggestion of President Davis, evoke a warm response. In it he declared that Maryland had been reduced to a conquered province by a ruthless enemy, especially through strong-armed measures like illegal arrests of citizens and suppression of freedom of speech and of the press. The Confederate army, he announced, had come to enable the Marylanders to throw off "the foreign yoke." He promised that the Confederate government would respect whatever choice that they should make as to their destiny.[13] At the same time Lee wrote to President Davis that the Confederate government should announce that it wished to negotiate for peace. Such a proposal, he observed, would be made from a position of strength and not from that of suppliants, and it might affect the Northern elections.

Faced by this crisis of a threat to Washington, President Lincoln restored McClellan to command of the defending army. The battle fought at Antietam Creek near the village of Sharpsburg, Maryland, on September 16–17, 1862, was sadly mismanaged by both sides. Its outcome illustrated how luck plays a large part in battles and how overconfidence of an army is a dangerous state of mind.

In the first place, there was an enormous amount of straggling in the Confederate army that Lee surely did not anticipate. This falling out of ranks and behind the army was not solely owing to footsore soldiers, one fifth of whom had no shoes; many of them were suffering from dysentery from eating green corn by the wayside. Lee had to use his cavalry to force them back into battle.

Then Lee had a terrible piece of luck. His marching orders for the concentration of his army fell into the hands of McClellan. Someone in D. H. Hill's troops had dropped a copy of the orders wrapped around three cigars, left in their camp at Fredericksburg. They had been picked up and taken to the federal commander. Although Lee learned of the lost orders in time to make some changes, which were helped along by the slowness of McClellan, he lost some momentum and coordination of his forces. Also, Jackson's arrival on the battlefield was held up by the unexpectedly stiff resistance of the garrison at Harpers Ferry before it surrendered. The battle of Antietam (or Sharpsburg) was one of the decisive battles of the Civil War. Though it is rated as a draw, the significant fact was that Lee was forced to retreat behind the Potomac River. Peter W. Harrison of the *Savannah Republican,* one of the ablest Confederate war correspondents, reported that the battle was by far the bloodiest of the war up to that date, and he pronounced the invasion of Maryland a mistake.[14]

While the Maryland campaign was going on the Confederates were hopefully invading Kentucky with two armies, one led by Braxton Bragg, and the other by Kirby Smith. Bragg had replaced Beauregard, who after the evacuation of Corinth had taken a sick leave without informing Richmond. Bragg proved eventually to be the evil genius of the western army. Born in North Carolina, he displayed few Southern characteristics, save for a strong sense of regional and personal honor. Handsome in his young manhood, the commander had become ugly as he advanced in age, with prominent black bushy eyebrows, and emaciated features that, according to a critic, made him look like a monkey. Fremantle described him as having a sickly, cadaverous appearance, with an iron gray beard, and stooped and very thin.[15] His sour disposition may have resulted from frequent attacks of migraine headache and dyspepsia. He was a superb disciplinarian—the only one of his generals, Davis said, who put down drunkenness among the officers and soldiers. Bragg did not hesitate to arrest and imprison high-ranking generals, as did Lieutenant General Leonidas Polk after the battle of Chickamauga. He had the habit of blaming his generals if things went wrong, and he seems to have been in a continuous state of depression. On the other hand, he knew his profession and was excellent in preparing his men for battle, but then he could not lead them to victory. He suffered from a nervous dread of defeat in battle and habitually retreated too soon.

There was a curious, drastic decline in the feeling of the army toward Bragg, from general approval when he took command in 1862 to condemnation, and even hate, toward the end of the war. On September 30, 1862, while Bragg's army was invading Kentucky, one of his soldiers expressed a very favorable opinion of the general: "Bragg is beyond doubt the best disciplinarian in the South. When he took command at Corinth the army was little better than a mob, he had one man shot for discharging his gun, with the result that there is excellent discipline now."[16] Soldiers love a victorious general regardless of how tough he is before or during their battles. The fundamental reason for the decline of respect for Bragg was his failure to win victories.

The object of the invasion of Kentucky was to capture Louisville, terminus of the important Louisville and Nashville Railroad, or Cincinnati. Bragg began his advance from Chattanooga, to which he had transported his army by rail by a long, indirect route from Tupelo, Mississippi, south to Mobile, then north to Chattanooga. At the same time Kirby Smith advanced from Knoxville, and the armies were supposed to cooperate with each other when they reached central Kentucky. Davis made a serious mistake in not forcing the two armies to operate in a coordinated plan, with Bragg distinctly in command. It turned out that Kirby Smith, who was young and ambitious, operated without much regard for his senior, Braxton Bragg.[17] Moreover, Bragg had not followed Davis's suggestion that he defeat Buell's strong army at Nashville before advancing into Kentucky.[18] Instead, Bragg decided to go around Buell and seize Louisville before the latter could catch up with him.

The Confederates believed that the Kentuckians would rise up and aid the invading army—an illusion similar to the one they had in invading Maryland. As Davis wrote to General Theophilus Holmes in Arkansas, after the campaign was over, the only justification for the invasion of Kentucky was the expectation that the Kentuckians would rise en masse to support the Confederate army.[19] But the Kentuckians were unwilling to make their state a battleground for the Union and Confederate forces. As Kirby Smith lamented, "the Kentuckians are slow and backward in rallying to our standard. Their hearts are evidently with us but their blue-grass and fat cattle are against us."[20] When Kirby Smith marched triumphantly with his army into Lexington in the heart of the Blue Grass country, however, they were received with cheers, and ladies waving handkerchiefs, but very few men joined the Confederate troops.

In the meanwhile, Bragg, having bypassed Buell's army at Nashville, was rushing toward Louisville, but he was too late. Buell beat him to the entrance to this strategic city on the Ohio River. Bragg had been held up by the stout resistance of a federal force at Munford, Kentucky, at the passing of the Green River. Then, realizing that he had lost out to Buell in capturing Louisville, he turned aside to inaugurate Richard Hawes as governor at Frankfort. Immediately afterward, he had to fight Buell's army at the battle of Perryville, October 8, 1862, without the proper support of Kirby Smith's army. This was an example of the typically indecisive nature of Bragg's battles. Thereupon, he retreated out of Kentucky to Murfreesboro, Tennessee. Here he was opposed by a large army under General William S. Rosecrans, a Catholic general not much different from Bragg in terms of slowness and vacillation.

While Bragg and Kirby Smith were invading Kentucky, generals Earl Von Dorn and Sterling Price undertook a campaign in northern Mississippi to divert federal forces from being sent to Kentucky against Bragg. Both generals were strongly individualistic, and both ambitious and impulsive, with the result that they did not cooperate harmoniously. Price, without waiting for Van Dorn who was his senior in rank, attacked and surprised Iuka, near Corinth, and easily captured the town. When Van Dorn arrived the two Confederate armies on September 19, 1862, attacked the federal armies at Corinth behind their strong defenses, but they were repulsed with staggering losses. Price wept at the fearful slaughter of his men, but the expedition did succeed in its diversionary purpose. Because Van Dorn had mismanaged the campaign, he was removed from the eastern command of Mississippi and assigned to command in the Trans-Mississippi, while General John C. Pemberton was sent from his post in South Carolina to replace him. Price could not get along with Pemberton, openly disdaining his fortifications at Vicksburg, and went to Richmond to plead his cause of being allowed to return to Arkansas with the eventual object of recovering Missouri, where he was still immensely popular.[21]

In addition to illusions concerning popular sentiment in both Kentucky and Maryland, there were special reasons for the failure of the two-pronged offensive of the Confederates in the fall of 1862. Lee did not pay proper attention to logistics before he invaded Maryland. He and his soldiers were overconfident; he was the victim of bad luck, in that his orders for the concentration of his divided army were discovered by the enemy; the Northerners fought just as staunchly and valiantly as did the Confederate soldiers; and Lee's coordination of the army units was poor. If Lee was overconfident and aggressive, Bragg in the invasion of Kentucky was the opposite; if Lee's coordination was faulty, Bragg's was worse. Moreover, Davis failed to exert sufficient control over the planning and execution of the two invading armies in Kentucky.

Antietam was one of the turning points of the Civil War. But it is doubtful that Lee, Davis, or the Southern people recognized its profound significance. It had a twofold impact: (1) on Confederate diplomacy, which will be discussed in the next chapter; and (2) on public opinion, both Confederate and Northern. It shook the confidence of the Southern people in Lee as invincible and in a favorable outcome of the war. Lincoln had already drawn up his Emancipation Proclamation, but he took Seward's advice and waited for an important victory before issuing it. Antietam was that victory, and shortly after the battle he issued it, to go into effect on January 1, 1863. Early in the war the House of Representatives had passed the Crittenden Resolution declaring that the war was for preserving the Union, and not to abolish slavery. Lincoln now changed its purpose: it had become a war both to save the Union and to abolish slavery. Thus Antietam afforded him the occasion to add a new objective to the war, a towering moral dimension, a universal element of idealism (although a minority of Copperheads were antagonized, and many Northern soldiers did not like fighting with Negroes for their freedom).

The President's Role in Diplomacy

*A*fter the Confederates drove McClellan's mighty army from the capital to defeat, they thought that the European countries would recognize the Confederacy and break the blockade. But President Davis and the representatives whom he sent to Europe had little diplomatic skill, and they failed to take immediate advantage of the favorable opportunity. Davis had never been to Europe (neither had Lincoln nor many other politicians, North or South, of that era), and he had a provincial view of the world. His personality was very undiplomatic, and he had a legalistic mind, which he applied to diplomacy. He simply couldn't understand why European nations ignored international law and instead consulted their own national interests in dealing with the recently emerged Confederate States of America. Furthermore, he was so busy directing military affairs that he had little time to devote to diplomacy, leaving that branch of governmental activity to his secretaries of state—Robert Toombs, Robert M. T. Hunter, and especially Judah P. Benjamin, in whom he had the utmost confidence. The history of Confederate diplomacy is, in large part, a matter of Judah Benjamin's conduct of the State Department.

Benjamin was much more urbane and cosmopolitan than Jefferson Davis or the other Confederate statesmen, with the exception of John Slidell, commissioner to France. He visited Paris annually to see his French Catholic Creole wife and his daughter. His wife refused to live in America with him, but he provided liberally for her maintenance in France. When he urged more economy on her she would reply "Don't talk to me of money; it is so fatiguing." Born in St. Croix of the Virgin Islands of a Jewish mercantile family, Benjamin grew up in Wilmington, North Carolina and went to Yale College, but he was forced to leave, accused, not of cheating, but of stealing, and finally landed in New Orleans. There he became a successful lawyer, acquired a splendid sugar plantation, Bellechasse, and was elected to the United States Senate.[1]

Benjamin was of short stature and stout, with black hair and eyes, and a short black beard. Though he dressed stylishly, usually carrying a gold-headed cane, he was also rather careless in his dress. He loved good food and society, and was a pleasant, always cheerful conversationalist. His only vice seemed to be indulgence in gambling. Despite his debonair manner and love of the repartee and wit of good society, he was a hard worker and an efficient and ready dispatcher of business. Although he had the intellectual equipment to be a superb secretary of state, the perspicacious Robert Kean, chief of the War Bureau, commented in his diary on August 13, 1863, that the secretary of state was a poor adviser. "He is a smart lawyer, a ready, useful drawer up of papers but perhaps the least wise of our public men." And on another occasion, Kean recorded unfavorably: "Mr. Benjamin is the most unreliable of news reporters, believes anything, and is as sanguine as he is credulous."[2]

But these unfavorable opinions were certainly not held by the president or the great majority of Southerners. Benjamin studied the president carefully, noting his likes and dislikes, especially the latter. He flattered him and was tactful and deferential. Davis liked to consult him, for he was always cheerful and optimistic. In contrast to the president, he was impervious to criticism and seldom voiced opposition. "His philosophy of life," wrote Rembert Patrick in his *Jefferson Davis and His Cabinet,* "was to live in and for the present, and it had a quality of Oriental fatalism."[3] He was, perhaps unfairly, called the president's factotum and alter ego. Yet, unlike Davis, he did not seem to have a deep attachment for any cause.

He was the cabinet member who seems to have had the greatest influence on Davis in the administration of government. Benjamin's influence grew gradually. When both he and Davis were in the U.S. Senate they were not friendly toward each other. In fact, in Senate debate Benjamin challenged Davis to a duel over certain words that implied that the Louisiana senator was a liar. But Davis quickly recognized the injustice of his remark and apologized before the Senate. "I cannot gainsay," Davis said, "that my manner implied more than my heart meant." Recognizing his hasty temper in the debate with his skillful and able opponent, he confessed that his behavior was "sometimes unfortunate, and is sometimes, as my best friends have told me, of a character which would naturally impress that I intended to be dogmatic and dictatorial."[4]

Varina noted the growing bond between the two men. "It was a curious spectacle," she wrote, "the steady approximation to a thorough friendliness of the President and his war minister. It was a very gradual approachment, but all the more solid for that reason." She explained Benjamin's helpfulness to the president as follows: "Mr. Benjamin was always ready for work; sometimes, with half an hour's recess, he remained with the executive from ten in the morning until nine at night and together they traversed all the difficulties which encompassed our beleaguered land.... Both the President and the Secretary of State worked like galley slaves, early and late. Mr. Davis came home fasting, a mere mass of throbbing nerves; perfectly exhausted; but Benjamin was always buoyant and fresh. There was one striking peculiarity about his temperament. No matter what disaster befell our arms, after he had done all in his power to prevent or rectify it, he was never depressed." This shrewd man carefully cultivated and courted Mrs. Davis as well as the president, believing that she exerted great influence with her husband.

The president's selection of the first commissioners to England and France were singularly inappropriate. The commissioner to Great Britain, William L. Yancey, was not only undiplomatic in speech, but the very symbol of the Southern devotion to slavery and an advocate of reopening the slave trade. Pierre Rost was an obscure former judge of Louisiana, whose chief qualification seemed to have been that he could speak French, and Ambrose Dudley Mann of Virginia, a personal friend of Davis, who had been in the U.S. diplomatic service, was a gentleman with charming manners, but pompous, egotistical, and lacking in ability. Secretary of State Toombs's instructions to them were first to state that the separation of the Confederate states was legal, that the Confederacy was a stable government, and that there was no chance of reunion. The commissioners were to make "a delicate allusion" to the King Cotton argument, and point out that the Confederacy would pursue a virtually free trade policy.[5]

On May 14, because of Lincoln's proclamation of a blockade of Southern ports, Great Britain, and shortly thereafter France, announced a policy of neutrality, carrying with it rights of belligerency. This policy was decided upon by Great Britain independently, with the Confederate envoys having virtually nothing to do with it. It was, however, really the only important concession made to the Confederacy by the European powers during the war. The commissioners did not at this time offer a liberal commercial treaty, as recommended by Robert Barnwell Rhett, chairman of the Foreign Relations Committee of Congress. He and his son, Robert Barnwell Rhett, Jr., blamed Jefferson Davis for the failure of the first mission on this account.[6]

Opposing the inept Confederate commissioners at the Court of St. James was one of the ablest foreign ministers in the history of the United States, Charles Francis Adams, son of President John Quincy Adams. Adams was urged by Secretary of State William H. Seward to take a bold stand in asserting American rights. The British minister for foreign affairs, Earl John

Russell, would not receive the Confederate commissioners officially, but held several informal conversations with them. Thereupon Adams on June 2, 1862, informed the British cabinet officer that any further conversations with the Confederate commissioners would be regarded as an unfriendly act, which caused Earl Russell to promise that he had no expectation of seeing them any more.[7]

Confederate diplomacy was based initially on a belief in the economic power of Southern cotton, upon which the British and French mills were dependent. This reliance on the power of cotton to force the European nations to recognize the Confederacy and come to its aid caused Frank L. Owsley to entitle his important study of Confederate diplomacy, *King Cotton Diplomacy.* Senator James H. Hammond of South Carolina had popularized the phrase, "Cotton is King," when he had predicted in the Senate, March 4, 1858, with the height of planter arrogance and provincialism, what would happen if the South stopped growing cotton for three years: "England would topple headlong and carry the whole civilized world with her, save the South. No, you dare not make war on cotton. No power on earth dares to make war upon it. 'Cotton is King.' "[8]

The president subscribed to the popular illusion that "Cotton is King." Mrs. Davis stated his belief in this way: "The President and his advisers looked to the stringency of the English cotton market, and the suspension of the manufactories, to send up a ground-swell from the English operators that would compel recognition, and grudged every pound exported."[9] Nevertheless, he did not recommend to Congress the passage of a law that prohibited such exports in order to produce a "cotton famine" in Europe, although some state laws did. Later, when serious opposition to him arose in Congress, he was accused of not rushing cotton to Europe to serve as a bank with which to buy munitions and supplies. Some prominent men—notably General Joseph E. Johnston, Alexander H. Stephens, and Governor Joseph E. Brown of Georgia —made this charge. Postmaster Reagan wrote in his memoirs that the question of the government buying the entire cotton crop was fully discussed and rejected in the cabinet. He noted that at the beginning of the war 3 million bales of the 3,849,000 bales of the crop of 1860–61 had been exported to England as well as 600,000 bales to New England spinners. Reagan supported Memminger's defense of the failure to send vast quantities of cotton abroad before the blockade became effective by observing that it would have taken 4,000 ships to carry the cotton remaining; and where could these "phantom ships" be obtained, he asked, and where could the Confederate government obtain the money for the purchase? He noted, moreover, that private enterprise shipped as much cotton as the government could have shipped.[10] Nevertheless, it seems that there was a lack of realization at this early stage of the war, when it was believed it would be a short war, of the need for rushing cotton to Europe. W. H. Russell, who traveled widely in the South at the beginning of the war, found that people everywhere believed that a cotton famine would bring Great Britain to her knees, and that her material interests would force her to come to the rescue of the South.[11] Judah Benjamin was described by Frank Owsley as "an ardent and unfaltering champion of the King Cotton doctrine."[12] Also Davis strongly opposed using cotton in trading between the lines at Memphis, with the enemy, which both his commissary general and quartermaster general thought was essential to get bacon and blankets for the army.[13]

William L. Yancey resigned as a commissioner to Great Britain in September, 1861, feeling that his task was futile; he returned to Richmond with the comment that the English had read *Uncle Tom's Cabin* and believed it. Yancey's replacement was a strange choice. Another strong advocate of slavery, the provincial Senator from Virginia James M. Mason was the author of the detested Fugitive Slave Law of 1850. When Mary Chesnut heard of the appointment of this tobacco-chewing aristocrat, she exclaimed in her diary: "My wildest imagination will not picture Mr. Mason as a diplomat. He will say 'chaw' for 'chew,' and he will call himself 'Jeems,' and he will wear a dress coat to breakfast. Over here whatever a Mason does is right. He is above law. Somebody asked him how he pronounced his wife's name. She was a Miss Chew from Philadelphia."[14]

But the appointment of John Slidell to the court of Louis Napoleon in Paris, taking the place of Rost, was excellent. Slidell was a shrewd and sophisticated New Yorker, who had emigrated to New Orleans after graduating from Columbia, married a French-speaking Creole, built up an unscrupulous political machine, and was elected to both the U.S. House and the Senate. Davis, however, made a very injudicious diplomatic appointment when he selected John T. Pickett as envoy to Mexico. Pickett had a swashbuckling manner and got into trouble with the Mexican authorities; his mail was intercepted, and he returned in disgrace to the Southern Confederacy. Nevertheless, he did a service to historians, for, after the war, unaccountably, he got hold of the whole diplomatic correspondence of the Confederacy and sold it to the U.S. government for approximately $75,000. It is now in the manuscript room of the Library of Congress, and the papers are known as the Pickett Papers.[15]

The Confederacy had a bit of luck on November 8, 1861, but it was only temporary. While Mason and Slidell were on their way to England, going out from Havana on the British mail steamer *Trent,* Captain Charles Wilkes of the U.S. Navy, commanding the *San Jacinto,* arrested them. He neglected, however, to seize their dispatches and, as required by international law, to take the ship into a port to be adjudged a prize. Public opinion in the North widely acclaimed him a hero and Congress voted him a gold medal, but Great Britain was outraged and issued an ultimatum. Prime Minister Palmerston, the very image of John Bull in appearance and overbearing manner, declared in a cabinet meeting: "You may stand for this but damned if I will."[16]

Great Britain issued an ultimatum and threatened war, sending 8,000 troops to Canada. President Davis in a message to Congress condemned it as a violation of rights, "for the most part held sacred even amongst barbarians." Davis and his secretary of state, however, did not exploit the seizure with effective propaganda. Lincoln and Seward at first seemed hesitant to back down, apologize, and hand over the prisoners to the British government, but at "Christmas Conference" of the cabinet they decided to do so, and Prince Albert shortly before his death used his influence to moderate the anger of his government.[17]

The three main objectives of Southern diplomacy were to get European nations formally to recognize the Confederacy, to secure their aid in breaking the blockade, and to negotiate international loans, with cotton as the security. After Lee drove McClellan from Richmond and down the peninsula, Mason and Slidell presented their notes for recognition at the end of July, 1862, but both England and France refused to grant their request. The Confederacy had strong friends in Parliament, notably William S. Lindsay, a shipbuilder, Lord Campbell, W. H. Beresford, and John A. Roebuck; and out of Parliament, James S. Spence, the ablest British propagandist for the Confederate cause. One of the strong cards held by the Confederacy was a protest against the illegal blockade, which Davis felt should be debated. Its diplomats maintained with some justice that Lincoln's blockade of the Southern ports was only a paper blockade, in violation of international law. They gave impressive statistics of vessels entering and leaving the Confederate ports, which in the first year amounted to only one tenth of those captured by the blockading squadron.[18] The British government, however, argued that the blockade was legal because it presented a substantial danger and deterrent to vessels entering the Southern ports. In addition to the diplomats whom the State Department sent over, it dispatched early in the war an extremely able propagandist, Henry Hotze, who established a Confederate propaganda journal, *The Index,* in London, as well as an inept propaganda agent, Daniel De Leon, to France.[19]

The Confederacy's best opportunity to win European support came in the fall of 1862 before the repulse of the Southern army at Antietam was known. Slidell persuaded Emperor Louis Napoleon to make a formal move to secure the cooperation of England and Russia, with France proposing mediation. The emperor had a special reason for so doing, since the French people loved glory and for this purpose he was seeking to establish a French empire in Mexico. Also, the French provinces had complained to the emperor of injuries inflicted on French cotton and exporting industries by the blockade.[20] The U.S. government was determined to enforce the Monroe Doctrine, but the Confederacy might accept his plan for imperial expansion. Accordingly, after preliminary conversations with the two great powers, Louis Napoleon on November 10, 1862, made a formal proposal of a six-months' armistice during which the blockade should be suspended. Lord John Russell, in September, had proposed to Prime Minister Palmerston that Great Britain should offer mediation "with a view to the recognition of the independence of the Confederates," and Gladstone, the chancellor of the exchequer, boldly declared in a speech at Newcastle on October 3: "Jefferson Davis and other leaders in the South have made an army; they are making, it appears, a navy, and they have made what is more than either, they have made a nation. We may anticipate with certainty the success of the Southern States so far as regards their separation from the North." But the defeat at Antietam, Lincoln's preliminary Emancipation Proclamation, and the opposition of Russia made the British cabinet cautious, with Palmerston advising on October 22 that "we must continue to be lookers-on until the war shall have taken a more decided turn."[21] Adams informed Lord John Russell that if Great Britain recognized the Confederacy, the United States would break diplomatic relations and he would leave England. France, fearful of war though continuing to be sympathetic to the Confederacy, would not act without the cooperation of Great Britain.

Another favorable opportunity to urge recognition and mediation from the British government occurred in the early summer of 1863 when once more Confederate military prospects were riding high. John A. Roebuck and W. S. Lindsay went to France and gained an interview with Emperor Louis Napoleon; they reported to Parliament that he was favorable to mediation, but would not again make a formal application since his first proposal had been rebuffed. Roebuck, who represented the manufacturing Sheffield district, presented his motion for recognition and mediation in Parliament on June 30, but it was opposed by Prime Minister Palmerston.[22] The Confederacy was unfortunate in having Roebuck present the motion for recognition, for he was one of the greatest eccentrics in England, a laughingstock without a political following in Parliament. Roebuck withdrew his resolution on July 13; shortly afterward, news of Lee's defeat at Gettysburg ended any chance that Great Britain and France would come to the aid of the beleaguered Confederacy.

James Mason believed that the Confederacy should stop supplicating European powers for recognition (a belief held by many proud Southerners). It should *demand* recognition, and if refused withdraw its representatives immediately. But the president and the secretary of state thought this tactic too extreme. Nevertheless, Davis wrote to Benjamin on August 4, 1863, that after reading the debates in Parliament he was forced to conclude that there was little hope for the Confederacy to obtain recognition from England; therefore, Benjamin should instruct Mason to leave his post in London unless he perceived a change in the British attitude.[23] Accordingly, the Confederate commissioner to England left for Paris, where Slidell remained on the job. Also, in the same month, while Davis was away from Richmond visiting the army in Tennessee, Benjamin called a cabinet meeting at which it was decided to expel the British consuls on the ground of their advising their nationals that they were not liable to Confederate military service. Davis concurred in this decision.[24] On December 7, 1863, the president in a message to Congress announced that there was no improvement in foreign relations, which were dominated by Great Britain, since that nation and France had agreed to act together.[25]

Nevertheless, the Confederacy did have two successes in Europe: namely, the opportunity to build commerce raiders in British shipyards without serious intervention of the government until April and October, 1863, and the negotiation in France of the Erlanger loan, to be discussed in a later chapter. The Confederacy sent to Europe James D. Bullock of Georgia, an uncle of Theodore Roosevelt, and Lieutenant James H. North to buy and have built commerce raiders and iron-clads for the Confederacy.[26] They succeeded in acquiring a number of wooden commerce raiders, the most notable of which was the *Alabama,* built in Scottish shipyards, but they obtained their crews and armament after leaving British ports. These armed ships destroyed and burned many United States ships—the *Alabama* alone, 65 in all—and especially whaling ships, which brought vital oil to lubricate Northern machinery. But on April 5, 1863, the British government stopped this building of Confederate cruisers in their shipyards by seizing the *Alexandra* after it had left the limits of Great Britain. Also, Charles Francis Adams obtained information which he presented to the British government that the Confederates were building two powerful iron-clad rams in the Laird shipyards, and he threatened war if they were allowed to leave. As a result, the British, in October, 1863, ordered that the Laird rams be seized by the government. The French government, however, encouraged the Confederacy to construct cruisers in French shipyards, but insisted that their destination must be kept secret. When a spy revealed their true destination the emperor ordered that they be sold to European powers.

Probably Davis exercised as little control over Confederate diplomacy as did Lincoln over U.S. diplomacy. Lincoln, however, had a great advantage over Davis in being president of a strong established nation, and he also had a very capable secretary of state in William H. Seward. But Lincoln himself made a great contribution to the diplomacy of his government through the Emancipation Proclamation—something that Davis did not do. Davis gave Congress and the Southern people very little information about Confederate diplomacy, and his anger and pride led him on rare occasions to throw diplomacy to the winds, as he did in April, 1864, when he received a letter from Lord Lyons, the British ambassador in Washington, conveying a message from the prime minister refusing to allow delivery of the Laird rams to the Confederacy. Davis was indignant that Lyons referred to the Confederacy as the "so-called Confederacy," which caused the Confederate president to inform him that "in the future any document in which the term may be repeated will be returned unanswered and unnoticed."[27] Moreover, he, Benjamin, and the Confederate Congress sought to appeal to the material interests of England and France, offering to France in the spring of 1862 a bribe of 100,000 bales of cotton and free trade if it would break the blockade.

Confederate diplomacy failed, not because of the ineptitude of Davis and his secretaries of state, but primarily because of conditions in Europe. On account of these conditions, England was not willing to risk a war with the United States, which Secretary of State Seward had threatened on several occasions if it recognized the Confederacy. The antislavery-based opposition to the Confederacy in Europe was very strong. Although the British working classes suffered from the cotton shortage, they supported the antislavery North. England had a two-year supply of cotton when the war began and increased its supplies from India and Egypt, and France increased imports from Algeria, so that the King Cotton argument did not work. The chief factor in the failure of Confederate diplomacy was the military defeats of the Confederate armies, especially at critical times. Moreover, the continuance of the war permitted Great Britain to make large war profits. A minor factor in causing Great Britain to maintain a neutral attitude was the failure of British wheat harvests at a critical time, so that they needed to import Northern wheat possibly even more than Southern cotton.

As a final desperate effort to get recognition and to break the blockade Davis sent Duncan Kenner, a wealthy sugar planter and member of Congress, on a secret mission to Europe to offer emancipation of the slaves in return for recognition and aid. Also Benjamin wrote instructions on December 27, 1864, to both Mason and Slidell to question the English and French governments directly as to whether the institution of slavery prevented them from granting recognition to the Confederacy. James Mason, having returned to England, had an interview of more than an hour with Lord Palmerston at Cambridge House on March 14, 1865. Indirectly he made the offer of emancipation, but the war was nearly over, and it had no effect. Slidell had a conference with the French emperor, who told him that with regard to slavery "he had never taken that into consideration" and that it had not and could not have any influence on his action, but that probably it had been considered differently by England. On March 26 Mason questioned a friend of the Confederacy, Lord Donoughmore, on whether the British government would recognize the Confederacy if slavery were abolished, and he replied that "the time had gone by" for that issue to influence his government.

Jefferson Davis seems never to have understood the realities that controlled England in its refusal to recognize the Confederacy and break the blockade. He had a curious psychological fixation, extending far back in his early life, that his opinions were the correct ones, and he took it for granted that others agreed with him. Although he knew that European opinion was antislavery he could not understand that it was based on deep-seated conviction, for he himself thought that Southern slavery was a just and beneficent institution. His brief discussion of Confederate diplomacy written years after the war, is legalistic. In it he pointed out how the nations of Europe, particularly Great Britain, proclaimed neutrality, but actually it was a one-sided neutrality favoring the federal government. This fact was demonstrated, he maintained, when they refused permission for the Confederate privateers to bring their prizes into their ports, and by their failure to observe international law in assenting to a paper blockade of the Southern ports. The British government had modified international law in regard to paper blockades, he wrote, by holding that a blockade was sufficient, provided it "created an evident danger" to neutral ships seeking to enter or leave Southern ports. Thus the South was deprived of the rights of a free nation seeking its independence against formidable odds by "the hollow profession of neutrality," especially by Great Britain.[28]

The Fateful Year of 1863

But victories lay ahead for the Confederacy, as Lincoln and his Secretary of War Edwin Stanton fumbled about to find a successful general: they tried a general for one battle; when he failed, they jerked him from command and experimented with another; McClellan they tried twice. On December 13, 1862, Ambrose E. Burnside, of the famous sideburns and whiskers, stormed the fortifications on the heights of Fredericksburg, Virginia, with his huge army, but Lee defeated him with such slaughter that he wept over his losses. Then in April of 1863 Beauregard, with the guns of his forts defending Charleston, defeated and humiliated Admiral Samuel F. Dupont commanding nine iron-clad warships. In the valley of the Mississippi both William Tecumseh Sherman and Grant failed in their attempt to take Vicksburg from the north.

To top it all, Lee and Jackson won the glorious victory of Chancellorsville in northern Virginia over "Fighting Joe" Hooker, who boasted of having "the finest army on this planet"—he certainly had the largest, with 130,000 men, while Lee's army was only half that strength. But it was also a fatal battle for the Confederates—"Stonewall" Jackson, whom Lee called his "right arm," was mortally wounded by his own troops as he was reconnoitering the position of the enemy late in the evening. Moreover, the victorious Confederates were, as usual, unable to destroy the federal army because of a lack of reserves. It retreated to Washington, where Fighting Joe Hooker resigned, and to replace him, three days before the army was to fight the decisive battle of Gettysburg, President Lincoln appointed General George Meade, a capable but colorless general, whom Lee predicted would not make a mistake in handling his army (Lee, however, did, in handling *his* army).

Military historians have hotly debated which battle marked the turning point of the Civil War: Chancellorsville seemed to Robert Selph Henry, whose judgment deserves respect, "the high noon of the Confederacy," and I agree with this assessment, but Bell Wiley, also a capable military historian, calls it "afternoon."[1] Wiley also deemphasizes the significance of Gettysburg as the decisive battle and regards the loss of Vicksburg as more important. Both were tremendously important strategically and psychologically. Again I agree with T. Harry Williams, who holds, "Actually, I think the South had a reasonable chance to win the war despite the 'superiority' of the North" (in economic resources and manpower).[2] That is, up to the middle of 1863, when Lee was defeated at Gettysburg and the Confederacy had to surrender Vicksburg, the key to the Mississippi River. Then the chance was lost. It was lost, fundamentally, because Davis, with the concurrence of most of his cabinet, yielded to the urging of Lee and made the dubious decision of allowing him to invade Pennsylvania instead of sending strong reinforcements from his army to defeat Grant at Vicksburg.

If Lee kept his eyes only on the eastern army and territory (which he usually did) he had good arguments for invading Pennsylvania. The army needed provisions badly, for the Virginia sources were depleted, the horses were weak because of lack of fodder, and the soldiers needed to keep active in order to maintain their high morale. Above all, Lee felt that a defensive policy could not end the war, and he hoped to do so by a decisive victory on Northern soil. Furthermore, Lee was one of the few aggressive-minded Confederate generals; he was willing to take risks to gain results.

Lee went to Richmond and presented his ideas to the Confederate cabinet in May 14–17, 1863, and it considered them very carefully, for the president and his cabinet officers had confidence in Lee's generalship. At the same time that Lee was arguing in favor of a Northern invasion, Vicksburg was gravely menaced by Grant, and generals Pemberton and Johnston sent urgent pleas for reinforcements. Lee argued, however, that the best way to rescue Vicksburg was to threaten Washington and Pennsylvania, which would lead to the recall of Grant's troops to protect the nation's capital. But the sober, comon-sense Postmaster General Reagan contended that the proposed action would not force Grant to give up the Vicksburg campaign, and that 25,000 to 30,000 of Lee's troops should be dispatched to Vicksburg.[3] Three high-ranking generals—D. H. Hill, James Longstreet, and Pierre Beauregard—also opposed the invasion of Pennsylvania, the latter two arguing for heavy reinforcement of Bragg in the West and sending his army north to capture Louisville and Cincinnati. Finally, the president, though reluctantly, and his cabinet made the fatal decision to let Lee go ahead with his plans.[4]

Accordingly, at the end of June, Lee's army turned its face toward Pennsylvania, supremely confident in both their leader and the invincibility of the army. But the army had serious weaknesses, particularly since Lee had to reorganize it after the death of Jackson. Only one of the three corps into which he divided the army was led by an experienced and dependable commander, and even Longstreet had developed a habit of questioning and dissenting from Lee's plans. The other two, A. P. Hill and Richard Ewell, were able fighting generals in subordinate positions who were not equal to their new responsibilities. Ewell was a relatively unknown quantity in a position of high responsibility though he had been very capable under the leadership of Jackson, whom he now succeeded. This bald-headed general was given to cursing and colorful expletives until he got religion in the middle of the war; he was in rather poor physical condition, having lost a leg in battle, yet with his wooden leg, and strapped in his saddle, he could ride horseback. A. P. Hill was a quiet, unimpressive man with a long auburn beard, who had the fire of a Crusader in his eyes.[5] In addition to these questionable corps leaders, Lee had not paid sufficient attention to logistics or to supplying his army.

Toward the end of June Lee sent part of his troops to march northward through the Shenandoah Valley and with his main army, after crossing the Potomac at Williamsburg, headed toward Chambersburg and Harrisburg, the capital of Pennsylvania. The troops had strict orders not to molest civilians or to take their property without paying for it (in Confederate notes that were worthless to Pennsylvania inhabitants). A young Confederate surgeon J. B. Clifton, who accompanied the army into Pennsylvania, recorded in his manuscript diary that despite orders against taking property, "hogs, sheep and poultry stand a poor chance [along the line of march] for their lives," and that the soldiers liked to tease the inhabitants.[6] The English military observer, Colonel Arthur Fremantle, who accompanied Lee's army, recorded that it had good morale and was well armed, but that the artillery was pulled by horses in poor condition. The soldiers, he observed, were well clothed, carrying their toothbrushes in the holes of their lapels, but there was no uniformity in their uniforms or, rather, lack of uniforms. Confident of success, they were eager for a fight. Their commander, Robert E. Lee, the Englishman noted, was "the handsomest man for his age" that he had ever seen. Lee and his second in command, General Longstreet, had no vices and carried no arms, not even swords.

Led by their Christian commander, Robert E. Lee, the teasing soldiers were the very opposite of a ferocious army. Lee paid a high compliment to his officers—they were gentlemen. Mrs. Davis thought Wade Hampton of South Carolina was the beau ideal of the Cavalier officers. One of these gentleman officers was James Johnston Pettigrew of South Carolina, who led the famous charge of Pickett's division on the last day of the battle of Gettysburg. Of him President David L. Swain of the University of North Carolina wrote on January 15, 1861: "No pupil has ever passed from under my hands in whose judgement, candour, and friendship I have so much confidence as yours."[7] After a brilliant career at the University of North Carolina, Pettigrew went to Italy to fight for Italian liberty—but only on a charging steed, not on foot.[8] To friends who remonstrated that he might be killed, he replied, "What is life to a young man without adventures?". When a South Carolina lady wished to send him delicacies while he was in the army, she heard "that you had determined with spartan-like self denial to fare no better than your men."[9] Not all of the officers in Lee's army, of course, were like the knightly Pettigrew, but many of them cherished the romantic ideals of warfare that they had read of in Sir Walter Scott's novels and in *Scottish Chiefs*. Their president, Jefferson Davis, was so inspired, and so was his young aide, William Preston Johnston, son of Albert Sidney, who told "Rosa" in a letter, written while riding on a train in Virginia, that he was reading *Scottish Chiefs*.[10]

The South was a leadership-oriented society, and it is quite likely that the ideals of chivalry of the upper class filtered down to the middle-class soldiers, if not to those of the lower class, who were often illiterate. Lee's army consisted mostly of these middle-class and lower-class soldiers. A Northern journalist, George A. Townshend, interviewed some captured prisoners from South Carolina during the summer of 1862 who may or may not have been typical, and found that they had little comprehension of what the war was about, but had volunteered because of a variety of reasons; some had enlisted for the honor of their family, whose ancestors had "fit in the American Revolution."[11]

It is unnecessary to describe the course or the technicalities of the battle of Gettysburg in a biography of Jefferson Davis, for he had no direct relation to it other than the all-important decision to invade Pennsylvania.[12] A high point of the battle, however, was an incident that revealed something significant about the type of people whom Jefferson Davis governed as Confederate president. It—namely, Pickett's famous charge—occurred on July 3, the last day of the battle. Lee in desperation had ordered the foolish charge, and Longstreet protested strenuously against it, saying that the force of 15,000 men was inadequate to storm the center of the Union line, well protected as it was on the high terrain by fortifications.[13] Nevertheless, the men marched as though on parade against the storm of cannon shells and the devastating firing of rifles. General Lewis Armistead of Virginia was in the forefront of the gallant charge, and his men had reached the ramparts of the federal army when he was mortally wounded. Colonel William R. Aylett took command of the shattered brigade as it retreated. His report of the brigade's action, is an epic of Confederate valor:

Conspicuous to all, 50 yards in advance of his brigade, waving his hat upon his sword, he led his men upon the enemy with a steady bearing which inspired all breasts with enthusiasm and courage, and won the admiration of every beholder. For in advance of all, he led the attack till he scaled the works of the enemy and fell mortally wounded in their hands, but not until he had driven them from their position and seen his colors planted upon their fortifications.[14]

How differently are battles fought today, and this was so even toward the end of the Civil War! The charging of massed men in close formation, as in Napoleon's day, was already obsolete, especially in the face of the firepower of the rifled artillery and the use of rifled muskets and guns. These weapons wrought deadly destruction on troops, as evidenced by the fact that at Gettysburg Lee lost one third of his army—25,000 men killed, wounded, and missing, out of 75,000 men—a loss so great that he never again had a chance for a successful offensive.

In accounting for Lee's defeat Confederates neglect to observe that Meade had a very strong army of 90,000 men, that he had been able to seize the strategic positions on the battlefield, that he made no great mistakes, and that he also had some superb officers, such as General Winfield Scott Hancock. Before the battle both Lee and his soldiers were undoubtedly overconfident, which often leads to a fall. Fremantle analyzed the defeat of the Confederate army as owing to "the utter contempt felt for the enemy by all the rank," and as the reason for its retreat the failure to coordinate the various units of the army. He was probably right.[15] For this condition Lee himself was largely to blame. He was in the habit of giving few orders during battle, relying on the judgment of his corps commanders, a practice which was all right as long as he had Jackson in place of Ewell and Hill. Longstreet also had a plausible explanation for the defeat. In a letter to Senator Louis Wigfall of Texas, he wrote: "Our failure in Pa, was due I think to our being under the impression that the enemy had not been able to get his forces up. Being under this impression, General Lee thought it best to attack at once, and we did attack before our forces got up and it turned out that the enemy was ready with his whole force, and ours was not."[16]

Lee did not blame Stuart, his cavalry leader, who had taken off on one of his daring exploits and lost contact with the main army, but he should have, for his cavalry was "the eyes of the army," and consequently Lee was surprised into fighting a battle in a location that he had not planned. This gave the Union army a decided advantage. Halsey, the young son of Senator Wigfall, who was in Stuart's cavalry, wrote to "Louly" that Stuart and his cavalry left the army on June 24 and did not contact Lee's army again until the afternoon of July 2, the second day of battle. Halsey Wigfall was in rags and tatters, but he had the interesting experience of meeting Dutch people, who had furnished refreshments, such as apple butter and milk—they did not know what to expect from Confederate troops, some expected the raping of women.[17]

A month after the battle, when the Army of Northern Virginia had re-treated safely across the Potomac River, and Meade did not follow him, Lee wrote a noble letter to the president, offering to resign the command of the army to a younger and abler man (Lee was fifty-six years old).[18] Davis re-plied that it was impossible for him to find a proper substitute for Lee, su-perior in ability and basking in the confidence of the army. He observed that the general had refused to stoop to planting articles in the public journals (which he condemned as generally partisan and venal) for the purpose of lauding himself. He expressed regret that Lee was still suffering from his illness of the spring (in the battle of Gettysburg, Lee was not well, but he did not plead this condition to condone his defeat) and wrote that he hoped his health would be fully restored so that he could lead the army in the struggles for independence that lay ahead.[19]

There were two important psychological effects of the battle. It shook the confidence of the Southern people in ultimate victory for the Confederate cause, ending any chance for European recognition. It also strengthened, as Davis later wrote, the malcontents, the critics—of him and of the peace advocates.[20] To General Theophilus Holmes, in command in Arkansas, he lamented that "the clouds are truly dark over us," but that he hoped the disasters would arouse the people to vigorous action against the enemy, and he expressed his belief that God would shortly reward "a just cause and faith-ful efforts with final success."[21] And to Governor H. Flanigan of Arkansas he wrote: "Our recent disasters will, I hope, only serve to nerve the men of the Confederacy to greater exertion."

Although Davis had put greater emphasis on the military effort in the invasion of Pennsylvania than in holding Vicksburg, there can be no doubt that he was vitally concerned with the defense of the Mississippi Valley. At the beginning of the war he had sent there Albert Sidney Johnson, whom he regarded as his best general, and when Johnston died he sent Pierre Beau-regard and Joseph E. Johnston to direct the defense of this region. Next to Lee and Jackson, they were regarded as the best generals available. As for Davis's overriding concern with the western theater of war, Josiah Gorgas, chief of Confederate ordnance, commented in his journal on March 23, 1863: "I spent an hour with the President. He is at present wholly devoted to the defense of the Mississippi and thinks and talks of little else."[22]

On the Tennessee front Braxton Bragg's army, after its retreat from Kentucky, lay encamped in December, 1862, near the middle Tennessee town of Murfreesboro. There was great disaffection toward the general among the men and officers, so much so that Davis felt it necessary to leave Richmond and find out for himself the extent of this feeling. The president was predisposed toward Bragg, to whom he wrote on August 5, 1862: "You have the mis-fortune of being regarded as my personal friend and pursued therefore with malignant censure."[23] On December 8, he wrote to Lee at Fredericksburg that he proposed to go to Tennessee immediately "with the hope that something may be done to bring out men not heretofore in service and to arouse all classes to united and desperate resistance." But the real object of his visit was to investigate the alarming rumors about the antipathy of Bragg's officers and men toward the commanding general. He must have been reassured, for less than two weeks before the impending battle of Murfreesboro, he wrote to Secretary of War Seldon that the troops at Murfreesboro were in good condition and fine spirits.

On the occasion of his visit to the army at Murfreesboro, a reporter from the *Chattanooga Rebel* reported the president's unassuming republican demeanor as he traveled with only one suitcase, marked "J.D.," and with one servant. He described Davis as "a man rather above the middle stature, of slight but well-proportioned figure; features decidedly handsome for a middle-aged gentleman, and wearing a perpetual expression of good humor. . . . His head is slightly sprinkled with grey and his whiskers are grey; yet he is a younger man in appearance and in feelings than we had conceived him to be; his voice, soft and persuasive, yet distinct and full-toned, and he is in the habit of speaking occasionally an exceeding good thing in a most quiet, accidental sort of way."[24]

Thirty miles from Murfreesboro, at Nashville, a strong Union army under the command of Major General William S. Rosecrans lay poised to strike Bragg's army. Shortly after Christmas, 1862, Rosecrans began his advance. Bragg had just participated in one of the glamorous social events of the Confederacy, the marriage of John Hunt Morgan, the handsome and dashing Kentucky cavalry leader, who was one of the most romantic figures of the war, to the Tennessee belle, Mattie Ready, a marriage performed by Bishop-General Leonidas Polk.

Bragg's army had been seriously weakened by an unwise order from Jefferson Davis to detach Stevenson's division of 11,000 men to aid General Pemberton in the defense of Vicksburg. Also Bragg had sent away on missions both Forrest's and Morgan's cavalry. At Stones River, two and a half miles from Murfreesboro, from December 31 to January 2, his army fought a staunch battle, but it was a drawn battle—no one knew who won—but then, as usual, Bragg retreated southward to Tullahoma, Tennessee.[25]

After Bragg's failure to follow up what seemed to his men a victory at Stones River, the disaffection with him grew alarmingly in the army. The newspapers, especially the *Chattanooga Rebel,* on whose staff was the brilliant young Henry Watterson, criticized him in caustic editorials early in January, 1863, saying that his officers and men had no confidence in him. Thereupon, on January 10, Bragg sent a circular to his generals, declaring that he would resign his command if they had no confidence in him. Their replies indicated that the majority thought the army needed a new leader.

Davis was now in a quandary; he disapproved of Bragg selecting this group of subordinate generals as a tribunal to decide whether he should resign. On

January 22 he ordered General Joseph E. Johnston to go to Bragg's head-quarters, investigate the charges, and report back to him. Unexpectedly, Johnston gave a glowing report of the general.[26] In the deep recesses of his mind, a variety of motivations were probably working; he knew that if he should recommend the removal of Bragg, he would probably be appointed to his place, and his personal pride forbade him from incurring the charge of seeking Bragg's place. It may be, also, that Johnston sincerely admired Bragg's military ability, for Bragg fought in the same style as Johnston. To his friend Senator Louis Wigfall, Johnston wrote in February and March, 1863, prais-ing Bragg "for gallantly and ably fighting" at Murfreesboro, asserting that he commanded extremely well in middle Tennessee, exhibiting great energy and discretion in his operations.[27] The president now had little choice other than to keep a man in command of an army that really hated him and had no confidence in his generalship.

While the military situation in Tennessee remained grave, Davis had to turn his attention to an even more dangerous confrontation at Vicksburg. When he removed General Earl Van Dorn from command there, he made the serious mistake of sending from Charleston Lieutenant General John C. Pemberton to take his place. Although Davis had respect for his military qualifications, he did not take sufficiently into account the human element. Pemberton was born in Pennsylvania but had joined the Confederacy. The fact that he was a Yankee counted against him. In addition, he had a brusque and repellent personality. The president admitted that Pemberton's manners were ungracious and that he quarreled with nearly every one with whom he came into contact, yet said he was a good soldier and an excellent man.[28] Realizing these faults of Pemberton, Davis wrote to him, three weeks before his surrender of Vicksburg, advising him to secure the cooperation of the people of Mississippi, and to use patience and listen to them.[29]

In view of the serious situation at Vicksburg, as early as November 11, 1862, Secretary of War George W. Randolph, grandson of Thomas Jefferson, had ordered General Theophilus Holmes, commanding the Confederate troops in Arkansas, to send 10,000 men across the Mississippi River to bolster Pemberton's defense of the strategic city. But the next day Davis revoked the order, for it violated the departmental organization of the army and infringed on his prerogative as commander-in-chief. Randolph's orders en-visaged a sensible movement of troops, but it was a bold act on the part of Jefferson's grandson. Davis ordered him thereafter to refer to him movements of troops between departments. The president was wrong in seeking to pre-serve departmental boundaries when common sense dictated otherwise, but he was right in insisting that in such important decisions he be consulted before-hand. The proud Virginian was stung by Davis's peremptory order and re-signed on November 15, 1862, leaving much unfinished business on his desk. Randolph wrote to his brother Thomas Jefferson Randolph that he had resigned because of the president's unwillingness to allow the secretary of war any discretion. He declared that he would not tolerate being merely a head clerk.[30]

Nevertheless, Davis himself on November 24, 1862, abandoned the rigid departmental system by appointing Joseph E. Johnston commander of a large territory, embracing the area between the Appalachian Mountains and the Mississippi River—the Department of the West. He was specifically given authority to take command, if he wished, of either Bragg's army or Pemberton's. Davis was reluctant to appoint Johnston to this command of such large responsibility, but he felt that he had no alternative among the senior generals of the army. Johnston was also reluctant, but accepted the appointment. Accordingly, he failed to rise to the great opportunity, maintaining, despite specific orders to the contrary, that he was not authorized to lead either of the armies in the Mississippi Valley, but had been assigned only to an empty job of geographical supervisor. It was a curious case of minimizing his considerable powers, and he did little to unify the defense of the West. Davis wrote a caustic letter to him, on July 15, after Vicksburg had been lost, reprimanding him for insisting on misinterpreting his orders (and perversely), and for maintaining that he had been given no real authority.

One valuable piece of advice that Johnston gave to Davis was not followed: Johnston wanted Pemberton reinforced from Holmes's army west of the river, but Davis, although he suggested it, would not order the western commander to do so. Johnston believed that it was foolish (and he was undoubtedly right) for Davis to transfer from Bragg's army 9,000 of his troops to Pemberton just before the battle of Murfreesboro, which he thought had prevented Bragg from winning a stunning victory over Rosecrans. Johnston was a Virginian, and his heart was not in commanding in the West; he was constantly writing to his friend Senator Louis Wigfall to get him transferred back to his old command in Virginia.[31]

After fruitless attacks on Vicksburg—which rested on a 200-foot-high promontory in a bend of the river—from the north, including efforts to cut through the bend, Grant decided on a new, bold plan. He transported his troops across to the west bank of the river, marched down past Vicksburg, and the Union gunboats and transports after running by Vicksburg in the night ferried Grant's army back to the east bank at Bruinburg, thirty miles below the city on April 30. He surprised the Confederates by this maneuver and by his risky decision to cut loose from his base of supplies and live on the country. The War Department at Richmond ordered Johnston to go immediately to Mississippi to take charge of the defense. Arising from a sickbed in Chattanooga, his headquarters, he arrived at Jackson on May 13, and telegraphed, "I am too late." Before this, he had advocated concentration of the Confederate forces in that area, even if it meant stripping the Mississippi River of its defenses.[32] He had asked President Davis to state his priorities. Which was most important, defense of the Confederate line in Tennessee, or

Vicksburg? Davis replied that both were vital and must be held, but Johnston believed that "without some great blunder of the enemy we cannot hold both."[33] Obviously, Johnston was not the man for a desperate situation.

While Johnston was attempting to gather an army at Jackson to aid Pemberton, Grant was marching northward toward both Vicksburg and Jackson. Thereupon followed a miserable sequence of untoward events for the Confederacy. Johnston ordered Pemberton to bring his army out of the city, or he would lose both Vicksburg and his army. Pemberton followed orders and was defeated at Champion's Hill while Johnston was trying to help him. Unfortunately, one of Johnston's orders in triplicate, outlining his plan to attack Grant's rear while Pemberton attacked the front, fell into the hands of a Union spy in Johnston's army, who took it to the federal commander. Thus, Grant was able to deal separately with the two uncoordinated Confederate armies and defeat them. Pemberton's vanquished army returned to its fortifications in Vicksburg, but Johnston again ordered him to try to cut his way out of the encircling federal army. The Confederate general was a victim of conflicting orders—Davis had ordered him to hold the strategic city at all hazards —and he obeyed the president.

On July 4 Pemberton felt forced to surrender his garrison of 30,000 men to Grant, who paroled them. In a long report in the *Official Records* defending himself from charges, Pemberton declared emphatically that he did not surrender on account of lack of food and supplies. He asserted that at the time of surrender, his army had remaining 40,000 pounds of bacon, 5,000 pounds of peas, and 51,000 pounds of rice. He surrendered because his men were exhausted and emaciated by continuous exposure for forty-seven days and nights in the trenches, and his position had become hopeless. He surrendered on the Fourth of July, he said, because he thought that on this day he could get better terms for his army from the Northern conqueror. But the Southern people condemned him for surrendering on this day, which they regarded as almost a sacred day—a quite different feeling from that of our more sophisticated age.

Davis was bitter over the surrender of Vicksburg, especially toward Johnston's ineffective role. When Gorgas observed to the president on July 17 that the garrison had surrendered apparently because of want of provisions, he replied, "Yes, from want of provisions, inside, and a general outside who wouldn't fight."[34] Did Davis realize, did the Southern people realize, that after this tragic loss of Vicksburg and the defeat at Gettysburg the Confederacy had little chance of winning the war, and therefore that the sensible policy was to make peace? The answer is decidedly no. There were some realists and some natural pessimists, such as Alexander H. Stephens, who thought otherwise, but, as far as one can tell, Davis and the Southern people were counting on a resurgence of the Southern spirit and on the war weariness of the Northern people to bring the war to a successful close for the Confederacy. Even Lee in his letter of August 8, 1863, offering to resign, wrote:

"Nothing is wanted but that their [the people's] fortitude should equal their bravery to insure the success of our cause." And on October 29, 1863, the realist, General Gorgas, wrote in his diary: "We are now in a condition to carry on the war for an indefinite period. There is breadstuff enough, and tho' the inadequacy of transportation makes prices high in some parts, there is an abundance for all if the total be considered. And we have war material sufficient—men, guns, powder—the real pinch is in the Treasury."[35]

Gettysburg and Vicksburg were depressing, yet all was not lost; so thought Confederate leaders such as Lee and Davis, and probably most of the Southern people. In the fall they were cheered by the news of the astonishing victory of Chickamauga in Tennessee. Before that cheering event the military situation looked gloomy, indeed, for the Confederates. Rosecrans, after six months of inactivity following the drawn battle of Stones River (or Murfreesboro), began to move against the equally passive army of Bragg at Tullahoma. With scarcely any hard fighting, he drove Bragg from his base at Tullahoma into Chattanooga. Then, by threatening his communication to the south, he maneuvered Bragg out of Chattanooga and occupied the city. As Gorgas observed, "Bragg has shown his usual readiness for retreating, and has retreated us out of the whole of East Tennessee—Rosecrans being in possession of Chattanooga and Burnside of Knoxville, without the pulling of a trigger."[36]

Bragg waited for reinforcements. The president at the beginning of September decided to strengthen him with a large portion of a corps of Lee's army.[37] Lee acquiesced in this mutilation of his army, which was facing the unaggressive federal army under Meade, who was threatening Richmond, on condition that the troops be returned quickly, but he declined the president's request that he go and take command there.[38] Instead Lee sent Longstreet, who was eager to go.

Longstreet's corps had to travel on the railroads by way of Atlanta and barely arrived on time to turn the tide of battle. Rosecrans made a serious blunder in maneuvering his troops, thereby leaving an opening in his line, through which Longstreet's troops rushed. The federal army was routed and Rosecrans fled headlong with his troops to Chattanooga. His army was saved from complete disaster by General George H. Thomas, who thereafter was called "the Rock of Chickamauga." It was one of the bloodiest battles of the war, leading to tremendous losses on both sides, amounting to about a third of both armies. Thomas Wolf's short story of "Chickamauga" portrays the desperate valor, the blood and sweat, of that battle. A ninety-five-year-old Confederate veteran told him: "But the biggest fight that I was ever in—the bloodiest battle anyone has ever fought—was at Chickamauga in that cedar thicket—at Chickamauga Creek in that great war." Chickamauga has been evaluated by General D. H. Hill as "the great battle of the West." Yet the Confederates, after all the loss of blood and sorely needed manpower, did not attempt to follow up their victory. It proved useless to them.

After the battle occurred one of the most disgraceful episodes in Confederate military history—one in which Davis did not show up at all well, owing to his friendship for Bragg. As was his wont, Bragg blamed his generals for his failures. He suspended Lieutenant General Leonidas Polk and later preferred charges against him for not attacking at sunrise, as well as preferring charges against General Thomas C. Hindman for disobeying orders; he also accused General John C. Breckinridge of drunkenness. On the other hand, Bragg's generals and his soldiers were bitter that a knockout blow of the routed Union army had not been delivered by a rapid pursuit. Pent-up feelings against Bragg resulted in a secret conference of his generals on the night of October 8, 1863, in which they resolved to draw up a petition to the president to remove him from command. Twelve generals signed it: the leaders seem to have been Longstreet and Buckner, both of whom were ambitious to succeed Bragg.

The president came from Richmond to investigate. He had already persuaded Bragg to relinquish the charges against his friend, General Leonidas Polk, who was sent to Mississippi. On October 9 Davis called a conference of the dissident officers at Bragg's headquarters, with Bragg present. Boldly, the officers told the president that Bragg would be of more use in another theater. Yet Davis seems to have decided before the meeting to retain Bragg in command, and he did. In so doing, he showed an insensitivity to public opinion, as well as to the feelings of the soldiers. He also brought with him on the train from Atlanta General John C. Pemberton, hated by both the army and the people for the surrender of Vicksburg on July 4, with the intention of placing him in command of Polk's corps, but when he found that officers and men were violently opposed to this he abandoned the idea.

Bragg still had a chance to capture Rosecrans' army, penned up in Chattanooga. But he foolishly weakened his forces by sending away his ablest general, Longstreet, with 20,000 men—one third of his strength—on an unsuccessful attempt to dislodge Burnside's army, well fortified at Knoxville. In the meantime Grant, realizing the desperate situation of the besieged army in Chattanooga, arose from a sickbed, journeyed to the beleaguered army, and removed Rosecrans from command, replacing him with the dependable General George Thomas. He ordered Hooker's corps of 23,000 men to journey from Alexandria, Virginia, by rail to Tennessee, which they accomplished in six days—a more spectacular use of the railroads than Longstreet's journey to join Bragg's army just before the battle of Chickamauga. Grant's energy and decisiveness then opened up a supply line to the federal army in Chattanooga and strongly reinforced the beleaguered troops.

The Confederate army was holding strong strategic positions on the low mountains surrounding Chattanooga. But the federal army was far more aggressive. On November 23, 1863, Hooker's men charged up Lookout Mountain through clouds and mist to attack a weak Confederate skirmish line of 2,000 men at the top and defeat them in an engagement romanticized as the "Battle above the Clouds." But the real disaster to the Confederate army occurred two days later in the battle of Missionary Ridge. Grant sent Sherman's army to capture the rifle pits at the bottom of the ridge, which they easily did, and then, inspired with martial enthusiasm, without orders from their officers, the men charged up to the top of the ridge, and the Confederate troops in a strange panic fled before them. President Davis, in a message to Congress on December 7, 1863, spoke of this humiliating defeat as follows: "It is believed that if the troops who yielded to the assault had fought with the valor which they had displayed on previous occasions, and which was manifested in this battle on other parts of the line, the enemy would have been repulsed with very great slaughter, and our country would have escaped the misfortune and the army the mortification of the first defeat that has resulted from misconduct of the troops."[39] His words were too mild; what he called "misconduct" was actually cowardice; but there was a general on another part of the line, General Patrick Cleburne, called "the Stonewall Jackson of the West," who led his troops with conspicuous valor in this battle. Bragg explained what he called "the shameful conduct" of part of his army as follows: "A panic which I had never before witnessed seemed to have seized upon officers and men, and each seemed to be struggling for his personal safety, regardless of his duty or his character."[40] He thought that they had become demoralized because they could plainly see the mobilization of the great numerical superiority of soldiers to be hurled at them.

Bragg then retreated to winter quarters at Dalton in northern Georgia. He was so thoroughly discredited in the eyes of the army and of the Southern people, that even the common soldiers shouted opprobrious epithets as he passed their lines, such as "Here is your mule!" and "Bully for Bragg, he's hell on retreat!" Bragg finally realized that the army did not want him to lead it and on November 28, 1863, he gave up and resigned. General W. J. Hardee succeeded him temporarily, but only temporarily, for he did not want the responsibility of the job, and on December 16 the president reluctantly reappointed Joseph E. Johnston. Bragg, in a letter to the president of December 8, 1863, recommended that new generals should be appointed to command the corps of the army in place of Frank Cheatham and John C. Breckinridge "who take to the bottle and drown their cares by becoming stupid and unfit for duty." The president did not take this advice, but he recalled Bragg to be his adviser on military affairs at Richmond.

Davis and the Trans-Mississippi West

It was a question of priorities with President Davis. At the same time that the trans-Mississippi West—consisting of Missouri, Arkansas, Texas, western Louisiana, and the Confederate territory of Arizona—needed his attention, he felt that the defending of the Tennessee, the Virginia, and the Mississippi River frontiers made even more imperative demands. Properly handled, the trans-Mississippi West could have furnished valuable resources in manpower and food, especially meat and wheat, to the Confederate fighting forces east of the Mississippi River. It failed to do so, however, in the first place because this vast region was only slightly connected by railroads with the rest of the Confederacy. Robert Black's railroad map of the Confederacy in June, 1861, shows that Arkansas had practically no railroads, Louisiana only a few scattered lines, the short lines in Texas were concentrated around Houston and Galveston, and the tiny part of southwest Missouri controlled by the Confederacy had no railroads.[1] When the Union army obtained control of the Mississippi River in 1863, that river severed the Confederacy into two parts as with a sword. There were no telegraphic communications. In addition to this lack of communication, the feeling for the Confederacy in this vast, remote region was decidedly lukewarm, and its soldiers were reluctant to serve across the Mississippi River. Furthermore, there was dissension among the southwestern generals, who often would not cooperate with each other. President Davis tried to act as a peacemaker, but with little effect.

Accordingly, the record of the Confederate armies in that region was one of failure, with few successes. General Josiah Gorgas in his journal of April 2, 1863, summarized these military engagements as follows: of the four considerable actions in Arkansas and Missouri, the victories of Wilson Creek, or Springfield, Missouri, and Lexington, Missouri, were accidental victories, and the battles of Pea Ridge, or Elkhorn Tavern, and of Prairie Grove in Arkansas in 1862 were disastrous retreats, if not positive defeats. "It is," he commented, "a lamentable record of bad management." Two weeks later he wrote, "Our affairs west of the Mississippi have never prospered, because nearly all our means and attention were concentrated on the great theatre east."[2]

The battle of Wilson Creek on August 10, 1861, came shortly after the victory of Bull Run, when Sterling Price, leading his Missouri troops, and Texas troops under General Ben McCulloch, former captain of the Texas Rangers, defeated a federal force under the command of Brigadier General Nathaniel Lyon, an abolitionist zealot, and Franz Sigel of the St. Louis Germans, resulting in the tragic death of Lyon. A month later Price captured the entire force of 3,500 men commanded by Colonel James A. Mulligan, shut up in a fort at Lexington, Missouri. These battles took place before the so-called "Rebel Legislature" of Missouri seceded October 31, 1861, and established the Confederate capital at Neosho in the extreme southwest corner of the state. Early in 1862 General Henry H. Selby was authorized by President Davis to recruit and organize an army in Texas, which proceeded to advance up the Rio Grande as far as Santa Fe. He had grandiose ideas of marching to California, obtaining the gold supply there for the Confederate Treasury, and extending Confederate authority and slavery over California and the Southwest, but in April he was disastrously defeated at Glorietta Pass in New Mexico, retreating with heavy losses back into Texas.

President Davis had difficult relations with the most prominent trans-Mississippi general, Sterling Price. Price's biographer, Professor Robert E. Shalhope, has described these relations under the chapter heading "A Thorn in Davis's Side." Price was a Virginian, educated at Hampden-Sidney College, who traveled with his family to Missouri, where they became tobacco planters on a large scale. He fought in the Mexican War and entered politics, being elected governor of Missouri in 1852. He was vain (Davis called him the vainest man he had ever met), but was immensely popular in Missouri and beloved by his soldiers, who called him "Pap." Missouri was a battleground of pro-Union and Confederate supporters, a strategic state that Davis apparently did not appreciate. Price had been a reluctant secessionist, but after Governor Claiborne Jackson refused Lincoln's call for troops, he joined the Confederate side. After Price's victories at Wilson Creek and Lexington, Davis transmitted to him a complimentary resolution passed by Congress. When the general requested additional troops and supplies, the president told him that he had none to give except McCulloch's Texas troops, but that he would do all in his power to save Missouri for the Confederacy. At the same time he expressed regret that the Missouri troops had enlisted for only short periods. At this time the relations between the president and the vain general, who was thirsting for glory, were cordial.

Price next participated in the disastrous battle of Pea Ridge, or Elkhorn Tavern, in northern Arkansas on March 18, 1862. He joined forces with General Ben McCulloch, leading Texas troops, and General Albert Pike, Indian diplomatist, and Chief Stand Watie, the only Indian brigadier in the Confederate army, leading a colorful force of Indians, most of whom had emigrated from the South. McCulloch did not think much of Price's military ability or of his undisciplined troops, but a West Pointer, General Earl Van Dorn, was placed in overall command. The three generals failed to coordinate their forces in attacking the federal army under General Samuel R. Curtis, being defeated in a decisive battle, in which McCulloch was killed, that lost the chance to recover Missouri.

Shortly after the battle of Pea Ridge, Price was ordered to cross the Mississippi and join Beauregard's army at Corinth, Mississippi. Much against his wishes, for he hoped to recover Missouri, he obeyed orders, put his troops on transports, crossed the river, and landed them at Memphis, proceeding by rail to Corinth. At Memphis his swollen ego was inflated by the enthusiastic welcoming crowd, to whom he delivered a flowery speech. To counteract the feeling in the West that it had been abandoned, Davis instructed Van Dorn to issue a proclamation that he would return with the Army of the West, but Price would not join in what he regarded as deception.

In June, 1862, he arrived in Richmond to confer with Davis, hoping to be placed in charge of the trans-Mississippi West, and advocating an immediate advance into Missouri. Davis's interview with Price was typically Davis. Although he promised eventually to transfer him to the West, he refused to commit himself on the question of giving Price, of whose military ability he had an unfavorable opinion, the command of the western armies. When Price hotly said he would resign, Davis replied he would willingly accept his resignation, and that he would be happy but "surprised" if Price carried out his threat of going back to Missouri, raising a new army of state troops, and winning victories for the Confederacy. But on the next day Davis relented, adopting a conciliatory attitude, and Price did not resign.[3]

After his defeat at Corinth, Price desired intensely to return to the trans-Mississippi to lead a campaign to recover Missouri. On February 23, 1863, he was granted his wish, and in the fall of 1864 led an undisciplined army of Confederates, poorly armed, into the heart of the state in hopes of attracting many recruits into the Confederate army. He succeeded in obtaining some recruits and 600 wagons of supplies, as well as a great herd of cattle. He waged some battles with promising results, but was finally defeated in the extreme western part of the state—at Westport on October 23, 1864. His army had plundered both foe and friend. He was removed from command by Kirby Smith, but his devotion to the Confederate cause remained so strong that when the Confederacy collapsed he exiled himself to Mexico to help found the Confederate colony of Carlotta. He has been fitly described by his biographer as "a military romantic," intrigued with the idea of the cavalier, impulsive, brave, neglectful of logistics, contemptuous of breastworks and fortifications, a charismatic figure, beloved by his soldiers. There were a number of officers in the Confederate command system much like him, but perhaps not quite so egotistical and vain.

The Confederates dreamed constantly of recovering Missouri, using their positions in Arkansas as a base. The Confederate commander in this region, General Thomas C. Hindman, was planning an advance into Missouri in the fall of 1862 when his superior, General Theophilus Holmes, prodded by the War Department, ordered him to bring his division of 11,000 men to Little Rock and from there to proceed to cross the river and go to the aid of Pemberton at Vicksburg. Before obeying the order Hindman decided to fight one more battle to recover Missouri. At Prairie Grove, near Fayetteville, Arkansas, he fought this battle on December 7, 1862, and was badly defeated. Thus the reserve of trans-Mississippi troops so desperately needed to defend Vicksburg was lost.

The trans-Mississippi region was in urgent need of a capable general to command the scattered Confederate forces. As early as September, 1862, the governors of the states in this region—Francis R. Lubbock of Texas, Claiborne F. Jackson of Missouri, Thomas Moore of Louisiana, and R. H. Rector of Arkansas—wrote a joint letter to Davis urging that a competent general and adequate supplies be sent to the Trans-Mississippi Department, and that a branch of the Treasury be established there. Davis replied on September 12 that he was sending Lieutenant General Theophilus Holmes, Richard Taylor (son of Zachary), Thomas C. Hindman, and Sterling Price, as well as the supplies requested.[4] Governor Lubbock wrote on November 13, 1862, that the people of Texas, alarmed by dangers from jayhawkers and Indians, could furnish no men for out-of-the-state service. Much the same situation existed in Missouri and Arkansas. The western politicians became so disillusioned over the mismanagement of General Holmes and the "odious conduct" of General Hindman that on January 20, 1863, the Arkansas delegation in Congress asked the president to withdraw them and appoint Kirby Smith as commander of the Trans-Mississippi Department.[5] Davis acceded to this request by transferring Hindman to Bragg's army and on February 9, 1863, appointing Lieutenant General Kirby Smith as commander of the department. Hindman, in a letter to Senator Louis T. Wigfall of Texas, wrote that when he went to Arkansas, he became the most popular man in the state, but that when he refused to be a demagogue or to ignore the interests of the service a clamor arose against him, leading to his recall.[6] Davis retained Holmes, who was given charge of the district of Arkansas under Smith.

The personality of Kirby Smith was important in this vast region of the trans-Mississippi after 1863, for he ruled virtually as a Persian satrap.[7] Smith was born in St. Augustine, Florida, and graduated from West Point, but with so low a ranking and so many demerits that his imperious father warned him "to reign in your prancing steed." So nearsighted was he that after finishing at West Point he was at first denied a commission, but his father got this decision reversed and he became a lieutenant. After he joined the Confederate army, he won distinction at Bull Run and in the Kentucky campaign of 1862. With his glossy black hair, handsome face, and ample whiskers, he was a striking-looking officer, who impressed President Davis with his dash. There have been many generals and statesmen who have impressed the public as masterful, who inside their homes were as meek as lambs. Kirby Smith was not one of these; his attractive wife said that everything he did was exactly right. Fremantle in his journal commented on Kirby Smith as being remarkably active and wearing large eyeglasses (very few Confederate officers or men did), but he became more of a civil governor than a fighting military officer.

The people and the politicians of the West complained constantly that they were being neglected by the Confederate government at Richmond.[8] They thought that they had special problems of jayhawkers, hostile Indians, and marauding bands of deserters. After Vicksburg, they feared that they would be forgotten and deserted. Davis tried to reassure them, by letters chiefly, such as the one he wrote to Senator Waldo Johnson of Arkansas on July 14, 1863. He commented that Johnson's letter to him found him in "the depths of gloom," but that "we must exercise charity in criticism and rely on God." He assured him that he had no intention of abandoning Arkansas. He suggested that the state try to seek self-sufficiency by establishing the desperately needed industries that would be so located as to be almost invulnerable to attack—to establish a foundry and rolling mill to make munitions, tanneries, and so on—and he would send to the state skilled mechanics and cards for household industries to make cotton and woolen cloth.[9]

Missouri, as well as Kentucky, maintained governments-in-exile, represented by stars in the Confederate flag, and sent full delegations to Congress. The letter book and papers of Thomas C. Reynolds, who succeeded Claiborne Jackson as governor of Missouri when he died in December, 1862, illustrate the problems of a Confederate government-in-exile. Reynolds was loyal to President Davis. When a Missouri senator died and he was urged to appoint Sterling Price, he refused to do so because he believed that Price aspired to the presidency and might become the leader of a party in the Senate hostile to Davis. As governor of the 15,000 or 20,000 Missourians within the Confederate lines (his estimate), Reynolds sought to recruit soldiers in south

Missouri to prevent guerrilla warfare in the state (it alienated the people from the Confederate cause), to alleviate the jealousies of Missouri officers and politicians, and to moderate the discontent among Missouri troops and politicians for his not upholding state rights as did Governor Joseph Brown of Georgia. He located the seat of his government at Marshall, Texas, from where he tried to unify the region and maintain its connection with the Confederate government at Richmond.[10]

Davis liked Kirby Smith, whose ability he respected, and tried to give him encouragement and support, but his energies and attention were monopolized by the danger in the eastern theater. When Kirby Smith asked him in 1863 to delegate the power of appointment in his isolated department, the president replied, "The power to appoint cannot be delegated," thus illustrating anew his jealousy of preserving his presidential prerogative.[11] Although Davis was frequently accused, especially toward the end of his administration, of being a "despot," he was careful to operate under the authority of the laws and of the Constitution. He had earlier written to General Mansfield Lovell at New Orleans on April 23, 1862: "Leave all State institutions, as far as possible, undisturbed."[12] He advised Kirby Smith to consult the governors of the trans-Mississippi region and secure their cooperation. Smith did call a conference of the governors and justices of this region at Marshall, Texas, on August 15, 1863. They gave discouraging reports, especially as to lack of means and the lukewarm spirit of the people. They recommended that slaves be impressed to serve as teamsters, that cotton be impressed for military necessities, that the commander interfere as little as possible with the state powers, and that a commissioner be sent to establish good relations with the Mexican and French authorities in Mexico.

Kirby Smith's most vexing problem in administering his Department of the Trans-Mississippi was to control the cotton trade for the benefit of the Confederacy. During the war, because of its accessibility to Mexico, Texas became the most important cotton-producing area in the Confederacy. Indeed, it became the center of an immense speculation for private traders, described as consisting largely of Jews and Yankees, who had no regard for the interests of the Confederacy, particularly in neglecting to import military supplies in exchange for cotton. Huge profits could be made in this illegal trade, for cotton could be bought in the interior of Texas for three cents a pound and sold at the border for fifty and sixty cents. To transport it, horses, mules, and wagons were required that were badly needed for the Confederate service. Smith set up a Cotton Bureau to supervise procuring cotton for the Confederacy and importing military supplies. When he used the power given him by the Impressment Act of 1863, seizing one half of the cotton of reluctant planters, allowing them to keep the other half, a storm of protest ensued, and all kinds of subterfuges and evasions were used to defeat his policy. The governor of Texas, Pendleton Murrah, contributed to this opposition to the activities of his Cotton Bureau by buying cotton for the state account, and in 1864 the impressment policy was abandoned. Accordingly, the Confederacy could not use the cotton trade in Texas effectively to supply its needs.

Kirby Smith's position as commander of the department involved exercising many civil functions; he declared that it was no bed of roses. One of his problems was financial, especially the lack of money to pay the troops, which was part of the reason for their low morale. The Confederate Treasury set up an independent branch west of the Mississippi, but it did not greatly alleviate the situation. Although Texas had vast herds of cattle and its wheat fields were so extensive that it was called the "Granary for the Confederate troops west of the Mississippi," the lack of transportation facilities hindered their effective use. Furthermore, as General Richard Taylor complained early in 1864, the planters withheld their grain from the army, and the tanners did not tan, because the Confederate agents paid only one half of the price to be obtained on the open market. Also, planters were alienated by the army burning their cotton to prevent it from falling into the hands of the enemy.[13]

Another of Smith's problems was General Theophilus Holmes, district commander of Arkansas. He had given Holmes permission to try to recover Helena, on the Mississippi River, but the attack, launched on the day that Vicksburg surrendered, failed. Holmes still occupied Little Rock, where he had located his headquarters, but on September 10, 1863, he was forced to evacuate this last Confederate stronghold in Arkansas. In the following March, Kirby Smith removed Holmes from command, which Governor Reynolds and the Arkansas delegation in Congress had unanimously requested.

The most important military engagement of the Confederates west of the Mississippi River occurred in the spring of 1864, when the politician General Nathaniel Banks invaded Louisiana by way of the Red River. It was a joint army and navy operation with Admiral David D. Porter commanding a large flotilla of gunboats. A dominating objective of the campaign was to obtain cotton. Admiral Porter described it as follows: "It was an army of cotton speculators, commanded by General Greed, General Avarice, General Speculation, and General Breach of Trust, with all their attendant staff of harpies, who were using the army and the navy for the vilest purposes."[14] Banks captured Alexandria, Louisiana, as the Confederates under Major General Richard Taylor retreated, but on April 8, 1864, when the Northern army had nearly reached Shreveport, Taylor attacked the strung-out army at Mansfield (also called Sabine Cross Roads) with forces less than half the strength of the invading army and defeated them, and after another clash at Pleasant Hall, the federal army retreated down the river valley. Taylor called on Kirby Smith at Shreveport to send reinforcements to complete the rout and destruction of the federal army.

But Smith feared a simultaneous advance of troops from Arkansas under General Frederick Steele, and first went after this less important army, planning to defeat it and return in time to participate in the destruction of Banks's army. He arrived too late, and Banks got away with his fleet, which was held up by low water at the falls at Alexandria, but was at last freed by a series of wing dams built by Wisconsin troops. Taylor was disgusted that the federal army and its fleet were allowed to escape, and became involved in a bitter controversy with Smith over this miscue. Taylor asked to be transferred out of the department, and was assigned to a command in Mississippi, but he could not take his troops with him for, he said, not only did they face formidable problems in crossing the Mississippi River, but so reluctant were his troops to serve east of the river that if the crossing had been attempted they would have melted away through desertion.

Taylor's intransigence illustrated the dissension among the officers in the Trans-Mississippi Department. It would have taken more than the peacemaking efforts of Davis, remote in Richmond, to settle their quarrels as long as he clung to retaining General Theophilus Holmes in that region. Blunt and realistic, General Richard Taylor strongly disapproved of Kirby Smith's policies, expressing his opinions in caustic letters to the departmental commander, so that, according to General John A. Wharton, commanding the Texas Corps of Cavalry, Smith had to relieve him to keep his self-respect.[15] Taylor thought that the commander was wasting his strength in seeking to recover lost territory to the neglect of areas that the Confederates possessed: "The substance of Louisiana and Texas was staked against the shadow of Missouri and northern Arkansas."[16] When Smith tried to follow orders from Davis to send troops to the aid of Vicksburg in the spring of 1863, Taylor thought the effort was impractical, and so it proved. After the fall of that city individuals could still cross the Mississippi, but crossing became virtually impossible for organized bodies of troops or supplies.

The tragedy of the trans-Mississippi was that it rendered very little assistance to the cause of the Confederacy. It did furnish at least two generals of ability who rendered notable service in the battles of the eastern theater—General Patrick Cleburne of Arkansas and General John B. Hood—and Texas troops fought valiantly at First Manassas, in the Seven Days battles around Richmond and in other battles. President Davis tried, as we have seen, to get troops from the trans-Mississippi to cross the river and aid in the defense of Vicksburg, and even afterward he constantly urged Kirby Smith to send troops across the river. Not only Smith, but Simon Bolivar Buckner and Richard Taylor, advised him that it was not practicable following the surrender of Vicksburg to dispatch troops from that region to the east. When Davis mildly criticized Kirby Smith for this failure, he offered to resign. But the time to have sent troops and large supplies of meat from the trans-Mississippi was before the loss of Vicksburg. Though Davis did not seem to realize that this opportunity had passed, he did not order the crossing. But it was not easy at any time for troops to do so, owing to the lack of railroads and the threat of formidable federal armies on their side of the river. Furthermore, the president was not superhuman, and he had to consider the priorities of his overall command, which clearly were the eastern front, the defense of the back door of the South through Tennessee, and keeping the Mississippi River under Confederate control. Yet when the surrender came in 1865, over 30,000 Confederate troops were under Kirby Smith, at a time when Lee's pitiful forces were deployed against the powerful army of Grant, and Beauregard and Johnston were trying to stop Sherman's advance with mere brooms of soldiers.

The trans-Mississippi region, in truth, seems to have had only an inchoate idea of a Southern nation. The people were separated in a geographical sense from the Confederate capital; their Southernism and desire to fight for Confederate independence were lukewarm. Kirby Smith complained that all the fighting men of the region had gone into the armies in the East, leaving mainly old men, women, and children, plus men who shirked military service. It was the most frontier-like region of the South in its society, only slightly organized, without much industry, where the private gun often prevailed. Although the region had plenty of wheat and cattle for meat and for tanning leather, its soldiers were frequently ill fed, ill shod, and ill paid. Speculation in cotton through the lines with Mexico and blockade-runners slipping into the port of Galveston with private goods tended to erode Southern patriotism. Kirby Smith was discouraged by conditions in the trans-Mississippi region when he assumed command. He found unusual problems, such as marauding Indians, jayhawkers, and criminals, notably William C. Quantrill, leading guerrilla bands who masqueraded as Confederate soldiers but were completely lawless. Other problems were mutiny, officers quarreling with and shooting each other in duels, and planters protesting against the government interfering with their profits from the illegal sale of cotton—it was certainly not a Confederate paradise, and far from the romantic legend of the Confederate soldiers.[17]

Davis's Neglect of the Home Front

Davis's neglect of the trans-Mississippi West was unfortunate, but not nearly as disastrous as his neglect of economic affairs, or of the home front. As president of the Confederate States of America his first priority of duty was, for the short run, the management of the war machine, for if the army should be unable to win victories, there could be no Confederacy. But, his second duty was to oversee the home front, which in the long run was just as important. Failure in this department explains in large part the collapse of the Confederacy. As the notable expert on the Confederacy, Charles W. Ramsdell, put it: "The Confederacy had begun to crumble or break down within long before the military situation appeared to be desperate."[1] The single greatest weakness of the Confederate government, he thought, was in the handling of finances, and General Josiah Gorgas and General Joseph E. Johnston agreed. The next greatest failure, Ramsdell thought, was in the handling of the transportation system.

To perform these tremendous tasks in an economy that had been geared to agriculture, business brains were needed. Davis certainly did not appear to appreciate the value of business acumen in managing either the government economy or the army. All his life he had dealt with planters and politicians and occasionally with cotton factors. He had been largely concerned with abstractions, such as state rights and constitutional liberties. Only two men in his cabinet, Memminger and George A. Trenholm at the very end, were businessmen. The antebellum South, indeed, lacked good businessmen; until recently Southerners have never properly valued the businessman, and in the Civil War this proved a great disadvantage.[2] The North, on the other hand, had able businessmen, both in government and in the army. Although Lincoln was a loose administrator, he had been a shrewd and successful corporation lawyer, and in administering the war economy he had the services of Thomas Scott, president of the Pennsylvania Railroad, as assistant secretary of war, and another efficient businessman, Montgomery Meigs, as chief of the Quartermaster Corps, plus two of the ablest businessmen in the country, Herman Haupt and Daniel McCallum, to manage the railroads.

By way of contrast the Confederate assistant of war was, first, Albert T. Bledsoe, professor of mathematics at the University of Virginia, a man absolutely controlled by abstractions—a ridiculous appointment—and, later, ex–Supreme Court Justice John A. Campbell. The continuance in office through most of the war of Lucius B. Northrop, an old West Point and army friend, as commissary general, was a disaster. The North, moreover, had a much abler secretary of the treasury than Memminger in Salmon P. Chase, who devised a system of national banks that aided in supporting its finances and the issue of viable paper money, or "greenbacks." But President Davis, even if he had tried energetically, would have had a harder time in recruiting good businessmen in the Confederate service than did Lincoln with a going government.

Davis was so busy with military affairs that he interfered very little with the conduct of the Treasury Department. He respected Memminger's financial judgment and the two men got along very well. Moreover, he knew that Memminger consulted the best financial brains in the Confederacy, especially Trenholm, who succeeded him in the summer of 1864. Trenholm was a Charleston businessman, probably the wealthiest man in the Confederacy, part owner of as many as fifty blockade-runners, and highly respected. Others who advised the president on financial matters were Howell Cobb, who had been secretary of the treasury under Buchanan, Robert M. T. Hunter, chairman of the Senate Finance Committee, and the able New Orleans banker, James A. Denegre.

Secretary of the Treasury Christopher Memminger had been an advocate of hard money before the war, but the necessities of war caused him to change drastically and to preside over a paper money economy. In the first place, he could obtain very little specie; the blockade prevented the tariff (although low) from bringing in much cash, and the specie existing in the Confederacy was very small. One source was the seizure of specie from the federal custom houses and mints; another was a windfall, when the specie in the six New Orleans banks amounting to $4,192,998.79 was rushed through the Confederate lines before the city fell, only to be appropriated by the Confederate government. The Confederacy fought for four years on the basis of approximately $27 million.

How did they do it? The only large loan that brought in cash was obtained from the Paris bankers, Erlanger and Company; ironically they, instead of the Confederate Treasury, proposed the loan in the fall of 1862, as a great cotton speculation. They proposed selling Confederate bonds worth $25 million, which the Erlangers would underwrite. But it seemed to Confederate authorities, Memminger and Benjamin, that the terms were too favorable to the Erlangers, and they foolishly scaled it down to $15 million. Baron Emile Erlanger then went to Richmond to persuade the Confederate authorities to increase the loan to the original amount proposed. Upon his return to Paris he told the Confederate agent, James G. Gibbs, that Memminger emphatically opposed the extension, saying that $15 million would provide sufficient funds. Erlanger said that he tried to induce President Davis to overrule his secretary of the treasury but that the president refused to do so, saying that he left it up to Memminger, but privately he agreed to extend the loan as much as possible. The evidence on this point is conflicting, for a letter quoted by Memminger's chief clerk in the first year of the war, Henry D. Capers, seems to contradict Erlanger's statement by claiming that Memminger advocated the increase of the credit of their government in Europe to the largest sum. Another version attributed the decision to reject the larger sum to the supposed shrewdness of Judah P. Benjamin.[3] Much of Confederate finance, both as to loans and taxation, was based on the hopeful belief that the Confederacy would win the war within a year.

A relatively recent study of the Erlanger loan maintains that, as advantageous as the issue of bonds appeared to be to the Erlangers, it was the best bargain that the unproved Confederate government could obtain in the European market. When the bonds were first put on the market in March, 1863, they were oversubscribed by five times, mainly by English investors who were attracted by the high rate of interest of 7 percent paid and by their convertibility into cotton at six pence a pound. But the bonds began to decline and the Erlangers persuaded the Confederate authorities to "bull the market" by secretly buying back bonds to the amount of over half of the original loan. Since the bonds were to be paid for in installments, the Erlangers and the Confederates feared that subscribers woud not pay further installments and, also, to allow the market to go lower would indicate lack of faith in the Confederate government's ability to survive. This secret selling proved ultimately to be a shrewd move. Older writers, particularly Frank L. Owsley, maintained that the Jewish bankers "fleeced" the Confederacy by the profits that they made from the loan and their commissions, and that the Confederacy received only $2,599,000 from the loan.[4] Ms. Judith Gentry, however, in her able analysis, shows clearly that Owsley was grossly wrong, and that the Confederacy obtained $8,535,486 from the sale of the bonds, for it later resold a large amount of the bonds obtained by bulling the market, and persuaded creditors, notably Saul Issac and Company in England, to accept them for purchases of supplies. Therefore, instead of the Erlanger loan being a sellout, it was a decided success.[5]

Unable to borrow much in Europe, Memminger tried to raise funds by bond issues bearing 8 percent interest, but the public showed slight interest in buying them, and, besides, they had little specie to pay for them.[6] Accordingly, Congress passed, on May 16, 1861, the Produce Loan Act providing for the sale of bonds to planters from the proceeds of their agricultural produce, which was changed on April 21, 1862, to permit direct exchange of agricultural produce for the bonds. Administered by J. D. B. DeBow, the famous New Orleans editor, it brought into the treasury something under 500,000 bales of cotton, much of which was ultimately captured by the enemy.

The other source of revenue was taxation. But Congress shied away from imposing heavy taxes on a people who before the war had been lightly taxed. Congress was controlled by planters and slaveholders, who were naturally reluctant to impose heavy taxation of their lands and slaves in order for the South to bear the financial burden of the war. Consequently two years passed before Congress passed the first comprehensive tax law: a tax in kind of one tenth, a light tax on incomes, and a series of license taxes on occupations. After the permanent constitution went into effect, Congress was prevented from taxing *ad valorem* the great source of wealth of land and slaves, which constituted two thirds of the wealth of the Confederacy, by the prohibition of direct taxes, except according to population, and taxes on property and slaves were so regarded. Again and again, Davis advocated taxation to prevent the government's dependence on paper money, and he was seconded in this advocacy by the vice president and Secretary Memminger.

Davis reported the financial condition of the government to Congress regularly. Until 1863 these reports were optimistic. In his message of August 18, 1862, for example, he observed that "the credit of the government securities [bonds] remains unimpaired, and ... this credit is fully justified by the small amount of accumulated debt, notwithstanding the magnitude of our military operations."[7] Nevertheless, he also recommended an increase in the issue of treasury notes (paper money), stating that there should be no fear on this account for they would be convertible into 8 percent bonds. But by December, 1863, the tone of his messages to Congress changed, and he issued grave warnings. He announced that the issues of treasury notes had so increased that the amount of currency circulating was more than $600 million—or more than threefold the amount required by the business of the country.

He recommended two ways to correct the evil, which he said had stimulated speculation and had exerted a corrupting influence on the morals of the country. He pointed out that Congress was prevented by the permanent constitution from levying taxes on land and slaves, except on the basis of the population of a state, to be determined by a census. But such a census was impossible to take because of the war. He recommended, therefore, disregarding this limitation and, acting by other provisions of the Constitution, passing a realistic law taxing slaves and property. Congress followed his advice, and on February 17, 1864, enacted a law taxing all property, real and personal (slaves), 5 percent, and jewelry and articles of luxury, 10 percent.[8] But the law came too late. The situation was so bad by February, 1865, that Davis implored Congress to pass some kind of an additional tax law. General Lee also appeared before Congress to ask it to do something for his men, who were starving outside of Richmond, but he bitterly commented, "They do not seem to do anything except to eat peanuts and chew tobacco."[9] According to E. M. Coulter, "The Confederacy raised throughout its existence about one per cent income in taxes!"[10] The exclamation point, unusual in history, is justified in this instance, for no responsible government would have acted in this way. The only condoning fact is that Congress and the Southern people never anticipated that the war would be a long one.

Consequently, an ever increasing flood of paper money poured forth from the government presses. The supply of fiat money was increased by the fact that the states issued large quantities of paper money and permitted railroads, cities, and insurance companies to issue such currency in small denominations, called "shinplasters." The result was the greatest inflation ever seen in America, with the possible exception of the revolutionary period. Surprisingly, though, Confederate currency did not fall drastically in value until after Gettysburg and Vicksburg. In April, 1863, Colonel A. J. L. Fremantle exchanged his English gold for Confederate currency at the rate of one for four; in August, though, it fell so rapidly that the Confederate dollar was equal to only eight cents in gold; in January, 1864, four and one-half cents; and in March, 1865, less than two cents.

In addition to the state of finances, the condition of the railroads deeply concerned the president, but his old theories of laissez-faire prevented him from taking firm action to force them to operate in the public interest. The failure to keep up the railroads caused Ramsdell to rank transportation difficulties next to finances in terms of deleterious consequences leading to breakdown of the home front.[11] When the war began the Confederate states had a congeries of small railroads operated by 104 companies, with varying gauges of track and in a number of cities no connections, a condition brought about by selfish local interests. There was a gap between railroads in Selma and Montgomery that was not closed until after the war was over and another serious gap of 48 miles between Danville, Virginia, and Greensboro, North Carolina, which broke rail communications in the Piedmont area between Richmond and Atlanta.

In a message to Congress on November 18, 1861, Davis urged the Confederate government itself to undertake the construction to close the Danville-Greensboro rail gap, and Congress appropriated a million dollars in bonds for this purpose. But the Confederate government encountered so many difficulties in constructing it, such as the reluctance of planters to furnish slaves as laborers, the difficulty of obtaining iron rails, and the refusal of Governor Vance and the North Carolina legislature to allow the same gauge on it as on the connecting Virginia railroad, that it was not completed until the summer of 1864.[12] State rights created opposition to the Confederate government building railroads, not only in North Carolina, but also to Senator Louis Wigfall's bill in 1862 to connect Louisiana with Texas by rail (New Iberia, La., to Orange, Tex.), but President Davis intervened in behalf of building the railroad and Congress appropriated $1.5 million worth of bonds for the project, which was never built.[13] There was also no link between the Georgia and Florida railroads, a condition that prevented General Joseph Finegan from following up his victory at Ulustee, Florida, on February 20, 1864; this fact caused the Confederate government to realize the necessity of such a link, but only after a terrific legal battle with ex–Senator David Levy Yulee, who opposed tearing up the tracks of his railroad, and after much delay the link was completed on March 4, 1865.

On December 3, 1862, a Yankee living in the lower South, William M. Wadley, who had made a career of managing railroads, was appointed supervisor of all railroads in the Confederacy, and he was under the control of the secretary of war and not under the quartermaster general. When Wadley called a meeting of the presidents of the railroads at Augusta, Georgia, for December 15, 1862, he could get no real cooperation from them.[14] President Davis gave Wadley support in his message to Congress on January 12, 1863, by urging the military necessity of government control of the railroads, but did not recommend the revolutionary action of taking direct control of them.[15] The railroads were seriously handicapped by the refusal of Confederate officers —even General Lee—to release much needed mechanics from the army. On May 1, 1863, Congress finally adopted a stiff railroad bill, providing for thorough schedules and impressment of railroads that would not cooperate but, strangely, at the same time, it dismissed the competent head of the Railroad Bureau.[16] His assistant, Lieutenant Colonel Frederick W. Sims of Georgia, was placed in charge of the railroads under the quartermaster general, in which position he served until the end of the war. Sims was more conservative than Wadley, and did not try to force the railroads to interchange their cars and engines. The railroads strenuously opposed letting their rolling stock get out of their control, destroying the possibility of through traffic of freight to Richmond.

Although after May 1, 1863, the Confederate government at last had an adequate railroad law, it did not use its powers to take control of the railroads. Davis advocated "cooperation" of the railroads rather than impressing them and taking direct control of them. Robert Kean sums up succinctly in his diary (April 1, 1863) a reason for the desperate situation of the railroads at that date, which became worse later: "The railroads are worn out. Wadley says that he can do nothing unless he is allowed to have mechanics. General Lee has fought all winter *against* this [the release of mechanics from the army], and now the evil, which much might have been done to remedy during the winter months, is nearly irremediable and the campaign about to begin. The truth is that the Secretary [Seddon] has been too deferential to the army officers. They have thwarted whatever of policy there was in supply by their clamor against details, and Mr. Seddon has 'recommended to favorable consideration of', where he might and should have given instant orders."[17] President Davis was also guilty of this weakness. It is amazing today to learn that, according to Colonel Sims, not a single iron rail was produced in the Confederacy after 1861, and very few were imported through the blockade.[18] When the rails wore out the simple expedient was adopted of tearing up the rails from less essential railroads, which led to conflicts, notably with Yulee of Florida, when Confederate authorities began tearing up the rails of his Florida Railroad.

The Northern army and cavalry made it a prime objective to destroy or interrupt the Southern railroads. When General Henry Halleck captured Corinth in the spring of 1862 the Confederacy lost the use of its main eastern and western line. The railroad from Richmond to Chattanooga was constantly being interrupted by Unionists in east Tennessee burning railroad bridges. Davis struggled manfully to protect this line as well as the Richmond-Weldon-Charleston line in the coastal plain and the important Western and Atlanta between Chattanooga and Atlanta, which remained in Confederate possession until near the end of the war. But Sherman's campaign through Georgia wrecked its lines completely in 1864.

The reports of railroad men and of officers supervising transportation in the last year of the war reveal the results of the government's inability to control the railroads and the selfishness of the people in using the railroads. Sewell L. Fremont, chief engineer and superintendent of the Weldon and Wilmington railroad, a vital supply line for Lee's army, wrote to Bragg as general-in-chief on March 11, 1864: "There seems to be the greatest selfishness about this absorption of transportation. The officer who wants something hauled does not seem to car [*sic*] whether others are suffering in consequence of his gratification or not. Trains to carry corn and meat to Lee's army are used for frivolous reasons. The railroads profit more from hauling freight than troops," regardless of the good of the country.[19]

Quartermaster General A. R. Lawton wrote to Secretary of War Breckinridge on March 10, 1865, pointing out the critical connection between supplying the army and keeping the railroads running. He observed that the destruction of the railroad lines in South Carolina by Sherman's troops destroyed the means of obtaining abundant supplies of grain from Georgia and Alabama. He remarked that neither locomotives nor rails had been imported into the Confederacy for four years. Even the lack of railroad spikes had severely hampered the operation of the trains, the superintendent of the Western and Atlanta railroad in Georgia reported to Bragg on June 22, 1864. Fremont wrote that if the railroads in Virginia and North Carolina could be protected from the enemy and used exclusively for transportation of supplies there would be no serious difficulty in providing supplies to the army. But lack of money was also a serious obstacle to delivering supplies, both for the commissary department and for the railroads, which were crippled by lack of funds even for daily expenses.[20]

Although the president failed to put pressure on the railroads to operate in the public interest, he made strenuous efforts to increase the production of food for the army, yet seemed much less concerned about supplying adequate food for the poor on the home front. When shortages developed in the army in northern Virginia and the soldiers complained of bad bread, Davis suggested that the officers have the soldiers build their own ovens and bake good bread. In the interests of producing larger food crops, a number of states, as observed, severely limited cotton and tobacco planting. But in the early spring of 1863 a notion spread among the farmers and planters that the war would be over within the year, and consequently they made plans to enlarge the production of the staple crops of cotton and tobacco. Congress and the president were alarmed over this assumption. In accordance with a resolution of Congress, President Davis issued a proclamation to the people of the Confederate states, dated April 7, 1863, warning them against this feeling of euphoria, and urging them to continue to reduce the planting of tobacco and cotton and to concentrate on producing food crops. He admitted that the wheat crop in the lower South had been good and that there was no want of bread in the Confederacy, but that meat was lacking. He told them that in fact the soldiers were on one-half rations of meat, and there was also danger of a short supply of corn and fodder for feeding the army horses and mules. He pointed out that the bad roads in winter, the lack of transportation, and "the attempt of groveling speculators to forestall the market and make money out of the life blood of our defenders" had led to the withdrawal of much needed supplies from the army.[21] One of the grave difficulties in the situation lay in delays in transportation, which caused large quantities of supplies to accumulate in the depots, only to rot and be wasted, while Lee's army in Virginia was near starvation.

One of the clichés about supplying the Confederate army has been that there was plenty of food in the Confederacy but that lack of transportation prevented proper distribution. Although this was partly true, the two men who should have known, Commissary General Northrop and Assistant Commissary Frank G. Ruffin, thought otherwise. Perhaps the origin of the controversial notion was the plentiful existence of food in middle Georgia when Sherman's army was marching through. The great shortage was in meat. During the summer of 1861, Commissary General Northrop wrote to President Davis: "There are not hogs in the Confederacy sufficient for the army and the larger force of the plantation negroes."[22] So precarious did the food situation appear to the Commissary Department on October 18, 1862, that the assistant commissary, Lieutenant Colonel Ruffin, wrote to Colonel Northrop: "With the whole Confederacy completely exhausted of supplies, we have only meat rations for 300,000 men for twenty-five days. As we feed by rough estimate not less than that number, including prisoners, and we cannot expect to commence on the new hog crop before 1st Jany., the condition of the commissariat is well described by Major [S. B.] French (Commissary officer at Richmond) as 'alarming.' "[23] By the fall of 1864 the daily ration of the Confederate army had been reduced to one third of a pound of bacon, as contrasted with three fourths of a pound, which was the standard ration of the U.S. soldier. On December 20, 1864, Commissary General Northrop wrote, "The idea that there is *plenty for all* in the country is absurd. The efforts of the enemy have been too successful . . . people have killed whole flocks of sheep, breeding stock of cattle, and young cattle."[24]

The shortage of corn and fodder for the army horses became critical in the logistics of the Confederate armies. The horse-breeding country of the South —Kentucky, West Virginia, Missouri, and middle Tennessee—fell early under the control of the Union armies. As early as the summer of 1862 a stringency occurred in the horse supply of the Confederacy. There was a heavy mortality among army horses: in the artillery and transportation services the average life of a horse was seven and a half months, but in the cavalry it was much shorter. An equine infirmary was established at Lynchburg, Virginia, to restore sick and worn-out horses, but only 15 percent were returned to the service. By the last year of the war the splendid horses of the Confederacy were used up and the ability of the cavalry to protect both the flanks of the army and the railroads had seriously deteriorated, while on the other hand the Northern cavalry became stronger and more dangerous. Furthermore, the army horses were so weak at times that they could not properly perform their functions, especially in Virginia. Lee complained of the failure of the railroads to deliver fodder to nourish them.[25]

The significant point to make about the food situation, as far as the Confederate army was concerned, was that it became primarily a problem of distribution, resulting from the breakdown of the railroads and also from the lack of acceptable money. Major Sidney B. French, the commissary at Richmond, Virginia, wrote to the new commissary general, Isaac St. John, as late as 1865, that with good acceptable money and adequate transportation the subsistence of the troops could easily be supplied, for the crops south of North Carolina—in Georgia, Alabama, and Mississippi—were never so large; but the great herds in Florida and Texas were not available for meat because it could not be transported.[26]

As a result the armies of Lee frequently lived from hand to mouth on a spartan diet. Lee himself once dined on only a small piece of bacon and cabbage. Lack of good food played an important role in the decline of morale during the last year of the war, resulting in illness and alarming desertions from the army. The city populations also suffered much from the uneven distribution of the Confederate food supplies, as J. B. Jones's diary in Richmond reveals in detail. Yet there was conflicting testimony about the food situation in the Confederacy, which is complicated by the story of imports penetrating the blockade and trade between the lines.

To make up for the apparent shortage, meat and dried vegetables were imported to a considerable extent through the blockade. For a region primarily agricultural, this fact seems ironical, eloquently illustrating the inefficiency and disorganization of the Confederacy. The cargo manifests of blockade-runners from Bermuda show that importing bacon, pork, dried beef, flour, sugar, peas, and onions had become prevalent in 1864. In one year—November 1, 1863, to December 8, 1864—there were imported through the blockade 8,632,000 pounds of meat, as well as 520,000 pounds of coffee on government account alone.[27] Furthermore, despite the fact that the South was an important corn-producing section of the nation, large quantities of whiskey and brandy were brought through the blockade instead of being manufactured in the Confederacy. If the Confederacy had been able to feed the army with its own resources, it could have used this space on blockade-runners for desperately needed railroad iron to keep the railroads operating. Moreover, Lee's invasion of Pennsylvania in 1863 was motivated in part by the need to feed his hungry army, and one objective of John Hunt Morgan's cavalry raids in Kentucky was to bring herds of cattle to feed Confederate soldiers. Although it was definitely against Confederate policy to trade with the enemy, this policy had to be partially abandoned: cotton and tobacco were exchanged with the enemy for bacon, pound for pound, despite Davis's strong objections.

The black slaves were the great producers of food in the Confederacy.[28] The question arises, Did they become markedly less productive when many of their masters were away in the army? The evidence indicates that they knew what the war was about, but they continued docilely to work, with no attempts at insurrection. Nevertheless, it would be only human nature for them to relax their work habits, and we have some evidence that the women on the small plantations had difficulty in managing them. So did Mrs. Warren Akin, wife of a Georgia congressman, and when her husband rebuked her for letting Rachel (a slave girl) have a dance, the wife replied that Rachel had been so good that she could not refuse her.

The proximity of a federal army usually disrupted the labor force of a plantation. The case of Brierfield illustrates this point. As soon as the overseer left, in the latter part of May, 1862, Joseph Davis reported to his brother that the slaves began robbing the house by breaking open the doors and carrying off every article of value; they would not remain to cultivate the cotton crop.[29] Joe managed to hire two of his brother's slaves and thirty of his own to hospitals and to the government. In June, Joe wrote that he had been able to take away from the plantations a part of his brother's slaves and of the Hurricane slaves; but he also reported that Confederate troops had burned 200 bales of his cotton and all of the Brierfield cotton to prevent them from falling into the hands of the federal army.[30] In November Jefferson sent Joseph Davis money to buy corn for feeding his slaves who still remained in his possession.

Susannah, the mother of Clement Clay, Jr., reported even worse demoralization of the slaves on the Clay plantation of Monte Vista near Huntsville, Alabama. Clement Clay placed most of his slaves with the Nitre and Mining Bureau, but eleven of them absconded. Those on the plantation refused to work and threatened to kill the overseer if he tried to whip any of them. Susannah wrote, "If we make bread under existing circumstances I will be content." She complained that she had spent two weeks at the plantation trying to bring some order, but that the Negroes were bold and did as they pleased. She tried moral persuasion to get them to do their duty, and sometimes it succeeded. "We cannot exert any authority," she lamented. "I beg ours to do what little is done."[31]

Slaves were impressed to work on fortifications despite the strong reluctance of planters; they continued to serve as blacksmiths, carpenters, coopers, bricklayers. They were employed in the Tredegar Iron Works, constituting more than half its labor force, in the Nitre and Mining Bureau, and to some extent in the factories.[32] In the Phineas Browne letters is one from a coal-and-iron mine owner protesting against the shortsighted policy of the governor of Alabama in not encouraging the mining of coal and iron in which Negro labor was badly needed. He could not hire slaves from the planters for this work because they did not want them to work underground.[33] It would seem that the states and the Confederate government did not efficiently utilize the vast reservoir of Negro labor, either to raise food crops or on government work. The Van Riper study of the Confederate civil service estimated that only 13,228 civilians, most of them slaves, were employed in the Nitre and Mining Bureau, while 11,500 civilians, a large proportion of them slaves, were in the Bureau of Engineers.

Rather, they adopted a stern impressment policy as to farm products. Davis strongly supported such a policy but Secretary of War Seddon appears to have been lackadaisical in enforcing it.[34] Moreover, serious abuses arose from army commanders using the power of impressment, for they usually paid below the market price for goods impressed and gave receipts instead of paying money. They stripped the country of supplies near encampments and along railroads, but left more remote areas untouched. To remedy these abuses Congress passed the Impressment Act of March 26, 1863, requiring appraisal of value of goods impressment by a fair tribunal, including a citizen of the neighborhood as well as a Confederate officer.[35] Nevertheless, abuses continued, with the result that farmers often refused to bring their produce to market in towns where it could be easily impressed. Of the impressment policy, Ramsdell wrote: "No other one thing, not even conscription, caused so much discontent and produced so much resentment in the Confederacy."[36]

Unfortunately, Davis and Congress gave little attention to trying to regulate speculators and hoarders, and this was one of the most serious failures of the government. Especially among the poor, the cry arose that speculators got rich while the poor starved. Bell Wiley quotes some letters of poor women who would wander from place to place seeking to buy food, but rich people and hoarders would not accept Confederate money and demanded inflated prices far above their ability to pay. The impressment officers would take from the farmers mules, horses, and wagons necessary to raise subsistence crops.[37]

Davis held to the old idea of laissez-faire in economics, and therefore opposed price controls, which modern nations regard as essential in times of war. He wrote to General Holmes in Arkansas on January 29, 1863, protesting against a policy of trying to compel people to sell or transport products at fixed prices. "Prices must always be determined," he wrote, "by the law of supply and demand, and no law which can be devised can change the effect which will be produced in the enhancement of the prices of food where the amount to be sold is too small for the number of consumers."[38]

Apparently he did not consider rationing, which the weak, undeveloped system of the Confederate government was not prepared to enforce. Extortion, he thought, could best be restrained by the state. He also wrote to Holmes in regard to relief for the poor families whose men were serving in the army: "I had hoped that the liberal provisions understood to have been made by the State legislature (of Arkansas) would to a great extent have relieved the sufferings of the poor, and have quieted the anxieties of the soldiers in regard to the condition of their families." Relief of poor families was at first a duty of the county governments, but it was so poorly administered that eventually the state governments took over providing relief for the families of poor soldiers.

Davis's laissez-faire philosophy operated against interference with businesses and manufacturers. He believed that government regulation of these aspects of the economy was the function of the states and not of the Confederate government. Nevertheless, the Confederate Congress passed laws limiting the profits of textile mills and other factories engaged in making war goods, usually to not more than 75 percent upon the cost of materials, and the Confederate government had a strong club to wield over them by its control over labor through exemptions and details. Few new industries were started up as a result of war demand, although in some cases the government advanced a third or a half of the capital needed to get going.[39]

The one important exception was the manufacture of munitions of war. Davis was fortunate in finding a Pennsylvania native, General Josiah Gorgas, to take charge of the Ordnance Department.[40] Gorgas established numerous arsenals and foundries in the principal cities of the South for the manufacture of rifles, sabers, cannon, iron plate for ships, and chemicals for munitions and powder factories. He had a brilliant success in establishing a large and efficient powder factory in Augusta, Georgia, in April, 1862, which was placed under the charge of Colonel George Washington Rains. He recruited college professors, notably John William Mallet, to head laboratories for making chemicals and established a Nitre and Mining Bureau under the charge of Isaac St. John. The Confederacy never lost a battle as a result of the lack of a superior grade of powder. Gorgas acquired blockade-runners that brought in military supplies to supplement his own production.

The two great manufacturers of munitions were the Tredegar Iron Works at Richmond and the Selma, Alabama, Iron Works, started by Colin McRae as a private enterprise in 1861. The Tredegar Iron Works expanded its work force, including many slaves, from 800 men in 1860 to 2,500 in 1863. But it constantly lacked iron and its president, Joseph R. Anderson, had to resign his brigadier generalship to go out in the valley of Virginia and elsewhere to stimulate iron production. Nevertheless, because of lack of iron, it operated far below capacity throughout the war.[41] At the peak of its production the Selma Works—which made gunboats and heavy ordnance for the navy as well as machinery and iron-plate for the *Tennessee* that defended Mobile, Alabama, in 1864—employed 3,000 workingmen.

In closing this chapter it is pertinent to ask to what extent President Davis was responsible for the woeful failure of the Confederacy on the home front. He considered his main duties to be military and diplomatic, and the job of providing for the home front, except insofar as it concerned producing munitions and food for the army, to be the function of the state governments. After all, he could do only so much. He was, moreover, severely limited by the state rights feeling in the Confederacy and the laissez-faire ideas of the people, which was also his own economic philosophy. He should be praised, however, for his stern enforcement of the Confederate blockade-running policy and for his efforts to increase food production. But he deserves criticism for his failure to exert the powers given him to regulate the railroads properly and also for not exerting strong pressure on Congress earlier to tax the people realistically.

Perhaps, instead of criticizing Davis personally for his neglect of the home front when he felt that military affairs required his attention, one should criticize the fundamental philosophy of the Southern people, who were not geared to carry on a revolution or to deal effectively with social problems. That society, in comparison with Northern society, was extremely conservative and disorganized, and would not tolerate any large movement toward the centralization that was absolutely needed in a revolutionary war, especially since the Confederacy was so much weaker than its opponent. Davis undoubtedly realized the needs of the occasion, but he, as well as his society, was restrained from effective action, not only by his devotion to constitutionalism and observing the law, but by the powerful, eluctable forces of tradition and state rights. He clearly changed as the war progressed, moving gradually toward a more centralized government and toward a nationalistic point of view when such a change was dictated by the necessity for the survival of the Confederacy.

Davis's Conflict with Congress

The American government—and the Confederate government supposedly —was based on three coordinated branches. Actually the Confederate government had no supreme court, and its Congress was remarkably weak. This situation arose from the fact that in wartime the power of the president is enormously increased, especially with the absence of a two-party system. In the beginning the Confederacy wished to demonstrate to the world a spirit of unity in which political parties would be intentionally suppressed. President Davis tried to inhibit the normal growth of an opposition party by making appointments from the ranks of the Secessionist and the Union or Cooperative parties. But the result was the development on the one hand, of irresponsible factions that gradually took shape as his supporters, or Southern nationalists, and, on the other hand, as his enemies, or roughly, the state righters. No strong leader arose in this latter group to form them into a party, although Alexander H. Stephens was the logical choice. But he was ailing most of the time and had a defeatist or profoundly pessimistic nature. On the infrequent occasions when he was in Richmond he chafed under the restriction of being the presiding officer of the Senate and was unable to make speeches. Nor did the Davis supporters have an effective leader in Congress, although Benjamin Hill of Georgia was perhaps the outstanding pro-Davis leader in the House of Representatives.

The Confederate Constitution, like the American Constitution, gave the president extraordinary powers in wartime, as commander-in-chief of the armed forces. But both President Davis and President Lincoln still had to deal with Congress—in Davis's case with a weak one, in Lincoln's case with a much stronger one. The United States Congress appointed a Joint Committee on the Conduct of the War; the Confederate Congress did not create such a supervisory body. Its control over military affairs, such as it was, was exerted through congressional investigations, such as into the causes of the surrender of New Orleans. Nevertheless, Lincoln, the consummate politician, was able to get his way most of the time, despite the noisy opposition of the radicals in his own party and of the discredited Democratic party, abetted by the Copperheads.

Davis also got along very well with the first legislative body, the Provisional Congress, that lasted until February 22, 1862. It was not elected by the people, but by state conventions that appointed delegates to Montgomery to found the Confederate government. The Montgomery convention, after its work of framing a constitution was over, instead of adjourning, converted itself into a unicameral congress. Varina Davis described its personnel in glowing terms to Clement C. Clay, Jr., of Alabama: "They are the finest set of men I have ever seen collected together, grave, quiet, and thoughtful-looking men, with an air of refinement which makes in my mind's picture gallery a gratifying pendant to Hamlin, Durkee, and Dolittle [sic] and Chandler" —[Northern political leaders of the U.S. Congress in 1861].[1] They seemed to justify the boast of Southerners that their slave-based society produced higher quality statesmen than did the bourgeois, industrial society of the North.

Indeed, the Provisional Congress of fifty members contained some of the South's most distinguished men, including President John Tyler (who died in 1862), Robert W. Barnwell of South Carolina, Harvard graduate and ex-president of South Carolina College, and U.S. Senator Charles M. Conrad, who had been secretary of war under Millard Fillmore. With few exceptions they were slaveholders and landholders, thus practically eliminating the representation of the poor people and the yeoman class. In fact, throughout the history of the Confederate congresses, the planting interest dominated the making of laws and prevented the fair taxation of the property of that class. Yet their control was exercised primarily through lawyers (42 of the original 50 members were lawyers) and 17 planters (large slaveholders).[2] Thirty-six had attended college and a large majority had had previous legislative experience.

During three congresses, there served in the Senate or House of Representatives, six Harvard men, six Yale men, four Princeton men, and others who attended less prestigious Northern colleges—such as Yancey, Williams College, Edward Sparrow, Kenyon College, and Robert Toombs, Union College —but their exposure to Northern education seemed to have little influence in nationalizing them.[3]

But as soon as the new congress (elected in November, 1861, fresh from the people) convened, they began to criticize the Davis administration. The two congresses elected by the people in 1861 and 1863 were far from being as impressive as the Provisional Congress, and gradually the members as a group came almost into contempt with a majority of the people. Robert Kean commented on the "smallness" of the members of Congress who refused to deal courageously with taxation, recording in his diary on March 15, 1863: "Certainly no deliberative body ever met in this state with less statesmanship in it." Louis Wigfall, fire-eater and senator from Texas, bemoaned the weakness of Congress, commenting, "What hope can any reasonable man draw from that source?"[4] In 1863 some of the best men were defeated for reelection, such as Jabez L. M. Curry of Alabama, a Harvard man (and after the war president of Richmond College), by the peace movement, and Clement C. Clay, Jr., because of his friendship with Davis and because he had voted against raising the pay for soldiers. James H. Hammond, former governor and U.S. senator from South Carolina, wrote in 1863 to Senator R. M. T. Hunter, president pro tem of the Senate: "Some malign influence seems to preside over your councils. Pardon me, is the majority always drunk? The people are beginning to think so."[5] Thomas Bragg noted in his journal as early as January 22, 1862, that Congress was full of factions and discontented men, who neglected the country's business—especially the old Union men complain that they do not get their share of offices, and demand that a new cabinet of the regular government not be confirmed unless the old Whig and Union parties be represented in it.[6]

There were, however, a number of reasons for the low repute and ineffectiveness of Congress. In times of war during our national history (as previously noted) Congress has taken a back seat, and the power of the president has been greatly enlarged. It was so during the Southern Confederacy; many people throughout the Confederacy regarded it as a weak, pusillanimous, and ineffective body. In addition, there were a number of special reasons for the low esteem of the Confederate Congress. Some of the ablest political leaders, such as ex-Governor Henry A. Wise, Howell Cobb, and Robert Toombs, went into the army, attracted by the superior glamor of that branch of service. Frequent secret sessions were an important cause of its poor public image. Congress was the scene of fisticuffs between some members and of disgraceful antics of other members, of the formation of cliques, such as the anti-Davis coalition, and of lobbies for favorite generals or for regions, notably the trans-Mississippi West. The Confederate Constitution had provided for cabinet members speaking on the floor of Congress and answering questions; however, this innovative provision was not implemented. If it had been adopted, it might have given Congress better information and guidance. Some members lacked the authority of speaking for valid constituencies: Simms of Kentucky and Vest of Missouri are examples. In addition to alcoholism, they were guilty of poor attendance, at times resulting in the lack of a quorum for business, of indulging their egos in florid oratory, and of wasting their time on trivialities. There was a serious lack of leadership—for instance, no recognized floor leader in the

House of Representatives—and of organization, since Davis's theory of government prevented him from taking the lead. Because of the failure to develop a two-party system, few caucuses were held.[7]

The life of a congressman in Richmond was not conducive to a calm and judicious consideration of laws that would advance the welfare of the whole Confederacy rather than that of their state or region. Their pay of $2,760 a year, plus twenty cents mileage for necessary traveling, hardly covered expenses even with strict economy; because of inflation Congress voted to double its pay in 1864. Although Congressman Warren Akin of Georgia, for example, apparently had sufficient to eat at his boardinghouse, he did not receive his accustomed dessert at the end of the evening meal, and paid a high price for board. To economize, he wore two shirts and one pair of socks a week; his drawers, flannels, and nightshirts lasted for two weeks, and he laboriously darned his socks, using an inkstand.[8] A religious man, who made a speech shortly after taking his seat in Congress in which he declared, "God is with us," he was appalled at the drunkenness of his colleagues and at the large number of women of ill fame on the streets.[9] It was dangerous, Akin wrote to his wife, for a member of Congress to walk on the unlighted or ill lighted streets at night so that he did not venture out then unless accompanied by one or two other congressmen; because of the dangers, Congress discontinued night sessions.[10] He was "almost crazy" to go home and see his wife, and he worried over the education of their children and over the danger of the burning of their cotton and homes by the Yankees.

The Congress must have been filled with very human men, like Josiah Turner, a Whig Unionist who had been editor of the *Hillsboro Recorder* of North Carolina. He wrote to his wife from Richmond that he had bought his children candy, then ate it all, being unable to trust himself with candy for the children.[11] His wife was a religious woman who asked him not to write to her on Sunday. Turner and James T. Leach of North Carolina were ardent peace men and Leach's resolution of May 23, 1864, while Lee was fighting his last campaign to save Richmond, proposed a ninety-day armistice, and stipulated that should peace terms be offered by the North they should be submitted to the states for ratification or rejection. This resolution was laid on the table by a vote of the House of Representatives, 62 to 21, 14 of the nay votes coming from North Carolina and Georgia.[12] On February 19, 1865, Turner wrote to his wife that he looked upon all as being lost and upon the country as subjugated. He would return home but for his determination to vote against the pending bill to arm the Negroes, which restrained him. The Congress refused to intervene and take away from Davis his constitutional right to conduct peace negotiations, and honor prevented Turner from begging for peace and mercy from the North. Turner wrote to his wife on May 5, 1864, that "there is nothing Congress can do to save us, it is all with the Lord and General Lee." He was so disgusted with the futility and contentiousness in Congress that he exclaimed, "I would rather plough and feed hogs than legislate for the Confederacy."[13]

In contrast to Turner, Clement C. Clay, Jr., may be taken as representative of the cultivated, aristocratic type in Congress. Educated at both the universities of Alabama and Virginia, Clay became a lawyer at Huntsville, Alabama, and a planter, owning eighty-nine slaves when he was elected by the legislature to the Senate. In the Senate he pursued a middle-of-the-road course between state rights and Southern nationalism.[14] Among the bills that he introduced was one imposing the death penalty on Northern officers or privates who imported counterfeit Confederate money (considered a heinous atrocity) and another denying Confederate citizenship to foreigners, except those serving in the army, thus excluding many much-needed mechanics. Since his home was invaded on several occasions, his wife, a society belle, who wrote *A Belle of the Fifties,* lived as a refugee, often with relatives or friends, but otherwise she lived very well, importing through the blockade or through the lines by friends, luxuries, especially corsets, the lack of which caused much mortification among Southern ladies of the upper class.

Congress was slow acting on Davis's recommendations and suggestions. He did not take the legislative body into his confidence or go to any pains to explain his plans or ideas. Warren Akin wrote to his wife on how slowly Congress acted. "You would be amazed," he wrote, "to see the differences of opinion that exist among the members. It seems, sometimes, that no proposition, however plain and simple, could be made that would not meet with opposition."[15] He observed that there were so many men holding different opinions that it took a long time in Congress to give expression to them. As a result bills that urgently needed expeditious action were held up by numerous amendments, parliamentary maneuvers, and long-winded speeches. Unfortunately, Davis did not exert any obvious leadership.

Davis's worst side came out in dealing with the 26 senators and 30 representatives of the first and second congresses (257 different congressmen held office during the four years of the life of the Confederacy) when it was obvious that he badly needed their confidence and support. These men were Southerners, possessed of a large share of egotism and pride. But Davis made few concessions in the line of duty to ordinary human nature. When congressmen came to see him, either singly or in delegations, he usually received them formally and with dignity, but he often antagonized them by his manner. He explained to one congressman, Garland of Arkansas, that the day was not long enough for him to see all who wished to be received: congressmen, department heads, generals, and casual visitors.[16]

Yet the cordiality of his reception seems to have depended on his mood. He was in a pleasant mood—it must have been one of the days when his physical ills had subsided—when Warren Akin, one of his very few Georgia supporters in Congress, called on January 9, 1865. Akin went away satisfied, relating an account of the visit to his wife as follows: "I had a long conversation with the President yesterday. He has been greatly wronged. He does not control the generals in the field. He did not send Hood after the Atlanta campaign to Tennessee. He has been trying to get General Lee to accept the command of all our armies but he declines. The President is not that stern, puffed up man he is represented to be. He was as polite, attentive and communicative to me as I could wish. He listened patiently to all I said and when he differed with me he would give his reasons for it. He was very cordial in his reception of me, and in his invitation to me to call again. And many gentlemen tell me the same thing as to his manner with them. His enemies have done him great injustice. He is a patriot and a good man I think. He will have to do something more than anything he has done before I can denounce him. He is the best man in the Government for his place. Many want him out of office. Were he removed today, we should be ruined in a few months and I fear we shall be any way."[17] In his reception of visitors, Davis seems to have been a man of moods, doubtless affected by fluctuating ill health and by nervous tensions. Frank Vandiver speaks of his charm with individuals: "Davis could persuade individual congressmen, he should have brought small groups to the White House on a regular basis for discussions, briefings, for mutual complaint." But he felt that such diplomacy smacked of politicking, which he could not bring himself to do.[18]

Some congressmen disliked his aloof personality and his autocratic way of dealing with Congress. William W. Boyce of South Carolina, who had attended South Carolina College, the University of Virginia, and Columbia University, was a leader of the opposition, who considered Davis as puffed up; others referred to his stubbornness; still others, such as Toombs, thought that the trouble with Davis was that he had too high an opinion of himself.[19] Senator W. E. Simms of Kentucky in a letter to Robert McKee, secretary of state of Kentucky—in exile, November 16, 1863—described the difficulties of Congress in getting along with the president: "We as Congressmen have forborne and tried to harmonize with the President. His friends have tried to get him to change his policy, give up bad generals and surrender his favorites in the army—neither they nor the pressure of public opinion have any effect—a vote of no-confidence in the cabinet will not have moved the President—the President controls everything—he has cabinet meetings, but his will prevails."[20]

Secretary Mallory made an acute observation explaining Davis's coolness to congressmen and visitors. So many in coming to him, he wrote, were motivated by self-interest rather than the interest of the country, "although they tried to disguise their unworthy motives under the protestations of patriotism. So he put on his defensive armor, suspecting that the Congressmen or visitors had 'axes to grind.' " Accordingly, he let the intruders know that they were encroaching upon his time: "Few men could be more chillingly, freezingly cold." Mallory, who was very sociable and agreeable, thought that Davis made a serious mistake in alienating good patriotic men of Congress with his forbidding demeanor. He wrote in his diary that the president made no attempt "to cultivate the good will of congressmen by little acts of politeness, attention, and deference ... not sacrificing a smile" to those that he disliked until they departed. But the secretary explained why Davis would not follow his friends' advice to adopt a different manner with congressmen: "It was not in his nature and his restless, manly, open, and turbulent spirit turned from what to him [seemed] as the faintest approach to seeking popularity and he scorned to believe it necessary to coax men to do their duty in the then condition of the country."[21]

Mrs. Davis corroborates Mallory's testimony in her memoir. The Davises did little entertaining, chiefly at breakfasts for a few of the president's friends. She admitted that her husband refused to flatter congressmen or to appear to confide in them when to do so would have exposed the army or navy to danger. She praised her husband as being too sincere to play the political game and for this reason, she wrote, she had deprecated his assuming the civil administration. His repellent manner toward congressmen she attributed to his being "abnormally sensitive to disapprobation" and to a feeling that he was misunderstood.[22] In a speech in Richmond after a visit to the army in the West, Davis apologized for not entertaining or engaging in social intercourse with the citizens because of the heavy burdens of his office, which gave him no time to do so.

The Confederate politicians, in truth, were a difficult lot with whom to deal, and the more one reads the sources, the more one realizes that human nature then was much like human nature today. Many congressmen were jealous, petty, and self-seeking. They fought among themselves; the most melodramatic incident occurred when Ben Hill of Georgia threw an inkstand at William L. Yancey in the Senate chamber, leaving a gash on his cheek. Shortly afterward Yancey died, but not from this cause. Yancey himself was a thorn in the flesh to Davis. He seems to have been alienated from the president because the latter would not appoint his candidate as postmaster of Montgomery and also refused Yancey's request to increase the number of brigadier generals from Alabama to accord with the number of troops furnished from the state. It is quite likely that both Yancey and Robert Barnwell Rhett, who were regarded as the fathers of the Confederacy, retained a secret hostility toward Davis because this reluctant secessionist occupied the position of president which they thought that they deserved. Yancey called Davis conceited, wrong-headed, wranglesome, and obstinate.

The two most virulent critics of Davis were Louis T. Wigfall, and his old enemy, Henry S. Foote, who had moved to Tennessee and been elected to the Confederate House of Representatives. Foote attacked practically everything that Davis proposed to Congress and even went so far in his malignity as to suggest deposing Davis as president and making Lee dictator. Foote, however, became thoroughly obnoxious to Congress, and after he was arrested trying to cross the Potomac River to the enemy and brought back, he was expelled from the House of Representatives.

Wigfall's hostility after 1862 represented a curious reversal of his ardent support of Davis at the beginning of his administration. Although a man of great ability, he was capable of deep, bitter prejudices over petty things. Secretary of the Treasury John H. Reagan explained that Wigfall's enmity began when he conferred with the president over the appointment of a new secretary of war, and the fact that Davis on this occasion did not confide in him that he had already chosen James A. Seddon angered the senator and turned him against his former friend; but there were other reasons for Wigfall's violent opposition to the president in the Senate,[23] such as Davis's veto of his plan to increase and upgrade the general staffs of each general (a good suggestion) and Davis's failure to heed Mrs. Wigfall's request for a promotion of her son in the army.[24] Despite Wigfall's frequent votes against Davis's appointments and his violent condemnations, he supported the president's main measures for vigorously waging war against the Yankees, whom he hated more than he did Davis.

On the other hand, the president had some strong supporters in Congress. In the Senate there were Howell Cobb of Georgia, R. M. T. Hunter of Virginia, Clement C. Clay, Jr., of Alabama, James Phelan of Mississippi, and George Davis of North Carolina. In the House of Representatives were Ben Hill of Georgia, Ethelbert Barksdale, who had been a prominent Mississippi editor, and Jabez L. M. Curry of Alabama, one of the most cultivated men in Congress. It should also be noted that, despite the developing opposition to him in Congress after 1863, Davis retained control over the legislative body nearly to the end. He vetoed thirty-nine bills and only one, a bill granting free postage on newspapers to soldiers, in the last year of the war, was passed over his veto. He justified this veto by explaining that the bill would prevent the Post Office Department from living up to its constitutional obligation to be self-sustaining. He vetoed a bill requiring quartermasters and commissaries under forty-five years of age to report for field service, on the ground that it would disrupt these important branches of the service, and that it would add relatively few to the ranks. He defeated by a pocket veto in January, 1865, a bill of George Vest of Missouri that would have conscripted Marylanders living in the Confederacy, in order to prevent the alienation of this neighboring state which was almost neutral. He requested Congress to establish a supreme court as provided by the Constitution, but primarily because of the appellate jurisdiction from state supreme courts that such a court would exercise, he failed to persuade Congress to grant his request.[25] The principal reason that Davis was able to keep his majority in Congress was the support of the congressmen from the border and occupied states—Kentucky, Tennessee, Mississippi, Arkansas, and Louisiana. They were in favor of strong measures to support the war and recover their homes. In 1863 these states, represented by forty-seven congressmen, contained only five opponents of the Davis administration.[26]

Peter W. Alexander, reporter of the *Savannah Republican,* who was a keen observer, wrote on November 26, 1862, that President Davis exerted greater power than had George III or Andrew Jackson. "He has exercised the veto power more frequently, perhaps, than all the Presidents of the United States did, and always with success. In no instance that has come to my knowledge, either in the Provisional or present Congress, did he ever fail to carry his point against Congress—nor is it known that he has ever been prevailed upon to yield to the public desire, when different from his own, except in the appointment of General [Sterling] Price and the transfer of Mr. Benjamin from the Department of War to that of Foreign Relations. No public man in our history ever stood closer to his friends, or conceded less to those who had crossed his path or arrayed themselves among his personal or political enemies. A man of great nerve and imperturbable coolness, combined with remarkable courtesy, or the most freezing politeness, as the occasion may require, he yet manages as the Chief Magistrate of a Confederacy of sovereign states under the limitations of a written constitution . . . to wield a power almost unlimited, and to exercise supreme control in every department of the government."[27] This report of the president's power, exaggerated as it was, portrays some of the qualities needed in a successful general, but not suited to leading a democracy. Abraham Lincoln, in contrast, vetoed few laws and knew how to work with his Congress.

One of the most independent members of Congress who stood up against Davis's power was Senator Edwin G. Reade of North Carolina. When Davis summoned the North Carolina delegates to meet him in the winter of 1864, he had a confrontation with them. The president began by reading a long letter in which he said that a prominent person of the state gave a bad account of North Carolina and advised the suspension of the habeas corpus writ, declaring that vigorous measures should be taken "to overawe and silence" the traitorous group in the state. When Reade defended the state, according to a letter that he wrote Governor Vance on February 10, 1864, the president "flared up," but Reade held his ground and told the president that such action as he proposed would make him a dictator. "Trust North Carolina and let her alone," he advised the president, but Reade left the interview feeling that Davis was prejudiced against the state. The North Carolina delegation was mortified at the attitude of the president, who was as "bitter as gall" toward the state.[28]

The center of opposition to Davis in Congress was from the Georgia representatives, eight of whom were his opponents after 1863. The most powerful anti-Davis personalities in the Confederacy were located in this state: Governor Brown, Alexander H. Stephens, and Robert Toombs, elected by the legislature as senator. Toombs was defeated in 1863 by Herschel Johnson, who reluctantly supported Davis at times for the sake of the cause but generally opposed him. Two of these men had been strong Unionists at the time of secession. In the election of 1863 in South Carolina, although Rhett was defeated, four of the state's six congressmen were opponents of the administration. In North Carolina only one member of the Second Congress, elected in 1863, supported the president. Senator R. M. T. Hunter of Virginia, who generally presided over the Senate as president pro tem because Vice President Stephens stayed away from Richmond, was at first a pro-Davis man but in the end turned against him because the president bitterly attacked Virginia. In the second and last Congress the opposition consisted of 40 percent of the membership.[29]

Congressional opposition to Davis was accentuated in March, 1863, by his dismissal of the veteran Quartermaster General Abraham C. Myers, who was well liked by the congressmen. Gossip, as noted, suggested that Davis's hostility toward him was owing to Mrs. Myers's statement that Mrs. Davis, with her dark skin, looked like a squaw, a remark that was reported to the president. When Congress tried to promote Myers to the rank of brigadier general, Davis circumvented that body by getting rid of him and appointing Brigadier General Alexander R. Lawton of Georgia to the post. The Senate Military Affairs Committee, however, by a vote of 15 to 6, declared that Myers still served, and 76 congressmen (nearly three quarters of the House) petitioned that Myers be retained.[30] Nevertheless, Davis had his way. He also successfully resisted congressional pressure to get rid of his friend, Commissary General Lucius B. Northrop, who was unpopular throughout the South. Foote in the House of Representatives declared in 1863 that the commissary general, whom he called a "pepper doctor from South Carolina," had injured the Confederacy more than the enemy and should be dragged from his position. The chairman of the Military Affairs Committee in the House, William Porcher Miles, also asserted that the president was responsible for keeping Northrop in his position after he had been rejected by the people.[31]

The strongest attack by Congress against Davis's power was made at the end of December, 1863, and in the early part of 1864. Senator Waldo P. Johnson of Arkansas introduced a bill limiting the term of cabinet members to two years, necessitating Senate approval of appointments after that term. The bill was really an attack on Davis, but although it was debated in Congress for two months, it never came to a vote.[32] There were four cabinet members toward whom Congress was hostile: Judah P. Benjamin (partly because he was a Jew), Secretary of the Navy Mallory, Secretary of the Treasury Memminger, and at the end, Secretary of War Seddon. Memminger, as we have seen, resigned in 1864 because of this hostility and because he could not get his program of taxation adopted. Seddon resigned early in 1865 because the Virginia delegation in Congress had commissioned the speaker of the House of Representatives, Thomas S. Bocock, to recommend to Davis a reorganization of the cabinet, warning him of the danger of Congress passing a vote of want of confidence in the cabinet and in the administration if he did not carry out this reconstruction, and predicting that such a resolution would pass by a three-fourths vote. Davis sharply replied that the legislature had no control over his cabinet.

Thomas B. Alexander and Richard E. Beringer have recently issued a valuable quantitative study in which they revealed some pertinent facts. The congressmen formed a rich man's Congress, the richest being Edward Sparrow of Louisiana, born in Ireland, owner of 460 slaves and an estate of $1,248,050, but Duncan Kenner, also of Louisiana, owned the most slaves, 473 in number. Sparrow was chairman of the Senate Committee on Military Affairs, while the chairman of the House Committee on Military Affairs, William Porcher Miles, a Charleston educator, owned no slaves. Alexander and Beringer maintain that Congress did not divide in their votes on the basis of rich and poor, but a division often did occur on the basis of regionalism within the Confederacy, which may have been a variation between the richer and the poorer members.[33] The upper South, with smaller farms and slaveholdings, sent poorer members to Congress than did the lower South, although Virginia's Senator R. M. T. Hunter owned 160 slaves. The largest delegation in Congress was from Virginia, with 35 men, while Arkansas, Florida, and Louisiana together had only 11 congressmen. The members were often connected by intermarriage and kinship relations. "Name recognition" seems to have been as important then as today, for in general the voters chose well-known men, previous officeholders, experienced in political affairs. The vast majority of the members were lawyers (77 percent), and the next vocation, numerically, was agriculture, with a large proportion of members being engaged in both vocations. Since political parties did not develop, the members acted without party discipline or programs. Many of them were like Clement C. Clay, Jr., voting on some issues as state rights men but on other issues as Southern nationalists. It cannot be denied, however, that the fact that a member had been a Whig or Unionist did have a predetermining effect on his voting in Congress or on his opposition to or support of President Davis. This phenomenon became especially noticeable after 1863 when the peace movement developed. Perhaps the most valuable lesson to be learned from the Confederate Congress's experience is the necessity of a two-party system for effective congressional action in a democracy.

Handling the Rebellious Governors

*J*efferson Davis's struggle with the rebellious governors illustrated one of the most important causes of the Confederate defeat. He had a new vision of a Confederate nation and of the means necessary to establish it. The governors, on the other hand, basically represented die-hard localism, or state rights, above the needs of the nation. Davis came gradually to this conception of an organized nation, and it was forced upon him by the pressure of circumstances. All his life he had been a staunch upholder of state rights, and in fact this philosophy was the legal basis of secession. In the early part of his administration he tried to carry out this philosophy and to deal tactfully with those governors who recognized no change in the status of the states. His significant change in this regard is the best refutation of those critics who maintained that he was stubborn and inflexible.

Judah P. Benjamin, when he was briefly secretary of war, in a letter to General Braxton Bragg on November 4, 1861, keenly analyzed the reasons for the obstructive tactics of some of the governors:

> The difficulty lies with the governors, who are unwilling to trust the common defense to one common head—they therefore refuse arms to men who are willing to enlist unconditionally for the war and put these arms in the hands

of a mere home militia who are not bound to leave the state. . . . Each governor wants to satisfy his own people and there are not wanting politicians in each state to encourage the people to raise the cry that they will not consent to be left defenseless.[1]

The most powerful and vocal upholder of state rights in the Confederacy was Governor Joseph E. Brown of Georgia. Though born in South Carolina, he grew up in the red hills of Georgia, where the yeomen had their stronghold. Although a graduate of the Yale Law School, he spoke the language of the people and shared their prejudices. In one important particular, however, he differed from them: he was an ardent secessionist. Very unimpressive in appearance, small, partially bald, with a short scraggly beard, he was pale, and had a sad expression on his face.

J. E. Brown dramatized his lowly origin and rapport with the common people by wearing a gray homespun suit instead of the pompous, aristocratic style of a broadcloth shadbelly coat, a stovepipe hat, and a vest adorned with a gold fob, but he did carry a gold-headed cane characteristic of the politician of the Old South. Religious, abstemious in habits, he did not smoke, chew, or drink alcoholic liquors, and in his first term as governor tried to prohibit Sunday mails and trains. His nature was very egotistical and combative, and he apparently loved to fight vigorously to get his own way regardless of the welfare of the Confederacy. It is somewhat of a mystery why this humorless, unattractive man could wield such power over the masses of Georgia, winning election to the governor's office in 1857 and continuously being reelected by overwhelming majorities. The aristocrats of Georgia—Howell Cobb, owner of many slaves, and Congressman Benjamin H. Hill—considered this plebeian a demagogue, and some facts in his career support this view and document his lust for power.[2]

Brown's course in the Civil War seems contradictory to a modern student. At the beginning of the war he was foremost among the governors in recruiting troops and sending them to the Virginia and Tennessee fronts. But he wished to appoint all of the officers from the state, including those above the ranks of regimental colonel and generals. Moreover, Brown wished to furnish "skeleton companies" with a large array of officers and relatively few soldiers, but the Confederate government would not accept them. Thus, from the very beginning, a source of friction appeared between the governor and the president, though at first it was not serious. Davis wired him on April 11, 1862, thanking him for his promptness in responding to the request for troops and telling him that even men armed only with pikes and knives would be acceptable.[3] When Brown urged the president to conduct an offensive war Davis telegrammed on May 5, 1862, that he had long desired to do so but that it was a question of lack of power.[4]

Friendly relations between the president and the Georgia governor were radically changed by Davis's determination to enforce the conscription act of

April 16, 1862.[5] Although Brown himself used a draft in the state at various times, he protested violently against the enactment of Confederate conscription, maintaining that it destroyed state sovereignty, that it was unconstitutional, and that he would not permit the militia officers to aid in the execution of a law that would strip the state of her constitutional military powers. He pointed out that Georgia had furnished more than her quota of soldiers to the Confederate army and, setting up his judgment over that of the president, he declared that there was no necessity for the conscription law. "The difficulty," he maintained, "has never been to get men. The States have already furnished the Government more than it can arm."[6] He notified the secretary of war that he would arrest any Confederate officer trying to enroll state militia officers. Apparently, Brown's principal reason for opposing conscription was his desire to appoint the higher officers commanding troops furnished by the state.

Davis replied to the recalcitrant governor on May 29, 1862, in a forceful letter. He observed that all the cabinet, as well as the attorney general, agreed with him as to the constitutionality of the conscription law and that it had been sustained by large majorities of both houses. He gave the governor an exposition of the powers held by the states and those by the central government, citing the *war powers* of the Confederate Constitution as granting ample authority for the law. He also defined the constitutional limits on the use of the state militia. He pointed out that the military situation in the face of the foe's superior numbers was critical, and that the conscription act was indispensable. But he complimented the governor on responding to every call made for troops, thanking him for his cordial and effective cooperation in the defense of "our common country."[7]

Brown continued to argue that conscription violated both state rights and the Confederate Constitution. Davis, in a letter of July 10, 1862, denied in "a most pointed manner" Brown's charge that he believed Congress to be the final judge of the constitutionality of a contested power. No, Davis held that only the courts possessed that power, and in regard to conscription, he did not share Brown's alarm over state rights.[8] In his struggle with the president over conscription, the governor appealed to the legislature to sustain him by not permitting the second conscription law of September 27, 1862, enrolling men between 35 and 45 years of age, to be enforced in Georgia, especially by preventing the enrollment of militia officers. Brown had the support of Alexander H. Stephens, Robert Toombs, and Stephens's brother, Linton, a powerful member of the legislature.[9] While the legislature was considering Brown's request to support him in his stand against conscription, Congressman Ben Hill came from Richmond to make a powerful address in support of conscription, and the legislature adjourned without making a decision. In the meanwhile the Georgia Supreme Court declared the Confederate conscription laws constitutional, and they were so declared by judges of several other states. Since the Confederacy did not have a supreme court to pass on the constitutionality of laws of Congress, the supreme court judges of the states exercised this power.

Brown was only temporarily halted by this setback. In the list of exemptions of the Confederate law of May 1, 1863, the state legislatures were permitted to decide what civil officers were necessary for the administration of the government, and these were exempt, but the later law of February 17, 1864, gave this decision to the governors of the states. Thereupon Brown, in a proclamation, certified every civil and military officer as indispensable to the proper administration of the state government. Major General Howell Cobb, who at this time was in command of the state reserve force consisting of those 17 to 18 years old and those 45 to 50 years old, protested against this wholesale exemption, pointing out that it included 2,000 justices of the peace, 1,000 constables, and 3,000 military officers who had practically no duties to perform.[10] In addition to the Confederate reserve forces, which were not to be used to serve out of the state, and which were hardly sufficient to guard the 30,000 federal prisoners at Andersonville, Brown reorganized the state militia to include those 16 years of age and those between 50 and 60 years of age. In the fall of 1864 he called out these men, known as Brown's "Ten Thousand Pets," to defend Georgia from Sherman's invasion, but after the fall of Atlanta on September 2, he furloughed them, as Sherman sarcastically remarked, to gather the sorghum and corn crops. The Bureau of Conscription reported in February, 1865, that Georgia had exempted 8,229 state and militia officers, North Carolina being next, with 5,589, and Virginia with only 1,894.[11]

The governor of Georgia also entered into a well-matured conspiracy with Alexander Stephens, Linton Stephens, and Robert Toombs to oppose Davis, not only on conscription, but even more so, to resist the enforcement of the power given to the president of suspending the writ of habeas corpus. On three occasions the president suspended the writ for limited periods in order to deal with spies and traitors.

Brown called the legislature into special session on March 10, 1864, to counteract the enforcement of the law suspending the writ of habeas corpus in Georgia. Alexander H. Stephens advised Brown on the governor's message to the legislature "from stern to stem."[12] In this message, Brown claimed that suspension of writ destroyed constitutional liberty and he warned against setting up a dictator, meaning Davis. The governor recommended that after every important victory the Confederate government should offer peace terms. Shortly afterward, Linton Stephens's resolutions in the legislature presented a similar proposal, as well as that the separate states in their state organizations and popular assemblies should strive to put an end to the civil war. The governor then engaged with the Stephens brothers in a vigorous propaganda campaign against the Davis government by sending at state expense copies of his message and of Linton Stephens's resolution to the captains and lieutenants of all the Georgia troops in the Confederate service.[13] He also distributed Alexander Stephens's address at private expense. The practical effect of this concerted opposition to the Davis government was to nullify the operation of the suspension of habeas corpus in Georgia and greatly to stimulate the peace movement.

Louise B. Hill, in a chapter of her study of Brown entitled, "Habeas Corpus: Second Major Assault on the Richmond Government," observes: "The opposition to the suspension of the writ of *habeas corpus* was even more disastrous to the Confederate cause than was the conscription controversy."[14] And she quotes Judge John Campbell, assistant secretary of war, as declaring in March, 1865, that "Georgia is in a state that may properly be called in insurrection against Confederate authority and that her public men had made the execution of its laws in the state nearly impossible."[15]

In the power struggle in the state between President Davis and Governor Brown, Linton Stephens played a signfiicant role.[16] Linton was a man of real ability, who had been educated at the University of Georgia (Franklin College), and at the Harvard Law School under Associate Supreme Court Justice Joseph Story. Tall, well formed, and handsome, Linton was a striking contrast to Alexander, who was eleven years older. The relationship between the brothers, maintained by a daily correspondence, was perhaps even more of a Jonathan-David one than that between Jefferson and Joseph Davis. Linton was brilliant and became an outstanding judge at the early age of thirty-five. He had sided with his brother in opposition to the secession of Georgia, but when the secession of the state was consummated he resigned his judgeship and briefly entered the Confederate army. An emotional man, he launched all of his intellectual and emotional force into a crusade against conscription and against the suspension of the writ of habeas corpus; his position as a powerful leader in the legislature, to which he was elected, gave him the leverage to carry out his and his brother's passionate opposition to Jefferson Davis. In furthering this purpose he became a strong ally of Brown.

Shortly after Brown had delivered his message to a special session of the legislature, Linton introduced his inflammatory resolutions as a part of the conspiracy against Davis. They asserted that there was no constitutional power to suspend the writ of habeas corpus, blamed Lincoln and the Northern states for the war, and proposed that immediately after signal successes of the Confederate army the government should make an official offer of peace to the enemy. At the same time the resolutions stated that Georgia would support the Confederate government until peace was made upon honorable terms.[17]

Brown's extreme assertion of state rights against the Confederacy was also displayed in his fight to keep control of blockade-runners in the interests of the state rather than of the Confederacy. He protested to the legislature that Davis's strict enforcement of the Confederate law of February 6, 1864, relating to blockade-runners, was a palpable assumption of unconstitutional power and an utter disregard of every principle of state rights and state sovereignty. The Confederate law required that one half of the cargo space of outgoing as well as incoming vessels be reserved for the Confederacy, but vessels wholly owned by the state were exempt from these regulations. In order to evade the law, private vessels owned by foreign interests were chartered by the owners to individual states. But Davis refused to allow such vessels to clear Southern ports without obeying the regulations. Brown chartered several such vessels and in April, 1864, wired the Treasury secretary for clearance of one of these vessels, *Little Ada,* loaded with cotton, none of it for the Confederate account.[18] Angered by the refusal of clearance, Brown called a conference of those governors east of the Mississippi River to seek a repeal of the Confederate blockade-runner law. Governors William "Extra Billy" Smith of Virginia and John Milton of Florida refused to attend, but Zebulon B. Vance of North Carolina, Thomas W. Watts of Alabama, and Charles Clark of Mississippi did attend, and on April 18, 1864, they issued a protest against the Confederate regulations. At the instigation of a Georgia representative, Congress passed a law that exempted ships owned in part by a state or chartered by it from the necessity to conform to the Confederate regulations, but on June 10 Davis vetoed it, and at this time it could not be passed over his veto. On March 4 and 8, 1865, however, the state righters won by passing a law removing all restrictions of the state on blockade-running. Nevertheless, it was futile, for in a month the Confederacy was at an end.

Although Brown had a real sympathy for the common people and tried to provide for the soldiers' families and for relief of the poor, the dominant motive in his struggle with Davis seems to have been a quest for personal power, even to the point of wanting to displace Davis as president. After the war, he turned Republican. He made a fortune by leasing convicts from the state to work in his mines at a nominal sum. When it seemed to his advantage, he returned to the Democratic party and was appointed to the U.S. Senate in 1880, serving until 1891.[19]

Usually equated with Brown as an extreme state rights man and obstructionist in regard to Confederate policies is Zebulon Baird Vance, the governor of North Carolina, but he should not be. Vance was a poor boy from the western hills of North Carolina who worked his way through the University of North Carolina, became a lawyer at Asheville, and was elected to Congress in 1858 as a Whig. He represented his section of North Carolina in opposing secession, but when his state seceded he raised a company of westerners who called themselves the Rough and Ready Company, was eventually elected colonel of a regiment, and participated in several battles in Virginia. In August, 1862, at the age of thirty-two, he was elected governor by the greatest popular majority in the history of the state, winning the solid soldier vote. Vance was a dynamic leader, tall, bushy-browed, handsome, a natural-born orator who spoke the language of the people and entertained them by his homely and at times coarse humor and anecdotes.[20]

As governor, unlike Brown, he loyally supported conscription and the

Confederate war effort, according to his lights. It was not he, but the chief justice of the state, Richmond H. Pearson, who seriously undermined the conscription laws by declaring them unconstitutional and indiscriminately issuing writs of habeas corpus in 1863–65. Vance explained the evil effects of Pearson's decisions in causing desertion and resisting the conscription acts in a long and respectful letter to President Davis dated May 13, 1863. Here he clearly demonstrated his loyalty to the Confederacy and his strenuous efforts to sustain it. He cited a decision of Judge Pearson, who released some murderers of a squad of his militia sent out to arrest deserters and draft evaders in Yadkin County, a western county, based on the ground that the governor had no authority to arrest deserters and conscripts, but that this authority pertained to Confederate authorities alone. The legislature, also on the same ground, refused a request from the governor to pass legislation definitely giving him the authority to arrest deserters and making it a penal offense to harbor and conceal them. The North Carolina generals had already appealed to Vance to aid in stopping wholesale desertions of their troops after Pearson's decisions were known. Vance wished the president to give him definite authority to use the militia in enforcing the conscription laws and arresting deserters, and also to request other governors to use their powers for this purpose. At the same time he outlined the principal reasons for desertion and the ways to remedy it.[21] Davis replied that it would be better to have deserters arrested by companies of volunteer exempts than by the militia.[22]

Davis's letters to the North Carolina governor were far more cordial and accommodating than those that he wrote to Brown; he praised Vance for patriotic efforts and cooperation. Nevertheless, Vance solicited the appointment of North Carolinians, and not citizens of other states, to Confederate offices in the state. In July, 1863, he had complained that the resident of another state had been appointed collector of the tax-in-kind for North Carolina. The president in replying patiently explained the reasons for the appointment. He ended his letter on a conciliatory note: "I am aware of the embarrassments you may have in carrying out your patriotic efforts to aid the Confederate Government in this struggle, and relying on your capacity and energy to overcome them I would be very far from willingly allowing any additional obstruction to be thrown in your way."[23] Earlier, when Vance sent him resolutions of the citizens of Onslow County asking Confederate protection from depredations, Davis replied that he had ordered General S. G. French to send mounted troops to protect the citizens, ending his letter in a flattering tribute to Vance: "I gratefully acknowledge the earnest and patriotic manner in which, since your assumption of the Executive authority in N. Carolina, you have labored to fill the battle-thinned ranks of her regiments, and recruit our armies in the field."[24] When Vance applied, however, for exemption from the draft of certain classes, such as police officers of towns, Davis insisted on strictly following the law, but wherever there were conflicting opinions as to the eligibility of constables and justices of the peace for exemption, he ordered enrolling officers to wait until a conference could be held with the governor. When Vance requested the return to North Carolina of a certain Eli Swanner, who had been arrested by the Confederate authorities as a traitor, Davis pointed out to the governor the danger to the Confederate government of releasing this man, but added that "with an earnest desire of promoting harmony and good feeling between the State and the Confederate authorities, I acceed to your request."

Up until the early part of 1864 Davis's relations with the North Carolina governor were cordial, even accommodating. But then the growing peace movement, the increase of the state rights feeling among the North Carolinians, and Vance's blockade-running policy created bad relations between the president and Vance. (The peace movement will be considered in the next chapter on declining Confederate morale.) The breaking point came apparently on February 29, 1864, when Davis replied to a critical letter from Vance. It was like a body blow to an enemy. Davis hotly denied that he had practiced a policy of exclusion of antisecessionists from the more important offices of the government and in the promotion of officers in the army. In a haughty fashion he asked Vance to specify cases and also to specify facts indicating that Davis "*suspected* the loyalty of North Carolina because of the reluctance with which they gave up the old Union." And finally Davis rejected Vance's accusations of his refusing to redress acts of "ruthless" conscription, and of the severity of the government in the impressment of property, "frequently entrusted to men unprincipled, dishonest, and filled to the overflowing with all the petty meanness of small minds, dressed in a little brief authority." Again Davis asked the governor to specify, accusing him of a singular misconstruction of his previous letter. He declared also that he would not misuse the power granted to him to suspend the writ of habeas corpus.[25]

When Vance sent him cases of three officers not promoted presumably because of their political opinions, Davis demolished him in a letter of March 31, 1864, citing facts in regard to the promotions and concluding the letter with a request that, because of Vance's unpleasant remarks and unprofitable discussion, he end his correspondence with him except for official matters. Davis was excessively proud and thin-skinned, and could never pass over criticisms and slights, as Lincoln did. Almost invariably his replies to criticisms of his conduct as president justified or rationalized his actions by saying that it was his duty to counteract criticisms that "would tend to create hostility to the Government and undermine its power to provide for public defense" or that would seriously weaken the confidence of the people in his direction of the government.

At approximately the same date as this hassle, the president began his quarrel with Vance over the latter's blockade-running activities. The governor wished the Confederate government to exempt citizens who had a part interest in the state's blockade-runners from complying with the federal law of 1864 that required one half of the cargoes of blockade-runners, either exporting or importing, to be reserved for Confederate supplies (those blockade-runners wholly owned by the state were excepted). Vance was defiant. He wrote to Senator William A. Graham on May 11, 1864: "I have ordered all our ships not to return unless restrictions are removed—large quantities of merchandise and machinery are laying at the islands and will I fear cause great loss to the state."[26] Davis replied that the law must be obeyed, and if Vance's request should be granted, individuals in other states would try to evade the law by buying a part interest in a state vessel, and "there would be nothing left for the Confederate government to regulate."[27] In a message to Congress, the president observed that so profitable was the blockade-running business that stock in the blockade-running companies originally selling for $2,000 a share had advanced to $20,000.

Despite Vance's obstructive tactics, motivated by a provincial concern for his state rather than for the Confederacy, he continued to be loyal to the Confederate cause in his own peculiar way. In fact, he made important contributions both to the supply of the Confederate army and to the recruitment of troops. He claimed that North Carolina furnished more soldiers to the Confederate army than any other state, but neglected to reveal also that its desertion rate was the highest in the Confederacy. He listed the supplies that he furnished as follows: leather for 250,000 pairs of shoes, gray woolen cloth for at least 250,000 uniforms, 12,000 overcoats, 2,000 Enfield rifles, 100,000 pounds of bacon, 500 sacks of coffee for hospital use, $50,000 worth of medicines at gold prices as well as 60,000 pairs of handcards, 10,000 grain scythes, and 200 barrels of bluestone for the wheat growers.[28] Vance neglected to mention that while Lee's army in Virginia was shivering in the cold winter of 1864 from inadequate clothing and many soldiers were barefoot, he hoarded large supplies of clothing and shoes not needed by North Carolina troops, such as 92,000 soldiers' uniforms.

Governor Andrew Magrath also became hostile to Davis because of the great expansion of the power of the central government. He corresponded with both Vance and Brown early in 1865 to get their support in preserving the power of the states, which, he wrote, had been eroded by their gradually acquiescing in the expansion of federal power. South Carolina at the end of 1864 had drafted youths 16 and 17 to serve in the militia which, together with the reserves, numbered 16,000 men. After Sherman defeated Hood and the safety of the state was gravely threatened, the legislature removed the restriction on these troops leaving the state. In desperation, the governor proposed the union of the militia of all the different states into one body for the common defense, and that General Joseph E. Johnston be placed in charge of both this united force and Hood's army. But Magrath wrote to Governor Brown and Alexander H. Stephens of the danger of calling a convention. Their activities in opposing the Confederate government had come so close to treason that General William T. Sherman had invited them to meet him for a peace conference, but both leaders refused.[29]

Though there may have been other governors like Vance and Brown who weakened the Confederate government and the war effort, the majority of governors loyally supported President Davis. When Brown was refused clearance for the blockade-runner *Little Ada*, the governor of Georgia sent out dispatches to the other governors asking them to unite with him in a protest to Congress against such regulations. Governor William "Extra Billy" Smith of Virginia refused, and Governor John Milton of Florida in his refusal rebuked Brown, saying that the safety of the people demanded "the utmost confidence and generous support [by] the State governments to the maintenance of the Confederate Government. . . . It is best, therefore, where it can be honorably done, to avoid all conflicts and competition between the State and Confederate authorities for political power, or commercial privileges, at all events during the existing war."[30]

Other governors besides Smith and Milton in general supported Davis in his administration. Although some of them, such as Governor Thomas O. Moore of Louisiana and J. J. Pettus of Mississippi, had some friction with the War Department in their zealous efforts to defend their states by retaining considerable bodies of militia, they rendered many valuable services to the cause. Practically all the governors were shortsighted in making numerous appeals to Davis for arms that the War Department could not furnish and for scattering the Confederate forces to protect the individual states. The president had constantly to contend with the virulent state rights feeling and the parochialism of viewpoint of both people and governors. As early as January 17, 1862, he was so irritated by states demanding the return of their arms that he said in the cabinet, according to Bragg's journal, if this was to be the attitude of the states toward the Confederate government it would be impossible to carry on the war, and that those with halters around their necks should flee.[31] And on February 15, when the delegation in Congress from North Carolina asked the president to withdraw North Carolina troops from the army to come home to protect the threatened eastern shore, he told them that for the states to withdraw their troops to their borders in every emergency would not give the country even a semblance of a Confederacy.

Jefferson Davis's attitude to state rights throughout the war was ambivalent. Before the war he had been an ardent state rights man, and much of that feeling remained. But as the successful prosecution of the war required greater and greater centralization, he was flexible enough to change in order to meet his responsibilities. He changed faster than most of the Southern people and, accordingly, one of his most serious problems was to combat or evade the blocks to the vigorous prosecution of the war set up by the upholders of traditional state rights. Some writers, especially Frank L. Owsley, have perhaps exaggerated the role of localism in the collapse of the Confederacy, without realizing that the North was also afflicted by excessive state rights feeling, though to a lesser degree than the South.[32] Owsley has gone so far as to propose an epitaph for the Confederacy: "Died of State Rights."

The state rights fetish was a part not only of the selfishness of human nature, but of a traditional ideology that hampered the Confederacy in forging a nation out of individualistic states. Its ill effects were displayed by the states' withholding a large part of their arms in the first year of the war so that the Confederacy, according to the secretary of war, lost the services of 200,000 volunteers because it could not provide them with arms. It was responsible for seriously hindering the enforcement of conscription, for enabling blockade-runners to evade Confederate regulations made to insure that the foreign trade be regulated for the benefit of the Confederacy instead of for greedy individuals, for indirectly encouraging draft evaders by the resistance to the suspension of the habeas corpus writ, for monopolizing the output of state cotton mills such as those in North Carolina for the benefit of its citizens and soldiers, for preventing the Confederacy from manufacturing whiskey in some corn-producing states for its hospitals and for the treatment of wounded soldiers, for interfering with building links in railroad lines to transport soldiers and supplies, and in general for weakening the efforts of the Confederacy to defeat the enemy. More subtly, the strength of the state rights feeling may have prevented Davis and his secretaries from attempting, or even conceiving, bolder and more revolutionary measures of concentrating the resources of the country and harnessing them to the herculean task of winning the War for Southern Independence.

Losing the Will to Fight, but Not Jefferson Davis

The struggle of Davis with the governors was simply a part of the morale problem of the Confederacy, for in general they reflected the will of the people. In the last year of the war the Southern people lost the will to fight for their independence as a nation. But it was not a one-way street; the Northern people also fluctuated in their morale and in their determination to continue the war. Because of war-weariness and the shocking casualties of Grant's army, President Lincoln feared that he would not be reelected.

The British ambassador in Washington, Lord Lyons, reported to his government on January 9, 1863, the war weariness of the Northern people, upon which the Confederates were counting to end the war. He wrote, "I have no hesitation in saying that all men of all parties have lost heart about the war. They are not confident of success."[1] The Democrats of New York, he thought, had given up the idea of restoring the Union by force, and he judged that "the difficulty of recruiting in the North may end the war." On March 2 he reported: "But the country is growing more and more tired of the war, and unless there is something to raise the war spirit again soon the Democrats may come out as a peace party."[2]

The letters of Frank McGregor, a Union soldier in the lower Mississippi river valley, to his sweetheart reflected the willingness of the soldiers to give up the fight as early as the middle of the war. To "Dearest Susie" he wrote from a point near Vicksburg on January 30, 1863: "The greater portion of our troops are so disaffected that they would make all kinds of concessions to an amicable adjustment of this affair." They did not like Lincoln's Emancipation Proclamation, "they holding it has come down to be a nigger war, fighting for the Blacks etc." They wished "peace at almost any price." But his mood changed in the fall of that year after the victories at Gettysburg and Vicksburg. He then wrote: "Now all is changed, the great North has shown its strength. . . . No one now, friend or foe, doubts our ultimate success."[3]

So the mood of the Southern people and their morale rose and fell with victory and defeat, and also with their estimation of the Northern will to persevere. It was this belief on the part of the Southerners, that the Northern people would soon get tired of the war and give up, forcing the government to abandon the attempt to drive the South back into the Union, that sustained their morale. J. R. Rogers, for example, wrote from Jonesville, Lee County, Virginia, on February 4, 1863: "Every one you meet is of the opinion that the war cannot possibly last *much* longer. This idea is based upon the political dissensions of the North, the rise and progress of the democratic party— its recent successes, aim, and object as a peace party—lack of success of Feds in the field—they blame it on incompetent generals—we, that we are fighting for life and liberty."[4]

Bell Wiley has plotted an interesting diagram of the curve of Confederate morale.[5] It was very high at the beginning of the war, and although it took a dip in February, 1862, after the surrender of Fort Donelson, it recovered considerably after the victories in April, 1862, of Shiloh, in August, 1862, of Second Bull Run, and in May, 1863, of Chancellorsville. It took a steep plunge downward in the autumn of 1862 after the failure of Lee's invasion of Maryland and defeat at Antietam and Bragg's failure in the invasion of Kentucky. It also fell drastically after the double defeat of Gettysburg and Vicksburg. It never recovered much afterward, according to Wiley, taking its sharpest dive in September, 1864, with the fall of Atlanta and the reelection of Lincoln in November of that year. From then on the morale of the country was very low, but the morale of the army was always higher. Thus the rise or fall of Confederate arms in battle was by far the decisive factor in keeping up or lowering Southern morale.

President Davis, in messages to Congress and speeches to the people, tried to inspire the Southerners to a heroic defense of their country. But almost invariably these efforts presented too roseate a picture of the condition of the country and minimized the serious defeats and economic deterioration of the Confederacy. His message of December 7, 1863, was the first to contain a serious note of gloom.[6] He admitted disappointment over the reverses at Gettysburg, Vicksburg, Port Hudson, Helena, and Little Rock, but he explained Lee's withdrawal from Pennsylvania after the battle of Gettysburg as caused by the extraordinary flooding of the Potomac River that prevented the supplies upon which he had relied from reaching the army. In this message also appeared a theme that increasingly dominated his public utterances, namely, that he and the country relied on God for victory, because their cause was just.

His speeches to the people in the last year of the war were the most inspiring of the period, for he abandoned his natural aloofness that had kept him from communicating freely with the people and opened his heart to them. The Confederate cause was desperate then, and he employed all of his splendid technical qualifications as a public speaker—sincerity, impressive dignified appearance, beautiful speaking voice, and command of a lucid, vigorous style of prose—in fact, his qualifications were superior to those of Lincoln, except for the fact that the Northern president had a superior moral cause that appealed to the world. As a result, Davis was magnificent. Alexander H. Stephens, though a bitter enemy, wrote of his speech in Richmond shortly before the collapse of the Confederacy: "It was not only bold and undaunted in tone, but had that loftiness of sentiment and rare form of expression, as well as magnetic influence in delivery by which the people are moved to their profoundest depths. Many who had heard this master of oratory in his most brilliant display in the United States Senate said they never before saw Mr. Davis so really majestic. The occasion . . . the circumstances . . . caused the minds of not a few to revert to like appeals by Rienzi and Demosthenes."[7] Still, for most of his presidency, Davis was too absorbed in military affairs to devote much time to communicating with and inspiring the people.

Davis's stirring appeals to the Southern people occurred mainly while he was on the trips that he made to the army in Tennessee, and later in Mississippi and Georgia, when the Southern cause was failing. On December 8, 1862, Davis wrote to Lee at Fredericksburg, Virginia, that he planned a trip to the Southwest immediately, "with the hope that something may be done to bring out men not heretofore in service, and to arouse all classes to united and desperate resistance." He did not mention that his main objective was to confer with Bragg and his generals in order to restore harmony among them. He arrived at Murfreesboro, Tennessee, where Bragg's army was stationed on December 17. Although he found the troops there in good condition and fine spirits he was disturbed by the fact that "the feeling in East Tenn., and North Alabama was far from what we desire. There is some hostility and much want of confidence in our strength."

In his speeches and messages to Congress Davis employed various devices to arouse the fighting spirit of the people, such as describing Northern atrocities—"Beast" Butler in New Orleans, the refusal to exchange prisoners, declaring medicines as contraband and thus making war on the sick, distributing counterfeit Confederate money, burning the barns and homes of peaceful civilians, the treatment of captured Southern soldiers in Northern prisons, Lincoln's Emancipation Proclamation, and outrages of Northern soldiers upon defenseless women. He declared that "every crime which could characterize the course of demons has marked the course of the invader." He predicted that horrible conditions in the South would result from a Northern victory.[8]

The president's appeals to the patriotism of the Southern women were characteristic expressions of Southern chivalry. He urged them to shame skulkers, evaders, and those able-bodied men who avoided military service by taking advantage of unnecessary exemptions into joining or returning to the army. He advised the young ladies looking for a husband to choose a war hero, or a man with an empty sleeve, rather than a man who had remained at home and grown rich by speculation.[9]

Other methods used to arouse the people were appeals to their sense of honor and to their religious feelings. Nine times during the war the president proclaimed a day of fasting, humiliation, and prayer, and General Gorgas noted that these religious days were generally observed in the Confederacy.[10] The ministers (not all of them) and the women appeared to be the most ardent supporters of the Confederate cause, staunch defenders of Jefferson Davis against his critics. James Silver concluded that in the waning months of the Confederacy, "there is overwhelming evidence that the preachers as a whole retained a higher degree of morale than they were able to instill in their parishioners."[11] Accustomed to warning sinners of the torments of Hell, they dramatically foretold what would happen if the Yankees won and the South was subjugated. Defeats were often explained away as the providence of God working to purify and chasten the people for their sins, and to inspire them to more heroic efforts to save the Confederacy. Such also was the Davis explanation of Confederate defeats. In 1863, especially, great religious revivals rocked the army.[12] Even the dashing, swashbuckling cavalry leader, John Hunt Morgan of Kentucky, who was captured on a raid into Ohio and imprisoned, wrote to his bride that she had been a good religious influence on him and that he read his prayerbook every night.

If religion gave a strong support to Davis and the Confederacy, the virulent attacks of certain influential newspapers against the president weakened his administration. Although at the beginning of the war there were approximately 800 newspapers in the Confederate states, the attrition among them during the course of the war, with its severe shortage of paper, is indicated by the fact that in February, 1865, the total number of editors exempted from the draft was only 123, plus 682 employees. The great majority of the newspapers loyally supported the president and the Confederate cause, but many were critical of certain generals. The *Chattanooga Rebel,* one of several peripatetic Confederate newspapers, had on its staff the brilliant Henry Watterson (who after the war became the powerful editor of the Louisville *Courier-Journal*). Noted for his wit and audacity, he attacked General Bragg so unmercifully that the general tried to get him dismissed. In general, the

Confederate newspapers tried to keep up the people's morale by holding back news of defeats, exaggerating victories, and describing in lurid detail atrocities committed by Northern troops.[13]

The two newspapers that were among the most bitter in their criticisms of Davis were the *Charleston Mercury,* controlled by the Robert Barnwell Rhett family, and the Richmond *Examiner,* edited by the brilliant John M. Daniel and later by Edward Pollard. Why Daniel was so hostile to Davis is a mystery. When the president came to Richmond to live at the end of May, 1861, Daniel's newspaper praised him profusely, but after the defeats at Roanoke Island and Fort Donelson it became critical of Davis's administration. For a short while Daniel was a military aide to General A. P. Hill, and the contrast in the appearance of the two men was striking, even ridiculous. The famous general was described by an observer as short and spare, dressed in a fatigue jacket of gray flannel, wearing a queer little hat with no plume and the least possible military insignia, while Daniel was dressed as a dashing cavalier with a plume waving in his hat. Daniel was tall, with long black locks, an aquiline nose, and a Jewish-looking face, while Hill wore a luxuriant reddish beard, and in battle had the fire of a Crusader in his eyes. Daniel was a misanthrope, egotistical and cynical; perhaps his morose personality was the basic cause for his disparagement of the Confederate president.

So damaging was his newspaper, as well as the *Richmond Whig,* to the administration that Secretary Mallory at a cabinet meeting suggested to the president the expediency of getting one of the Richmond dailies to explain editorially the wisdom of some administration measures that were making the people unhappy, but Davis paid no attention to this advice. Attorney General Thomas Bragg also disapproved of Davis's ignoring the press. In his journal of January 8, 1862, he noted that the Richmond *Examiner* was assailing the administration almost daily and that the administration was not defended by the *Whig* or the *Dispatch,* with its large circulation, and only very seldom and then faintly by the *Richmond Enquirer.* Bragg related that on February 5, 1862, there was a discussion in the cabinet of having a newspaper in Richmond that would defend the government, but he commented that the *Enquirer* could not be purchased and that the *Dispatch* wanted conditions in return for supporting the president.

Robert Kean recorded in his diary on September 1, 1863: "The Examiner and Whig in their persistent malice toward the President do only less harm than the Raleigh Standard" (which as early as 1862 was advocating making peace with the U.S. government). Though Kean confessed that he was far from being a universal admirer of the president, nevertheless he could not understand what good these papers hoped to accomplish by stirring up opposition, distrust, and hatred of him. The *Examiner,* for example, used such occasions as the controversy with Joseph E. Johnston, the dismissal of the quartermaster general, and the appointment of Bragg as an adviser to attack the president with the sharpest irony.

But the tremendous decline of morale in the Confederacy was revealed most frankly, not in the newspapers, but in private diaries and private letters and by the disgraceful amount of desertion in the army. A graph could be drawn showing the decline of morale on the basis of slave ownership, reaching its lowest point in the mountains and hill country where slavery was weak and antagonism to the planter class was strong, and its highest point in the lowlands, where slavery was strongly entrenched and the planter class preserved traditions of honor. Susannah Clay, the mother of Senator Clement Clay, Jr., wrote from Huntsville, Alabama, to her distinguished son on July 25, 1863: "Our citizens seek to save individual property more than country." She observed that young men who should be fighting for their country "appear plenty here," leading her to ask, "Are our people false?" And Clay's brother Hugh Lawson, who was in the army, also wrote in deep gloom over new military disasters, that now there was no chance for recognition of the Confederacy by England. He had thought that it would come after McClellan was driven from the environs of Richmond. Now, however, he feared that the patriotism of the people was limited to the pocket rather than to the honor of the flag and the independence of the country. David Clopten, writing from Tuskegee, capital of Alabama, to Mrs. Clement Clay, Jr., was more hopeful, though depressed over the surrender of Vicksburg, for he relied on Providence.[14]

But long before the double disaster of Vicksburg and Gettysburg, in February, 1862, Attorney General Thomas Bragg saw signs of deteriorating morale, such as the apathy toward the Confederate cause of the people of Tennessee, who were making no effort to help defend the state, but depended entirely on the Confederate troops. He commented also as early as February 15, 1862, that he feared the Confederacy would "go under."[15] One of Davis's strong supporters in Congress, Clement C. Clay, Jr., of Alabama, expressed his own discouragement and commented on the people's loss of morale after the surrender of Vicksburg in a letter to Senator Wigfall. He observed that "the papers are beginning to open upon Davis and his 'pets' and I am quite surprised to see how many of them are abusing him.... The burthen of the charge of all is that he is sacrificing the country to his personal likes and dislikes." He noted a lack of patriotism and an unwillingness to give up fortunes that pervaded the South. Georgia, he commented, was full of refugees from Mississippi, Tennessee, and north Alabama fleeing with their Negroes to some safe place: "They cling to their flesh pots while the country crys to them for help." In another letter to Wigfall, he declared that he was "sick of the selfishness, demagogism, and bigotry that characterize a large percentage of those in office," and when he saw "how many are growing rich in the Commissary and Qr. Master's Departs. by defrauding the Government and the people and yet are unchecked," and how many "cheating impressing agents" there were, he wished to retire from public life.[16]

An important cause of the decline of morale was a feeling among the poorer members of society that the burdens of war were borne unequally by rich and poor. Governor Vance received letters, ignorant and ungrammatical, but full of bitterness, from poor wives of soldiers. They complained that those who had plenty of corn would not sell it for Confederate money and were hoarding it, and that half of the women of Rutherford County in North Carolina stayed away from church because they were barefoot. One woman wrote ominously of the resentment among the poor that "the common people is drove of[f] in the ware to fight for the big mans negro & he at home making nearly all the corn that is made & then becaus he has the play in his own fingers he puts the price on his corn so as to take all the Solders wages for a fiew bushels."[17]

Profiteering, speculation, and hoarding, indeed, did much to undermine patriotism and morale. Gorgas wrote on July 17, 1863, concerning the siege of Charleston: "The sins of the people of Charleston may cause that city to fall; it is full of rottenness, every one being engaged in speculations."[18] On March 25, 1863, he wrote again of the vast profits that the firm of the Crenshaws were making from their flour contract and woolen factories in Richmond and that the firm of Frazer and Company of Charleston, of which Secretary of the Treasury (in 1864-65) George A. Trenholm was a leading partner, had made a colossal fortune from blockade-running. The farmers, too, Kean accused (April 21, 1863) of being the worst extortioners in the Confederacy. Since the enforcement of the Impressment Act by which the government often paid at 50 percent below market prices, he wrote that "the instant impressment of flour, corn, and meat, as soon as they are brought to any of the inland towns to be put in market, is causing universal withholding of surplus—secreting and non-production."[19] The profound selfishness of many Southern people about their material interests was reflected by Warren Akin, who wrote to his wife in Georgia of their inconsistency in being willing to give up husbands and sons to the army, but "let one of their negroes be taken and what a houl[sic] you will hear—the love of money is the greatest difficulty in our way to independence."[20]

The depressing condition of the Confederacy in the fall of 1863 and winter of 1864 led to a movement among the legislatures and soldiers to boost morale. In early December, 1863, the legislature of South Carolina passed a resolution commending the president's official conduct, expressing its unabated confidence in him and its "unalterable determination to sustain the Government in its efforts to conquer an honorable peace, and maintain the liberties of the people" (yet within a year sentiment in the state had so changed that it elected an anti-Davis governor, Judge Andrew Magrath).[21] The Mississippi legislature followed in the same month with a similar resolution. On January 9, 1864, Davis received the resolutions of the Georgia legislature expressing its "determination to prosecute the present war with the utmost vigor and energy."[22] A year later, the Virginia legislature in a resolution requesting that Lee be appointed to take command of all the Confederate armies, assured him at the same time of its confidence in his patriotic devotion to the welfare of the country. Davis in his reply of January 18, 1865, testified to the unhesitating spirit with which Virginia had consecrated throughout the war "the blood of her children" as well as all her natural resources to achieve independence."[23] Also resolutions of confidence in and support of the president from various units of the army, such as the resolutions of the Twelfth Battalion of the Georgia artillery and the resolutions of Stewart's brigade of Virginia infantry, began to be received in his office.[24] Individual soldiers, too, such as Johnny Green of the Kentucky "Orphan Brigade," expressed sentiments of loyalty to the Confederate cause: "Our cause is just & will surely prevail"; "The boys are all of one mind. Fight on until death."[25]

Nevertheless, the rise and growing strength of the peace movement during the last two years of the war were undermining morale. At first it was an underground movement carried forward by secret organizations, such as the "Heroes of America" with rituals, handgrips, and passwords, that elected some sheriffs and justices of the peace. The movement extended throughout the Allegheny peninsula, or the back country, where the Unionists had always been strong. It was joined by armed bands of deserters and was especially strong in northern Alabama, western Virginia, and western North Carolina.[26] Its spread in western North Carolina, where Governor Vance was born, especially alarmed Davis. Vance tried to combat it by writing to the president on December 30, 1863, suggesting a way to remove "the sources of discontent" in his state by making an attempt to negotiate directly with President Lincoln for concluding a peace. Davis replied that he had made three distinct efforts to communicate with the Northern president, but had been rebuffed. Lincoln's terms for ending the war—namely, the emancipation of the slaves and the return of the Confederate states to the Union—were so objectionable that he felt sure the people of North Carolina would reject them.[27] The president asked the governor not to delay in using his influence firmly to suppress the traitorous movements of some bad men in his state. Rather than trying to conciliate them, he urged the governor to crush treason in its incipient stages, not allowing it to mature.

Vance was in a tight spot in regard to the peace movement that began to gain headway in the summer of 1863, led by W. W. Holden, editor of the Raleigh *North Carolina Standard*. Holden was agitating for calling a convention to withdraw the state from the Confederacy through a series of public meetings of the Conservative party. Although Vance was staunchly opposed to this, he realized that in order to keep the good will of the people he must move carefully. He thought that Holden was playing a demagogic role in catering to the peace movement, and that he really wished to displace him as governor. Accordingly, Vance tried to get the support of powerful conservative leaders who had opposed the secession movement, such as E. J. Hale, the editor of the *Fayette Observer,* and ex-governor and ex-senator William A. Graham of Hillsboro, to come out in the press in opposition to Holden. In a letter to Graham dated January 1, 1864, he wrote: "I will see the Conservative Party [to which he himself belonged] blown into a thousand atoms and Holden and his under-strappers in hell (if you will pardon the violence of the expression) before I will consent to a course which I think would bring dishonor and ruin upon both State and Confederacy! We are already ruined, almost, but are not yet dishonored."[28] Vance declared that the peace meetings in the state would cause the army to melt away by desertion. In April, 1864, he visited the North Carolina troops and was pleased by his reception. In August he ran for reelection against Holden, the peace candidate, and won an overwhelming, nearly four-to-one victory.[29]

A clear indication of the loss of the will to fight was the alarming increase in desertions from the army. The enormous number of desertions in the last year of the war not only seriously weakened the army's ability to resist the enemy, but told the story that the Confederate states were not unified in their desire to wage a "sacred" war for Southern independence. Braxton Bragg, commander of the western army, wrote to President Davis on November 16, 1863, that rigid legislation was necessary to cure the evil of officers and their men remaining absent from the army. This evil was so great, he observed, that his present effective force did not exceed 40 percent of the aggregate strength on the muster rolls. This dereliction from duty, he noted, was a frightful condition, revealing that the sense of honor in the army was low.[30] General Richard Taylor, son of Zachary Taylor, who commanded an army in the trans-Mississippi West said that his men were so reluctant to serve east of the river that he was fearful his army would disintegrate if he tried to lead them across the Mississippi River.[31] Desertion became so appalling after the defeat at Gettysburg that, in order to attract the deserters to return, Davis offered amnesty to those who would return to their posts within thirty days. In his speech at Macon, Georgia, on September 29, 1864, the president said that two thirds of Hood's army were absent—some sick, some wounded, but most absent without leave (deserters)—and at Columbia a few days later he said that if half of the men absent from the army would return, Sherman would be disgracefully defeated.

Desertion deprived the Confederacy not only of sorely needed men, but of the guns that they often took with them. There were many reasons for desertion, not the least of which was the failure for long periods to pay the soldiers, and then to pay them in depreciated currency that would buy little. The pitiful letters of wives to soldiers, complaining that they and their children were starving, or constantly endangered by marauders, the inability, as the war went on, to get furloughs, and the hard life of the soldiers, who marched frequently without shoes and had little to eat, caused many to desert. The relative impunity for absences without leave and the remarkable laxity in granting furloughs in the early days of the war encouraged desertion. Although some deserters were shot, court-martials in the Confederate army were generally lenient and imposed less severe penalties for this dangerous crime, such as flogging with thirty-nine lashes. J. R. P. Ellis, however, who had been conscripted in North Carolina, wrote to his wife from Kinston, North Carolina, on June 8, 1864, that he had recently seen seven deserters hanged, that some of the boys were nearly naked, and that he was dirty and "mighty tired of the war."[32]

The decision of Chief Justice Richmond Hobson Pearson of North Carolina declaring the Conscription Act unconstitutional and his release of conscripted men by habeas corpus process caused, according to General W. D. Pender, "a disgraceful desertion of North Carolina troops." Then, also, the troops throughout the Confederate army developed a sense of the hopelessness of continuing the struggle since the North constantly renewed its armies with immigrants enticed by huge bounties and the opportunity of acquiring a homestead, which the poor Confederacy could not offer. Soldiers in Lee's army came to feel that it was practically useless to kill a Yankee soldier, for his place would be quickly filled. Southerners contended, with some truth, that they were being beaten by the importation of foreigners into the Yankee army. Ella Lonn, in her able study of foreigners in the two armies, estimated conservatively that foreign-born soldiers constituted from one fifth to one fourth of the strength of the Union army, but only a very small element in the Confederate army. Faced by all these difficulties, soldiers, especially from the hill and mountain country, where Union feeling had been strong, deserted in droves during the last year of the war. The official reports fixed the number of deserters at 103,400, but actually the number was far greater. Modern studies indicate that there was one desertion for every nine enlistments in the Confederate army, but an even greater desertion rate in the Union army (one deserter to every seven enlistments).[33]

In the last year of the Confederacy, the people were becoming weary of the struggle, worn out by constant defeats and by being deprived of the ordinary comforts of life. General Gorgas wrote in his diary on October 6, 1864: "Our poor harrowed and overworked soldiers are getting worn out with the campaign. They see nothing before them but certain death, and have, I fear, fallen into a sort of hopelessness, and are dispirited. Certain it is that they do not fight as they fought at the Wilderness and Spotsylvania."[34] As the shadows of war began to darken the lives of the civilian population, many longed for peace, and meditated on the dubious value of a war for the preservation of Southern independence. In her diary on July 26, 1864, Mrs. Chesnut voiced the feeling of many of her sex as she contemplated the death of so many fine young men: "Is anything worth it—this fearful sacrifice; this awful penalty we pay for war?"[35] Another wife of a Confederate officer wrote from Richmond to Mrs. Roger A. Pryor during the latter dark days of the war: "I am for a tidal wave for peace—and I am not alone."[36]

Like the defeated soldiers and many dispirited Southern women, Davis also had periods of gloom over the way the war was going, but his morale continued firm to the very end. Reagan in his memoirs tells how tears ran down the president's cheeks as he discussed with the cabinet the perilous condition of Richmond in May, 1862, when McClellan's army had advanced so close to the Confederate capital. He declared, "Richmond must not be given up—it shall not be given up." Reagan observed that he had never seen the president show such deep emotion as he did on this occasion.[37] General Gorgas also noted his determination never to surrender. He recorded that Lee's chief of staff, General R. H. Chilton, reported his commander as saying in October, 1864, "If we can't get the men, all that is left for us is to make peace on the best terms we can." Gorgas commented, "He must be subject to fits of despondence. Our brave president never wavers thus in act or thought."[38]

Davis overworked his frail physique for the cause of Confederate independence, but in the end the people did not appreciate his efforts. On March 2, 1865, Gorgas commented in his diary: "The President has alas! lost every vestige of the public confidence. Had he been successful his errors and faults would have been overlooked, but adversity magnifies them." Jefferson Davis's devotion to the Confederate cause was magnificent, but he could not inspire the Southern people with a similar selfless devotion. If he had been able to do so, he might possibly have turned the tide of defeat to victory.[39]

Davis as War Leader

The dream of glory—Jefferson Davis never really gave it up after he had attained fame in the Mexican War. Stephen Mallory, commenting on his Civil War career, wrote that the president "spoke and acted habitually as if conscious of possessing military genius, embracing the qualities of a great soldier."[1] Although Davis made suggestions to his generals, he did not interfere with their plans of battle. He once indicated that if he could take command of the western army and Lee of the Army of Northern Virginia, together they could win.[2] During Lee's invasion of Maryland, he began a trip to join him, but the general sent his aide, Major W. H. Taylor, to dissuade him. Varina writes in her memoir that when Grant was besieging Richmond in 1864, "he bitterly resented his executive position that prevented him from participating in the battle."

The president, wrote Gorgas on July 1, 1864, "likes to talk of matters purely military, especially about guns, etc. which he used to pay attention to as Secretary of War under Pierce."[3] Also Mallory in his diary noted that "military affairs, however minute, rarely failed to command his patient industry, no labours at the War Office were too small for his attention, and appointments and promotions of officers, questions of rank, military laws and usage, routine, etc. very often engrossed it, notwithstanding his unbounded

242

confidence in the experience and judgment of General Cooper [the Adjutant General] upon all such subjects."[4] This absorption in military details that drained his energy needed for larger subjects was undoubtedly one of the reasons for his irritability and frequent ill health and his serious neglect of the home front.

Mallory thought that Davis's interest in and familiarity with military affairs was a handicap in his administration of the presidency. It "induces his desire," he wrote, "to mingle in them all and to control them; and this desire is augmented by the fear that details may be wrongly managed without his constant supervision."[5] An example of this constant supervision of military details that should have been left to capable subordinates was his overruling of Robert Kean, chief of the Confederate Bureau of War, in assessing a disputed election for colonel of a Mississippi regiment in May, 1862.[6] The president wished to be sure that a just decision had been made.

In his brilliant diary, probably the best contemporary insight into the Confederate government, Robert Kean recorded some of the unfavorable aspects of Davis as a war leader. Kean noted his exceedingly poor judgment of men, his habit of frittering away his time and energy on details that should have been left to subordinates, his failure to delegate authority, his West Pointism, his adherence to a rigid departmental organization of the army, which contributed largely to the loss of Vicksburg, and his "facility for converting friends into enemies." But Kean was prejudiced against Davis.

Furthermore, Davis was jealous of the slightest infringement on his prerogatives as president and commander-in-chief of the army and navy. The *Richmond Whig,* an anti-Davis newspaper, observed on this point on March 9, 1864:

> The President never for a moment relinquished his rights as Commander-in-chief, and never entertained the first thought of doing so. This earth holds not the human being more jealous of his constitutional rights than Mr. Davis, and among those rights that to which he clings with death-like tenacity is well-known to be the supreme and exclusive control of military operations.[7]

Davis's fundamental strategy for the war was defensive—the South lacked the men and resources to wage an offensive war, and his political position was that the South wished only to be left alone by the North. To Gustavus Smith, who complained of the moral effect on the Southern troops of "repressing the hope of volunteers for an advance against the enemy into Maryland," he excused his defensive policy, as of October 10, 1861, on the ground of the numerical weakness of the Confederate army and its lack of arms.[8] To General Joseph E. Johnston he wrote on November 9, 1861, that he "looked hopefully forward to the time when your army can assume the offensive." To W. M. Brooks of Alabama he wrote on March 13, 1862, that he had not chosen a "purely defensive policy" but that it was dictated by lack of means. And to Governor Brown of Georgia he replied on May 5, 1862, that "such a campaign as you suggest has long been desired," but that an offensive campaign was a question of means, not of desire.

The great advocate of offensive warfare in the Confederate army was General Beauregard, with his elaborate, but often impracticable, plans. The "Hero of Sumter" was so irked by the inactivity of the army in northern Virginia under the command of Joseph E. Johnston that in the fall of 1861 he wrote to Secretary of War Benjamin (October 5, 1861) asking that he be transferred to New Orleans (unfortunately for the Confederacy his request was refused, for he might have saved that vital seaport from capture). He was right, however, in opposing the president's policy of dispersing Confederate troops to protect relatively unimportant places. General Beauregard wrote in 1862: "Our only hope of success lies in throwing all of our forces into large armies, with which to meet and successfully overthrow our adversary. The result of one such victory would be worth more to us than [would be] the occupation of all our important cities to the enemy." Beauregard had the sound idea, which Lincoln ultimately grasped, that the military objective should be to destroy the army of the enemy.[9]

Davis's policy of dispersing troops was one of expediency rather than of thought-out policy. He admitted in his (previously noted) message to Congress of February 25, 1862, that "the Government had attempted more than it had power successfully to achieve. Hence in the effort to protect by arms the whole of the Confederate State, seaboard and inland, we have been so exposed as to encounter serious disasters." But did he learn from these disasters the lesson of the need for concentration? The pressure exerted by the governors to scatter military strength in defending their territory was so great that frequently he felt forced to yield. The first year of the war was a time of learning the American art of war for both combatants—for Lincoln, as well as Davis—and although Davis and his generals read French books on the art of war far more than did Lincoln, these treatises were written before the railroads came into prominence as a means of waging war. Both presidents as well as the generals had to learn what was effective for American warfare largely through experience, by a trial-and-error method.

The Confederate generals, and apparently Davis as well, were disciples of Napoleon and Baron Henri Jomini, the interpreter of Napoleon's art of war. They studied carefully Frederick the Great's campaigns. At West Point they were taught the importance of fortification by the superintendent; thus the Confederate and Union officers shared the same background in military science. In the Northern army, General Henry Halleck's, *Elements of Military Art and Science* was strongly influenced by Jomini, and in July, 1862, Halleck became general-in-chief of the Union army, stationed in Washington as military adviser. The great exponent of Napoleon's military ideals in the Confederate army was General Beauregard, who published his *Principles and Maxims of War,* based on Napoleon and Jomini. Beauregard laid down three basic principles: (1) place masses of your army in contact with fractions of your enemy, (2) operate as much as possible on the communications of your enemy without exposing your own, and (3) operate always on interior lines (or shorter ones in terms of time).[10] The Confederate General W. J. Hardee had also written a popular textbook on infantry tactics. Although the Civil War generals had learned something of war movements from the Mexican War, none of them had managed sizable armies in the field.

Davis's policy of sending to the Senate the nominations of military officers for promotion was intelligent, but not popular. There was a great rush to secure commissions as officers. The volunteer soldiers elected the company officers, the state governors appointed the colonels of regiments, and the president selected the officers above that rank. Davis was accused of "West Pointism," namely, of favoring West Point graduates or men of some professional training instead of politicians. The politicians who were tried proved, in general, to be unsuitable officers—notably, Robert Toombs, ex-Governor Henry A. Wise, John Floyd, and others—but some good officers with no professional training were developed in the army, such as Nathan Bedford Forrest, Wade Hampton, and possibly John C. Breckinridge. Davis had to deal constantly with ambitious officers such as Jeremy Gilmer of North Carolina, assigned to the Engineer Department, who wrote to his wife on March 12, 1862: "If not given the rank of colonel soon I will quit the service."[11] Or Humphrey Marshall, of a prominent Kentucky family, who demanded that he be placed in charge of all troops from his home state. Davis's refusal caused him to resign. The president's policy in regard to choosing generals and directing their actions in the field was clearly stated in a letter to Major General Benjamin Huger, commanding at Norfolk, Virginia, dated February 26, 1862: "My rule has been to seek for the ablest commanders who could be obtained and to rely on them to execute the purposes of the Govt. by such plans as they should devise, and with such means as could be made available."[12] To General Joseph E. Johnston, whose army was backed up against Richmond, he wrote on May 17, 1862: "As on all former occasions my design is to suggest, not direct." Postmaster General Reagan in his memoirs tells how Davis refused to interfere with Joseph E. Johnston's conduct of operations in the Peninsula campaign, saying that when he entrusted a command to a general, he assumed that in battle with all the facts before him the commander would know what was best to be done, and that it would be unsafe to control military operations from the capital. "This," Reagan wrote, "I know to have been his policy throughout the war, adverse critics to the contrary notwithstanding."[13]

But Davis did not always carry out this rule, especially as the war progressed. He seldom interfered with Lee, or Albert Sidney Johnston, in whom he had great trust, but he seriously interfered with Joseph E. Johnston's command, or so Johnston maintained, in the Atlanta campaign. Furthermore, he often displayed poor judgment in selecting prominent army officers—notably Braxton Bragg, Theophilus Holmes, and John C. Pemberton—and in retaining Commissary General Lucius Northrop when it was evident that he was not up to the job. Also he retained the incompetent Adjutant General Samuel Cooper, who failed to keep decent records of the number or location of troops and was a slave to red tape.

As commander-in-chief of the armed forces Davis was greatly concerned with keeping up the morale of the soldiers after they had enlisted. As a means to this end he wrote on October 10, 1861, to Major General Gustavus W. Smith suggesting small expeditions to keep up the spirit of the men, and also that the generals should look after the health of the men and seek to command troops from their home states.[14] He also mentioned another important point: that the staff officers for volunteers should display forbearance and urbanity, for "many of the privates are men of high social position, of scholarship and fortune. Their pride furnishes the motive for good conduct, and if wounded, is turned from an instrument of good to one of great power for evil."[15] To Beauregard, who objected to catering to the state rights feeling in organizing brigades and divisions, the president replied that it was advisable, as far as practicable, to keep regiments from the same state together and to assign generals to command the troops from their own state. Thus the flame of state pride could be utilized to inspire soldiers to greater effort, and it was valuable to have lonely men from the same neighborhood in the same regiment so that they could comfort and console each other.

Davis was also deeply concerned over the complaints of "the shocking neglect of the sick, who were sent down from the battlefields in cars such as those used to transport horses without cleansing them and then left without water, food, or attention."[16] Reports of such callous neglect, he said, were spread among the people and chilled the ardor for volunteering. But, oppressed by many other affairs, he seems to have done nothing but mouth words about it. This care was left to the surgeon general, Samuel Preston Moore. The youthful Alice Ready, sister-in-law of John Hunt Morgan, visited a soldiers' hospital in Murfreesboro, Tennessee, in 1863, recording in her diary that she was shocked by the conditions she found and the indifference shown to dying men—"no more notice taken of them than if they had been dogs."[17] The Confederacy had nothing like the effective United States Sanitary Commission under the direction of Frederick Law Olmsted. Furthermore, as the war progressed, people became more callous to wounded and dying soldiers. Some noble women acted as volunteer nurses, especially at the great army hospital of Chimborazo, but usually they were untrained and rendered mostly psychological succor to the soldiers, putting hot or cold compresses on their brows, writing notes for them, reading them the Bible, and holding their hands to console them.[18]

Moral conditions among the soldiers also concerned the president. Drinking was the great vice of the soldiers' life. They were paid only $11 a month, and quickly spent this small amount in riotous living when they got to cities such as Richmond. Attorney General Thomas Bragg noted in his diary that: "The city is crowded with drunk and lawless soldiers."[19]

Davis had observed at a cabinet meeting as early as January 8, 1862, that drinking could not be stopped in the army unless the officers set an example and, as mentioned, he praised General Braxton Bragg for stopping drinking among his troops. The attorney general noted that a part of Brigadier General Henry A. Wise's army were drunk when they left Richmond for the front at Roanoke Island. Much of the soldiers' drinking in Richmond arose from the fact that inflation was so great that they could not pay for a night's lodging at a hotel and were virtually forced to wander at night about the streets, populated by prostitutes (many with venereal disease), an unmentionable and generally hidden fact. In an attempt to control drinking in the army Senator Clement C. Clay, Jr., introduced a bill that was passed providing for dismissal, suspension, or public reprimand of officers guilty of intoxication, whether on or off duty.[20]

One of Davis's serious early mistakes was his organization of the departmental system of the army, with each department reporting to him. Such an organization prevented the development of an adequate unity of command and the proper movement of reserves. As Robert Kean observed on July 12, 1863: "The radical vice of Mr. Davis' whole military system is the separate departmental organization, each reporting only to him. It makes each department dependent on its own strength."[21] It was constantly criticized by the chief of the Confederate Bureau of War after Secretary of War George W. Randolph resigned in 1862, following a reprimand from Davis for his failure to observe the departmental system. It gave Kirby Smith the chance to avoid cooperating with Bragg by uniting his army with that of his rival in the invasion of Kentucky, resulting in the failure of this promising campaign. The damage done to the Confederate war effort by Davis's departmental system has been pointed out by Connelly and Jones, who observed that when Lee surrendered on April 9, 1865, with his pitiful army of 27,800 troops, there were still an amazing number of troops scattered in other sections of the Confederacy: General Richard Taylor's 42,293 men in the Southwest who surrendered at Mobile, General Kirby Smith's trans-Mississippi army of 60,000 troops, as well as several thousands elsewhere, totaling 174,233, of which approximately two thirds gave no support to the armies of Lee and Jackson.[22] This isolation of troops within the broad expanse of the Confederacy seems to have been an enormous waste of manpower that, properly concentrated and led, might have defeated Grant and Sherman.

It should be noted in defense of Davis that he abandoned the rigid departmental system when he realized that it worked badly. On two occasions he tried to unify the forces between the Appalachian mountain barrier and the Mississippi River. The first time was in October, 1862, when he appointed Joseph E. Johnston in command of that region with authority to move troops from one of the large armies in Mississippi to the other in Tennessee and even to take command of either army. But, as we have seen, Johnston's intransigence defeated this plan, though Johnston's biographers defend their subject by maintaining that the president did not understand the situation in the West: both armies in this region were so threatened that they could not transfer troops to each other.[23] Johnston's suggestion of getting reinforcements from Holmes's army on the other side of the Mississippi River, nevertheless, was sound advice. The other time that Davis tried to establish a unified command system over a large geographical area was when, after Hood's defeat at Atlanta, he placed Beauregard in charge, but this change from departmental command to theater command came too late.

The three major invasions of the North were initiated not by Davis, but by the boldness of Lee and the western generals. As noted, the president was dubious about the invasion of Kentucky unless Bragg first defeated Buell's army stationed at Nashville, and only his faith in Lee caused him to consent to the invasions of Maryland and Pennsylvania. He was overpersuaded, against his better first judgment. Davis did all he could, however, to furnish the armies with reinforcements and munitions. He cannot justly be blamed for the defeat at Fort Donelson, but in the defense of New Orleans it would seem that he relied too much on his secretary of the navy and did not send an adequate army under an able commander to that strategic city. Furthermore, Davis made serious blunders in keeping Bragg in command of the army in Tennessee despite the strong objections of a majority of Bragg's officers, and in mishandling the defense of Vicksburg. After the war Bragg said that he had advised Johnston's adjutant, General Thomas Jordan, to abandon Vicksburg and Port Hudson and to concentrate the Confederate troops to attack Grant, and that holding these fortified positions was based on a point of honor (to which Davis's whole career had been devoted) and violated all military principles.[24]

Davis had been an innovative secretary of war, alert to new inventions, but as commander-in-chief of the Confederate armed forces, he seems to have lost his boldness and feared trying new things. Secretary of the Navy Mallory had by far the most innovative mind in the administration, introducing ironclad war vessels, torpedoes, the Brooke cannon, and the submarine *H. L. Hunley,* which in 1864 sank the federal warship *Housatonic* in Charleston harbor. Yet both Davis and General Gorgas disparaged him, Gorgas writing in his journal on November 20, 1864: "Mr. Mallory lacks earnestness and devotion to his duty. He is too good company and too generally informed to be worth much at any one thing tho' a man of undoubted ability." He was a sort of Rhodes scholar in the Confederate cabinet, Gorgas observed, who beat the secretary of war in every discussion that arose, for he was "too smart for Mr. Seddon."[25]

The president, though earnest and devoted to duty, no longer had an innovative mind. At the time a rifle was invented that could have given the Confederacy a quick victory over the North if it had been adopted—the Spencer repeating, breech-loading rifle (invented in 1860). The Gatling gun, which proved so deadly in World War I, was manufactured in Indianapolis as early as 1862 by Richard J. Gatling of North Carolina. General Gorgas, chief of ordnance, mentions neither of these weapons in his journal. The North did not appreciate them either, yet at the very end of the war a Northern brigade armed with the Spencer rifle inflicted appalling damage at the battle of Franklin, Tennessee. "Casemont's brigade with these arms," wrote the artillery officer, General E. P. Alexander, "decided that battle with terrific slaughter."[26]

As commander-in-chief, Davis held some surprisingly old-fashioned ideas. He favored the cavalry being armed with long swords, or sabers, so that they could engage the enemy's cavalry in close contact. He vetoed in September, 1862, Senator Wigfall's bill providing for an adequate modern staff for commanding generals who, instead of the president, were to select their staff, giving the more important members the rank of brigadier general. This proposal would have put Southern staffs, both in numbers and rank, on a parity with the staffs of Northern generals.[27] Davis vetoed this progressive bill partly because he was unwilling to give up any of his military prerogatives.

Despite mistakes of omission and commission, he displayed many virtues as a war leader.[28] When conscription became obviously necessary, he used all his powers to get conscription laws expanded. He opposed short enlistments, tried to minimize the use of elections to select officers, and opposed frequent furloughs. Wisely he chose West Point men as major officers and, except in a few instances, adhered to a policy of promoting officers on the basis of the recommendations of their superiors in rank. Toward the end of the war he advocated detailing men from the army, rather than exemption, as the fairest way to secure the services required for nonfighting tasks. And finally he pushed hard for Congress to enlist and train Negroes for fighting. Spiritually, he tried, particularly in the last year of the war, to inspire the Southern people through his speeches to show the same fighting spirit and exalted patriotism that he himself possessed. Unfortunately, he had bad relations with the press, did not cultivate them, and would not have resorted to propaganda as we understand and practice it today.

What was Davis's gravest mistake as the military leader of the South? It was probably his failure earlier in the war, until Congress and the Virginia legislature pressured him, to appoint a general-in-chief as did Lincoln. The president had great admiration for Lee and depended on him for military advice. But Thomas Connelly and Archer Jones in their provocative study, point out serious weaknesses of Lee, who was the choice of Congress and the country for the position of general-in-chief.[29] Perhaps because he did not have the responsibility of directing all the Confederate armies until the end of the war, he paid almost exclusive attention to the Virginia front and gave relatively little attention to the important far western front. Lee may not have realized the seriousness of the problem of the West until it was too late and may not have understood the overall geography of the Confederacy. Hence, his constant plea for reinforcements was a "one-way street," begrudging sending any troops to provide relief in the West. His offensive strategy and tactics, like those of Grant, caused an excessive loss of men, but both men won victories, while Joseph E. Johnston's defensive tactics saved his men and won their love but won no victories. Lee presented no grand strategy for the Confederate military effort, confining his attention largely to his own army in Virginia. Davis offered him the position of commander-in-chief, but he did not want the responsibility. As the cause became desperate toward the end of the war, Congress insisted that the president appoint Lee general-in-chief, and in February, 1865, he did so, nearly a year after Lincoln had put Grant in command of all the federal armies. Although Davis rejected Lee's advice to strengthen the Virginia frontier at the expense of the West, partly because of a lobby of western generals and politicians, he did try to meet Lee's pleas to draw reinforcements from other areas in the Atlantic seaboard states.

Perhaps the remark of General Josiah Gorgas in his diary, dated January 15, 1865, sums up the final judgment of his own day as well as that of many historians of our time in regard to Davis as a war leader: "I have cherished and long ago expressed my conviction that the President is not endowed with military genius, but *who would have done better?*" (author's italics).[30] The wisdom of this judgment was demonstrated in one of the last campaigns of the Confederacy.

25

Taps for the Southern Confederacy

———◆———

It is amazing how the spirits of the soldiers, the people, and, in general, the Confederate officials, recovered in 1864 after the disastrous year of 1863. Historians who look at the statistics and have the hindsight of a later generation count the Confederacy out after the double defeats of Vicksburg and Gettysburg. But not the Southern people. Perhaps only the more intelligent realized the full implications of those defeats. One important consideration that modern historians fail to take into account in the psychology of the Southern folk and their leaders was their strong religious background. This firm religious faith helps to explain why they did not despair. During Sherman's invasion of Georgia, General Gorgas recorded in his diary, June 9, 1864: "What the issue will be is in God's hands."[1] Moreover, all classes placed tremendous confidence in Lee. On January 25, 1865, Gorgas confided in his diary: "I have outlived my momentary depression, and feel my courage revive when I think of the brave army in front of us, sixty thousand strong. As long as it holds we need not fear." When periods of depression came over him, as on June 4, 1864, he exclaimed in his diary: "What have we done that the Almighty should scourge us with such a war?"[2]

Although this Pennsylvania-born general was a realist, he was hopeful amidst adversity, as were many Southern people. In the fall of 1863, nearly four months after Vicksburg and Gettysburg, he wrote, "We are now in a condition to carry on the war for an indefinite period," noting that there was breadstuff enough and sufficient war material—men and gun powder—"but the real pinch is in the Treasury."[3] On September 29 he commented that the Confederacy was better off than it was two years before, "when no one doubted our ability to wage the war. The only point against us is the scarcity of men to fill up our Armies," and to do this the Confederacy had to arm the Negroes and give them their freedom.

Despite crushing defeats, Gorgas recorded in his diary as late as the New Year in 1865 that there was much gaiety in Richmond among the young people when soldiers were on furlough, with many quick marriages and parties. Young girls wished to marry the soldiers despite the risk of their being killed in battle. The older people were not so irresponsible or bent on pleasure. Everywhere one saw women wearing the mourning veils and the long black dresses that indicated that some close relative had been killed. Yet even the older people played cards and had dinner parties in the evening, while during the day the women tended the sick, knitted socks for the soldiers, and made long underwear for them that was often unskillfully cut and sewn, looking monstrous. When General John S. Preston entertained at a dinner for three generals, a senator, and Mrs. Chesnut on Christmas Day, 1863, the menu consisted of oyster soup, roast mutton, ham, boned turkey, wild duck, partridge, plum pudding, Sauterne, Burgundy, sherry, and Madeira. "There is life in the old land yet!" Mrs. Chesnut exclaimed.[4] But a year later life had become exceedingly hard for the poor, as the journal of J. B. Jones, the Confederate war clerk, describes. And in the president's mansion there was deep sorrow over the death of little Joe, his son, who while playing fell from a high porch of the White House.

The war began to change when in March, 1864, Lincoln appointed Ulysses S. Grant general-in-chief commanding all the Union armies. In May, Grant began his campaign to capture Richmond, and sent Sherman to capture Atlanta. Lee opposed him with an army half as strong as the federal army and often half starved. The great Confederate general countered the Northern advance with superb skill, constantly fighting behind breastworks and in entrenchments. By this time Southern soldiers had abandoned their cavalier disregard for entrenchments and breastworks. Gorgas commented on June 4, 1864, of the troops defending Richmond: "Our troops were lying behind triple lines of breastworks. They have acquired a respect for this sort of entrenchment, and work like beavers when they take up a new position. They began the war with a contempt for the spade, but now thoroughly believe in it."[5] Grant was determined to hammer on the Army of Northern Virginia in a war of attrition, regardless of terrible casualties, but it was to take nearly a year to defeat Lee and capture the Confederate capital.

In the meanwhile William Tecumseh Sherman was leading his mighty army toward Atlanta. The Confederate army opposing him, beaten and humiliated at Missionary Ridge near Chattanooga, had retreated to Dalton, close to the northern border of Georgia. It received a new commander in General Joseph E. Johnston, who infused a new spirit among the soldiers opposing Sherman. After Bragg had resigned on December 1, 1863, Hardee took temporary command, but refused the responsibility of regular command, and Davis reluctantly recalled Johnston to command the army. The soldiers were delighted that "Uncle Joe" was to command them. One of them, Sam Watkins of "Company Aytch," wrote: "A new era had dawned; a new epoch had been dated.... [General Johnston] restored the soldier's pride; he brought the manhood back to the private's bosom.... The revolution was complete. He was loved, respected, admired; yea almost worshipped by his troops."[6] By the spring of 1864 Johnston commanded a confident and well-trained army of 40,000 troops in defense of Atlanta.

Grant's appointment of Sherman to lead an army to invade Georgia and capture Atlanta, the great rail center of the lower South and the repository of huge supplies, was a lucky break for the Union cause. This redheaded Northern general was ideally suited for the task ahead, being not only militarily competent but possessed of a determined fighting spirit and a ruthless philosophy of total war. He advanced from Chattanooga toward his goal along the Western and Atlantic Railroad, owned and operated by the state of Georgia, and this and other railroads extending back to the Ohio River constituted his line of supply. "That single stem of railroads 473 miles supplied an army of 100,000 men and 35,000 animals for the period of 196 days, viz: from May 1 to November 12, 1864," he wrote in his memoirs.[7] "The Atlanta campaign was an impossibility without these railroads, and possible only then because we had the means and the men to maintain and to defend them in addition to what was necessary to overcome the enemy." Thus Sherman, whom Robert Selph Henry calls "most modern of Civil War soldiers," advanced against an able Southern general of the old school. At Kennesaw Mountain Johnston took a valiant stand against the Northern army, and Sherman lost 3,000 men by hurling his troops against the entrenched Confederates. The heroism displayed at Kennesaw Mountain made Johnston proud of his troops, whose courage and fighting qualities had been doubted in comparison with Lee's eastern army. He declared that his soldiers were unsurpassed by Napoleon's famous "Old Guard" or by the troops of Wellington.

With only 40,000 men Johnston's army was vastly inferior in numbers to Sherman's troops. He felt that he could not risk a direct encounter with the stronger army, so he began a strategic retreat toward Atlanta, fighting only behind breastworks, abatis, and redoubts and seeking to delay Sherman's advance by pursuing a strategy of attrition. Grant in his memoirs praised Johnston's method of fighting as sensible.

Nevertheless, the constant retreat of the Confederate army alarmed Davis and the people of Georgia. Johnston would not take the president and his commander-in-chief into his confidence and refused to reveal his plans. The governor of Georgia became nervous and on July 5 sent a telegram to the president urging him to use the cavalry of Forrest and John Hunt Morgan to cut Sherman's communications. The Governor bluntly warned: "If your mistake should result in loss of Atlanta and the occupation of other strong points in this State by the enemy, the blow may be fatal to our cause and remote posterity may have reason to mourn over the error."[8] Davis sent a sharp reply reprimanding the governor for trying to control the disposition of Confederate troops in different parts of the Confederacy and requesting the source of his information as to what the whole country expected and what posterity will judge. But the governor was correct in advising the use of cavalry to attack the enemy's long line of communications. In his letter he had observed: "We do not see how Forrest's operations in Mississippi or Morgan's raids as conducted in Kentucky interfere with Sherman's plans in this State, as his supplies continue to reach him." General Johnston requested the same thing, but not until it was too late was this suggested plan carried out.

Davis was getting more nervous as Johnston kept on retreating until at last his army crossed the Chattahoochee River. On July 9 he sent General Braxton Bragg, his adviser at Richmond, to confer with Johnston to learn when he intended to fight for Atlanta. Bragg wired: "I cannot learn that he has any more plans in the future than he has had in the past."[9] In the meanwhile, Congressman Benjamin H. Hill, one of the president's strongest supporters, urged Davis to dismiss Johnston and appoint a fighting general to oppose Sherman. Davis then wired Johnston directly asking whether he intended to abandon Atlanta without a battle. Johnston's reply was evasive, and Davis decided that the time had come to change commanders.

But he was troubled by the problem of finding a replacement among the senior generals available. He requested Lee's advice as to the wisdom of appointing one of Johnston's corps commanders, the thirty-three-year-old John B. Hood. Hood had established a reputation as a bold aggressive fighter, but he was physically handicapped, having lost both an arm and a leg in leading his troops.[10] Unfortunately, Lee gave an indefinite reply to the president's request, warning that it was dangerous to remove a commanding general before a battle, suggesting, though, that if it was necessary, it should be done, but also stating that General Hardee had had more experience in directing an army. On July 18 Davis appointed Hood. Sherman was delighted at the change in commanders, for he had a low opinion of the young general. He remarked that Hood had ranked near the bottom of his class at West Point while two of his corps commanders, J. B. McPherson and John M. Schofield, ranked number one and number seven in the same class of 1853.

Davis's removal of Johnston and appointment of John B. Hood of Mount Sterling, Kentucky, met with the unanimous concurrence of his cabinet. Today Hood's appointment is controversial among historians, but the consensus regards it as a serious mistake.[11] The president felt, however, that he must act quickly, for a critical battle was impending, and his choice was limited by the exigency to the three corps commanders of Johnston's army: John Bell Hood, A. T. Stewart, who at the beginning of the war was a professor in the tiny Cumberland College of Tennessee, and William J. Hardee, famed as author of the textbook *Rifle and Infantry Tactics*. Stewart, called "Old Straight" by his soldiers, was lacking in dynamic qualities, and although Hardee seemed the most suitable choice he had refused the command of the Army of Tennessee nine months before. Hood had never directed an army, but Davis chose him primarily because he was known as a fighter, in contrast to the timid and conservative Johnston. When Kirby Smith in the far West heard of this change of commanders he remarked: "Hood is a soldier, Johnston the General—Hood is bold, gallant, will always be ready to fight but will never know when he should refuse an engagement. Hood is a man of ordinary intellect, Johnston's brain soars above all that surround him."[12]

This fighting general did exactly as he was supposed to do, and waged a series of hotly contested battles for the defense of Atlanta. He has generally been condemned as rash and reckless, but an eminent English military historian, Alfred H. Burne, has judged Hood's fight for Atlanta "sound—even brilliant," observing that he lost those battles by an extremely narrow margin.[13] Hood blamed his men for his defeats, accusing them of lacking fighting spirit. To General Bragg he wrote on September 4: "It seems that the troops (under Johnston) had been so long confined to trenches and had been taught to believe that entrenchments cannot be taken that they attacked without spirit and retired without proper effort,"[14] a condemnation that was disproved by their brave attack later at the battle of Franklin, Tennessee. Needed to oppose Sherman was a general who combined the experience and judgment of Johnston with the fighting spirit and charismatic leadership qualities of Hood. Perhaps Pat Cleburne of Arkansas had these qualities, but he was not a West Pointer and was only a major general. He also seemed very young for such a responsible position, being only thirty-five years old despite his gray hair, but Hood, at the age of thirty-three, was even younger.[15]

After Hood retreated forlornly into Atlanta, Sherman conducted a thirty-day siege of the city. Finally, the Northern general moved his army to the south of the besieged city, cutting Hood's vital supply lines to the south and causing him to abandon the city. Then, on September 2, Sherman's veterans occupied Atlanta. The ruthless Northern general shocked Southerners when he ordered the complete evacuation of the Southern city of 12,000 inhabitants, saying that he needed all the houses for his army. Margaret Mitchell's graphic novel, *Gone With the Wind* (based on years of research), has portrayed the human drama of the historic siege of Atlanta and of the forced, sad flight of its citizens.[16]

After the abandonment of Atlanta by Hood, Jefferson Davis had a grave problem to solve, namely, how to use Hood's army against the enemy. On September 25, three weeks after the loss of Atlanta, he journeyed to Palmetto,

Georgia, Hood's headquarters, to plan strategy for the defeated army. Hood proposed to move north to threaten Sherman's long line of communications from Chattanooga to Atlanta, believing that this maneuver would force Sherman to follow him. Davis approved of this maneuver. While in the lower South, he made four major speeches—as noted, at Macon, Montgomery, Augusta, and Columbia—seeking to arouse the people to heroic resistance and to inspire the numerous absentees from the army to return to their commands. He promised the Southern people that Sherman would meet a disastrous defeat similar to Napoleon's at Moscow. In Augusta, Georgia, before his return to Richmond, he conferred with Beauregard who approved of the strategy that he and Hood had devised of Hood's army leaving Georgia and attacking Sherman's line of communications. In order to have a more experienced head to supervise the young general, he appointed Beauregard as commanding general of a broad territory, entitled "Division of the West," a theater command similar to the organization in World War II.

For nearly a month Sherman played the part expected of him by the Confederates, following Hood's army northward. Finally, the Northern general concluded it would be folly to pursue Hood further; he turned back to Atlanta, leaving General George H. Thomas to handle the Confederate army. He then put into operation a bold plan of ignoring his line of communications and living on the country while his army marched toward the sea, 62,000 men carrying pontoons moving in four parallel columns. While Hood was far away on a "wild goose chase," Sherman's army in early November, 1864, abandoned Atlanta, burning it to the ground before they left, and marching with little opposition through central Georgia toward the sea. In this campaign Sherman demonstrated the modern conception of total war, as opposed to the Southern conception of chivalric war. The victorious commander grimly announced: "If the people raise a howl against my barbarity and cruelty, I will answer that war is war, and not popularity seeking." On another occasion he declared that "war is cruelty and you can not refine it." Still, again, he said: "We are not only fighting hostile armies, but a hostile people, and must make old and young, rich and poor, feel the hand of war, as well as their organized armies."[17]

He carried out exactly that doctrine, cutting a swath of destruction sixty miles wide in some places, burning private homes, barns, state buildings, destroying crops, seizing the sheep, chickens, mules, oxen, and cows of the people, and especially wrecking railroads by heating the rails and twisting them around tree trunks—"Sherman's neckties," as they were called. For years the inhabitants of the invaded states retained bitter memories of the outrages of Sherman's army, especially from the stragglers and bummers, as well as from the cavalry commanded by General Judson Kilpatrick, who seems to have been somewhat of a sadist, although few charges of rape and murder were substantiated. Sherman occupied Milledgeville, the capital of Georgia, and on December 10 captured Savannah, presenting it as a Christmas present to President Lincoln. Then, turning northward, he marched through Columbia, where the Southerners accused him of burning a large district of the city. He avoided detouring to Charleston and marched into North Carolina, where near Bentonville General Joseph E. Johnston, commanding a remnant of the Southern army on March 19, 1865, fought heroically but futilely—a gesture of honor—against the overwhelmingly superior Northern army.

What of the fate of Hood's army as it invaded Tennessee? Beauregard's condition for approving Hood's plan of marching into Tennessee was that he should move quickly before the Union forces under Major General George H. Thomas could reorganize and acquire new reinforcements. Instead, Hood tarried at Tuscumbia, Alabama—three weeks—before he crossed the Tennessee River into Tennessee on November 16, 1864. It was unlike the dynamic, dashing Southern leader to be so lethargic. Although various excuses were offered to explain the delay, it is still somewhat of a mystery. By the time that he "got going," the enemy was ready for him; his orders were inefficiently executed and he had bad luck. He was defeated at Franklin, Tennessee, with a terrible loss of twelve generals, including the Irish-born general, Pat Cleburne, called "the Stonewall Jackson of the West," as well as numerous lesser officers. On December 15 Thomas attacked Hood's army in the environs of Nashville and shattered it in the most complete victory of a Union army during the war. Davis had gambled in permitting Hood to abandon Sherman's army around Atlanta and go off on a risky campaign into Tennessee, and as a result the Confederates lost a vital campaign. Following this disaster Hood resigned and the remnant of his army was placed under the command of General Richard Taylor, Davis's brother-in-law by his first marriage.[18]

In Virginia, in the late spring of 1864, General Lee permitted Grant's army to cross the Rapidan River, a tributary of the Potomac, without molestation, and awaited him in the hilly and tangled woods of "the Wilderness." Here he attacked the Northern invaders, inflicting terrible losses on them. But Grant did not turn back as earlier commanders had done but, regardless of loss of life, moved doggedly forward, fighting two ferocious battles—at the "Bloody Angle" near Spotsylvania Court House, and at Cold Harbor, June 1–3, near Richmond. Grant lost over 10,000 men in the latter battle, where he ordered a frontal assault against the Confederates, strongly entrenched, but as was his custom, he refused to ask for a truce to bury the dead and attend to the wounds of his stricken soldiers.

The loss of life was so great in such reckless attacks that Grant began adopting a sidling tactic to get around Lee's army. On June 14 the Union army crossed the James River and approached Richmond from the south, attacking Petersburg, an important railway center, lying twenty miles below the Confederate capital. Lee did not realize that Grant had transported his army across the James, and Petersburg was saved only by the prompt and heroic action of General Pierre Beauregard in the battle of Drewry's Bluff. Previously Beauregard had stopped an army under the command of General

Ben Butler that was moving toward the capital from Fort Monroe. Grant now began the siege of Petersburg, which lasted nine months. In desperation, his soldiers tunneled under the Confederate lines and on July 30 set off a mine of powder that blasted a huge hole in the Confederate lines. But when Grant sent troops, including a division of Negro soldiers, into the "crater" to attack the Confederates, the latter massacred them, restoring their breastworks and lines. As long as Fort Stedman, the Confederate strong point, held and the Confederates controlled the South Side Railroad that brought them supplies, they could endure.

As the Confederacy continued to weaken before the onslaughts of a foe that could replace its losses and add new reinforcements from its pool of immigrant soldiers and its recruitment of over 100,000 Negro soldiers, some realistic Southerners began to advocate the enlistment of Negro troops. While the western army was at Dalton, Georgia, only one week after Joseph E. Johnston took command in the latter part of December, 1863, Major General Patrick Cleburne circulated a document among the officers supporting the recruitment of Negro soldiers. This fascinating and eloquent document, dated January 2, 1864, stated a gloomy view of the Confederacy, held by the army and many other people, if a large accession of manpower were not added to the Southern army to counterbalance the growing strength of the Union army. Cleburne pointed out the need of immediately commencing to train a large reserve of the most courageous slaves and asked that freedom be promised not only to the slave soldiers but to the whole race that was loyal to the South. He observed that, despite the cliché that the Negroes were content under slavery, actually they had been dreaming of freedom, and that the Confederacy should offer the slave soldier immediate freedom not only for himself but for his wife and children, and also "make his marriage and parental relations sacred in the eyes of the law and forbid their sale." He maintained that the slaves would fight bravely for the Confederacy if they had these incentives. The adoption of this plan of slave enlistment and emancipation, he asserted, would also influence foreign nations to recognize the Confederacy and give the South its independence. But, he warned, the training of the Negroes for soldier duties would require much time, and "there is danger that this concession to common sense may come too late."[19] The document was signed by fourteen officers of higher grade and sent to General Johnston. Johnston refused to forward it to the president, but one of the opposing officers, Major General W. H. T. Walker, obtained a copy and sent it to the president.

Davis replied cautiously: "Deeming to be injurious to the public service that such a subject be mooted, or even known to be entertained by persons possessed of the confidence and respect of the people, I have concluded that the best policy under the circumstances will be to avoid all publicity." He ordered General Johnston to persuade Cleburne to suppress it, which he did.

But the ominous subject could not be swept under the rug. Davis himself took an important step toward utilizing the slaves and free Negroes in the army.[20] On February 17, 1864, he signed a law providing for the employment of free Negroes and slaves by the army to be used as teamsters, cooks, servants in hospitals, and laborers on fortifications to the number of 20,000, to be obtained from masters voluntarily offering their services, but if they could not be obtained voluntarily in sufficient numbers, they must be impressed, with the condition, however, that not more than one in five slaves of an owner could be thus impressed. And on November 7, 1864, he proposed to Congress the employment of 40,000 slaves to be used as pioneers and engineer laborers, giving them instruction in the manner of encamping, marching, and parking trains.

The attempt to enlist the slaves was the last desperate effort to obtain soldiers for the dwindling Confederate army. The only sure way, however, was to hold those who were absent without leave to their duty in the army and to inspire them with the fighting spirit. When Davis, speaking in Macon in late 1864, told the enemy that two thirds of Hood's army were absent without leave, when a year earlier Bragg reported that only 40 percent of the men on his rolls were present for duty, and long before Lee surrendered his last pitiful remnant of 8,000 infantrymen and 5,000 cavalry at Appomattox Court House, the moving hand had written the fate of the Confederacy on the wall.[21]

While Petersburg was being besieged in January, 1865, the old Jacksonian editor, Francis P. Blair, came across the lines to Richmond on a peace mission. He talked with Davis and prominent Confederate leaders about his project to bring about a return of the Southern states to the Union on the basis of a joint war against the French in Mexico to enforce the Monroe Doctrine. Davis finally agreed to a conference between Confederate commissioners and President Lincoln because he believed that its likely failure would arouse Southerners to fight more desperately than ever to preserve the Confederacy. Shrewdly, he appointed the most prominent advocate of such a conference, Alexander H. Stephens, to lead the Southern commission, the other members being ex-Supreme Court Justice John A. Campbell and Senator R. M. T. Hunter. They met with Lincoln and Secretary of State Seward on the steamer *River Queen* at Hampton Roads at the mouth of the James River on February 3, 1865. Stephens urged the wisdom of the two nations concluding a peace treaty and then together enforcing the Monroe Doctrine. He observed that history showed examples of nations at war laying aside a quarrel and cooperating in matters of mutual interest. Lincoln replied that he knew nothing of history: "You must talk history to Seward," he said. Brushing aside protocol, Lincoln insisted on the restoration of the Union of all the states and the abolition of slavery as indispensable peace terms. Such proposals the Confederates refused even to consider, and peace negotiations ended in failure, as Davis had expected. But the president had won a coup over his crestfallen critic, the vice president of the Confederacy, and had established the fact that only by fighting on could the Confederacy avoid "subjugation" with all its imagined horrors.

The siege of Petersburg came to an end on April 2, after Philip Sheridan's cavalry had ravaged the Shenandoah Valley and cut the lifeline of Lee's army by seizing control of the South Side Railroad. President Davis was in his pew at St. Paul's Episcopal Church when a messenger from Lee notified him that Richmond must be evacuated. He received the message of doom stoically and immediately gave orders for the removal of the government documents and the scanty supply of specie to Danville, Virginia, where he, his family, and the cabinet followed.

Lee evacuated Petersburg with an army of 28,000 men and marched westward to Lynchburg, with the objective of joining Joseph E. Johnston's small force in North Carolina. Expected supplies did not arrive at Amelia Court House and his men were left with little food. By the time he had reached Appomattox Court House near Lynchburg a large part of his army had disappeared. Thus he had only the alternatives of surrender or of resorting to guerrilla warfare, and this he opposed, for he believed that it could lead only to the needless sacrifice of many gallant young soldiers. He met General Grant at the McLean house near Appomattox Court House on April 9. In the full dress uniform of a Confederate general, Lee was still a magnificent looking man, while the leader of the victorious army, clad far less simply, a small man, wearing false teeth that often clenched a cigar, did not look or act at all like a conquerer. Grant's terms of surrender were generous: Lee was allowed to keep his sword, the officers their sidearms, and the soldiers their horses (with which to do the spring plowing). Johnston surrendered his army to Sherman on April 18 at Durham, North Carolina, and Sherman offered the vanquished army even more generous terms than had Grant. But they were revoked by Washington.

From Danville, President Davis and his party traveled on the train to Greensboro, North Carolina, a city that disgracefully refused hospitality to the little band. At Greensboro he summoned Governor Vance to a conference with his cabinet and General Johnston. On this occasion, Vance related in a lecture entitled "The Last Days of the Confederacy," the president was bold, defiant, and determined to cross the Mississippi River and continue the fight there. He asked Vance to accompany him, but Secretary of War Breckinridge and Joseph E. Johnston, with a stronger sense of reality than the president, opposed the quixotic plan.

The president then traveled on with a small military escort to Abbeville, South Carolina, where his family joined him, and thence to Washington, Georgia, where the last cabinet met. In the meanwhile the news had arrived of the assassination of President Lincoln on the night of April 14, and Davis was officially charged with being implicated. A price of $100,000 was offered for his arrest. As Davis fled southward, urged by his wife to separate from her and the children, he heard that his family was threatened by a band of desperate marauders, and decided to remain to defend them. In the dawn of May 10 a troop of federal cavalry caught up with them near Irwinville,

Georgia, approximately fifty miles from the Florida line.[22] Davis rushed from his tent toward a saddled horse to escape. He seized a raglan, which happened to be his wife's, and she threw her shawl over him. The cartoonists represented him as fleeing in a feminine disguise. Davis, his wife and children, and Clement C. Clay, Jr., were taken on a ship from Savannah to prison at Fort Monroe, and the vice president to Fort Warren in Boston harbor. Thus, for the Confederates, their cause, and Jefferson Davis, it is appropriate to cite the Latin phrase, *"Sic transit gloria mundi."*

The Sphinx of the Confederacy

By the time that Davis was captured by federal troops he had become very unpopular in the Confederacy; he was called a "despot." But his cruel treatment as a prisoner at Fort Monroe made a martyr of him in the eyes of the Southern people, restoring him to immense popularity. Brigadier General Nelson A. Miles, before the war a clerk in a Massachusetts shoe store, was his jailor, but above Miles was the malignant secretary of war, Edwin M. Stanton. Davis was a proud man, so that when a blacksmith was called in to put an iron manacle with a ball and chain on his leg he resisted furiously. He was highly nervous but his jailers kept a soldier in his cell at all times, and guards walked monotonously to and fro in front of it. A lamp was kept lighted in his room, and this he found especially distressing. These unnecessary precautions tortured his nerves and his only eye that had retained its sight. Furthermore, he was kept incommunicado from family and friends and not until three months after his imprisonment was he allowed to write to his wife or to receive letters from her. As a result of this inhumane treatment the ex-president became very ill, but the army surgeon at the fort, Dr. John Craven, did what he could to secure better treatment for the distinguished prisoner of war. Craven and he held many conversations. The doctor came to admire him, and in 1866 published *The Prison Life of Jefferson Davis.*[1]

Davis's main consolations were reading the Bible and being allowed to smoke his meerschaum pipe. Letters received from his wife, living on a plantation in Georgia, from which state she was forbidden to leave, as well as his letters to her, reveal a beautiful relationship between them. In these prison letters, now preserved in Transylvania University Library (which Hudson Strode published with no indications of passages left out), Davis is philosophical. He referred, for example, to Horace's satire on the desire of people for change, and commented, "In all affairs of life, we are reduced to choosing evils, every situation having its disadvantages."

Early in 1866 Varina was permitted to visit her children in Canada, who were under the supervision of her mother. After her return she began a campaign to secure her husband's release from prison. President Johnson and Secretary Stanton gave her little encouragement, but on September 2, 1866, she wrote to Horace Greeley, the editor of the powerful *New York Tribune,* to enlist his efforts on behalf of Davis's release. Greeley wrote a vigorous editorial advocating the immediate release of the fallen Confederate leader and rebuking President Johnson for not withdrawing his earlier charge that Davis was implicated in a conspiracy to assassinate President Lincoln. The able New York lawyer, Charles O'Conor, volunteered his legal services to secure Davis's release. Varina also went to Baltimore and persuaded John W. Garrett, president of the Baltimore and Ohio Railroad, who had great influence with the government, to try to secure the release of her husband from prison. Her efforts were successful, and on May 11, 1867, Davis was brought before the federal court at Richmond, Virginia, and released on bail. The bail of $100,000 for his appearance at a formal trial was signed by Horace Greeley and Gerrit Smith, both of whom had been prominent abolitionists before the war, but the trial was never held.[2]

After his release from prison Davis went to see his children in Canada, and afterward he and Mrs. Davis traveled to England, where they were hospitably entertained by former Confederates living there and by warm-hearted British friends who had supported the Confederate cause. Davis made several trips to Europe to obtain employment and to place his youngest child Varina Anne in school. He was unsuccessful in establishing a business connection in Great Britain, either with a commission house, an insurance company, or a company to develop mines in the Southern states or to finance immigration into that "land-poor" region. In seeking employment Davis was restrained by his pride and was not very aggressive. He wrote to Varina from London on April 26, 1867, that his personal dignity as well as the dignity of being ex-president of the Southern Confederacy would not permit him, as others might do, "to ask employment by personal application."[3] Finally in November, 1869, he secured a job in Memphis, Tennessee, as president of the Carolina Life Insurance Company. He was very happy in this occupation until the company failed as a result of the panic of 1873, and on August 25 of that year he resigned. But in Memphis his eldest daughter Maggie found a husband,

J. Addison Hayes, a young bank cashier in that city; she and Hayes were married on January 1, 1876.

Davis's latter days were plagued by the litigation to recover his plantation of Brierfield and by attacks on his Confederate record by disgruntled former Confederates, notably General Joseph E. Johnston.[4] His brother Joseph died in 1870, and since before he died, strangely, he had made out no written deed to his brother Jefferson for the plantation of Brierfield, which he had given him, Joseph's granddaughter Lise Mitchell Hamer and her brother Joe Mitchell claimed the inheritance of Brierfield. Jefferson made no attempt to establish his claim to the plantation legally until he lost his job as president of the Carolina Insurance Company, and then he went to court to obtain possession of his plantation.

Davis's lawyers had quite a struggle to reclaim Brierfield. Lise Mitchell declared in court that the reason her grandfather did not execute a deed to the Brierfield plantation was that he disliked Varina and did not wish her to inherit the land, and that he abhorred the thought of the needy and shiftless Howells (Varina's family) having anything to do with the property (which was probably true). Lise and Joe Mitchell, Jefferson wrote to his wife on October 23, 1874, "had filed an answer to my bill, and by bold statements and by seeking advantage of my kindness heretofore shown to them, have denied my claims and pleaded an estoppel." In the summer of 1877, however, Davis won his suit, but he had to go finally to the Supreme Court of Mississippi to do it. He employed his son-in-law Addison Hayes to manage the property, but he and Davis were constantly worried by the difficulty of controlling free Negro laborers, by a succession of corrupt and inefficient overseers, and, above all, by the overflowing of the Mississippi River, and therefore Davis made very little money from his restored ownership of Brierfield. In 1884 Addison Hayes developed tuberculosis, and the family moved to Colorado Springs, leaving Davis to exercise general supervision over his estate from afar.

Davis was rescued from near poverty by a stroke of fortune. One of his ardent admirers and a devotee to the Confederate cause was a wealthy widow, Sarah Anne Dorsey, who rented to him early in 1877 a small cottage on her estate of Beauvoir for a nominal sum. Varina was jealous of Mrs. Dorsey and at first refused to join her husband at Beauvoir, staying with the Hayeses in Memphis. Jefferson, Jr., lived here for a short while with his father after flunking out of VMI, but he soon obtained a job in a bank at Memphis. Here he died shortly afterward from yellow fever—the last of Davis's four sons, the others having died in early childhood.

Mrs. Dorsey was a cultivated woman, and she encouraged Davis to write both an account of the Confederacy and an autobiography. In March, 1877, he dictated the manuscript that was published in two volumes in 1881 as *The Rise and Fall of the Confederate Government*.[5] Mrs. Dorsey aided him by taking dictation on this work, which made Varina furious. Davis also had the aid of Major W. L. Waltham, who looked up references, gathered documents, and even made a trip to Washington, D.C., to obtain information for the historical project. Realizing that Varina's jealousy would interfere with Jefferson's enjoying the peace and quiet that he needed to complete his history, Mrs. Dorsey gave up her favorite home, selling Beauvoir to him at great financial sacrifice for $5,500, to be paid in three installments. Before she died from cancer on July 4, 1879, she made Jefferson Davis her executor, willing to him not only Beauvoir but her entire estate. In the Jefferson Hayes–Davis Papers is a letter from Davis to Varina, telling her of the death of his friend and expressing his gratitude for her many kindnesses to him, while noting the meanness of her near-kin to her.[6]

Davis's *The Rise and Fall of the Confederate Government* does not do him credit. It was written under very difficult circumstances. He apologized that his "labors in preparing his reminiscences have been much obstructed by the loss of my books and papers" and also by the reluctance of those who participated in the war to answer his inquiries.[7] He confessed frankly that the work was designed to present "our side" of the War for Southern Independence. An excessive number of pages were devoted to proving that the Southern states had the constitutional right to secede from the Union. He made a strong legal case for this point of view, but to most people it had become irrelevant by 1880. What was lacking in the volumes, what people of that day and historians of a later day wished to know, was something more than a legal argument or a rather colorless account of military events—they wished to know the internal and personal history of the Confederacy, of which he was a first-hand observer. Davis declared that the Confederates fought not to preserve slavery but for "constitutional liberty," which the United States government under Lincoln had constantly violated. Many questions that would be asked today were ignored by Davis: for example, what was his analysis of the causes of the Confederate collapse? Certainly he did not take upon himself any responsibility for this collapse; he was probably incapable of doing so. But the reader may glean from his account that he believed that the superior forces and equipment of the enemy were the main cause. Also, Davis made statements inferring that during the last twelve months of the war the people lost the will to fight. The reception of the volumes was a disappointment; they did not sell well; the publisher did not promote them, and they were barely noticed by Northern reviewers.

Davis's last years were brightened by the admiration and affection that the Southern people displayed toward him in his role as the martyr of the South. When in the spring of 1886 he was invited to speak at the laying of the cornerstone of a Confederate monument, in Montgomery, Alabama, he at first declined, but the bearer of the invitation appealed to him to do so because it would give his youngest daughter Varina Anne ("Winnie") an opportunity to see how her father was loved and honored by the Southern people. The ovation in Montgomery and along the route was so thunderous that he said, "Your demonstration now exceeds that which welcomed me then" [at his inauguration as Confederate president]. From Montgomery, accompanied by Winnie, he rode by special train to Atlanta, where he had been invited to speak at the unveiling of a statue to Ben Hill, his ardent supporter in the Confederate Congress. It is unlikely that he realized that his invitation to Atlanta by Henry W. Grady and a group of Georgia politicians was motivated by a desire to elect John B. Gordon, the former Confederate general, as governor by stimulating Confederate emotion and appealing to a host of ex-Confederate soldiers. As Henry Grady remarked, it was a "sure-fire" way to reelect Gordon, whose connection with western railroad promoters was far from ethical.[8] There was an outpouring of Confederate emotion such as the South had not witnessed for years, and Gordon was returned to the Senate.

From Atlanta, Davis traveled in a special car to Savannah to make two speeches. Wherever he went his path was strewn with roses by Confederate women, and the veterans in their eagerness to shake his hand almost crushed him. He returned to Beauvoir very happy, and Varina Anne had seen demonstrated how beloved her father had at last become, and she herself was called the "Daughter of the Confederacy." Shortly after his return he journeyed to his birthplace at Fairview, Kentucky, to receive a gift of the land on which he had been born, and a tall monument was erected on the site of his birthplace. In 1887 he attended his last reunion of Confederate veterans, meeting at Macon, Georgia. The effort was too much for the seventy-nine-year-old man; he became ill but rallied and was able to return to Beauvoir.

Although Davis remained true to the principles and virtues of the Old South, he did not become a reactionary. Like Robert E. Lee, he opposed the emigration of Southerners after the war to Mexico and Brazil. In prison he wrote to Varina condemning the expatriation of defeated Confederates: "All cannot go," he observed, "and those who must stay need the help of all who can go away."[9] He supported the movement by capitalists to secure federal aid for the Texas and Pacific Railroad in order that the South might have a railroad to the Pacific. He opposed the movement to enact prohibition laws as an invasion of personal liberty and not the proper way to control intemperance. To a young Northern reporter who visited him in 1883, he observed that one day in the future the supply of Northern lumber would be exhausted, and then the South with its vast forests of pine and its hardwoods would come into its own. The South would also develop its rich sources of coal and iron, which were already being exploited at Birmingham, and new cities would be built up, with the result that the South's future was bright—its prosperity would be far greater than when it depended on cotton. Although Davis refused the request of reporters to comment on the political situation, in his last speech, made before a convention of young men at Mississippi City in March, 1880, he urged them to let the past bury its dead, to lay aside all sectional rancor, and to work for the consummation of a reunited country.

Nevertheless, in his attitude toward women Davis remained a man of the

Old South. He was a Victorian. When Mrs. Davis and he sought a school in Europe for Winnie, Davis vetoed sending her to Paris. He wrote to his wife from Paris, February 7, 1869, of his disgust at the display of "prints and toys expressive of amorous passions. The population which remunerates for such work and the exhibition of such types of general sentiment cannot be favorable to the cultivation or preservation of modesty."[10] So Winnie was sent to a wholesome but fashionable school in Carlsruhe, Germany, operated by the Misses Friedlander. In the year before her father died Winnie fell in love with a Northerner, Alfred Wilkinson, Jr., an attractive twenty-eight-year-old man, a patent attorney of Syracuse, New York, good looking, well educated, and refined in manners. But he was the grandson of one of the most prominent abolitionists. The young Northerner came to Beauvoir in September, 1888, to get Davis's consent to marry his daughter, and Davis invited him to stay several days. He liked Wilkinson but finally said no to his request, and Winnie accepted without question her father's decision, which was apparently based on a desire to avoid the shock that would come to the Southern public if the daughter of the ex-president of the Confederacy should marry a Yankee. Following this traumatic decision, Winnie's health declined so seriously that her father assented to the match, but she never married, dying in 1898 at the age of thirty-four.

The death of Jefferson Davis early in November, 1889, was a consequence of exposure to a sleety rain on a trip to Brierfield. In New Orleans, while waiting to take the *Annie Laurie* to his plantation, he developed a severe cold that turned to bronchitis. He was seriously ill, too ill even to look at his plantation, and returned to New Orleans. On December 9 he died a stoic's death, expressing the wish that he might have lived to finish his incomplete autobiography, but saying that he was not afraid to die. Sadly, Winnie was away on a trip to Paris. After an elaborate state funeral that he would surely not have wished, he was buried temporarily in New Orleans. In 1893 his body was reburied in Hollywood Cemetery, Richmond, where many great Southerners of the past lay buried. After Varina had completed the memoir of her husband in 1890, she lived on in New York City until her death in 1905.

For whom the bell tolls, whether he be famous or obscure and humble, the same question arises: Did the dead man serve his society well or ill? In this book I have sought to answer the question for Jefferson Davis, particularly what kind of man he was beneath the façade that he presented to his contemporaries and whether he was largely responsible, as some critics hold, for the collapse of the Southern Confederacy. A penetrating observer, Clement C. Clay, Jr., of Alabama, wrote to Senator William L. Yancey in 1863 that the president was a strange compound, an inscrutable man. "He would not ask or receive counsel—he was predisposed to go exactly the way that his friends advised him not to go."[11] This patriotic statesman lamented that he had tried hard to be friends with the president, but that "he will be in a minority." Even today this sphinx-like, complex man, with so many virtues and so many faults, is not really understood by modern historians.

"Comparison is the key to understanding," Professor Arthur M. Schlesinger, Sr., used to tell his classes at Harvard University. Perhaps if a comparison were made between the Confederate president and other leading personalities of his period, especially in the South, it might lead to a better understanding of Jefferson Davis. Davis and President Lincoln have often been compared, usually to the disadvantage of Davis. But a less hackneyed and more fruitful comparison can be made with the leading Southern statesmen of the period, especially with the men considered by the Montgomery convention for the presidency. Such a comparison may help answer the question: Was Jefferson Davis the best *available* man for president of the Confederacy?

The two outstanding personalities who were seriously considered, along with Davis, for the job of Confederate president were Howell Cobb and Robert Toombs of Georgia. Cobb was chosen president of the Montgomery convention that founded the Confederacy. He was a rich man, the owner of many slaves, somewhat corpulent, and self-indulgent. He was hostile to Toombs, whose jests got under his skin, and he used his influence against Toombs. Cobb wrote to his wife that he did not want the job of Confederate president, considering it "a most undesirable position."[12] He had some excellent qualifications for leading the Confederate people that Davis did not have. He had been Buchanan's secretary of the treasury, as well as governor of Georgia, whereas Davis had had no executive experience. The Confederate congressman, Jabez L. M. Curry, a graduate of the Harvard Law School, testified to his admirable qualities: "Governor Cobb had a noble, generous affectionate nature, shrewdness, sagacity, common sense, a real and sincere judgment to lean on, was unselfish to an extreme degree, and few public men had a larger group of devoted friends."[13] But his strong fight in 1851 to prevent the secession of Georgia and his advocacy of the acceptance of the Compromise militated against his choice as president by the Montgomery convention, and he had the formidable competition of Toombs. Lawrence Keitt, a delegate to the convention from South Carolina, preferred Cobb to Davis, remarking to Mrs. Chesnut that "Howell Cobb's common sense might have saved us."[14] His talents were largely wasted during the course of the war; he would have made a first-rate cabinet officer, but Davis was inhibited from appointing two men from the same state, and Toombs got the job; Cobb was a senator for a short while and then an inconspicous brigadier general in the army.

If Cobb did not aspire to the presidency, Toombs, on the other hand, was ambitious and let it be known that he would accept the post. He was a strong contrast to Davis both physically and in personality. Whereas Davis was thin, emaciated, and sickly, Toombs was a large, burly man with striking black eyes and glossy black hair that he tossed about like Danton. He loved liquor and sometimes got "high" or drunk, but he shone on convivial occasions.[15] Varina Davis has drawn a vivid and apparently objective portrait of this tall Georgia aristocrat. She had an excellent opportunity to observe him since the Davises and the Toombses had rented a house together in Washington and belonged to the same congressional mess.

Toombs and her husband, she wrote, were never congenial in their tastes, and their habits and manners were entirely diverse. Davis was serious, quiet, and dignified; Toombs was Rabelaisian, regarded by some as a braggart. Toombs could be a delightful companion, witty and cultivated, who arose at daybreak to study French with his daughters; Varina once found him roaring over Molière's play *Le Médecin Malgré Lui*.[16] Davis concentrated on reading works of government, history and politics and seldom relaxed his taut nerves by social life and entertainment or by the outlet of earthy humor, which Toombs and Lincoln used to such advantage.[17]

Davis was a far more stable personality than the Georgian, whose good judgment was too often warped by his impetuosity, his love of liquor, and his rash speech. Senator Thomas Bragg from North Carolina, a moderate, noted in his diary on January 7, 1861, the contrast between Stephen A. Douglas's conciliatory speech in the Senate and the one by Toombs that poured hot lava on the Republicans.[18] Toombs displayed a strong streak of selfishness and waywardness, except with regard to his family, while Davis was utterly devoted to the cause of the South and later to the Confederacy. Davis's self-control and self-discipline were remarkable. Both men were intensely proud and gratuitously guarded their honor, a characteristic of the Southern aristocrat of this period. In terms of education both were far above the average politician, and both were accomplished orators. At times Toombs would display excellent judgment, but he was unpredictable, and would lose his sense of balance and common sense as a result of his belligerency and impetuosity.

Mrs. Chesnut's account of Toombs being thrown from his horse at the fair grounds in Richmond in 1861 does not inspire confidence in the egotistical Georgian as a suitable person for president of the Confederacy. She commented in her diary on August 1, 1861: "That bold Brigadier, the Georgia General Toombs, charging about too recklessly, got thrown. His horse dragged him up to the wheels of our carriage. For a moment it was frightful. Down there among the horses's hoofs was his face turned up towards us, purple with rage. His foot was still in the stirrup, and he had not let go the bridle. The horse was prancing and plunging. . . . However, he soon got it all straight, and though awfully tousled and tumbled, dusty, rumpled, and flushed, with redder face and wilder hair than ever, he rode off gallantly, having to our admiration bravely remounted the recalcitrant charger."[19]

A recent and perceptive biographer has concluded that if Toombs instead of Davis had been elected president of the Confederacy, he would have adopted a more dynamic, less defensive military policy and would probably have taken a big offensive gamble at the beginning of the Civil War.[20] By such a policy the Confederacy might have won but, more likely, might have collapsed early, sparing the South much bloodshed and years of bitter suffering.

Davis had many notable virtues that have often been overlooked by historians who are severely critical without taking proper account of the tremendous difficulties that beset him as president of the Confederacy—far greater than those that harassed President Lincoln. Running through the personal life of Davis and his speeches in the Senate was the theme of honor. If one had to choose an outstanding trait of Davis's, it would have to be the high value that he placed on honor. It was not simply a regard for his personal honor, but for his duty as a soldier, for the American flag, and as a statesman for the honor of the South. In this quality Davis and the upper-class Southerners contrasted with Northern leaders such as Lincoln, Ben Wade, and Thaddeus Stevens and with some of the senators in opposition; they spoke often of democracy and liberty, but seldom of honor. It would have been an oddity during this period to hear a New Englander speak of "the honor of New England," as Southerners spoke so fervently of "the honor of the South."[21]

Shaped largely by his upbringing, Davis became an outstanding exponent of Southern honor and Southern rights in the Senate. His whole life, indeed, was a commentary upon the virtues and defects of this conception of conduct. We have seen early examples of it at West Point in his contempt for the parsimonious life style of the Northern cadets, in his resentment and defiance when reprimanded by his commanding officer in the army, and in his support of dueling as a necessary means of protecting a man's honor. Nor did he escape the romanticism that lay back of the concept of Southern honor, as he showed in his love for the novels of Sir Walter Scott, in his courtships, and in his relations with women in general.

Scornful of expediency in politics, Davis was a man devoted to abstractions that he called "principles." Moreover, he was a man of legality and of inflexible belief in constitutionality, which was clearly indicated throughout his *The Rise and Fall of the Confederate Government*. The North might change in its conception of the Constitution owing to economic and social changes, but not the South, not Davis. In the speech at Faneuil Hall, Boston, in 1858 he held that the states were bound by obligations of honor to live up to the compact of the Constitution. Again, he said that it belonged to the honor of the states to execute the Fugitive Slave Law. In a speech in the Senate on May 16–17, 1861, he declared that it was "not the way of honor" to repress opinions for the sake of the victory of his party. He asserted also that the honor of Mississippi, as well as his own honor, would not permit him to be a secessionist and still hold his position in the Senate.

As Confederate president one of Davis's important virtues was his ability to act decisively in a crisis, and to carry out his decision with a strong will (his critics called it stubbornness). An example of this quality was his decisive action in dispersing a menacing mob, mostly of women, in Richmond during the famous "Bread Riot" of April 2, 1862. He first made a speech appealing to their patriotism and pointing out that many stole jewelry instead of bread. Gorgas in his journal described it as "a real women's riot whose motive was licence rather than desire for bread."[22] But when this appeal did not work, Davis dramatically turned his pockets inside out and threw his money to the crowd, saying that this was all the money that he had. Then, taking out his watch, he announced in a firm, resolute tone that he would give orders for the troops to fire on the mob within five minutes if they did not disperse. They dispersed. Yet the riot resulted in the distribution of some food to the poor.

To those who were close to Davis and whom he liked, he appeared as an admirable person. John H. Reagan commented in his memoirs that during sixty years he had known many distinguished citizens of the North, "but taking into view the combined elements of character and ability, I regard him as the ablest man I have ever known." This encomium was excessive praise, but in another part of his book, Reagan gives a more balanced estimate of the Confederate president. "My conclusion is," he wrote, "that he had two characters—one for social and domestic life and the other for official life. In the first he was one of the most pleasant and genial men that I ever knew, a remarkable agreeable conversationalist and all women [though not Lydia Johnston, the wife of the general, or Mrs. Wigfall] and children seemed instinctively to love him. In the second he was wholly given to duty. When a subject came up for consideration as important, his habit was to exhaust all available sources of information before reaching a conclusion. The conclusion once reached, that ended it."[23] Davis would not further discuss such questions, causing his critics to accuse him of being self-willed and stubborn. Thomas Bragg, the attorney general in the early years of the war, wrote in his manuscript diary on January 17, 1862: "He [Davis] is an able and honorable man —somewhat irritable when opposed—wants to have his way, but left to himself would conduct things more wisely, safely, and energetically than he can now." To the public he appeared to be lacking in humor, although on occasions he displayed an ironic wit and a cutting sarcasm; in private life, however, he was different, telling jokes, mimicking, and on jovial occasions, even singing Indian songs that he had learned as a frontier soldier.

William Preston Johnston, son of Albert Sidney, and an aide to the president, writing from the "President House" to Rosa on May 19, 1862, gave an intimate, close-up picture of Davis. The president, he wrote, was reserved, impatient of opposition, and somewhat irascible. He had a contempt for meanness, subterfuge, and dodges. He also despised demagogism and therefore was not popular with the common run of politicians.[24] This intelligent young man, who after the war became president of Tulane University, thought that Davis did not sufficiently conciliate this powerful class of society, the politicians. The evidence piles up to support Varina's judgment that her husband would not succeed as president because he did not know how to deal with the politicians.

Mixed with virtues, however, there were some serious faults in Davis's personality that hampered his effectiveness as a revolutionary leader. In order to succeed in the desperate struggle to win the war for Southern independence, it was essential to establish teamwork in the government and in the military forces. But Davis's rigid sense of pride, which contrasted with President Lincoln's humility, and his quick resentment of criticism interfered with the efficient carrying out of his duties. He was aware of this failing, as he revealed in a letter to Mrs. Davis who had written about the admirable conduct of their little daughter, Maggie, in dealing with her fractious cat. He replied: "Maggie is a wise child. I wish I could learn to let people alone who snap at me, in forbearance and charity to turn away as well from cats as the snakes."[25] But he never learned.

A principal cause of Davis's failure as president was owing to the fact that he was not a flexible politician, like Lincoln, who knew when to bend and when to stand firm. Those who visualize Lincoln in the context of the Second Inaugural and the Gettysburg Address know only part of the man. His law partner, William H. Herndon, observed: "He was always calculating, always planning ahead. His ambition was a little engine that knew no rest."[26]

Davis was a different sort of man, who scorned to use the arts of the politician—to his own loss and to the loss of the Confederacy—yet there is something admirable about his high-minded attitude. Allan Nevins, in his study of the statesmanship of the Civil War, maintained that Davis lacked great passion and therefore was incapable of stirring his nation with winged words that would endure as those of Lincoln and Churchill.[27] Davis did not really lack passion, but he was stoical and self-controlled, and failed to express it until nearly the end of the war. It was difficult for him to open his heart to the people, to depart from his dignity in order to express public emotion, which he had been trained to suppress. His defects and mistakes as Confederate president have been brilliantly dissected by David Potter in an essay assessing Davis's responsibilities for Confederate defeat.[28] One of the serious defects that Potter has criticized was Davis's conservative mind, but in this respect he faithfully represented the mind of the Old South. Allan Nevins, also, presented a very unfavorable portrait of Davis, describing him as proud, arrogant, and austere, and asserting that most politicians thought him "too much of a martinet, too moody, and too metaphysical" to be a good candidate for the Democratic nomination in 1860.[29]

Bell Wiley, in his introduction to an edition of *The Rise and Fall of the Confederate Government,* has rendered a severe judgment against the Confederate president, listing what he considers to have been the serious faults of Jefferson Davis, which included: (1) inability to get along with people; (2) lack of administrative capacity; (3) aloofness from the people; and

(4) neglect of civil functions in favor of military matters. Wiley considers him not equal to the responsibilities of his position—"The presidency of the embattled Confederacy took him beyond his depth."[30]

Did Davis grow in the presidency? In some respects he did, especially in freeing himself from the incubus of his original state rights obsession and arising as a true statesman to a conception of the growth of an organic nation and the development of realistic policies to attain Southern nationalism. Also, he seems to have grown in his grasp of a sound military policy, but not to the extent that Lincoln did. Furthermore, he attained a new public stature in his noble speeches made during his trip to the lower South at the end of 1864 and at Richmond. His character strengthened under the blows of adversity. There were some debits, however—areas in which he did not grow—notably in his ability to get along with people, particularly with Congress, and in his continued neglect of the home front. Unlike Lincoln, he did not grow in respect to humility and ability to appeal to the moral idealism of his section. To the end he remained the proud, sensitive Southerner; his mentality remained conservative and legalistic, his strong will unbroken.

Jefferson Davis appeared to change noticeably as the stresses and strains of being a war president told upon him. He developed a closed, sphinx-like personality that may have been latent, but was unrecognized before he became president. As this high-strung, sensitive, and often neurotic man encountered severe criticism and adversity, he presented a façade of stoicism, an impenetrability, a sort of defensive armor. Frank Vandiver observed that Davis was "a strangely muffled man."[31] Increasingly he retreated into himself, and Varina explained this by saying that he felt he was not understood by the people he was leading in a struggle against tremendous odds. Yet the clue, the key to the riddle of Davis's self-defeating personality, may well have been an invincible pride—far beyond that of ordinary individuals—that was closely associated in his mind with the notion of honor. Indeed, he remains a sphinx-like personality, imperturbable on the outside, a furnace of emotions inside, an enigma to historians. If, in the improbable case that his armies had won decisive victories and the Confederate States of America had become an established nation, he would doubtless have been hailed as a great man, his defects condoned and his virtues celebrated. Lincoln then, almost surely, would not be rated today as the number one president.

But if Lincoln's armies, instead of those of Davis, had been defeated, still Lincoln's noble speeches and messages to Congress had a quality that Davis's lacked. In back of the noble speeches of Lincoln, moreover, was a vision of America's destiny as a world leader for democracy; he had a sense of history, looking down on the nation as it engaged in a struggle to prevent the government of the people, by the people, and for the people from perishing from the earth. Davis had a sense of history, too, but it looked backward to 1789, and because of the limitations of his cause he could not appeal to universal principles of human liberty—except as to the principle of self-determination of peoples—a moving force today. Although he was an excellent public speaker, he did not have the gift of moving, unforgettable phrases or of communicating with the common people.

That Davis contributed to the defeat of the Confederacy is likely, especially in his failure to obtain teamwork both in the government and in the army. He grew up in a decentralized, nonindustrial society that lagged far behind the North in efficiency and organization. He is blamed for the defects of his society. Moreover, those scholars who severely criticize Davis as responsible for the Confederate defeat fail properly to appreciate the tremendous difficulties against which he struggled—much greater than Lincoln's problems —and the limited alternatives at his disposal. A rather recent article by William J. Cooper, Jr., of Louisiana State University, has ably presented these difficulties and limited alternatives as they applied to the campaigns around Atlanta and to the invasion of Tennessee in 1864–65.[32] Without entering into the military controversy on this subject, it is pertinent to this study of the character and ability of Davis to observe that in this critical hour for the Confederacy, far from being rigid, he consulted the best minds available to him and acted with decisiveness, and the plan that was adopted almost succeeded. It was not solely a defensive policy, but a defensive-offensive policy that involved leaving the defensive when a good opportunity presented itself for attacking the enemy. If Toombs was a gambler, Davis also proved at times to be a cautious gambler, especially in the Atlanta and Tennessee campaigns.

When Davis is compared with some of the egotistical, costive, and self-seeking men with whom he had to deal, his steadfast character and unselfish devotion to the cause of the Confederacy are shining lights. Indeed, in his diary Robert Kean takes the glamor from many of those men who led and fought for the lost cause, and illustrates the ever recurring fact that human nature is fallible; even the exalted General Robert E. Lee, Kean thought, was not exempt.[33]

In the years following the Civil War, Davis's reputation suffered at the hands of both contemporaries and historians. Because of the overwhelming importance and drama of the war years, he is often remembered only as the president of the Confederacy—as the leader of the lost cause. His honorable and distinguished service in both houses of Congress, in the Mexican War, and in Franklin Pierce's cabinet is often forgotten.

Andrew Johnson's pardon of 1865, the First and Supplementary Reconstruction Acts of 1867, and the Fourteenth Amendment to the United States Constitution denied the rights of citizenship to many who had supported the Southern cause. Although Davis was finally released from prison in Fort Monroe in 1867, he was excluded from both the 1872 and 1876 amnesties, and the rights of citizenship were never restored to him.

In recent years, efforts have been made to restore the citizenship of leaders of the Confederacy. In 1976, Congress passed a bill that restored those rights to Robert E. Lee. Currently, Congress is considering a joint resolution to "restore posthumously full rights of citizenship to Jefferson Davis." Introducing the resolution to the Senate, Mark Hatfield of Oregon praised Jefferson Davis, saying that "with this joint resolution I seek to keep his memory green and restore the rights due an outstanding American."[34] It was a significant expression of broad Americanism that came, not from a Southern senator, but a liberal Western senator.

In summation: Jefferson Davis was an admirable, honorable, but misguided man of exceptional ability and force who accepted the assumptions of his society—in fact, they were the only basis upon which he could have risen in politics. Nevertheless, despite his own faults and those of his society, he led the Southern Confederacy in enduring for four years against the overwhelming superiority of the federal government in manpower and matériel, and this fact alone speaks eloquently for the quality of his leadership and for the indomitable spirit of the Southern people.

$\mathcal{N}otes$

———◆———

CHAPTER 1: "THE IMPRINT OF KENTUCKY AND MISSISSIPPI" (pp. 1–11)

1. Jefferson Davis to "Joe," September 22, 1855, Duke University Library.

2. See H. A. Davis, *The Davis Family (Davis and David) in Wales and America* (Washington, 1927), II, 289–303.

3. Clement Eaton, *A History of the Old South: The Emergence of a Reluctant Nation* (New York, 1975), 46.

4. Jefferson Davis, "Autobiographical Sketch," in H. M. Monroe, Jr., and J. T. McIntosh (eds.), *The Papers of Jefferson Davis* (Baton Rouge, 1971), I, lxviii.

5. Varina Howell Davis, *Jefferson Davis, Ex–President of the Confederate States of America. A Memoir by His Wife* (New York, 1890), I, 200.

6. Monroe and McIntosh (eds.), *The Papers of Jefferson Davis,* I, lviii.

7. *Ibid.*

8. W. W. Jennings, *Transylvania, Pioneer University of the West* (New York, 1955); and Robert and Johanna Peter, *Transylvania University, Its Origin, Rise, Decline and Fall* (Louisville, 1896).

9. Monroe and McIntosh (eds.), *The Papers of Jefferson Davis,* I, lxxvii.

10. Jefferson to Joseph Cabell, January 22, 1820, in P. L. Ford (ed.), *The Works of Thomas Jefferson* (New York, 1912), XII.

11. N. H. Sonne, *Liberal Kentucky, 1780–1828* (New York, 1939); and John D. Wright, Jr., *Transylvania: Tutor to the West* (Lexington, 1975).

12. Charles Caldwell, *A Discourse on the Genius and Character of the Rev. Horace Holley, LLD* (Boston, 1828).

13. Monroe and McIntosh (eds.), *The Papers of Jefferson Davis,* I, lxxvii.

14. Varina Davis, *Memoir,* I, 27–29.

15. Clement Eaton, "A Law Student at Transylvania University in 1810–1812," *Filson Club History Quarterly,* XXXI (July, 1957).

16. Monroe and McIntosh (eds.), *The Papers of Jefferson Davis,* I, 10.

17. M. N. Wagers, *The Education of a Gentleman: Jefferson Davis at Transylvania, 1821–1824* (Lexington, 1943).

18. Monroe and McIntosh (eds.), *The Papers of Jefferson Davis,* I, lxxviii.

19. William Preston Johnston, *Life of Albert Sidney Johnston* (New York, 1878), 5–13.

20. Hudson Strode (ed.), *Jefferson Davis: Private Letters, 1823–1889* (New York, 1966), 6–7.

21. Hudson Strode, *Jefferson Davis, American Patriot, 1808–1861* (New York, 1955), 29–30.

22. Monroe and McIntosh (eds.), *The Papers of Jefferson Davis,* I, 11.

23. *Ibid.,* I, 10.

24. Clement Eaton, "Social Structure and Social Mobility in the Old Southwest," in L. F. Ellsworth (ed.), *The Americanization of the Gulf Coast, 1803–1850* (Pensacola, 1972), 53–62.

25. Susan Dabney Smedes, *Memorials of a Southern Planter,* ed. by Fletcher Green (New York, 1965).

26. Mack Swearingen, *The Early Life of George Poindexter, a Story of the First Southwest* (New Orleans, 1934).

27. Reuben Davis, *Recollections of Mississippi and Mississippians* (Boston, 1889).

28. Dunbar Rowland (ed.), *Jefferson Davis, Constitutionalist, His Letters Papers and Speeches* (Jackson, Miss., 1923), IV, 236–37.

29. William E. Dodd, *Jefferson Davis* (Philadelphia, 1907), 124–25.

30. D. R. Hundley, *Social Relations in Our Southern States* (New York, 1860).

31. Frederick Law Olmsted, *A Journey in the Back Country, 1853–1854,* with an Introduction by Clement Eaton (New York, 1970), 26–27.

32. Eugene L. Schwaab (ed.), *Travels in the Old South Selected from Periodicals of the Time* (Lexington, 1973), II, 289–303.

33. See J. A. Ramage, *John Wesley Hunt, Pioneer Merchant and Manufacturer* (Lexington, 1974).

24. Clement Eaton, *Henry Clay and the Art of American Politics* (Boston, 1957) chap. 5, "Kentucky Planter."

35. Bernard Mayo, "Lexington: Frontier Metropolis," in Eric F. Goldman (ed.) *Historiography and Urbanization* (Baltimore, 1941).

36. William Reynolds Journal, 1839–40, University of Kentucky Library.

37. James H. Atherton Letters, 1832–36, University of Kentucky Library.

38. Monroe and McIntosh (eds.), *The Papers of Jefferson Davis*, I, Introduction, p. ix.

CHAPTER 2: "A WEST POINT CADET AND FRONTIER SOLDIER"
        (pp. 12–20)

1. H. M. Monroe, Jr., and J. T. McIntosh (eds.), *The Papers of Jefferson Davis* (Baton Rouge, 1971), I, lxvii, lxix.

2. John Hope Franklin, *The Militant South, 1800–1861* (Cambridge, Mass., 1956).

3. Clement Eaton, *The Freedom-of-Thought Struggle in the Old South* (New York, 1964), chap. 4, "The Fear of Servile Insurrection."

4. Monroe and McIntosh (eds.), *The Papers of Jefferson Davis*, I, lxxix.

5. Charles P. Roland, *Albert Sidney Johnston, Soldier of Three Republics* (Austin, 1964); and William M. Polk, *William Leonidas Polk: Bishop and General* (New York, 1893), 2 vols.

6. Monroe and McIntosh (eds.), *The Papers of Jefferson Davis*, I, 17–18.

7. Douglas Southall Freeman, *R. E. Lee, A Biography* (New York, 1934–35), 4 vols.; and Gilbert E. Govan and James W. Livingood, *A Different Valor: The Story of General Joseph E. Johnston, C.S.A.* (New York, 1956).

8. Monroe and McIntosh (eds.), *The Papers of Jefferson Davis*, I, 37.

9. *Ibid.*, I, 37, 39–40.

10. *Ibid.*, I, 60–84.

11. Joseph E. Parks, *General Leonidas Polk, C.S.A.: The Fighting Bishop* (Baton Rouge, 1962).

12. Monroe and McIntosh (eds.), *The Papers of Jefferson Davis*, I, 95–101.

13. Ellsworth Eliot, *West Point in the Confederacy* (New York, 1941), chap. 1; R. E. Dupuy, *West Point: The First 150 Years of the United States Military Academy* (New York, 1951).

14. Monroe and McIntosh (eds.), *The Papers of Jefferson Davis*, I, 106.

15. L. J. Lasswell (ed.), "Jefferson Davis Ponders His Future, 1829," *Journal of Southern History*, XLI (November, 1975), 516–22.

16. Varina Howell Davis, *Jefferson Davis, Ex-President of the Confederate States of America. A Memoir by His Wife,* (New York, 1890), I, 81.

17. Monroe and McIntosh (eds.), *The Papers of Jefferson Davis*, I, 153, 164.

18. *Ibid.*, I, 156, 164.

19. *Ibid.*, I, 220.

20. For a discussion of this question, see *ibid.*, I, 240–42, 482–86.

21. *Ibid.*, I, 296–97.

22. Varina Davis, *Memoir,* I, 89–90.

23. Monroe and McIntosh (eds.), *The Papers of Jefferson Davis*, I, 283.

24. *Ibid.*, I, 276.

25. J. S. Chambers, *The Conquest of Cholera* (New York, 1931).

26. Monroe and McIntosh (eds.), *The Papers of Jefferson Davis*, I, 317.

27. *Ibid.*, I, 391; Varina Davis, *Memoir*, chaps. 6–10, tells many anecdotes of his life that her husband related to her.

28. Dunbar Rowland (ed.), *Jefferson Davis, Constitutionalist, His Letters, Papers and Speeches* (Jackson, Miss., 1923), III, 186.

29. Monroe and McIntosh (eds.), *The Papers of Jefferson Davis*, I, 379.

30. *Ibid.*

31. *Ibid.*, I, 378.

CHAPTER 3: "THE WOMEN IN DAVIS'S LIFE"
(pp. 21–32)

1. See engraving of Davis as a young man, in H. M. Monroe, Jr., and J. T. McIntosh (eds.), *The Papers of Jefferson Davis* (Baton Rouge, 1971), frontispiece.

2. Hudson Strode (ed.), *Jefferson Davis: Private Letters, 1823–1889* (New York, 1966), 10–12.

3. Monroe and McIntosh (eds.), *The Papers of Jefferson Davis*, I, 406–07.

4. *Ibid.*, I, liv.

5. Hudson Strode, *Jefferson Davis, American Patriot, 1808–1861* (New York, 1955), 103.

6. Strode, *Jefferson Davis, American Patriot*, 104.

7. Varina Howell Davis, *Jefferson Davis, Ex–President of the Confederate States of America. A Memoir by His Wife* (New York, 1890), I, 165–66.

8. For a pleasant account of Varina Howell, see Eron Rowland, *Varina Howell, Wife of Jefferson Davis* (New York, 1931).

9. Varina Davis, *Memoir*, I, 191–92.

10. Strode (ed.), *Jefferson Davis: Private Letters*, 19.

11. *Ibid.*, 21.

12. *Ibid.*, 19.

13. *Ibid.*, 23, 25.

14. *Ibid.*, 30.

15. *Ibid.*, 56.

16. *Ibid.*, 35.

17. *Ibid.*, 42.

18. *Ibid.*, 35.

19. *Ibid.*, 42.

20. *Ibid.*, 38.

21. For a perceptive and critical evaluation of Varina as the wife of the Confederate president see Bell I. Wiley, *Confederate Women* (Westport, Conn., 1975), chap. 3.

22. Mary Boykin Chesnut, *A Diary from Dixie,* ed. by B. A. Williams (Boston, 1949), 46, 89.

23. Strode (ed.), *Jefferson Davis: Private Letters,* 36.

24. *Ibid.,* 109–10.

25. Varina Davis to her mother, December 16, 1857, University of Alabama Library, cited by Wiley, *Confederate Women,* 93.

26. Varina Davis, *Memoir,* I, 200.

27. Monroe and McIntosh (eds.), *The Papers of Jefferson Davis,* I, 303–304.

28. *Ibid.,* I, 270–72.

29. Clement Eaton, "Breaking a Path for the Liberation of Women in the South," *Georgia Review,* June, 1974; and Anne F. Scott, *The Southern Lady: From Pedestal to Politics 1830–1930* (Chicago, 1970).

30. Quoted from John Hartwell Cocke Papers, Alderman Library, University of Virginia in Clement Eaton, *The Mind of the Old South* (Baton Rouge, 1967), 32–33.

31. Avery Craven, *Rachel of Old Louisiana* (Baton Rouge, 1975).

32. Susan Dabney Smedes, *Memorials of a Southern Planter* (New York, 1890), 233–34.

33. Dunbar Rowland (ed.), *Jefferson Davis, Constitutionalist, His Letters, Papers and Speeches* (Jackson, Miss., 1923). III, 311.

34. Jefferson Davis to Varina Davis, July 29, 1846, Jefferson Hayes–Davis Papers, Transylvania University Library.

35. Wiley, *Confederate Women,* 119–22.

36. Edward Younger (ed.), *Inside the Confederate Government: The Diary of Robert Garlick Hill Kean* (New York, 1957), 89–90.

37. Stephen Mallory, Diary and Reminiscences, University of North Carolina Library.

38. William H. Russell, *My Diary North and South* (Boston, 1863), 177.

39. Frank E. Vandiver (ed.), *The Civil War Diary of General Josiah Gorgas* (University, Ala., 1947), 22.

40. Strode (ed.), *Jefferson Davis: Private Letters,* 39.

41. D. Giraud Wright, *A Southern Girl in '61* (New York, 1915), 29.

42. Virginia Clay-Clopton, *A Belle of the Fifties,* ed. Ada Sterling (New York, 1905), 68.

43. Chesnut, *A Diary from Dixie,* 69, 345.

CHAPTER 4: "SLAVERY ON THE DAVIS PLANTATIONS"
    (pp. 33–46)

1. Frank E. Everett, *Brierfield: Plantation Home of Jefferson Davis* (Hattiesburg, Miss., 1971).

2. Frederick J. Turner, *The Rise of the New West, 1819–1829* (New York, 1906).

3. Varina Howell Davis, *Jefferson Davis, Ex–President of the Confederate States of America. A Memoir by His Wife* (New York, 1890), I, 165.

4. H. M. Monroe, Jr., and J. T. McIntosh (eds.), *The Papers of Jefferson Davis* (Baton Rouge, 1971), I, 462.

5. Hudson Strode (ed.), *Jefferson Davis: Private Letters, 1823–1889* (New York, 1966).

6. Monroe and McIntosh (eds.), *The Papers of Jefferson Davis*, I, 450.

7. Strode (ed.), *Jefferson Davis: Private Letters*, 79.

8. *Ibid.*, I, 247–48, n. 2.

9. Varina Davis, *Memoir*, I, 192–94.

10. Monroe and McIntosh (eds.), *The Papers of Jefferson Davis*, I, 304.

11. Varina Davis, *Memoir*, II, 305.

12. Monroe and McIntosh (eds.), *The Papers of Jefferson Davis*, I, 465.

13. U. B. Phillips, *Life and Labor in the Old South* (Boston, 1929), 177; chart of prices in New York.

14. Dunbar Rowland (ed.), *Jefferson Davis, Constitutionalist, His Letters, Papers and Speeches* (Jackson, Miss., 1923), IV, 561.

15. Jefferson Davis to Varina Davis, July 20, 1857, Jefferson Hayes–Davis Papers, Transylvania University Library.

16. Strode (ed.), *Jefferson Davis: Private Letters*, 83, 89.

17. Varina Davis, *Memoir*, I, 479.

18. Fogel and Engerman, *Time on the Cross* (Boston, 1974), I; for opposite views see C. S. Sydnor, *Slavery in Mississippi* (Baton Rouge, 1966, first published in 1933), 200; and U. B. Phillips, *The Slave Economy of the Old South*, ed by Eugene D. Genovese (Baton Rouge, 1968).

19. Eugene D. Genovese, *Roll, Jordan, Roll: Afro-Amercian Slaves in the Making of the Modern World* (New York, 1974).

20. Monroe and McIntosh (eds.), *The Papers of Jefferson Davis*, I, 463.

21. *Ibid.*, II, 245, 311.

22. Records of Bureau of the Census, 1850 and 1860, Schedule 4, Agricultural Production of Mississippi, Warren County, p. 21; courtesy of the editor of *The Jefferson Davis Papers*, James T. McIntosh, and Mississippi Department of Archives.

23. *Ibid.*, Schedule 4, Warren County, 1850, pp. 815; 1860, n. 21.

24. Strode (ed.), *Jefferson Davis: Private Letters*, 109.

25. Rowland (ed.), *Jefferson Davis, Constitutionalist*, II, 17.

26. Fogel and Engerman, *Time on the Cross*, I, 211; and William K. Scarborough, *The Overseer: Plantation Management in the Old South* (Baton Rouge, 1966), 10.

27. Herbert Weaver, *Mississippi Planters, 1850–1860* (Nashville, 1945).

28. H. G. Gutman, *Slavery and the Numbers Game: A Critique of Time on the Cross* (Urbana, Ill., 1975), 65–69; and P. A. David (ed.), *Reckoning with Slavery: Critical Essays in the Quantitative History of American Negro Slavery* (New York, 1976).

29. Information furnished to the author by Professor Engerman, April, 1976.

30. Strode (ed.), *Jefferson Davis: Private Letters,* 103, 108, 112.

31. Hudson Strode, *Jefferson Davis, American Patriot 1808–1861* (New York, 1955), 113.

32. Rowland (ed.), *Jefferson Davis, Constitutionalist,* IV, 240.

33. J. H. Franklin, *The Free Negro in North Carolina, 1790–1860* (Chapel Hill, 1943), 168–69.

34. Carter Woodson, *The Education of the Negro prior to 1861* (Washington, 1919); and Clement Eaton, *The Freedom-of-Thought Struggle in the Old South* (New York, 1964), 212.

35. Varina Davis, *Memoir,* I, 178.

36. Strode (ed.), *Jefferson Davis: Private Letters,* 101.

37. Jefferson Davis to M. B. Howell, April 18, 1859, Jefferson Hayes–Davis Papers, Transylvania University Library.

38. John W. Daniel (ed.), *Life and Reminiscences of Jefferson Davis by Distinguished Men of His Time* (Baltimore, 1890), 134.

39. Strode (ed.), *Jefferson Davis: Private Letters,* 223.

40. Charles S. Sydnor, "The Southerner and the Laws," *Journal of Southern History,* VI (1940), 1–23.

41. Varina Davis, *Memoir,* I, 176.

42. Rowland (ed.), *Jefferson Davis, Constitutionalist,* II, 176.

43. R. M. Myers (ed.), *The Children of Pride, A True Story of Georgia and the Civil War* (New Haven, 1972), 255, 267.

44. Fogel and Engerman, *Time on the Cross* (1974), which is based on their interpretation of statistics and their use of the computer, have presented a much milder view of Southern slavery than the harsh and stark one held by some modern liberals. Although I am incapable of dealing with the results of historical material fed into the computer, I agree in general with their findings and conclusions. My basic views have been arrived at independently from planters' papers, travelers' observations, interviews of ex-slaves in the Library of Congress, and belief in the continuity of human nature. I think, however, that Fogel and Engerman have perhaps overstated their conclusions.

45. Kenneth M. Stampp, *The Peculiar Institution; Slavery in the Ante-Bellum South* (New York, 1956), chap. 4.

46. Genovese, *Roll, Jordan, Roll.*

47. J. F. H. Claiborne, *Life and Correspondence of John A. Quitman* (New York, 1860), I, 190.

48. On this highly controversial question of the extent of the flogging of Southern slaves, I take a moderate position: see Clement Eaton, *A History of the Old South: The Emergence of a Reluctant Nation* (New York, 1975), chap. 14; for opposite views, see J. H. Blassingame, *The Slave Community: Plantation Life in the Ante-Bellum South* (New York, 1972), 62–64; N. R. Yetman (ed.), *Life under the Peculiar Institution: Selections from the Slave Narrative Collection* (New York, 1970); and E. A. Davis (ed.), *Plantation Life in*

the Florida Parishes of Louisiana, 1836–1846, as Reflected in the Diary of Bennett H. Barrow (New York, 1943).

49. Frederick Law Olmsted, *A Journey in the Back Country, 1853–1854,* with an Introduction by Clement Eaton (New York, 1970), 48.

50. Scarborough, *The Overseer,* 96; see also B. H. Wall, "African Slavery," and J. C. Bonner, "Plantation and Farm," chaps. 6 and 8, in Arthur Link and Rembert W. Patrick (ed.) *Writing Southern History* (Baton Rouge, 1965).

51. Cited from Clement Eaton, *The Waning of the Old South Civilization* (New York, 1969), chap. 2, "Characteristics of the Planter Aristocracy in 1860," pp. 32–34.

52. (Catherine C. Hopley), *Life in the South from the Commencement of the War, by a Blockaded British Subject* (London, 1863), II, 248.

53. Davis (ed.), *Plantation Life in Diary of Barrow.*

54. Fogel and Engerman, *Time on the Cross,* I, 32–33.

55. Avery Craven, *Rachel of Old Louisiana* (Baton Rouge, 1975), 40, 58.

56. Photostats of manuscript slave returns, 1850 census, Schedule 2, National Archives, courtesy of Larry Ashton, archives technician.

57. Photostats of manuscript slave returns, 1860 census, Schedule 2, National Archives, courtesy of Cooper L. Davis.

58. Conversation over telephone with Professor William K. Scarborough and letter from him to author, dated March 9, 1976.

59. Stanley L. Engerman to the author, April 15, 1976.

60. See Clement Eaton, *The Freedom-of-Thought Struggle in the Old South,* chap. 11.

61. Strode (ed.), *Jefferson Davis: Private Letters,* 88.

62. Boynton Merrill, *Jeffersons Nephews: A Frontier Tragedy* (Princeton, 1976).

63. Mary Boykin Chesnut, *A Diary from Dixie,* ed. by B. A. Williams (Boston, 1949).

64. See Myers (ed.), *The Children of Pride;* Betsy Fleet and John Fuller (eds.) and Clement Eaton, Editorial Consultant, *Green Mount: A Virginia Plantation Family during the Civil War* (Lexington, 1962); Susan Dabney Smedes, *Memorials of a Southern Planter* (New York, 1890); Eaton, *The Mind of the Old South* (Baton Rouge, 1967), chap. 2, and *The Waning of the Old South Civilization,* chap. 2; and Genovese, *Roll, Jordan, Roll,* 64, for a few printed examples. The very extensive John Hartwell Cocke Papers in the Alderman Library, University of Virginia and the Alexander H. Stephens Papers in the Library of Congress are only two of the many planters' papers that reveal the paternal master.

CHAPTER 5: "THE YOUNG POLITICIAN"
(pp. 47–56)

1. B. W. Folsom, II, "The Politics of the Elites: Prominence and Party in Davidson County, Tennessee, 1835–1861," *Journal of Southern History,* XXXIX (August, 1973), 359–78.

2. J. T. McIntosh (ed.), *The Papers of Jefferson Davis* (Baton Rouge, 1974), II, 15.

3. *Ibid.,* II, 37.

4. Dallas C. Dickey, *Seargent S. Prentiss, Whig Orator of the Old South* (Baton Rouge, 1946).

5. McIntosh (ed.), *The Papers of Jefferson Davis,* II, 47.

6. J. P. Shenton, *Robert Walker, A Politician from Jackson to Lincoln* (New York, 1961).

7. McIntosh (ed.), *The Papers of Jefferson Davis,* II, 73.

8. *Ibid.,* II, 40.

9. C. C. Sellers, *James K. Polk* (Princeton, 1966), II.

10. McIntosh (ed.), *The Papers of Jefferson Davis,* II, 19.

11. *Ibid.,* II, 188.

12. *Ibid.,* II, 176, 216.

13. Varina Howell Davis, *Jefferson Davis, Ex–President of the Confederate States of America. A Memoir by His Wife* (New York, 1890), I, 198.

14. McIntosh (ed.), *The Papers of Jefferson Davis,* II, 166, 180.

15. *Ibid.,* II, 166, 180.

16. Varina Davis, *Memoir,* I, 199.

17. Reuben Davis, *Recollections of Mississippi and Mississippians* (Boston, 1889), 196.

18. McIntosh (ed.), *The Papers of Jefferson Davis,* II, 151–52.

19. *Ibid.,* II, 202.

20. *Ibid.,* II, 263–82.

21. *Ibid.,* II, 286–87.

22. *Ibid.,* II, 357–60.

23. Varina Davis, *Memoir,* I, 206.

24. Herbert Wender, *Southern Commercial Conventions, 1837–1859* (Baltimore, 1930); and Charles M. Wiltse, *John C. Calhoun, Secessionist, 1840–1850* (Indianapolis, 1951).

25. Varina Davis, *Memoir,* I, 210.

26. *Ibid.,* I, 215.

27. Dunbar Rowland (ed.), *Jefferson Davis, Constitutionalist, His Letters, Papers and Speeches* (Jackson, Miss., 1923), I, 5.

28. Hudson Strode (ed.), *Jefferson Davis: Private Letters, 1823–1889* (New York, 1966), 56.

29. McIntosh (ed.), *The Papers of Jefferson Davis,* II, 389–91.

30. Varina Davis, *Memoir,* I, 225.

31. Edwin A. Miles, " 'Fifty-four Forty or Fight'—an American Political Legend," *Mississippi Valley Historical Review,* XLIV (September, 1957), 291–309.

32. John H. Franklin, "The Southern Expansionists of 1846," *Journal of Southern History*, XXV (August, 1959), 323–38.

33. McIntosh (ed.), *The Papers of Jefferson Davis*, II, 438–63; *Congressional Globe*, 29th Cong., 1st Sess., p. 319.

34. Strode (ed.), *Jefferson Davis: Private Letters*, 37.

35. McIntosh (ed.), *The Papers of Jefferson Davis*, II, 675.

36. *Ibid.*, II, 627–28.

37. For an account of the Tennessee congressman, see R. W. Winston, *Andrew Johnson, Plebeian and Patriot* (New York, 1928); and E. L. McKitrick, *Andrew Johnson and Reconstruction* (Chicago, 1960).

38. McIntosh (ed.), *The Papers of Jefferson Davis*, II, 627–28.

39. Varina Davis, *Memoir*, I, 245.

CHAPTER 6: "FOR GLORY AND FOR COUNTRY"
          (pp. 57–66)

1. J. H. Schroeder, *Mr. Polk's War: American Opposition and Dissent, 1846–1848* (Madison, 1973).

2. Dunbar Rowland (ed.), *Jefferson Davis, Constitutionalist, His Letters, Papers and Speeches* (Jackson, Miss., 1923), I, 46.

3. J. T. McIntosh (ed.), *The Papers of Jefferson Davis* (Baton Rouge, 1974), II, 608–09.

4. *Ibid.*, II, 670.

5. Hudson Strode (ed.), *Jefferson Davis: Private Letters, 1823–1889* (New York, 1966), 38–39.

6. *Ibid.*, 40.

7. Rowland (ed.), *Jefferson Davis, Constitutionalist*, I, 52–58.

8. Strode (ed.), *Jefferson Davis: Private Letters*, 37.

9. Reuben Davis, *Recollections of Mississippi and Mississippians* (Boston, 1889), 220.

10. McIntosh (ed.), *The Papers of Jefferson Davis*, II, 700.

11. Strode (ed.), *Jefferson Davis: Private Letters*, 42.

12. Varina Howell Davis, *Jefferson Davis, Ex–President of the Confederate States of America. A Memoir by His Wife* (New York, 1890), I, 282–89.

13. H. M. Monroe, Jr., and J. T. McIntosh (eds.), *The Papers of Jefferson Davis* (Baton Rouge, 1971), I, lv.

14. Strode (ed.), *Jefferson Davis: Private Letters*, 43–44.

15. Robert S. Henry, *The Story of the Mexican War* (Indianapolis, 1950), 83.

16. Holman Hamilton, *Zachary Taylor, Soldier of the Republic* (Indianapolis, 1941), 230.

17. Charles L. Dufour, *The Mexican War, A Compact History, 1846–1848* (New York, 1968), 60; and for a recent study of the military campaigns, see K. J. Bauer, *The Mexican War, 1846–1848* (New York, 1974).

18. William Preston Johnston, *Life of Albert Sidney Johnston* (New York, 1878), 138; the Vicksburg *Sentinel,* November 24, 1846; Rowland (ed.), *Jefferson Davis, Constitutionalist,* I, 61–63.

19. General Cadmus Wilcox, *History of the Mexican War* (Washington, 1892), chap. 6. Wilcox was fresh out of West Point when he joined Taylor's army.

20. Strode (ed.), *Jefferson Davis: Private Letters,* 42–43.

21. Rowland (ed.), *Jefferson Davis, Constitutionalist,* I, 63–65.

22. Varina Davis, *Memoir,* I, 310.

23. Justin Smith, *The War with Mexico* (New York, 1919), 352–62.

24. For a study of the Mexican leader, see Wilfred H. Calcott, *Santa Anna* (Norman, Okla., 1936).

25. Dufour, *The Mexican War, A Compact History,* 166.

26. Rowland (ed.), *Jefferson Davis, Constitutionalist,* I, 149–56.

27. *Ibid.,* I, 78.

28. *Ibid.,* I, 147–48, and Varina Davis, *Memoir,* I, 328, 354.

29. Rowland (ed.), *Jefferson Davis, Constitutionalist,* I, 308–9; Robert McElroy, *Jefferson Davis, the Real and the Unreal* (New York, 1937), I, 125–27.

30. Rowland (ed.), *Jefferson Davis, Constitutionalist,* III, 341–42.

31. J. D. P. Fuller, *The Movement for the Acquisition of All-Mexico, 1846–1848* (Baltimore, 1936).

32. F. N. Garber, *The Gadsden Treaty* (Philadelphia, 1923).

33. Rowland (ed.), *Jefferson Davis, Constitutionalist,* II, 189.

CHAPTER 7: "THE CHAMPION OF SOUTHERN RIGHTS"
          (pp. 67–80)

1. Varina Howell Davis, *Jefferson Davis, Ex–President of the Confederate States of America. A Memoir by His Wife* (New York, 1890) I, 362.

2. Hudson Strode (ed.), *Jefferson Davis: Private Letters, 1823–1889* (New York, 1966), 60.

3. Dunbar Rowland (ed.), *Jefferson Davis, Constitutionalist, His Letters, Papers and Speeches* (Jackson, Miss., 1923), I, 379.

4. *Congressional Globe,* 30th Cong., 1st Sess., p. 871.

5. *Congressional Globe,* 30th Cong., 1st Sess., p. 927.

6. Clement Eaton, *A History of the Old South: The Emergence of a Reluctant Nation* (New York, 1975), 388.

7. *Congressional Globe,* 30th Cong., 1st Sess., Appendix, pp. 907–14.

8. *Ibid.,* Appendix. The whole speech is printed on pp. 907–14.

9. *Congressional Globe,* 31st Cong., 1st Sess., pp. 52–54.

10. *Ibid.,* 136.

11. Strode (ed.), *Jefferson Davis: Private Letters,* 58.

12. *Congressional Globe,* 30th Cong., 2nd Sess., p. 209.

13. Rowland (ed.), *Jefferson Davis, Constitutionalist,* I, 214.

14. Grady McWhiney, *The Southerners and Other Americans* (New York, 1973).

15. *Congressional Globe,* 30th Cong., 2nd Sess., pp. 670, 677.

16. Margaret L. Coit, *John C. Calhoun, American Portrait* (Cambridge, Mass., 1950), 476.

17. Leon Litwack, *North of Slavery: The Negro in the Free States, 1790–1860* (Chicago, 1961).

18. William E. Dodd, *Jefferson Davis* (Philadelphia, 1907), 123, quoting the Jackson *Mississippian* report of October 20, 1849.

19. Cleo Hearon, "Mississippi and the Compromise of 1850," *Mississippi Historical Society Publications* , XIV (1914), 63–68

20. *Congressional Globe,* 31st Cong., 1st Sess., pp. 942–43; see also Charles M. Wiltse, *John C. Calhoun, Secessionist, 1840–1850* (Indianapolis, 1951).

21. Rowland (ed.), *Jefferson Davis, Constitutionalist,* I, 323.

22. Clement Eaton, *Henry Clay and the Art of American Politics* (Boston, 1957), chap. 12.

23. Holman Hamilton, *Prologue to Conflict: The Crisis and Compromise of 1850* (Lexington, 1946), chap. 7.

24. Coit, *John C. Calhoun,* 48.

25. Jefferson Davis, *The Rise and Fall of the Confederate Government* (Memorial ed., Richmond, original ed., 1881), I, 13–14.

26. Rowland (ed.), *Jefferson Davis, Constitutionalist,* I, 251.

27. *Ibid.,* I, 382.

28. The speech is given in its entirety in the Appendix to the *Congressional Globe,* 31st Cong., 1st Sess., pp. 907–14.

29. William L. Barney, *The Road to Secession; A New Perspective on the Old South* (New York, 1972), chaps. 1, 2.

30. Rollin G. Osterweis, *The Myth of the Lost Cause, 1865–1900* (Hampden, Conn., 1973).

31. See Eaton, *Henry Clay and the Art of American Politics,* chap. 12; Hamilton, *Prologue to Conflict;* and R. W. Johannsen, *Stephen A. Douglas* (New York, 1973).

32. James Ford Rhodes, *History of the United States from the Compromise of 1850 to the End of the Roosevelt Administration* (New York, 1928), I, 185.

33. Albert Gallatin Brown to Jefferson Davis, May 1, 1852, Jefferson Hayes–Davis Papers, Transylvania University Library.

34. Rowland (ed.), *Jefferson Davis, Constitutionalist,* I, 602–03, IV, 79.

35. See Clement Eaton, "Southern Senators and the Right of Instruction," *Journal of Southern History,* XVIII (August, 1952).

36. Rowland (ed.), *Jefferson Davis, Constitutionalist,* I, 597–98.

37. *Ibid.,* II, 71–82.

38. Henry S. Foote, *Casket of Reminiscences* (New York, 1968).

39. See discussions in Avery Craven, *The Growth of Southern Nationalism*

1848–1861 (Baton Rouge, 1953) chap. 1; and Eaton, *History of the Old South,* 472–75.

40. Edward Mayes, *Lucius Q. C. Lamar: His Life, Times and Speeches, 1825–1893* (Nashville, 1896), 51–54.

41. Strode (ed.), *Jefferson Davis: Private Letters,* 64.

CHAPTER 8: "THE POWER BEHIND THE THRONE"
        (pp. 81–88)

1. Dunbar Rowland (ed.), *Jefferson Davis, Constitutionalist, His Letters, Papers and Speeches* (Jackson, Miss., 1923), II, 335.

2. Hudson Strode (ed.), *Jefferson Davis: Private Letters, 1823–1889* (New York, 1966), 67.

3. Rowland (ed.), *Jefferson Davis, Constitutionalist,* II, 177–78, 179.

4. See Roy F. Nichols, *Franklin Pierce* (Philadelphia, 1931).

5. Strode (ed.), *Jefferson Davis: Private Letters,* 97.

6. Varina Howell Davis, *Jefferson Davis, Ex–President of the Confederate States of America. A Memoir by His Wife* (New York, 1890), I, 535.

7. John W. Daniel (ed.), *Life and Reminiscences of Jefferson Davis by Distinguished Men of His Time* (Baltimore, 1890), 32.

8. Virginia Clay–Clopton, *A Belle of the Fifties,* ed. by Ada Stirling (New York, 1905), 68.

9. Rowland (ed.), *Jefferson Davis, Constitutionalist,* II, 393.

10. *Ibid.,* III, 28, 29.

11. Autobiography in H. M. Monroe, Jr., and J. T. McIntosh, (eds.), *The Papers of Jefferson Davis* (Baton Rouge, 1971), I, lx.

12. Rowland (ed.), *Jefferson Davis, Constitutionalist,* II, 288–90, 461–62, 464–66; see also W. P. Webb, *The Great Plains* (Boston, 1931), 199–200.

13. Report of secretary of war to President Franklin Pierce, December 1, 1853; Rowland (ed.), Jefferson Davis, *Constitutionalist,* II, 310–17.

14. Report of secretary of war to President Franklin Pierce, December 3, 1855.

15. Rowland (ed.), *Jefferson Davis, Constitutionalist,* III, 565. A report was also submitted to Congress.

16. *Ibid.,* III, 116–18.

17. *Ibid.,* II, 350–51, 368–69.

18. *Ibid.,* III, 511–24, 573–82, 590–603.

19. James B. Ranck, *Albert Gallatin Brown; Radical Southern Nationalist* (New York, 1937), 122.

20. Culver Smith, *The Press, Politics and Patronage* (Athens, 1976), chap. XVI.

21. Jefferson Davis, *The Rise and Fall of the Confederate Government* (memorial ed., Richmond, original ed., 1881), I, 25.

22. James Ford Rhodes, *History of the United States from the Compromise of 1850 to the End of the Roosevelt Administration* (New York, 1928), 430.

CHAPTER 9: "THE ARISTOCRATIC TYPE OF SOUTHERN POLITICIAN"
(pp. 89–98)

1. Dunbar Rowland (ed.), *Jefferson Davis, Constitutionalist, His Letters, Papers and Speeches* (Jackson, Miss., 1923), II, 584–85.

2. *Ibid.,* IV, 94.

3. Charles S. Sydnor, *Gentlemen Freeholders: Political Practices in Washington's Virginia* (Chapel Hill, 1952), 53–54.

4. J. F. H. Claiborne, *Mississippi as a Province, Territory, and State* (Jackson, Miss., 1880), 425–26.

5. Virginia Clay-Clopton, *A Belle of the Fifties,* ed. by Ada Stirling (New York, 1905), 22.

6. W. H. Russell, *My Diary, North and South* (Boston, 1863), 89.

7. See R. W. Dubay, *John Jones Pettus, Mississippi Fire-Eater: His Life and His Times, 1813–1867* (Jackson, Miss., 1975).

8. James Phelan to Jefferson Davis, July 18, 1853, Jefferson Hayes–Davis Papers, Transylvania University Library.

9. James Phelan to Jefferson Davis, July 19, 1853, *ibid.*

10. Rowland (ed.), *Jefferson Davis, Constitutionalist,* II, 337.

11. James B. Ranck, *Albert Gallatin Brown; Radical Southern Nationalist* (New York, 1937), 136.

12. J. J. Pettus to Jefferson Davis, June 6, 1857, Jefferson Hayes–Davis Papers, Transylvania University Library. Davis's recollection is different. In *The Rise and Fall of the Confederate Government* (memorial ed., Richmond, original ed., 1881) 328, he writes within two weeks after his repudiation at the polls in 1851 that the State Rights party regained its majority position in the state. If this is true, it represented a remarkable reversal of public sentiment in such a short time.

13. Rowland (ed.), *Jefferson Davis, Constitutionalist,* III, 172–73.

14. Ranck, *Albert Gallatin Brown.*

15. Reuben Davis, *Recollections of Mississippi and Mississippians* (Boston, 1889), 351–52; William E. Dodd, *Jefferson Davis* (Philadelphia, 1907), 152–53.

16. R. A. Wooster, *The People in Power: Courthouse and Statehouse in the Lower South, 1850–1860* (Knoxville, 1969), 142–43.

17. Clement Eaton, *The Mind of the Old South* (Baton Rouge, 1967), 287.

18. J. T. McIntosh (ed.), *The Papers of Jefferson Davis* (Baton Rouge, 1974), II, 574.

19. Rowland (ed.), *Jefferson Davis, Constitutionalist,* III, 339–60.

20. A. J. L. Fremantle, *Three Months in the Southern States* (New York, 1864), 68–69.

21. John William DeForest, *A Union Officer in the Reconstruction* (New Haven, 1948).

22. Thomas B. Alexander, *Sectional Stress and Party Strength* (Nashville, 1967).

23. See Herbert Wender, *Southern Commercial Conventions, 1837–1859* (Baltimore, 1930).

24. Rowland (ed.), *Jefferson Davis, Constitutionalist,* III, 313.

25. See Charles G. Sellers, *The Southerner as American* (Chapel Hill, 1960), and R. McColley, *Slavery and Jeffersonian Virginia* (Urbana, Ill., 1973).

26. David Donald, "The Pro-Slavery Argument Reconsidered," *Journal of Southern History,* XXXVII (February, 1971).

27. John Berkeley Grimball Diary, December 17, 1860, Southern Collection, University of North Carolina Library.

28. Donald G. Matthews, "Charles Colcock Jones and the Southern Evangelical Crusade to Form a Biracial Community," *Journal of Southern History,* XLI (August, 1975), 202–205.

29. Rowland (ed.), *Jefferson Davis, Constitutionalist,* IV, 61–68.

30. P. S. Klein, *President James Buchanan, A Biography* (University Park, Pa., 1962), 346–47.

31. Rowland (ed.), *Jefferson Davis, Constitutionalist,* III, 517, 521.

32. *Ibid.,* IV, 207.

33. *Ibid.,* IV, 229.

34. *Congressional Globe,* 31st Cong., 1st Sess., pp. 890, 2059.

35. *Ibid.,* 227.

36. David Potter, *The South and the Concurrent Majority* (Baton Rouge, 1972).

CHAPTER 10: "THE SOUTHERN IMPERIALIST"
          (pp. 99–107)

1. J. G. Baldwin, *The Flush Times of Alabama and Mississippi* (New York, 1853).

2. William E. Dodd, *Jefferson Davis* (Philadelphia, 1907), 161.

3. Dunbar Rowland (ed.), *Jefferson Davis, Constitutionalist, His Letters, Papers and Speeches* (Jackson, Miss., 1923), III, 389.

4. *Ibid.,* III, 392–93.

5. *Ibid.,* III, 513.

6. *Ibid.,* III, 410–13.

7. *Ibid.,* IV, 565. Speech in Senate January 5, 1861.

8. See A. A. Ettinger, *The Mission to Spain of Pierre Soulé, 1853–1855* (London, 1932).

9. H. S. Commager, *Select Documents on American History* (New York, 1963), I, 12–19, 333–34.

10. Clement Eaton, "Henry A. Wise and the Virginia Fire Eaters of 1856," *Mississippi Valley Historical Review* (March, 1935).

11. Rowland (ed.), *Jefferson Davis, Constitutionalist,* III, 172–73.

12. *Ibid.,* III, 271–73.

13. *Ibid.,* III, 274–81.

14. There is a letter in the Bowdoin College Library, dated July 3, 1889, in which Davis expressed gratitude that his name was still enrolled among those who had received honorary degrees from Bowdoin College. Photostat sent to the author by Professor Emeritus Ernst Helmreich, my roommate at Harvard University.

15. Rowland (ed.), *Jefferson Davis, Constitutionalist,* III, 315–31.

16. *Ibid.,* III, 332–38.

17. *Ibid.,* III, 339–60.

18. Rowland (ed.), *Jefferson Davis, Constitutionalist,* IV, 84.

19. *Congressional Globe,* 35th Cong., 2nd Sess., p. 1354.

20. Rowland (ed.), *Jefferson Davis, Constitutionalist,* IV, 84.

21. *Congressional Globe,* 35th Cong., 2nd Sess., 542–43.

22. Robert W. Johannsen, *Stephen A. Douglas* (New York, 1973), 215–17, 328–32.

23. Rowland (ed.), *Jefferson Davis, Constitutionalist,* III, 313.

24. Frederick Merk, *Manifest Destiny and Mission in American History: A Reinterpretation* (New York, 1963); and Albert K. Weinberg, *Manifest Destiny: A Study of Nationalist Expansion in American History* (Baltimore, 1935).

25. See Robert E. May, *The Southern Dream of a Caribbean Empire, 1854–1861* (Baton Rouge, 1973), 194.

26. Norman Graebner (ed.), *Manifest Destiny* (Indianapolis, 1968), 220–53; and C. M. Wiltse, *John C. Calhoun, Secessionist, 1840–1850* (Indianapolis, 1951), chap. 19.

27. J. G. Nicolay and J. Hay (eds.), *Complete Works of Abraham Lincoln* (Lincoln Memorial University, 1894), VI, 77–78; and Eaton, *A History of the Old South: The Emergence of a Reluctant Nation* (New York, 1975), 497–98.

CHAPTER 11: "THE MOMENTOUS SPLIT OF THE DEMOCRATS"
(pp. 108–117)

1. Jefferson Davis to "Joe," September 22, 1855, Duke University Library.

2. W. B. Hesseltine (ed.), *Three Against Lincoln: Murat Halstead Reports the Caucuses of 1860* (Baton Rouge, 1960), 119–21.

3. *Ibid.,* 185.

4. Barton, H. Wise, *The Life of Henry A. Wise of Virginia, 1846–1876* (New York, 1899), 236–39, 264–65; and Clement Eaton, "Henry A. Wise, a Liberal of the Old South," *Journal of Southern History,* VII (November, 1941).

5. See R. W. Johannsen, *Stephen A. Douglas* (New York, 1973); and Gerald Capers, Jr., *Stephen Douglas, Defender of the Union* (Boston, 1959).

6. Dunbar Rowland (ed.), *Jefferson Davis, Constitutionalist, His Letters, Papers and Speeches* (Jackson, Miss., 1923), IV, 496.

7. James Ford Rhodes, *History of the United States from the Compromise of 1850 to the End of the Roosevelt Administration* (New York, 1928), II, 84–85.

8. R. W. Johannsen (ed.), *The Lincoln-Douglas Debates of 1858* (New York, 1965), 88.

9. P. S. Klein, *President James Buchanan, A Biography* (University Park, Pa., 1962), chap. 23.

10. Roy F. Nichols, *The Disruption of American Democracy* (New York, 1948), 173–74.

11. U. B. Phillips (ed.), "The Correspondence of Robert Toombs, Alexander H. Stephens, and Howell Cobb," *Annual Report of American Historical Association for the Year 1911* (Washington, 1913), II, 461.

12. D. L. Dumond (ed.), *Southern Editorials on Secession* (New York, 1931), 40–48.

13. *Ibid.,* 48–50.

14. C. W. Ramsdell, "The Natural Limits of Slavery Expansion," *Mississippi Valley Historical Review,* XVI (1929), 151.

15. Phillips (ed.), "Correspondence of Robert Toombs, Alexander H. Stephens, and Howell Cobb," II, 454.

16. Varina Howell Davis, *Jefferson Davis, Ex–President of the Confederate States of America. A Memoir by His Wife* (New York, 1890), I, 58.

17. Rhodes, *History of the United States,* II, 380.

18. S. B. Oates, *To Purge the Land with Blood: A Biography of John Brown* (New York, 1970), 360–61.

19. *U.S. Senate Committee Reports,* 1859–60, II, Majority report 1–19; minority report 21–25.

20. C. V. Woodward, *The Burden of Southern History* (Baton Rouge, 1960), chap. 3, "John Brown's Private War."

21. *Congressional Globe,* 36th Cong., 1st Sess., p. 935.

22. James B. Ranck, *Albert Gallatin Brown, Radical Southern Nationalist* (New York, 1937), 186–87.

23. Phillips (ed.), "Correspondence of Robert Toombs, Alexander H. Stephens, and Howell Cobb," II, 461.

24. Rowland (ed.), *Jefferson Davis, Constitutionalist,* IV, 293.

25. Jefferson Davis, *The Rise and Fall of the Confederate Government* (memorial ed., Richmond, original ed., 1881), I, 38; Phillips (ed.), "Correspondence of Robert Toombs, Alexander H. Stephens, and Howell Cobb," II, 481.

26. R. W. Johannsen, "Stephen A. Douglas and the South," *Journal of Southern History,* XXXIII (February, 1967), 26–50.

27. Rowland (ed.), *Jefferson Davis, Constitutionalist,* IV, 339.

28. *Ibid.,* IV, 94, 185; William E. Dodd, *Jefferson Davis* (Philadelphia, 1907), 173 n. 1, quoting from the Andrew Johnson Papers.

29. For excellent accounts of the breakup of the Democratic convention at Charleston, see Nichols, *Disruption of American Democracy,* chap. 15; Ollinger Crenshaw, *The Slaves States in the Presidential Election of 1860* (Baltimore, 1945); and David Potter, *The Impending Crisis, 1848–1861* (New York, 1976), chap 16.

30. Phillips (ed.), "Correspondence of Robert Toombs, Alexander H. Stephens, and Howell Cobb," II, 478–79.

31. Edward Mayes, *Lucius Q. C. Lamar: His Life, Times, and Speeches, 1825–1893*(Nashville, 1896), 83; see also William L. Barney, *The Secessionist Impulse: Alabama and Mississippi in 1860* (Princeton, 1974), 106.

32. Jefferson Davis, *Rise and Fall of the Confederate Government,* I, 45; for Douglas's Southern campaign, see Johannsen, *Stephen A. Douglas,* 786–91.

CHAPTER 12: "BRAKING SECESSION'S MOMENTUM"
        (pp. 118–123)

1. D. L. Dumond, *The Secession Movement, 1860–1861* (New York, 1931), 112, and Appendix D.

2. Dunbar Rowland (ed.), *Jefferson Davis, Constitutionalist, His Letters, Papers and Speeches* (Jackson, Miss., 1923), IV, 87.

3. *Ibid.,* IV, 541–42.

4. D. E. Reynolds, *Editors Make War: Southern Newspapers in the Secession Crisis* (Nashville, 1970).

5. P. L. Rainwater, *Mississippi, Storm Center of Secession, 1856–1861* (Baton Rouge, 1938), 162–65, 172.

6. U. B. Phillips, *The Life of Robert Toombs* (New York, 1931), 205.

7. Rainwater, *Mississippi, Storm Center of Secession,* 152–53.

8. Edward Mayes, *Lucius Q. C. Lamar: His Life, Times, and Speeches, 1825–1893* (Nashville, 1896), quoting Lamar's account of the meeting, p. 87.

9. Reuben Davis, *Recollections of Mississippi and Mississippians* (Boston, 1889), 391–92.

10. "Personal Reminiscences of Jefferson Davis," MS in Confederate Memorial Hall, New Orleans. Quoted in Rainwater, *Mississippi, Storm Center of Secession,* 168–69.

11. Jefferson Davis, *The Rise and Fall of the Confederate Government* (memorial ed., Richmond, original ed., 1881), I, 171.

12. *Ibid.,* I, 51.

13. H. M. Monroe, Jr., and J. T. McIntosh (eds.), *The Papers of Jefferson Davis* (Baton Rouge, 1971), I, lxi.

14. A. D. Kirwan, *John J. Crittenden: The Struggle for the Union* (Lexington, 1967), chaps. 18, 19; G. G. Van Deusen, *Thurlow Weed: Wizard of the Lobby* (Boston, 1947), and *William Henry Seward* (New York, 1967); and B. P. Thomas, *Abraham Lincoln, A Biography* (New York, 1952).

15. Rowland (ed.), *Jefferson Davis, Constitutionalist,* IV, 561, 564–65.

16. Laura A. White, *Robert Barnwell Rhett: Father of Secession* (New York, 1931), 194.

17. Varina Howell Davis, *Jefferson Davis, Ex–President of the Confederate States of America. A Memoir by His Wife* (New York, 1890), I, 696–98.

18. *Congressional Globe,* 36th Cong., 2nd Sess., Part I, p. 487.

19. David Potter, *The Impending Crisis, 1848–1861* (New York, 1976), 496; Clement Eaton, *A History of the Old South: The Emergence of a Reluctant Nation* (New York, 1975), 507–10.

20. Ralph A. Wooster, *The Secession Conventions of the South* (Princeton, 1962).

21. Lawrence Keitt to "Sue," February 19, 1861, Lawrence Keitt Papers, Duke University Library.

22. Rowland (ed.), *Jefferson Davis, Constitutionalist,* II, 564.

CHAPTER 13: "ELECTED PRESIDENT OF THE CONFEDERATE STATES"
        (pp. 124–134)

1. Diary of Thomas Bragg, January 12, 1861, Southern Collection, University of North Carolina Library.

2. See Clement Eaton, "The Role of Honor in Southern Society," *Southern Humanities Review,* Bicentennial Issue, 47–58.

3. Charles R. Lee, Jr., *The Confederate Constitutions* (Chapel Hill, 1963), chap. 2.

4. E. M. Coulter, *The Confederate States of America, 1861–1865* (Baton Rouge, 1950).

5. John H. Reagan, *Memoirs with Special Reference to Secession and the Civil War,* ed. by Walter F. McCaleb (New York, 1906), 122–23.

6. Henry Cleveland, *Alexander Stephens in Public and Private* (Philadelphia, 1866), 721–23.

7. Diary of Thomas Bragg, January 1, 1862, Southern Collection, University of North Carolina Library.

8. See James Z. Rabun, "Alexander H. Stephens and Jefferson Davis," *American Historical Review,* LVIII (1953), 290–321, and Rudolph von Abele, *Alexander H. Stephens, a Biography* (New York, 1946).

9. Varina Howell Davis, *Jefferson Davis, Ex–President of the Confederate States of America. A Memoir by His Wife* (New York, 1890), I, 12.

10. Dunbar Rowland (ed.), *Jefferson Davis, Constitutionalist, His Letters, Papers and Speeches* (Jackson, Miss., 1923), V, 49–53.

11. Clement Eaton, *A History of the Southern Confederacy* (New York, 1954), 60–61.

12. Rembert W. Patrick, *Jefferson Davis and His Cabinet* (Baton Rouge, 1944), chap. 3.

13. Mary Boykin Chesnut, *A Diary from Dixie,* ed. by B. A. Williams (Boston, 1949), 230.

14. J. B. Jones, *A Rebel War Clerk's Diary at the Confederate States Capital* (New York, 1953), I, 38–39.

15. Frank E. Vandiver (ed.), *The Civil War Diary of General Josiah Gorgas* (University, Ala., 1947), 172.

16. Jones, *Rebel War Clerk's Diary,* I, 54.

17. Burton J. Hendrick, *Statesmen of the Lost Cause: Jefferson Davis and His Cabinet* (Boston, 1939), 193.

18. Henry D. Capers, *Life and Times of C. G. Memminger* (Richmond, 1893), 323–25.

19. William H. Russell, *My Diary North and South* (Boston, 1863), 174.

20. Patrick, *Jefferson Davis and His Cabinet,* chap. 4.

21. See Robert D. Meade, *Judah P. Benjamin, Confederate Statesman* (New York, 1943).

22. Reagan, *Memoirs,* 146; For a biography of Reagan, see Ben Proctor, *Not Without Honor; the Life of John H. Reagan* (Austin, 1962).

23. Russell, *My Diary North and South,* 173.

24. Rowland (ed.), *Jefferson Davis, Constitutionalist,* V, 216–17.

25. Stephen R. Mallory, Diary and Reminiscences, Southern Collection, University of North Carolina Library.

26. Diary of Thomas Bragg, March 17, 1862, Southern Collection, University of North Carolina Library.

27. Edward Younger (ed.), *Inside the Confederate Government: The Diary of Robert Garlick Hill Kean* (New York, 1957), 72.

28. *Ibid.,* 87, 101.

29. Vandiver (ed.), *Civil War Diary of Gorgas,* 59.

30. Mallory, Diary and Reminiscences, I, 175, Southern Collection, University of North Carolina Library.

31. P. O. Van Riper and H. N. Scheiber, "The Confederate Civil Service," *Journal of Southern History, XXV* (November, 1959), 448–70.

CHAPTER 14: "THE FIRST GREAT DECISIONS"
                (pp. 135–145)

1. See W. A. Swanberg, *First Blood: the Story of Fort Sumter* (New York, 1957).

2. P. W. Klein, *President James Buchanan, A Biography* (University Park, Pa., 1962), 379.

3. Clement Eaton, "The Confederacy," in J. A. Garraty (ed.), *Interpreting American History: Conversations with Historians* (New York, 1970), I, 319–20.

4. An admirable study of the Fort Sumter crisis is presented in David H. Potter, *Lincoln and His Party in the Secession Crisis* (New Haven, 1942).

5. See Charles W. Ramsdell, "Lincoln and Fort Sumter," *Journal of Southern History,* III (August, 1937), 259–88; Kenneth Stampp, "Lincoln and the Strategy of Defense in the Crisis of 1861," *ibid.,* XI (August, 1945), 297–323; Ludwell H. Johnson, "Fort Sumter and Confederate Diplomacy," *ibid.,*

XXVI (November, 1960), 441–77, and R. N. Current, *Lincoln and the First Shot* (Philadelphia, 1963).

6. W. Y. Thompson, *Robert Toombs of Georgia* (Baton Rouge, 1966), 168.

7. J. G. Randall and David Donald, *The Civil War and Reconstruction* (Boston, 1961), 176.

8. Robert S. Henry, *The Story of the Confederacy* (New York, 1936), chap. 4.

9. Joseph H. Parks, *General Edmund Kirby Smith, C.S.A.* (Baton Rouge, 1954), 131–36.

10. Bell I. Wiley (ed.), *The Rise and Fall of the Confederate Government by Jefferson Davis* (New York, 1958), I, 346–47.

11. *Ibid.,* I, 354.

12. T. Harry Williams, *Napoleon in Gray, P. G. T. Beauregard* (Baton Rouge, 1954), 96.

13. Dunbar Rowland (ed.), *Jefferson Davis, Constitutionalist, His Letters, Papers and Speeches* (Jackson, Miss., 1923), V, 121.

14. Williams, *P. G. T. Beauregard,* 97.

15. Mary Boykin Chesnut, *A Diary from Dixie,* ed. by B. A. Williams (Boston, 1949), 100.

16. Russell F. Weigley, "The Civil War," unpublished MS, 86–88.

17. Rowland (ed.), *Jefferson Davis, Constitutionalist,* V, 156.

18. *Ibid.,* V. 132.

19. Mallory, Diary and Reminiscences, II, 207, Southern Collection, University of North Carolina Library.

20. William H. Russell, *My Diary North and South* (Boston, 1863), 174.

21. John Hope Franklin, *The Martial South, 1800–1861* (Boston, 1964); Marcus Cunliffe, *Soldiers and Civilians, the Martial Spirit in America, 1775–1865* (Boston, 1969; New York, 1973).

22. Daniel R. Hundley, Diary, Southern Collection, University of North Carolina Library.

23. John H. Reagan, *Memoirs, with Special Reference to Secession and the Civil War,* ed. by Walter F. Caleb (New York, 1906).

24. James M. Matthews (ed.), *Public Laws of the Confederate States of America* (Richmond, 1862–64); A. B. Moore, *Conscription and Conflict in the Confederacy* (New York, 1924); and Clement Eaton, *A History of the Southern Confederacy* (New York, 1954), 90–91.

25. Andrew Magrath to the governors of Georgia and North Carolina, January 9, 1865, carried by William H. Trescot, McGrath Papers, Southern Collection, University of North Carolina Library.

26. William Gilmore Simms to Governor Magrath, Mary C. Oliphant (ed.), *The Letters of William Gilmore Simms* (Columbia, S.C., 1953–54), IV, 475–76.

27. Frank E. Vandiver (ed.), *The Civil War Diary of General Josiah Gorgas* (University, Ala., 1947), 77.

28. Rowland (ed.), *Jefferson Davis,* Constitutionalist, V, 109–10.

29. Mallory, Diary and Reminiscences, I, 249, Southern Collection, University of North Carolina Library.

30. Rowland (ed.), *Jefferson Davis Constitutionalist,* V, 409.

31. Reagan, *Memoirs,* 164.

32. William A. Graham to David A. Swain, November 6, 1864, William A. Graham Papers, North Carolina State Department of Archives.

33. Vandiver (ed.), *Civil War Diary of Gorgas,* 164.

34. Weigley, "The Civil War," unpublished MS, 137.

CHAPTER 15: "EARLY DISASTER"
(pp. 146–154)

1. J. Cutler Andrews, *The South Reports the Civil War* (Princeton, 1970), 96.

2. Stanley F. Horn, *The Army of Tennessee* (Indianapolis, 1941), and Thomas L. Connelly, *Army of the Heartland: The Army of Tennessee, 1861–1862* (Baton Rouge, 1967).

3. Stephen R. Mallory, Diary and Reminiscences, August 11, 1862, Southern Collection, University of North Carolina Library.

4. See Charles P. Roland, *Albert Sidney Johnston, Soldier of Three Republics* (Austin, 1964), chap. 16.

5. Dunbar Rowland (ed.), *Jefferson Davis, Constitutionalist, His Letters, Papers and Speeches* (Jackson, Miss., 1923), V, 198–203.

6. Diary of Thomas Bragg, II, 169–70, Southern Collection, University of North Carolina Library.

7. Walter Lord (ed.), *Fremantle Diary, Being the Journal of Lieutenant Colonel James Arthur Lyon Fremantle, Coldstream Guards, of his Three Months in the Southern States* (Boston, 1954), 221.

8. Rowland (ed.), *Jefferson Davis, Constitutionalist,* V, 225.

9. *Ibid.,* V, 203.

10. Jefferson Davis, *The Rise and Fall of the Confederate Government* (memorial ed., Richmond, original ed., 1881), II, 31.

11. *Ibid.,* II, 27, 28.

12. Rowland (ed.), *Jefferson Davis, Constitutionalist,* V, 216.

13. Horn, *Army of Tennessee;* Connelly, *Army of the Heartland;* and Kenneth P. Williams, *Lincoln Finds a General: A Military Study of the Civil War* (New York, 1956), III.

14. "Albert Sidney Johnston at Shiloh," by W. P. Johnston, 540–68, and "The Campaign of Shiloh" by P. G. T. Beauregard, 569–93, in R. U. Johnson and C. C. Buel (eds.), *Battles and Leaders of the Civil War* (New York, 1887), I.

15. William J. Hardee to Mrs. Felicia L. Shover, April 9, 1862, W. J. Hardee Papers, Library of Congress.

16. Roland, *Albert Sidney Johnston,* chap. 18.

17. Robert S. Henry, *The Story of the Confederacy* (New York, 1936), 129.

18. Davis, *Rise and Fall of the Confederate Government,* II, 188.

19. Captain Beverley Kennon, "Fighting Farragut Below New Orleans," in Johnson and Buel (eds.), *Battles and Leaders,* II, 80.

20. David D. Porter, "The Opening of the Lower Mississippi," in *ibid.,* II, 39.

21. J. T. Durkin, *Stephen R. Mallory, Confederate Navy Chief* (Chapel Hill, 1954), chap. 10.

22. Diary of Thomas Bragg, January 6, 1862, Southern Collection, University of North Carolina Library.

23. Durkin, *Stephen R. Mallory,* 208.

24. Joseph Davis to Jefferson, June 18, 1862, Jefferson Hayes–Davis Papers, Transylvania University Library.

25. Mary Boykin Chesnut, *A Diary from Dixie,* ed. by B. A. Williams (Boston, 1949), 215.

Chapter 16: "The Capital Saved and the Two-Pronged Offensive" (pp. 155–163)

1. For a scholarly portrait of McClellan, see T. Harry Williams, *Lincoln and His Generals* (New York, 1952), 63–135.

2. William H. Russell, *My Diary North and South* (Boston, 1863), 576.

3. Varina Howell Davis, *Jefferson Davis, Ex–President of the Confederate States of America. A Memoir by His Wife* (New York, 1890), II, 273.

4. William Preston Johnston to "Rosa," June 2, 1862, William Preston Johnston Papers, Tulane University Library.

5. Douglas Southall Freeman, *R. E. Lee, A Biography* (New York, 1935), II, 22.

6. Mary Boykin Chesnut, *A Diary from Dixie,* ed. by B. A. Williams (Boston, 1949), 175.

7. G. E. Govan and J. W. Livingood, A *Different Valor: The Story of Joseph E. Johnston C.S.A.* (Indianapolis, 1956).

8. Dunbar Rowland (ed.), *Jefferson Davis, Constitutionalist, His Letters, Papers and Speeches* (Jackson, Miss., 1923), V, 222, 240.

9. Diary of Thomas Bragg, January 31, 1862, Southern Collection, University of North Carolina Library.

10. Frank E. Vandiver, *Mighty Stonewall* (New York, 1957).

11. Freeman, *R. E. Lee,* II, 62.

12. *Ibid.,* II, 409.

13. *Ibid.,* II, 357–58.

14. J. Cutler Andrews, *The South Reports the Civil War* (Princeton, 1970), 207–16.

15. Walter Lord (ed.), *Fremantle Diary, Being the Journal of Lieutenant Colonel James Arthur Lyon Fremantle, Coldstream Guards, of his Three Months in the Southern States* (Boston, 1954), 145.

16. John Buie to his father, John Buie Papers, Duke University Library.

17. See Joseph H. Parks, *General Edmund Kirby Smith, C.S.A.* (Baton Rouge, 1954), chap. 8.

18. Thomas L. Connelly, *Army of the Heartland: The Army of Tennessee, 1861–1862* (Baton Rouge, 1967), 221.

19. Rowland (ed.), *Jefferson Davis, Constitutionalist.*

20. R. U. Johnson and C. C. Buel (eds.), *Battles and Leaders of the Civil War* (New York, 1887), III, 13.

21. See Robert E. Shalhope, *Sterling Price, Portrait of a Southerner* (Columbia, Missouri, 1971), 221–23.

CHAPTER 17: "THE PRESIDENT'S ROLE IN DIPLOMACY"
(pp. 164–173)

1. See R. D. Meade, *Judah P. Benjamin, Confederate Statesman* (New York, 1943), Pierce Butler, *Judah P. Benjamin* (Philadelphia, 1907), Gamaliel Bradford, *Confederate Portraits* (Boston, 1914), chap. 5, and Burton J. Hendrick, *Statesmen of the Lost Cause* (Boston, 1939), chap. 6.

2. Edward Younger (ed.), *Inside the Confederate Government: The Diary of Robert Garlick Hill Kean* (New York, 1957), 55, 93.

3. Rembert W. Patrick, *Jefferson Davis and His Cabinet* (Baton Rouge, 1944), 157.

4. *Congressional Globe,* June 9, 1859, p. 2823.

5. For Confederate diplomacy see J. M. Callahan, *The Diplomatic History of the Southern Confederacy* (Baltimore, 1901); E. D. Adams, *Great Britain and the American Civil War* (2 vols., London, 1925), and D. Jordan and E. J. Pratt, *Europe and the American Civil War* (Boston, 1931).

6. R. U. Johnson and C. C. Buel (eds.), *Battles and Leaders of the Civil War* (New York, 1887), I, 109–10.

7. Yancey wrote with scorn of the British foreign minister "truckling" to Adams. Yancey to R. M. T. Hunter, December 31, 1861, Pickett Papers (Confederate State Department A: Great Britain), Library of Congress.

8. Frank L. Owsley, *King Cotton Diplomacy* (revised, Chicago, 1959), 16.

9. Varina Howell Davis, *Jefferson Davis, Ex–President of the Confederate States of America. A Memoir by His Wife* (New York, 1890), II, 160.

10. John H. Reagan, *Memoirs, with Special Reference to Secession and the Civil War,* ed. by Walter F. McCaleb (New York, 1906), 115.

11. William H. Russell, *My Diary North and South* (Boston, 1863), 43, 51–52, 64.

12. Owsley, *King Cotton Diplomacy,* 18–19.

13. Younger (ed.), *Diary of Kean,* 32.

14. Mary Boykin Chesnut, *A Diary from Dixie,* ed. by B. A. Williams (Boston, 1949), 123–24, 131.

15. Burton J. Hendrick, *Statesmen of the Lost Cause: Jefferson Davis and His Cabinet* (Boston, 1939), 138.

16. Allan Nevins, *The War for the Union* (New York, 1959), I, 388.

17. James A. Rawley, *Turning Points of the Civil War* (Lincoln, Neb.), chap. 3.

18. Yancey, Rost, and Mann to Earl Russell, November 29, 1861, Pickett Papers (Confederate State Department A: Great Britain), Library of Congress; also see J. D. Richardson (ed.), *A Compilation of the Messages and Papers of the Confederacy* (Nashville, 1905), II, 128.

19. See Henry Hotze to R. M. T. Hunter, February 23, April 24, 1862, Letterbook of Henry Hotze, October 1, 1862 to June 16, 1865, Library of Congress,

20. Yancey and Rost reported, October 5, 1861, that distress in France owing to the blockade of the Confederate states was greater than in England; cotton mills were working little more than half time. Pickett Papers (Confederate State Department A: Great Britain), Library of Congress. Also see L. M. Case (ed.), *French Opinion on the United States and Mexico, 1860–1867* (New York, 1936), and Case and W. F. Spencer, *The United States and France: Civil War Diplomacy* (Philadelphia, 1970).

21. See Adams, *Great Britain and the American Civil War*, II, 54–55.

22. *Hansard's Parliamentary Debates,* 3rd Ser. CLXXI, 1771–80.

23. Patrick, *Jefferson Davis and His Cabinet,* 185.

24. M. L. Bonham, *The British Consuls in the Confederacy* (New York, 1911).

25. Dunbar Rowland (ed.), *Jefferson Davis, Constitutionalist, His Letters, Papers and Speeches* (Jackson, Miss., 1923), VI, 93–129.

26. See J. D. Bulloch, *The Secret Service of the Confederate States in Europe* (2 vols., New York, 1883).

27. Hudson Strode, *Jefferson Davis, Tragic Hero* (New York, 1964), III, 26–27.

28. Jefferson Davis, *The Rise and Fall of the Confederate Government* (memorial ed., Richmond, original ed., 1881), II, chap. 38.

CHAPTER 18: "THE FATEFUL YEAR OF 1863"
         (pp. 174–186)

1. Bell I. Wiley, Review of Clement Eaton, *A History of the Southern Confederacy, New York Times Book Review,* July 4, 1954.

2. T. Harry Williams, "The Civil War" in J. A. Garraty (ed.), *Interpreting American History: Conversations with Historians* (New York, 1970), I, 297.

3. John H. Reagan, *Memoirs, with Special Reference to Secession and the Civil War,* ed. by Walter McCaleb (New York, 1906), 150–57.

4. Douglas Southall Freeman, *R. E. Lee, A Biography* (New York, 1935), III, 19.

5. See D. S. Freeman, *Lee's Lieutenants: A Study in Command* (3 vols., New York, 1944).

6. J. B. Clifton Diary, June 20, 1863–August 12, 1864, Southern Collection, University of North Carolina Library.

7. David L. Swain to J. J. Pettigrew, January 15, 1861, Pettigrew Papers, Library of Congress.

8. Clement Eaton, *The Freedom-of-Thought Struggle in the Old South* (New York, 1964), 54–56.

9. Mrs. L. Porcher to Pettigrew, January 12, 1861, Pettigrew Papers, Library of Congress.

10. William Preston Johnston to "Rosa," May 3, 1862, William Preston Johnston Papers, Tulane University Library.

11. George A. Townsend, *Rustics in Rebellion* (Chapel Hill, 1950), 83–87.

12. For a scholarly account of the battle, see Edwin B. Coddington, *The Gettysburg Campaign, a Study in Command* (New York, 1968).

13. D. B. Sanger, *James Longstreet* (Baton Rouge, 1952), chap. 13; George R. Stewart, *Pickett's Charge* (Boston, 1959).

14. Report of Col. William R. Aylett, Commanding Armistead's Brigade, July 12, 1863, Miscellaneous Confederate MSS, Huntington Library.

15. A. J. L. Fremantle, *Three Months in the Southern States* (New York, 1864), 274.

16. Longstreet to Louis T. Wigfall, August 2, 1863, Wigfall Papers, Library of Congress.

17. Halsey Wigfall to "Louly," July 18, 1863, Wigfall Papers, Library of Congress.

18. Dunbar Rowland (ed.), *Jefferson Davis, Constitutionalist, His Letters, Papers and Speeches* (Jackson, Miss., 1923), V, 586–87.

19. *Ibid.,* V, 588–89.

20. Jefferson Davis, *The Rise and Fall of the Confederate Government* (memorial ed., Richmond, original ed., 1881), II, 378.

21. Rowland (ed.), *Jefferson Davis, Constitutionalist,* V. 563–65.

22. Frank E. Vandiver (ed.), *The Civil War Diary of General Josiah Gorgas,* (University, Ala., 1947), 27.

23. Rowland (ed.), *Jefferson Davis, Constitutionalist,* V, 312.

24. J. Cutler Andrews, *The South Reports the Civil War* (Princeton, 1970).

25. Thomas L. Connelly, *Autumn of Glory: The Army of Tennessee, 1862–1865* (Baton Rouge, 1971), 44–68.

26. Rowland (ed.), *Jefferson Davis, Constitutionalist,* V, 420.

27. Johnston to L. T. Wigfall, February and March 1863, Wigfall Papers, Library of Congress.

28. Vandiver (ed.), *Civil War Diary of Gorgas,* 164.

29. Rowland (ed.), *Jefferson Davis, Constitutionalist,* V, 483.

30. Randolph to Thomas Jefferson Randolph, Nov. 25, 1862, Edgehill-Randolph Collection, University of Virginia Library.

31. Letters in Wigfall Papers, Library of Congress.

32. Joseph E. Johnston, *Narrative of Military Operations,* ed. by F. E. Vandiver (Indianapolis, 1959), 200.

33. Archer Jones, *Confederate Strategy from Shiloh to Vicksburg* (Baton Rouge, 1961), chap. 12.

34. Vandiver (ed.), *Civil War Diary of Gorgas,* 50.

35. *Ibid.,* 68.

36. *Ibid.,* 62.

37. For a scholarly study of Bragg's generalship, see Grady McWhiney, *Braxton Bragg and Confederate Defeat* (New York, 1969), I.

38. Connelly, *Autumn of Glory,* chap. 10.

39. Rowland (ed.), Jefferson Davis, *Constitutionalist,* VI, 95–96.

40. R. U. Johnson and C. C. Buel (eds.), *Battles and Leaders of the Civil War* (New York, 1887), III, 727.

CHAPTER 19: "DAVIS AND THE TRANS-MISSISSIPPI WEST"
        (pp. 187–195)

1. Robert C. Black, *The Railroads of the Confederacy* (Chapel Hill, 1952), map in the back.

2. Frank E. Vandiver (ed.), *The Civil War Diary of General Josiah Gorgas* (University, Ala., 1947), 34.

3. Robert E. Shalhope, *Sterling Price, Portrait of a Southerner* (Columbia, Missouri, 1971), chap. 14.

4. Dunbar Rowland (ed.), *Jefferson Davis, Constitutionalist, His Letters, Papers and Speeches* (Jackson, Miss., 1923), V, 342.

5. *Ibid.,* V, 369–70.

6. T. C. Hindman to Louis T. Wigfall, June 26, 1864, in Louis T. Wigfall Papers, Library of Congress.

7. See Joseph H. Parks, *General Edmund Kirby Smith, C.S.A.* (Baton Rouge, 1954), *passim.*

8. For an over-all view of the trans-Mississippi in the Civil War, see Robert L. Kerby, *Kirby Smith's Confederacy: The Trans-Mississippi, 1863–1865* (New York, 1972).

9. Rowland (ed.), *Jefferson Davis, Constitutionalist,* V, 548–50.

10. Thomas C. Reynolds Papers, Library of Congress.

11. Parks, *General Edmund Kirby Smith,* 317.

12. Rowland (ed.), *Jefferson Davis, Constitutionalist,* V, 234.

13. Parks, *General Edmund Kirby Smith,* 349.

14. E. M. Coulter, *The Confederate States of America, 1861–1865* (Baton Rouge, 1950), 359n.

15. John A. Wharton to Louis Wigfall, July 20, 1864, Wigfall Papers, Library of Congress.

16. Richard Taylor, *Destruction and Reconstruction: Personal Experiences of the Late War* (New York, 1878), 126.

17. See Kerby, *Kirby Smith's Confederacy,* chap. I.

CHAPTER 20: "DAVIS'S NEGLECT OF THE HOME FRONT"
(pp. 196–208)

1. Charles W. Ramsdell, *Behind the Lines in the Southern Confederacy* (Baton Rouge, 1944), 85.
2. Clement Eaton, "The Confederacy," in J. A. Garraty (ed.), *Interpreting American History: Conversations with Historians* (New York, 1970), I, 328.
3. H. D. Capers, *The Life and Times of C. G. Memminger* (Washington, 1893), 358.
4. Frank L. Owsley, *King Cotton Diplomacy* (revised, Chicago, 1959), 380–82.
5. Judith F. Gentry, "A Confederate Success in Europe: the Erlanger Loan," *Southern Historical Review*, XXXVI (May, 1970), 157–88.
6. See Richard C. Todd, *Confederate Finance* (Athens, 1954).
7. Dunbar Rowland (ed.), *Jefferson Davis, Constitutionalist, His Letters, Papers and Speeches* (Jackson, Miss., 1923), V, 323.
8. *Ibid.,* VI, 112.
9. Douglas Southall Freeman, *R. E. Lee, A Biography* (New York, 1935), III, 538.
10. E. M. Coulter, *The Confederate States of America, 1861–1865* (Baton Rouge, 1950), 182.
11. Ramsdell, *Behind the Lines,* p. x.
12. Robert C. Black, *The Railroads of the Confederacy* (Chapel Hill, 1952), 160–61.
13. A. L. King, *Louis T. Wigfall, Southern Fire-eater* (Baton Rouge, 1970), 152–53.
14. Black, *Railroads of the Confederacy,* 110.
15. Rowland (ed.), *Jefferson Davis, Constitutionalist,* V, 413.
16. Black, *Railroads of the Confederacy,* 121.
17. Edward Younger (ed.), *Inside the Confederate Government: The Diary of Robert Garlick Hill Kean* (New York, 1957), 47–48.
18. Black, *Railroads of the Confederacy,* 124.
19. Sewell L. Fremont to Braxton Bragg, March 16, 1864, Jefferson Davis Papers, Duke University Library.
20. A. W. Lawton to Secretary of War Breckinridge, March 10, 1865, *ibid.*
21. Rowland (ed.), *Jefferson Davis, Constitutionalist,* V, 469–73.
22. Northrop to Davis, August 21, 1861, Frank G. Ruffin Papers, Virginia Historical Society.
23. Frank G. Ruffin to Northrop, October 18, 1862, *ibid.* These commissary letters are cited in Clement Eaton, *A History of the Southern Confederacy* (New York, 1954), chap. 7.
24. Northrop to Secretary of War Seddon, December 20, 1864, Frank G. Ruffin Papers, Virginia Historical Society.
25. Charles W. Ramsdell, "General Robert E. Lee's Horse Supply, 1862–1865," *American Historical Review*, XXV (July, 1930), 758–77.

26. Sidney R. French to Isaac St. John, March 10, 1865, Jefferson Davis Papers, Duke University Library.

27. Frank E. Vandiver, *Confederate Blockade-Running through Bermuda 1861–1865* (Austin, 1947), 109–48.

28. See Benjamin Quarles, *The Negro in the Civil War* (Boston, 1953); Bell I. Wiley, *Southern Negroes, 1861–1865* (New Haven, 1938), and James H. Brewer, *The Confederate Negro: Virginia's Craftsmen and Military Laborers* (Durham, 1969).

29. Joseph Davis to Jefferson Davis, May 22, 1862, Jefferson Hayes–Davis Papers, Transylvania University Library.

30. Joseph Davis to Jefferson Davis, June 1, 1862, *ibid.*

31. Ruth K. Nuermberger, *The Clays of Alabama: A Lawyer-Planter-Politician Family* (Lexington, 1958), 211–15.

32. Charles B. Dew, *Ironmaker to the Confederacy: Joseph R. Anderson and the Tredegar Iron Works* (New Haven, 1966).

33. Phineas Browne letters, Alabama State Department of Archives and History.

34. Younger (ed.), *Diary of Kean,* 46–47.

35. Wilfred B. Yearns, *The Confederate Congress* (Athens, 1960), chap. 9.

36. Ramsdell, *Behind the Lines,* 117.

37. Bell I. Wiley, *The Plain People of the Confederacy* (Baton Rouge, 1943).

38. Rowland (ed.), *Jefferson Davis, Constitutionalist,* V, 425.

39. Louise B. Hill, *State Socialism in the Confederate States* (Charlottesville, 1936) and Charles Ramsdell, "The Control of Manufacturing by the Conderate Government," *Mississippi Valley Historical Review,* VIII (1921), 231–49.

40. Frank E. Vandiver (ed.), *The Civil War Diary of General Josiah Gorgas* (University, Ala., 1947), *passim.*

41. Dew, *Ironmaker to the Confederacy.*

CHAPTER 21: "DAVIS'S CONFLICT WITH CONGRESS"
              (pp. 209–219)

1. Varina Davis to Clement C. Clay Jr., May 10, 1861, Clement C. Clay Papers, Duke University Library.

2. Charles R. Lee, Jr., *The Confederate Constitutions* (Chapel Hill, 1963), chap. 2.

3. Wilfred B. Yearns, *The Confederate Congress* (Athens, 1960), 236–44; see also Ezra Warren, *Biographical Register of the Confederate Congress* (Baton Rouge, 1975).

4. A. L. King, *Louis T. Wigfall, Southern Fire-eater* (Baton Rouge, 1970), 176.

5. Hammond to Hunter, April 9, 1863, R. M. T. Hunter Papers, University of Virginia Library.

6. Diary of Thomas Bragg, March 6, 1962, Southern Collection, University of North Carolina Library.

7. See Thomas B. Alexander and R. E. Beringer, *The Anatomy of the Confederate Congress* (Nashville, 1972).

8. Bell I. Wiley (ed.), *Letters of Warren Akin, Confederate Congressman* (Athens, 1959), 79.

9. *Ibid.,* 46, 52, 56.

10. For conditions in Confederate Richmond, see Emory M. Thomas, *The Confederate State of Richmond; a Biography of the Capital* (Austin, 1971) and A. H. Bill, *The Beleaguered City; Richmond, 1861–1865* (New York, 1946).

11. Josiah Turner to His Wife, Richmond, June 6, 1864, Josiah Turner Papers, North Carolina State Department of Archives.

12. Yearns, *Confederate Congress,* 176.

13. Josiah Turner to His Wife, May 5, 1864, Josiah Turner Papers, Southern Collection, University of North Carolina Library.

14. See Ruth K. Nuermberger, *The Clays of Alabama: A Lawyer-Planter-Politician Family* (Lexington, 1958), chaps. 7–10.

15. Wiley (ed.), *Letters of Warren Akin, Confederate Congressman,* 66.

16. Dunbar Rowland (ed.), *Jefferson Davis, Constitutionalist, His Letters, Papers and Speeches* (Jackson, Miss., 1923), V, 459.

17. Wiley (ed.), *Letters of Warren Akin,* 75.

18. Frank E. Vandiver, "Jefferson Davis—Leader Without a Legend," *Journal of Southern History,* XLIII (February, 1977), 9.

19. See Rosser H. Taylor (ed.), "Boyce–Hammond Correspondence," *Journal of Southern History,* III (1937), 348–54.

20. W. E. Simms to Robert McKee, November 16, 1863, Robert McKee Papers, Alabama State Department of Archives and History.

21. Mallory, Diary and Reminiscences, September 27, 1865, Southern Collection, University of North Carolina Library.

22. Varina Howell Davis, *Jefferson Davis, Ex–President of the Confederate States of America. A Memoir by His Wife* (New York, 1890), II, 163.

23. John H. Reagan, *Memoirs, with Special Reference to Secession and the Civil War,* ed. by Walter F. McCaleb (New York, 1906), 161.

24. King, *Louis T. Wigfall,* 159.

25. Yearns, *Confederate Congress,* 37, 76.

26. *Ibid.,* 225.

27. J. Cutler Andrews, *The South Reports the Civil War* (Princeton, 1970), 220–21.

28. Edwin G. Reade to Governor Vance, February 11, 1864, Zebulon Baird Vance Papers, North Carolina State Department of Archives.

29. Yearns, *Confederate Congress,* 55, 234.

30. *Ibid.,* 233.

31. F. E. Vandiver (ed.), "Proceedings of the First Congress, Fourth Session, 1863–1864," in *Southern Historical Society Papers* (Richmond, 1953), 21, 23–24, 196.

32. Yearns, *Confederate Congress,* 231.

33. Alexander and Beringer, *Anatomy of the Confederate Congress,* chap. 12.

CHAPTER 22: "HANDLING THE REBELLIOUS GOVERNORS"
(pp. 220–230)

1. Photostat from the original in the University of Rochester Library, North Carolina State Department of Archives.

2. See Louise B. Hill, *Joseph E. Brown and the Confederacy* (Chapel Hill, 1939) and Joseph H. Parks, *Joseph E. Brown of Georgia* (Baton Rouge, 1977).

3. Dunbar Rowland (ed.), *Jefferson Davis, Constitutionalist, His Letters, Papers and Speeches* (Jackson, Miss., 1923), V, 236.

4. *Ibid.,* 24.

5. See Joseph H. Parks, "State Rights in a Crisis: Governor Joseph E. Brown versus President Jefferson Davis," *Journal of Southern History,* XXII (February, 1966), 3–24.

6. *Official Records,* III, 192–98; Hill, *Joseph E. Brown and the Confederacy,* 80.

7. Rowland (ed.), *Jefferson Davis, Constitutionalist,* V, 254–62.

8. *Ibid.,* V, 292–93.

9. U. B. Phillips (ed.), "The Correspondence of Robert Toombs, Alexander H. Stephens, and Howell Cobb," *Annual Report of American Historical Association for the Year 1911* (Washington, 1913), II, 597–99.

10. *Official Records,* III, 504–09.

11. Hill, *Joseph E. Brown and the Confederacy,* 96.

12. Rowland (ed.), *Jefferson Davis, Constitutionalist,* V, 202.

13. Hill, *Joseph E. Brown and the Confederacy.*

14. *Ibid.*

15. *Ibid.,* 239; *Official Records,* I, 106.

16. James D. Waddell, *Biographical Sketch of Linton Stephens, Containing a Selection of His Letters, Speeches, State Papers, etc.* (Atlanta, 1877), 257–59.

17. Waddell, *Biographical Sketch of Linton Stephens,* 269–75.

18. Frank L. Owsley, *States Rights in the Confederacy* (Chicago, 1925), 140–59.

19. See C. Vann Woodward, *Origins of the New South 1877–1913* (Baton Rouge, 1951), 15, 215.

20. See Foreword by Frontis W. Johnston (ed.), *The Papers of Zebulon Baird Vance* (Raleigh, 1963), I (1843–1862), and Richard E. Yates, *The Confederacy and Zeb Vance* (Tuscaloosa, 1958).

21. Rowland (ed.), *Jefferson Davis, Constitutionalist,* V, 485–88.

22. *Ibid.,* V, 492–94.

23. *Ibid.,* V, 354–56.

24. *Ibid.,* V, 545–46.

25. *Ibid.,* VI, 193–97.

26. Vance to William A. Graham, May 11, 1864, William A. Graham Papers, North Carolina State Department of Archives.

27. Owsley, *States Rights in the Confederacy,* 148.

28. Clement Dowd, *Life of Zebulon B. Vance* (Charlotte, 1897), 489–90.

29. Andrew Magrath to Governor Brown, January 9, 11, 1865, Andrew Magrath Papers, Southern Collection, University of North Carolina Library.

30. John Milton to Governor Brown, April 14, 1864, John Milton Letter Book, Florida State Department of Archives and History.

31. Diary of Thomas Bragg, January 17, 1862, Southern Collection, University of North Carolina Library.

32. Owsley, *States Rights in the Confederacy, passim.*

CHAPTER 23: "LOSING THE WILL TO FIGHT, BUT NOT JEFFERSON DAVIS"
(pp. 231–241)

1. Lord Lyons to Earl Russell, January 9, 1863, Lord John Russell Papers, PRO 30/22: United States, 1863, Public Record Office, London.

2. Lord Lyons to Earl Russell, March 2, 1863, *ibid.* Researched by the author when a Fulbright Professor in England, and cited in Clement Eaton *A History of the Southern Confederacy* (New York, 1954), 76.

3. Frank McGregor, *Dearest Susie, A Civil War Infantryman's Letters to His Sweetheart,* ed. by C. E. Hatch (New York, 1971), 37, 65. Professor Charles Roland called my attention to these published letters.

4. J. R. Rogers to his sister, February 4, 1863, J. R. Rogers Papers, University of Kentucky Library.

5. Bell I. Wiley, *The Road to Appomattox* (Memphis, 1956).

6. Dunbar Rowland (ed.), *Jefferson Davis, Constitutionalist, His Letters, Papers and Speeches* (Jackson, Miss., 1923), VI, 94–95.

7. Louis Pendleton, *Alexander H. Stephens* (Philadelphia, 1907), 340–41.

8. Some of his accusations of atrocity are found in Rowland (ed.), *Jefferson Davis, Constitutionalist,* V, 114, 292, 393, 408.

9. *Ibid.,* VI, 343.

10. Frank E. Vandiver (ed.), *The Civil War Diary of General Josiah Gorgas* (University, Ala., 1947), 175.

11. James Silver, *Confederate Morale and Church Propaganda* (Tuscaloosa, 1957), 65, 69.

12. J. W. Jones, *Christ in Camp or Religion in Lee's Army* (Richmond, 1888), 46, 233, 283–84.

13. J. Andrews Cutler, *The South Reports the Civil War* (Princeton, 1970), 43.

14. Clement C. Clay, Jr., Papers, Duke University Library.

15. Diary of Thomas Bragg, February 15, 1862, Southern Collection, University of North Carolina Library.

16. Clement C. Clay, Jr. to Louis T. Wigfall, August 15, 1863, Wigfall Papers, Library of Congress.

17. See Bell I. Wiley, *The Life of Johnny Reb, the Common Soldier of the Confederacy* (Indianapolis, 1943), and *The Plain People of the Confederacy* (Baton Rouge, 1943), 48.

18. Vandiver (ed.), *Civil War Diary of Gorgas,* 51.

19. Edward Younger (ed.), *Inside the Confederate Government: The Diary of Robert Garlick Hill Kean* (New York, 1957), 41, 53.

20. Bell I. Wiley (ed.), *Letters of Warren Akin, Confederate Congressman* (Athens, 1959), 33.

21. Rowland (ed.), *Jefferson Davis, Constitutionalist,* VI, 31.

22. *Ibid.,* 192.

23. *Ibid.,* 453–54.

24. Charles W. Ramsdell (ed.), *Laws and Joint Resolutions of the Last Confederate Congress* (Durham, 1941), 37–38, 43.

25. A. D. Kirwan, *Johnny Green of the Orphan Brigade* (Lexington, 1956), 85.

26. See Georgia L. Tatum, *Disloyalty in the Confederacy* (Chapel Hill, 1934); Eaton, *A History of the Southern Confederacy,* 266; and Ella Lonn, *Desertion during the Civil War* (Chapel Hill, 1934).

27. Rowland (ed.), *Jefferson Davis, Constitutionalist,* V, 143–46.

28. Z. B. Vance to William A. Graham, January 1 and February 25, 1864, William A. Graham Papers, North Carolina State Department of Archives.

29. See Richard E. Yates, *The Confederacy and Zeb Vance* (Tuscaloosa, 1958).

30. Braxton Bragg to Davis, November 16, 1863, Jefferson Davis Papers, Duke University Library.

31. Vandiver (ed.), *Civil War Diary of Gorgas,* 137.

32. J. R. P. Ellis to His Wife, June 8, 1864, Southern Collection, University of North Carolina.

33. See Ella Lonn, *Foreigners in the Confederacy* (Chapel Hill, 1940), and *Desertion during the Civil War* (Chapel Hill, 1934).

34. Vandiver (ed.), *Civil War Diary of Gorgas,* 145.

35. Mary Boykin Chesnut, *A Diary from Dixie,* ed. by B. A. Williams (Boston, 1949), 422.

36. Mrs. Roger A. Pryor, *Reminiscences of Peace and War* (New York, 1905), 293.

37. John H. Reagan, *Memoirs, with Special Reference to Secession and the Civil War,* ed. by Walter F. McCaleb (New York, 1906), 139.

39. Vandiver (ed.), *Civil War Diary of Gorgas,* 146.

39. The Spirit of the Southern people as they faced the hardships and adversity of the war is faithfully portrayed in the letters of the Jones family of Georgia. See R. M. Myers (ed.), *The Children of Pride, A True Story of Georgia and the Civil War* (New Haven, 1972).

CHAPTER 24: "DAVIS AS WAR LEADER"
            (pp. 242–250)

1. Stephen R. Mallory, Diary and Reminiscences, December 8, 1865, II, 203–09, Southern Collection, University of North Carolina Library.

2. Varina Howell Davis, *Jefferson Davis, Ex–President of the Confederate States of America. A Memoir by His Wife* (New York, 1890), II, 494.

3. Frank E. Vandiver (ed.), *The Civil War Diary of General Josiah Gorgas* (University, Ala., 1947), 122–23.

4. Mallory, Diary and Reminiscences, II, 147, Southern Collection, University of North Carolina Library.

5. *Ibid.,* II, 249.

6. Confederate War Department Papers, Letters Received, 1862, Box 10, National Archives, Washington.

7. Douglas Southall Freeman, *R. E. Lee, A Biography* (New York, 1935), II, 7.

8. Dunbar Rowland (ed.), *Jefferson Davis, Constitutionalist, His Letters, Papers and Speeches* (Jackson, Miss., 1923), V, 138.

9. See T. Harry Williams, *Napoleon in Gray, P. G. T. Beauregard* (Baton Rouge, 1954), 93–95, 100–01, 181–82, 214–17, and *Official Records*, XV, 744–45.

10. Thomas Connelly and Archer Jones, *The Politics of Command* (Baton Rouge, 1973), 29.

11. Jeremy F. Gilmer to "Loulie," March 12, 1862, Jeremy F. Gilmer Papers, Southern Collection, University of North Carolina Library.

12. Rowland (ed.), *Jefferson Davis, Constitutionalist,* V, 207.

13. John H. Reagan, *Memoirs, with Special Reference to Secession and the Civil War,* ed. by Walter F. McCaleb (New York, 1906), 137.

14. Rowland (ed.), *Jefferson Davis, Constitutionalist,* V, 138.

15. *Ibid.,* V, 140.

16. *Ibid.,* V, 148.

17. Diary of Alice Ready, Southern Collection, University of North Carolina Library.

18. Francis B. Simkins and J. W. Patton, *The Women of the Confederacy* (Richmond, 1936).

19. Diary of Thomas Bragg, February 21, 1862, Southern Collection, University of North Carolina Library.

20. Ruth K. Nuermberger, *Clays of Alabama: A Lawyer-Planter-Politician Family* (Lexington, 1958), 194.

21. Edward Younger (ed.), *Inside the Confederacy: The Diary of Robert Garlick Hill Kean* (New York, 1957), 80.

22. Connelly and Jones, *The Politics of Command,* 88.

23. G. E. Govan and J. W. Livingood, *A Different Valor: the Story of Joseph E. Johnston C.S.A.* (Indianapolis, 1956), 176.

24. A. M. Broom (ed.), "We Sowed and We Have Reaped: A Post–War Letter from Braxton Bragg," *Journal of Southern History*, XXXI (February, 1965), 77–78.

25. Vandiver (ed.), *Civil War Diary of Gorgas*, 151.

26. E. P. Alexander, *Military Memoirs of a Confederate* (New York, 1907), 53.

27. A. L. King, *Louis T. Wigfall, Southern Fire–eater* (Baton Rouge, 1970), 158–61.

28. See Frank E. Vandiver, *Rebel Brass: The Confederate Command System* (Baton Rouge, 1956).

29. Connelly and Jones, *Politics of Command,* chap. II.

30. Vandiver (ed.), *Civil War Diary of Gorgas*, 165.

CHAPTER 25: "TAPS FOR THE SOUTHERN CONFEDERACY"
              (pp. 251–261)

1. Frank E. Vandiver (ed.), *The Civil War Diary of General Josiah Gorgas,* (University, Ala., 1947), 114.

2. *Ibid.,* 113.

3. *Ibid.,* 143.

4. Mary Boykin Chesnut, *A Diary from Dixie,* ed. by B. A. Williams (Boston, 1949), 341.

5. Vandiver (ed.), *Civil War Diary of Gorgas,* 112.

6. Sam R. Watkins, *"Co. Aytch," Maury's Grays, First Tennesee Regiment . . .* (Jackson, Tenn., 1952), 194.

7. Quoted in Robert S. Henry, *The Story of the Confederacy* (New York, 1936), 376.

8. Dunbar Rowland (ed.), *Jefferson Davis, Constitutionalist, His Letters, Papers and Speeches* (Jackson, Miss., 1923), VI, 280; Davis's reply, 281.

9. Henry, *The Story of the Confederacy,* 388.

10. Hood's side of the story is told in John B. Hood, *Advance and Retreat, Personal Experiences in the United States and Confederate Armies* (New Orleans, 1880); also John P. Dyer, *The Gallant Hood* (Indianapolis, 1950).

11. For the Atlanta campaign see Thomas L. Connelly, *Autumn of Glory: The Army of Tennessee, 1862–1865* (Baton Rouge, 1971), chaps. 12–15.

12. Joseph H. Parks, *General Edmund Kirby Smith, C.S.A.* (Baton Rouge, 1954), 429.

13. W. J. Cooper Jr., "A Reassessment of Jefferson Davis as War Leader: the Case from Atlanta to Nashville," *Journal of Southern History,* XXXVI (May, 1970), 197.

14. Hood to Bragg, September 4, 1864, Jefferson Davis Papers, Duke University Library.

15. See Ezra Warren, *Generals in Gray; Lives of the Confederate Commanders* (Baton Rouge, 1959).

16. See Margaret Mitchell's defense of the historical accuracy of her novel. She wrote to Henry S. Commager, who had reviewed it favorably, that she

cringed when a noted historian, such as he, should review her novel, "though I knew the history in my tale was as water proof and air tight as ten years of study and a lifetime of listening to participants would make it." Richard Harwell (ed.), *Margaret Mitchell's Gone With the Wind Letters, 1936–1949* (New York, 1976), 39.

17. William T. Sherman, *Memoirs* (New York, 1875), II, 111, 126; and Lloyd Lewis, *Sherman, Fighting Prophet* (New York, 1932).

18. See Connelly, *Autumn of Glory,* and T. R. Hay, *Hood's Tennessee Campaign* (New York, 1929).

19. Robert F. Durden, *The Gray and the Black; the Confederate Debate on Emancipation* (Baton Rouge, 1972), 53–63.

20. *Ibid.,* chap. 4.

21. Rudolph von Abele, *Alexander H. Stephens, a Biography* (New York, 1946), 235–43.

22. Varina Howell Davis, *Jefferson Davis, Ex-President of the Confederate States of America. A Memoir by His Wife* (New York, 1890), II, 633–46.

CHAPTER 26: "THE SPHINX OF THE CONFEDERACY"
            (pp. 262–275)

1. John Craven, *The Prison Life of Jefferson Davis* (New York, 1866) and Varina Howell Davis, *Jefferson Davis, Ex-President of the Confederate States of America. A Memoir by His Wife* (New York, 1890), II, chap. 67, "The Tortures Inflicted by General Miles."

2. See Hudson Strode, *Jefferson Davis, Tragic Hero* (New York, 1964).

3. Hudson Strode (ed.), *Jefferson Davis: Private Letters, 1823–1889* (New York, 1966), 396.

4. See G. E. Govan and J. W. Livingood, *A Different Valor: The Story of Joseph E. Johnston C.S.A.* (Indianapolis, 1956), 391–92.

5. Davis to Winnie, March 17, 1877, in Strode (ed.), *Jefferson Davis: Private Letters,* 451.

6. Jefferson Davis to Varina, July 4, 1879, Jefferson Hayes–Davis Papers, Transylvania University Library.

7. Davis to The Rev. Mr. Frank Stringfellow, June 4, 1878, *ibid.*

8. R. B. Nixon, *Henry W. Grady, Spokesman of the New South* (New York, 1943), 226.

9. Strode (ed.), *Jefferson Davis: Private Letters.*

10. *Ibid.,* 297.

11. C. C. Clay, Jr., to W. L. Yancey, 1863, William L. Yancey Papers, Alabama State Department of Archives and History.

12. U. B. Phillips (ed.), "Correspondence of Robert Toombs, Alexander H. Stephens and Howell Cobb," *Annual Report of American Historical Association for the Year 1911* (Washington, 1913), 537.

13. J. L. M. Curry, *Civil History of the Confederate States* (Richmond, 1901), 47.

14. Mary Boykin Chesnut, *A Diary from Dixie,* ed. by B. A. Williams (Boston, 1949), 65.

15. See William Y. Thompson, *Robert Toombs of Georgia* (Baton Rouge, 1966).

16. Varina Davis, *Memoir,* I.

17. For judgment of Toombs, in addition to Thompson, see U. B. Phillips, *The Life of Robert Toombs* (New York, 1913), and Rembert W. Patrick, *Jefferson Davis and His Cabinet* (Baton Rouge, 1944), 78–90.

18. Diary of Thomas Bragg, January 7, 1861, Southern Collection, University of North Carolina Library.

19. Chesnut, *A Diary from Dixie,* 99.

20. Thompson, *Robert Toombs,* 163.

21. See Clement Eaton, "The Role of Honor in Southern Society," *Southern Humanities Review,* Bicentennial Issue.

22. Frank E. Vandiver (ed.), *The Civil War Diary of General Josiah Gorgas* (University, Ala., 1947), 29.

23. John H. Reagan, *Memoirs, with Special Reference to Secession and the Civil War,* ed. by Walter F. McCaleb (New York, 1906), 120.

24. William Preston Johnston to "Rosa," May 19, 1862, William Preston Johnston Papers, Tulane University Library.

25. Varina Davis, *Memoir,* II, 274.

26. Benjamin P. Thomas, *Abraham Lincoln* (New York, 1952), 153.

27. See Allan Nevins, *The Statesmanship of the Civil War* (New York, 1953), chap. 3.

28. David Potter, "Jefferson Davis and the Political Factors in Confederate Defeat," in David Donald (ed.), *Why the North Won the Civil War* (Baton Rouge, 1960), 91–114.

29. Allan Nevins, *The Emergence of Lincoln* (New York, 1950), I, 141, 264.

30. Bell I. Wiley (ed.), *The Rise and Fall of the Confederate Government by Jefferson Davis* (New York, 1958), I, Foreword.

31. Frank E. Vandiver, *Their Tattered Flags: The Epic of the Confederacy* (New York, 1970), 35.

32. William J. Cooper, Jr., "A Reassessment of Jefferson Davis as War Leader: The Case from Atlanta to Nashville," *Journal of Southern History,* XXXVI (May, 1970), 197.

33. Edward Younger (ed.), *Inside the Confederate Government: The Diary of Robert Garlick Hill Kean* (New York, 1957), 94 and *passim.*

34. Cited from the speech of Senator Mark Hatfield on the Senate floor introducing a joint resolution of Congress restoring citizenship to Jefferson Davis, Senate Calendar No. 80, 1st Sess., 95th Cong., Report No. 95–100.

Bibliographical Note

───◆◄●►◆───

MANUSCRIPTS

My biography of Jefferson Davis is based on manuscript sources to a much greater degree than any previous biography. The particular value of using manuscript sources is that they give a more intimate view of the subject—relatively free of self-consciousness—than do the formal printed sources. Among the most important manuscript collections used in preparing this book are those listed below.

Alabama State Department of Archives and History
  Phineas Browne Papers
  Robert McKee Papers
  William L. Yancey Papers

Library of Congress
  Pierre G. T. Beauregard Papers
  Breckinridge Family Papers
  James H. Hammond Papers and Diary
  William J. Hardee Papers
  Henry Hotze Letter Book and Papers
  Robert Todd Lincoln Papers
  Pettigrew Papers
  John A. Pickett Papers (Confederate State Department Papers)

Thomas C. Reynolds Papers
Alexander H. Stephens Papers
Louis T. Wigfall Papers

Duke University Library
John Buie Papers
Clement C. Clay, Jr., Papers
Jefferson Davis Papers
Lawrence Keitt Papers
Josiah Turner Papers

Filson Club Library, Louisville
Diary of William Little Brown

Florida State Department of Archives and History
Ives Papers
John Milton Letter Book and Papers

Huntington Library, San Marino
Brock Collection
Miscellaneous Confederate Papers

University of Kentucky Library
James H. Atherton Letters
William Reynolds Journal
J. R. Rogers Papers
Soldiers of the Civil War Letters

National Archives
Confederate War Department, Letter Book of Bureau of Conscription
Confederate War Department Papers, Letters Received, 1862
Photostats of Manuscript Census Reports for 1850 and 1860, relating to Davis
    Plantations

North Carolina State Department of Archives
Judah P. Benjamin Letter (photostat from original in University of Rochester
    Library)
William O'Brien Branch Papers
William A. Graham Papers
David L. Swain Papers
Josiah Turner Papers
Zebulon Baird Vance Papers

University of North Carolina Library, Southern Collection
E. P. Alexander Papers
Thomas Bragg Diary
J. B. Clifton Diary
Jerry Gilmer Papers
John B. Grimball Diary and Papers
Daniel R. Hundley
Andrew McGrath Papers
Stephen Mallory Diary and Reminiscences

William Porcher Miles Papers
John Hunt Morgan Papers
Alice Ready Diary
Josiah Turner Papers

Public Records Office, London
Earl John Russell Papers

South Carolina Department of Archives and History
J. H. Hammond, Secret Diary and Papers

South Carolina Historical Society
Thomas B. Chaplin Plantation Journal

Transylvania University Library
Jefferson Hayes–Davis Papers

Tulane University Library
William Preston Johnston Papers

Virginia Historical Society
Frank G. Ruffin Papers

University of Virginia, Alderman Library
John Hartwell Cocke Papers
Edgehill-Randolph Papers
Richard Eppes Diary
R. M. T. Hunter Papers

BIOGRAPHIES

Of the biographies of Jefferson Davis the one published seventy years ago by Professor William E. Dodd is the most scholarly, but it is not deeply researched and is dated. The earliest, by Edward Pollard and Frank H. Alfriend, contemporaries of Davis, are bitterly prejudiced, on the one hand, and adulatory, on the other. A similar lack of objectivity is present in the superficial biographies of Elizabeth Cutting, Robert W. Winston, Allen Tate, and Hamilton J. Eckenrode, the latter being the best one of this group. Professor Robert McElroy, a history professor at Princeton University, published *Jefferson Davis, the Real and the Unreal* in 1937, but it is superficial and undistinguished. Hudson Strode, a professor of English at the University of Alabama, wrote three volumes of a Davis biography, beginning in 1950, which are pleasant and interesting, but they are all-admiring and written in a political vacuum.

DIARIES AND TRAVEL ACCOUNTS

Much light is thrown on Davis's personality, Southern plantation life, and the Confederacy by the printed diaries and travel accounts, a selection of which is cited below.

Mary Boykin Chesnut, *A Diary from Dixie,* ed. by B. A. Williams (Boston, 1949).

E. A. DAVIS (ed.), *Plantation Life in the Florida Parishes of Louisiana, 1843–1846* (New York, 1943).

CLEMENT EATON, ed. and introduction to Frederick Law Olmsted, *A Journey in the Back Country, 1853–1854* (New York, 1970).

A. J. L. FREMANTLE, *Three Months in the Southern States* (New York, 1864).

FLETCHER GREEN (ed.), *The Lides Go South and West: The Record of a Planter Migration in 1835* (Columbia, 1952).

[CATHERINE C. HOPLEY], *Life in the South from the Commencement of the War, by a Blockaded British Subject,* 2 vols. (London, 1863).

W. L. ROSE, *A Documentary History of Slavery in North America* (New York, 1976).

W. K. SCARBOROUGH (ed.), The Diary of Edmund Ruffin, 2 vols. (Baton Rouge, 1972–76).

F. E. VANDIVER (ed.), *Ploughshares into Swords* (Austin, 1952).

EDWARD YOUNGER (ed.), *Inside the Confederate Government: The Diary of Robert Garlick Hill Kean* (New York, 1957).

PRINTED PRIMARY SOURCES AND DOCUMENTS

The printed sources on Jefferson Davis and especially on the Confederacy are too extensive for inclusion, except to list the most important.

Congressional Globe (Washington, 1846–61).

HENRY S. COMMAGER (ed.), *The Blue and the Gray: The Story of the Civil War as Told by Participants,* 2 vols. (Indianapolis, 1950).

JEFFERSON DAVIS, *The Rise and Fall of the Confederate Government,* 1st ed. (New York, 1881), 2 vols.; an elaborate edition (Richmond memorial ed.) and the edition edited by Bell I. Wiley (New York, 1958).

VARINA HOWELL DAVIS, *Jefferson Davis, Ex–President of the Confederate States of America. A Memoir by His Wife,* 2 vols. (New York, 1890).

JAMES T. McINTOSH (ed.), *The Papers of Jefferson Davis* (Baton Rouge, 1974), II.

JAMES MATTHEWS (ed.), *Statutes at Large of the Provisional Government of the Confederate States of America* (Richmond, 1864).

JAMES MATTHEWS (ed.), *Public Laws of the Confederate States of America* (Richmond, 1862–64).

HASKELL M. MONROE, JR., and JAMES T. McINTOSH (eds.), *The Papers of Jefferson Davis* (Baton Rouge, 1971), I.

Official Records of the Union and Confederate Navies in the War of Rebellion, 30 vols. (Washington, 1894–1927).

"Proceedings of the Confederate Congress," *Southern Historical Society Papers,* XI–LII, *passim,* the last three volumes of which have been edited by Frank E. Vandiver.

CHARLES W. RAMSDELL (ed.), *Laws and Joint Resolutions of the Last Session of the Confederate Congress* (November 7, 1864–March 18, 1965) (Durham, 1941).

J. P. RICHARDSON, *A Compilation of the Messages and Papers of the Confederacy* (Washington, 1905).

DUNBAR ROWLAND (ed.), *Jefferson Davis, Constitutionalist, His Letters, Papers and Speeches,* 10 vols. (Jackson, Miss., 1923).

The War of Rebellion: A Compilation of the Official Records of the Union and Confederate Armies, 128 vols. (Washington, 1880–1901), referred to as "O.R."

SECONDARY SOURCES

Since the literature on the Confederacy and the Civil War, in which Jefferson Davis had such an important role, is so vast, I have concluded that the sensible procedure is to list here only the general works, leaving the particular volumes cited for inclusion in the notes section. For a bibliography, see Allan Nevins, Bell I. Wiley, and James I. Robertson, Jr., *Civil War Books: A Critical Bibliography* (Baton Rouge, 1967).

E. M. COULTER, *The Confederate States of America, 1861–1865* (Baton Rouge, 1950).

CLIFFORD DOWDY, *Experiment in Rebellion* (New York, 1946).

CLEMENT EATON, *A History of the Southern Confederacy* (New York, 1954).

ROBERT S. HENRY, *The Story of the Confederacy* (Garden City, N.Y., 1931).

A. D. KIRWAN, *The Confederacy* (New York, 1959).

PETER J. PARISH, *The American Civil War* (New York, 1975).

J. G. RANDALL and DAVID DONALD, *The Civil War and Reconstruction* (Boston, 1961).

CHARLES P. ROLAND, *The Confederacy* (Chicago, 1960).

BELL I. WILEY and H. D. MILHOLLEN (eds.), *Embattled Confederates: An Ilustrated History of Southerners at War* (New York, 1964).

Index

Index